THE CLUSTERING OF AMERICA

THE CLUSTERING OF AMERICA

Michael J. Weiss

A TILDEN PRESS BOOK

1817

HARPER & ROW, PUBLISHERS, New York
Cambridge, Philadelphia, San Francisco, London
Mexico City, São Paulo, Singapore, Sydney

This book is based on the PRIZM cluster system developed by the Claritas Corporation of Alexandria, Virginia, which provided demographic statistics, maps, tables and bar charts. In addition, this book contains PRIZM-coded data drawn from Simmons Market Research Bureau (SMRB), Mediamark Research Inc. (MRI), R. L. Polk & Co. and Targeting Systems, Inc., under an agreement with Claritas Corp. Used with permission.

FIRST EDITION

Designed by Joan Greenfield

Library of Congress Cataloging-in-Publication Data

Weiss, Michael J., 1952–
  The clustering of America.

  "A Tilden Press book."
  Includes index.
  1. United States—Social conditions—1980–   . 2. United States—Social life and customs—1971–   . 3. Postal zones—Social aspects—United States.   4. Social surveys—United States.   I. Title.
  HN59.2.W45   1988   306 '.0973   88-45070
  ISBN 0-06-015790-9

  89 90 91 92 CC/MPC 10 9 8 7 6 5 4 3 2

FOR MY WIFE, PHYLLIS STANGER, AND MY
PARENTS, VIVIAN AND SIDNEY WEISS, WITH
LOVE AND THANKS

CONTENTS

INTRODUCTION

This is the story of lifestyles in contemporary America, but its origins are rooted in an unlikely source: the bottom right corner of virtually every piece of mail.

The story begins in late 1962 when the U.S. Postal Service proposed a novel idea to speed mail delivery: the Zone Improvement Plan, alias the ZIP code. Created for businesses to presort their mail in preparation for automated post offices, zip codes found ready acceptance in the corporate world but wary reluctance among many Americans. Civil libertarians feared the five-digit code could become a national identification number, and some media commentators worried that it would reduce people to a handful of digits.

The critics, of course, were ignored. But surprisingly, twenty years later, their predictions have come true.

During the last decade, your zip code—actually the community it represents—has come to reveal more about you and your neighbors than any postal clerk ever thought possible. Those five digits can indicate the kinds of magazines you read, the meals you serve at dinner, whether you're a liberal Republican or an apathetic Democrat. Retailers use zips to decide everything from where to locate a designer boutique to what kind of actor to use in their TV commercials—be it Mean Joe Green, Morris the Cat or Spuds MacKenzie. College and military recruiters even rely on a city's zip codes to target their efforts to attract promising high-school graduates. Your zip code is no longer just an innocuous invention for moving the mail. It's become a yardstick by which your lifestyle is measured.

Obviously, your post office can't take credit for these high-tech uses of zips. As American society has become increasingly fragmented due to shifts in family composition, labor distribution and the economy, marketing companies have pioneered many ingenious methods to quantify the changes and incorporate them into their product strategies. In 1974, a computer scientist turned entrepreneur named Jonathan Robbin devised a wildly popular target-marketing system by matching zip codes with census data and consumer surveys. Christening his creation PRIZM (Potential Rating Index for Zip Markets), he programmed computers to sort the nation's 36,000 zips into forty "lifestyle clusters." Zip 85254 in Northeast Phoenix, Arizona, for instance, belongs to what he called the Furs & Station Wagons cluster, where surveys indicate that residents tend to buy lots of vermouth, belong to a country club, read *Gourmet* and vote the GOP ticket. In 02151, a Revere Beach, Massachusetts, zip designated Old Yankee Rows, tastes lean toward beer, fraternal clubs, *Lakeland Boating* and whoever the Democrats are supporting. With PRIZM and a zip code, Robbin can draw on thousands of census and consumer statistics to produce accurate portraits of any neighborhood, right down to the cereal in the cupboard and the antacid in the medicine cabinet.

By the time I caught up with Robbin in early 1983 to profile him for the American Airlines in-flight magazine, he was the latest guru of the target-marketing industry and known as the "King of the Zip Codes." His Alexandria, Virginia–based company, Claritas Corporation, was earning $1 million a year by helping clients like *Time,* General Motors and American Express tailor their products and pitches to the forty lifestyle clusters. And in a true indication of Robbin's success, other companies were offering imitations of the PRIZM system.

Although my article focused on the business uses of the clusters, I remained intrigued by the cultural implications of this computer vision of America. Here was a new way of looking at the nation—not as fifty states but rather forty neighborhood types, each with distinct boundaries, values, consuming habits and political beliefs. If your choice in luxury cars or liberal causes could be linked to your neighborhood type, I reasoned, what other social and cultural phenomena were lifestyle-related? How does the structure of the forty neighborhood types affect the way Americans meet, settle down and raise families? What do the clusters mean to political alliances? How have they changed, and what are the current trends? In other words, what does the existence of the forty lifestyles reveal about who we are, where we came from and were we're going?

The Clustering of America explores these questions by piecing together the mosaic of the nation's forty neighborhood types. It combines census data, nationwide consumer surveys and interviews with hundreds of people across the country to produce a composite understanding of American lifestyles. For statistical data, Claritas let me tap into its data bases of buyer behavior, media patterns and lifestyle habits, while the consulting firm of Targeting Systems gave me access to its political polls on voting and ballot concerns. But the raw statistics provided only clues to the way people live; numbers simply can't convey a sense of place, the mood of a community, why life in one town revolves around its churches and in another its bohemian bars. So to meet the people behind the cold numbers, I went on the road and visited archetypical communities in each neighborhood type. I wanted to know if Young Influentials really do sip Perrier while watching "St. Elsewhere" after a tough workout at the club. And do Back-Country Folks actually chew tobacco and keep chain saws in their garages? I wanted to know why these lifestyles developed and why they endure.

My investigation into American lifestyles was far different from the televised trips through the boudoirs of the rich and famous by that breathless Englishman, Robin Leach. A dispassionate computer produced my itinerary, sending me to communities that mirrored the demographic profile of each neighborhood type. These cluster hotspots, while rarely starred in Fodor's guide, at least offered socioeconomic diversity —from the exclusive estates of Gibson Island, Maryland, to the struggling farmsteads of Early, Iowa, to the ramshackle rowhouses of Southeast Portland, Oregon. Between December 1985 and February 1987, I visited seventy-five communities, criss-crossing the country a dozen times and logging 50,000 miles by airplane and automobile. At each stop, I interviewed local politicians, reporters, shopkeepers, librarians, clergymen and typical residents—typical, at least, by cluster standards. My goal, while not a systematic investigation of every significant aspect of community life, was to present an accurate portrayal of forty quintessentially American lifestyles, each representing millions of people.

Ultimately, *The Clustering of America* explores the diversity of the way Americans really live: which issues concern us in local elections, how we define our dreams and aspirations, what we eat for Sunday brunch. It takes a little digging to learn that status in a Blue Blood Estates community like Malibu, California, is having a famous designer decorate your bedroom, while in the Hispanic Mix barrio of San Antonio's West Side, it's just having a son finish high school. In the Middle America town of Marshall, Michigan, Mayor Allen Bassage told me about his biggest headache—kids cruising the main drag—while we rested on lawn chairs at a summer evening's band concert (interrupted by the occasional blast from a souped-up Chevy). In the Mississippi Delta town of Belzoni, Mississippi, Herbert Allen described the segregated conditions facing black families of Tobacco Roads. As he did, two scrawny chickens danced around us and occasionally pecked at my tape recorder. "Looking back on my life," said the 57-year-old cotton farmer and father of nine, "I'm proudest of the fact that none of my children ended up in jail."

In the course of my fieldwork, people frequently asked whether the computer-based statistical portraits of their neighborhoods truly reflected the gritty reality. On most counts, the answer must be yes. Naturally, not everyone fits their neighborhood identity; Americans come in a marvelous variety and even those with similar demographics don't necessarily exhibit the same lifestyle.

But most people tend to move where they can afford to live, among people who are like themselves. Take the nation's book lovers. Last year, some 30 million Americans—17.5 percent of the population—each purchased more than six hardcover books. But book buyers are not evenly distributed across all American neighborhoods. The heaviest concentration lives in the affluent, suburban neighborhoods of college-educated, white-collar professionals—places like Highland Park in Dallas (a Money & Brains community) and Glendale, Colorado (Young Influentials). Cluster surveys show they also tend to belong to health clubs, enjoy foreign travel, attend the theater and engage in sports like skiing, hiking and sailing at rates well above national averages. On the other hand, they're not likely to booze much, enjoy pro wrestling, throw Tupperware parties, buy disco records or watch much TV. When America's book lovers aren't reading, chances are they're not turning into couch potatoes either.

Marketers find such insights fascinating and useful in their work, yet for others they can be unsettling. It is something in the nature of Americans to shun stereotypes and cherish distinctiveness. As noted economics writer Robert Samuelson has observed, "We favor equality yet clutch to diversity." But while the cluster system disputes the notion of a global village and the "malling" of America, it also reveals that there are hundreds of neighborhoods all over the country filled with households just like our own home, sweet home. However unique we may feel, we are not alone in our lifestyles.

Looking at the nation through a different prism is hardly a new idea. America has been examined from different vantages in every age—from Alexis de Tocqueville's *Democracy in America* and Joel Garreau's *The*

AMERICA'S BOOK LOVERS

The greatest concentration of American book buyers lives in suburban areas with high educational levels though not necessarily big incomes. In the starter-home neighborhoods of Young Suburbia, the middle-class residents are among the nation's leading readers—typically of Gothic romance novels. In contrast, the poorest and least-educated citizens of urban and rural America have the lowest rates of book buying. These are the nation's biggest TV watchers.

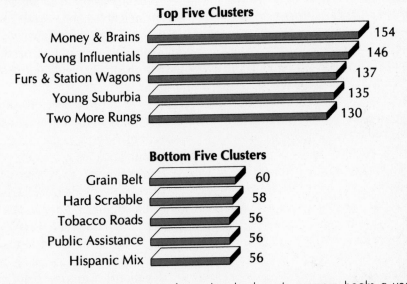

Top Five Clusters

Money & Brains	154
Young Influentials	146
Furs & Station Wagons	137
Young Suburbia	135
Two More Rungs	130

Bottom Five Clusters

Grain Belt	60
Hard Scrabble	58
Tobacco Roads	56
Public Assistance	56
Hispanic Mix	56

Numbers indicate percentages of people who buy six or more books a year, indexed against the national average. An index of 100 equals the U.S. average: 17.5%. An index of 154 means a cluster has 1.54 times the national average, or a book-buying population of about 27%. Source: SMRB 1985/86, Claritas Corp., 1987.

Nine Nations of North America to Ben Wattenberg's and Richard Scammon's *This U.S.A.* and Louis Harris's *Inside America*. While the first two works relied on the substantial powers of observation of their authors and the other two on the latest findings of the Census Bureau and syndicated surveys, *The Clustering of America* incorporates both perspectives: a journalistic work for the computer age. Most of us have an anecdotal sense of our community—whether the streets are filled with young singles, Japanese subcompacts and gourmet cookie shops or established families, domestic station wagons and the latest Tonka toys.

But *The Clustering of America,* with its aggregation of statistics and interviews, can confirm or contradict what we think is happening. A computer defined the boundaries of America's forty neighborhood types, but human beings determine the lifestyles within them.

One caveat: Like the people and communities it describes, the cluster system is dynamic, always changing as cities expand and contract, planned communities sprout and lifestyles shift. Thus the observations in this book reflect the progress and trends of our culture only at this point in time, America in the late 1980s. With every new consumer and census survey, the cluster portraits become clearer, the trends of American society more distinct. And as businesses and political organizations increasingly turn to cluster technology in the future, more Americans will understand the shared values of their lifestyle neighbors throughout the country.

Whether you're in the shadow of a skyscraper or a grain elevator, *The Clustering of America* demonstrates that where you live determines how you live.

1

THE CLUSTERING OF AMERICA

"Tell me someone's zip code, and I can predict what they eat, drink, drive—even think."
—Jonathan Robbin, creator of the PRIZM cluster system

It's enough to make the Statue of Liberty scratch her head.

In the tiny logging community of Molalla, Oregon, zip code 97038, residents ride through dusty streets on horseback or in pickup trucks, their deer rifles loaded in gun racks. Work grinds to a halt when hunting season begins, and the biggest holiday of the year isn't Christmas but the Buckaroo Rodeo, when locals gather to rope cattle, ride bulls and parade through town in spurs and leather-fringed cowboy outfits. Funerals are observed with a solemn procession of mammoth logging trucks.

A continent away, another American Dream dwells inside a renovated townhouse two blocks from a subway stop and a chic little Caribbean restaurant. In Dupont Circle, a downtown section of Washington, D.C., zip 20036, residents frequent shops that offer fresh squid-ink pasta, imported goat cheese and gourmet ice cream. Nightlife revolves around the abundant bars, outdoor cafes and leftist bookshops. The highlight of the social calendar for many is Gay Pride Day, when the local homosexual community celebrates itself with a parade of colorful floats, the drag queens decked out in sequined gowns and elbow-length white gloves.

Molalla and Dupont Circle may seem like peculiar pockets on the American landscape. But the truth is, more than 7 million people around

1

the country share these disparate lifestyles in their own communities. Throughout the nation, Americans live in distinctive community types, refusing to blend into the mythical melting pot. According to a population classification system linking census data to marketing and opinion surveys, America is made up of forty kinds of neighborhoods as different from each other as Molalla and Dupont Circle.

Call it the clustering of America, a new and revealing way to describe how U.S. citizens really live. From Beverly Hills to the Bronx, the nation resembles a patchwork quilt of lifestyles. Every one of America's 36,000 residential zip codes belongs to one of the forty neighborhood types— or "clusters." And each cluster has been dubbed with a descriptive nickname like Pools & Patios, Back-Country Folks and Norma Rae-Ville —monikers that summarize the characteristic lifestyle.

In Blue Blood Estates, which consists of America's richest neighborhoods, super-affluent suburbanites live in graceful mansions, drive luxury cars and avidly support political candidates and cultural charities. The poorest, most isolated of America's hamlets are called Hard Scrabble and can be found in areas ranging from the hollows of Appalachia to the Indian reservations of the Black Hills, where residents barely scratch out an existence living in tarpaper shacks. In between are clusters of city dwellers and small-town folk, college students and retirees, big families with Tonka toys and Weber grills and childless yuppies blending guacamole in their state-of-the-art Cuisinarts.

Taken together, the forty clusters reveal a surprisingly vivid portrait of America. In a nation that prides itself on being a classless, egalitarian society, the cluster system reflects the roaring diversity of how we live. Unlike the fifty states, whose boundaries were decided by rivers and surveyors' chains, the forty clusters of America are defined by demographic data and lifestyle surveys. What magazines do we read? Which cars do we drive? Are we more likely to buy pocket calculators or personal computers, drink domestic whisky or imported beer? Do we vote liberal or conservative, Republican or Democrat?

Within each cluster of neighborhoods, inhabitants tend to lead similar lives, driving the same kinds of cars to the same kinds of jobs, discussing similar interests at similar social events—cocktail parties here, backyard barbecues there, stoop-sitting elsewhere. In God's Country, a cluster of high-tech Silicon Valleys outside the nation's metropolitan areas, affluent city dwellers have taken their urban tastes to the countryside. Their clothes are Ralph Lauren, their cars are Saab and Subaru and their magazines are *Ski* and *Food & Wine*. Though 70 percent voted for President Reagan in 1984, many are sharply critical of his administration's laissez-faire environmental policies. Having made a conscious decision to settle in rustic surroundings, they guard their peaceful panoramas from toxic waste, developers' bulldozers and other unsightly intrusions.

Indeed, each cluster has a personality all its own, a perspective from which its residents view the world. In Bohemian Mix, composed of neighborhoods like Greenwich Village in New York and Haight-Ashbury in San Francisco, progressive ideas and liberal attitudes breed among its well-read and well-educated residents. In Coalburg & Corntown, a cluster of small towns in heartland America, locals socialize at American Legion halls and approach the Fourth of July with a sense of history. Bohemian Mixers smoke pot with their kids. The parents of Coalburg & Corntown worry about pot smoking among theirs. Sponsors of a Planned Parenthood fundraiser aim their pitches at Bohemian Mix neighborhoods. A smart conservative candidate running on a pro-family platform would bypass Bohemian Mix to canvas the blue-collar families of Coalburg & Corntown.

"A politician just can't say the same thing to all voters when some live in Bohemian Mix and others live in Coalburg & Corntown," says Charles Welsh, a political consultant who's employed the clusters in dozens of lobbying and election campaigns. "They speak a different language. Hell, they won't even drink in the same bar together."

You are where you live, according to *The Clustering of America*. And understanding the competing cluster viewpoints can help us sort out and assess the complex issues that divide a community. In Blue-Collar Nursery neighborhoods, composed of child-rearing suburban families, parents petition to build more schools for their children. In Pools & Patios subdivisions with older, empty-nesting households, residents vote to reduce the school tax and debate whether to convert closed schools into retirement homes or office condominiums. Cities with appreciable numbers of both neighborhood types often find themselves embroiled in battles over Proposition 13–type tax-cutting bills.

The clusters provide a framework for making sense of our pluralistic society and for finding our way around in it. Singles seeking Mr. or Ms. Right would increase their odds by moving to the cluster with the greatest concentration of singles—Bohemian Mix. Senior citizens old enough to retire but young enough to live a little would look for a Gray Power settlement like Sun City, Arizona, where residents spend their days jogging between golf courses and crafts lessons. Study the clusters and you'll discover why one local politician supports free trade while another from a neighboring town lobbies for stiffer tariffs, why one

AMERICA'S FORTY NEIGHBORHOOD TYPES

Cluster	Thumbnail Description	Percent U.S. Households
Blue Blood Estates	America's wealthiest neighborhoods includes suburban homes and one in ten millionaires	1.1
Money & Brains	Posh big-city enclaves of townhouses, condos and apartments	0.9
Furs & Station Wagons	New money in metropolitan bedroom suburbs	3.2
Urban Gold Coast	Upscale urban high-rise districts	0.5
Pools & Patios	Older, upper-middle-class, suburban communities	3.4
Two More Rungs	Comfortable multi-ethnic suburbs	0.7
Young Influentials	Yuppie, fringe-city condo and apartment developments	2.9
Young Suburbia	Child-rearing, outlying suburbs	5.3
God's Country	Upscale frontier boomtowns	2.7
Blue-Chip Blues	The wealthiest blue-collar suburbs	6.0
Bohemian Mix	Inner-city bohemian enclaves à la Greenwich Village	1.1
Levittown, U.S.A.	Aging, post–World War II tract subdivisions	3.1
Gray Power	Upper-middle-class retirement communities	2.9
Black Enterprise	Predominantly black, middle- and upper-middle-class neighborhoods	0.8
New Beginnings	Fringe-city areas of singles complexes, garden apartments and trim bungalows	4.3
Blue-Collar Nursery	Middle-class, child-rearing towns	2.2
New Homesteaders	Exurban boom towns of young, midscale families	4.2
New Melting Pot	New immigrant neighborhoods, primarily in the nation's port cities	0.9
Towns & Gowns	America's college towns	1.2
Rank & File	Older, blue-collar, industrial suburbs	1.4
Middle America	Midscale, midsize towns	3.2
Old Yankee Rows	Working-class rowhouse districts	1.6

Cluster	Thumbnail Description	Percent U.S. Households
Coalburg & Corntown	Small towns based on light industry and farming	2.0
Shotguns & Pickups	Crossroads villages serving the nation's lumber and breadbasket needs	1.9
Golden Ponds	Rustic cottage communities located near the coasts, in the mountains or alongside lakes	5.2
Agri-Business	Small towns surrounded by large-scale farms and ranches	2.1
Emergent Minorities	Predominantly black, working-class, city neighborhoods	1.7
Single City Blues	Downscale, urban, singles districts	3.3
Mines & Mills	Struggling steeltowns and mining villages	2.8
Back-Country Folks	Remote, downscale, farm towns	3.4
Norma Rae-Ville	Lower-middle-class milltowns and industrial suburbs, primarily in the South	2.3
Smalltown Downtown	Inner-city districts of small industrial cities	2.5
Grain Belt	The nation's most sparsely populated rural communities	1.3
Heavy Industry	Lower-working-class districts in the nation's older industrial cities	2.8
Share Croppers	Primarily southern hamlets devoted to farming and light industry	4.0
Downtown Dixie Style	Aging, predominantly black neighborhoods, typically in southern cities	3.4
Hispanic Mix	America's Hispanic barrios	1.9
Tobacco Roads	Predominantly black farm communities throughout the South	1.2
Hard Scrabble	The nation's poorest rural settlements	1.5
Public Assistance	America's inner-city ghettos	3.1

Household percentages are based on 1987 census block groups and estimated to the closest 0.1 percent. Source: PRIZM (Census Demography), Claritas Corp., 1987.

marketer will hawk a new product via Hal Holbrook and another will hire Max Headroom.

In the last decade, social commentators hearing a Muzak drumbeat have complained that the country has homogenized itself into a monotonous two-lane highway, a land where gas station follows burger joint follows video store. Quaint New England towns boast Tex-Mex drive-ins where lobster shacks once stood. Newspapers like *USA Today* transmit the latest trends to readers in rural sections of the country, and syndicated talk shows have become national forums for debate on everything from racial unrest to child abuse. Across the land, shopping malls sprout overnight like concrete mushrooms.

But anyone who's traveled this country outside its metropolitan sprawl soon discovers that America is too full of local charms and contradictions to be reduced to a single pale village. A youngster can grow up in the Middle America town of Marshall, Michigan, without ever experiencing the controlled atmosphere of a shopping mall. The Hard Scrabble folk who live in the Appalachia community of New Milton, West Virginia, must travel 25 miles for a fast-food burger—and then the choice is limited to whatever Wendy's is serving. "Americans are made of some alloy that won't be melted," observes Charles Kuralt, CBS-TV's wandering correspondent, who, after a million miles and two decades of "On the Road" interviews, should know.

And yet, for all our local idiosyncracies, *The Clustering of America* shows that neighborhoods separated geographically can be virtually identical in lifestyle. California and New Jersey may be thousands of miles apart, but the cluster system illustrates that Palo Alto and Princeton have much in common. Both classified as Money & Brains communities, they share a populace of white-collar professionals and technocratic executives, swank homes valued at more than $200,000 and high subscription rates to *Architectural Digest* and *Town & Country.* Perrier fizzes in their fridges. Invitations to Republican fundraisers arrive in the mail. On a cluster map, people who live 3,000 miles apart yet share the same neighborhood type have more in common with each other than with those people who live only three miles away.

And the map is always changing—through gentrification, urban decay and demographic shifts. The swing from a manufacturing nation to a service economy, for instance, has battered Mines & Mills, a cluster of coal- and steel-based factory towns located throughout the Northeast. Consumer surveys show that the union workers who used to buy new luxury sedans now drive stripped-down subcompacts like Dodge Omnis and AMC Eagles. Once-crowded bars and bowling alleys have locked their doors, their patrons moved away. The population in the cluster

CLUSTER DISTRIBUTION

Displayed on a map, America's lifestyle clusters resemble a vast patchwork quilt cut from forty pieces of cloth. While some neighborhood types—like Young Suburbia (top)—are widely distributed around the country, others—like Urban Gold Coast (bottom)—are concentrated in a few regions. The boundaries represent the nation's 200 TV markets, those reception areas reached by stations in a major city. An entire TV market will be shaded even if a neighborhood type is concentrated in only a small portion of its area. The Washington, D.C., TV market, for example, which includes parts of Maryland and Virginia, is shown to have a heavy concentration of Urban Gold Coast neighborhoods, even though they are concentrated in only a few sections of town.

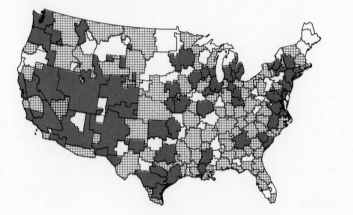

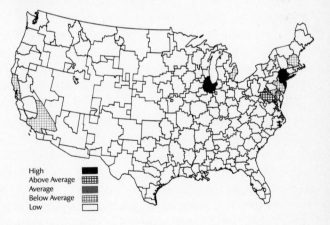

High
Above Average
Average
Below Average
Low

SOURCE: Claritas Corp., 1987.

community of Monessen, Pennsylvania, tumbled to 11,000 after the 1986 shutdown of the Wheeling-Pittsburgh steelworks—down from nearly 25,000 in the early 1960s. Laid-off workers now pass the time drinking Iron City beer on street corners, and pharmacists report that the most often prescribed drug is one for stress.

Still, the bad news in Mines & Mills is good news for New Home-steaders, which comprises Sunbelt boomtowns filled with assembly-line exiles. In a cluster town like Loveland, Colorado, the local population doubled during the 1970s to 31,000, as workers sought computer-based jobs with such firms as Hewlett-Packard. The rush of newcomers has forced some to take temporary jobs until new positions open up. In Loveland, scratch a waiter and you'll find an ex-autoworker from De-troit.

These trends represent just the latest chapters in what sociologist Nathan Glazer calls "the permanently unfinished story of America." For every fading factory town, a new community emerges to take up the social and economic slack. The emergence of the Black Enterprise cluster during the last decade marked the first significant presence of upper-middle-class black communities in the United States. Typically created in white, middle-class suburbs emptied by "white flight," Black Enterprise suburbs today are racially mixed, with middle- to upper-middle-class incomes and consumption patterns to match. Cascade Heights, on the western edge of Atlanta, presents a classic Black Enter-prise street scene: shady boulevards home to Montessori schools, ten-nis courts, BMW repair shops and a diner, basking in a pink neon glow, that unpretentiously calls itself the Beautiful Restaurant. The only dis-turbing aspect is what Cascade represents: the top of the heap for America's largest minority group. Except for a few exclusive areas, such as the Money & Brains community of Crenshaw in Los Angeles, there are virtually no predominantly black wealthy neighborhoods in the United States.

From boomtowns to ghost towns, *The Clustering of America* cap-tures our patchwork-quilt society in motion, producing a portrait colored by our habits, attitudes and values. To be sure, the forty neighborhood types don't reflect the living standard in fringe communities such as back-to-nature communes, gay enclaves or religious communities like the late Rajneeshpuram. Statistically speaking, there simply aren't enough people who've congregated into these kinds of communities to be counted among the nation's forty most common lifestyles. Yet the cluster system can discriminate among eleven distinct types of suburban communities, all at different socioeconomic levels and each with its own way of looking at the world. And the cluster system explains why two demographically similar neighborhood types behave in drastically different ways when it comes to solving local civic problems.

A while ago, the normally sedate Minneapolis suburb of Coon Rapids faced the problem of mischievous teenagers who had no hang-outs for blowing off steam. The youths roared through the streets in turbo-charged muscle cars, gunning the engines like latter-day James Deans and scaring the younger children who, too, had no place to play but in the street. The parents of Coon Rapids handled the situation in a manner appropriate for this and other Blue-Chip Blues communities filled with high-school-educated, blue-collar families. Baseball bats in hand, a posse of fathers cornered the hot-rodders one night and threatened bodily harm to life and machine if they persisted in using the neighborhood as a drag strip. The teenagers got the message and never returned.

Only a few miles across town in the suburb of Eagan, residents in a newly developed Young Suburbia subdivision faced a similar problem. The owner of a beat-up truck spent every Saturday tinkering with it, gunning the engine for hours at a stretch and disrupting the neighborhood's peace and quiet. In this community of college-educated, white-collar professionals, creative nonviolence was the answer. Several residents called the town clerk's office, learned of a local statute that barred such work outside an enclosed garage, and contacted the police to issue a citation. "We told them they'd have to live up to our standard of living because we weren't going to stoop down to theirs," one neighbor put it. Some months later, the truck owner and his family moved out.

"But why write about either place?" sniffed an urbane 50-year-old Minneapolitan when told of these incidents. Standing in the restored parlor of an 1897 Victorian house in the city's Lowry Park section, she dismissed both communities with a wave of her hand. "They're both so ishy, so tacky," she said. Indeed, from her perspective, a hip Bohemian Mix world, there was no reason to venture beyond the interchanges into the suburban world of unsophisticated, child-rearing families. She had chi-chi boutiques nearby, a gourmet deli down Hennepin Avenue and the nightly parade of joggers and roller skaters around Lake of the Isles. And yet those features that would make most American yuppies salivate were precisely the amenities that residents of Blue-Chip Blues and Young Suburbia wanted no part of. As one Coon Rapids resident put it, "Out here, we don't have to dress up to go anywhere—and we don't want to."

Obviously, when Saul Steinberg drew his famous *New Yorker* cover of the self-centered Manhattanite who saw the nation as a wasteland beyond the Hudson River, he wasn't just expressing the sentiments peculiar to the Big Apple. Variations of that illustration have popped up in virtually every other city—and would be applicable for small towns and rural hamlets as well. Most Americans don't know how the other 95 percent of the populace live—much less the other half. Yet none of us wants to feel like a stranger in our own land. *The Clustering of America* attempts to illuminate the many versions of the American Dream and explain why we do the things we do.

TAMING THE MARKETPLACE JUNGLE

For all its whimsy, this lifestyle portrait of America is grounded in the disciplines of sociology and statistical analysis. The forty clusters were created by Jonathan Robbin, a 57-year-old social scientist turned entrepreneur who pioneered a computer-powered marketing technique called geodemographics in the 1970s. At the time, consumer researchers were frustrated by the sudden ungluing of the mass market, driven by such demographic trends as skyrocketing divorce rates and double-income households. Standard demographic surveys that classify consumers by age, sex and income had lost their edge. Females aged 18 to 35 and earning over $15,000 annually simply no longer behaved predictably. Those who grew up eating fluffy white bread might one day start scouring the supermarket for croissants, rye bread or English muffins.

Robbin, a Harvard-educated computer whiz, maintained that consumers could be more efficiently grouped in neighborhood-sized markets. He believed that the U.S. Census held a treasure trove of information about the social class and economic status of the nation—and computers held the key. When the government released the first magnetic tapes of the 1970 census, Robbin set out to translate census data, then gathered in arcane units called "tracts," into a vernacular everybody understands, the zip code.

A short, stocky, professorial type equally at home quoting Baudelaire and R. Crumb, Robbin is not your typical Madison Avenue huckster. As a programmer during the 1950s when computers were in their infancy, he developed ways for reducing vast amounts of research data into a few clusters of meaningful numbers. For one project, he helped a geologist classify Bahamian sea-bed fossils according to salt content, temperature

THE ZOOM LENS: PINPOINT TARGET MARKETING

Cluster targeting enables marketers to pinpoint locations of people who reflect the ideal customer profile—areas as small as one of the nation's 254,000 census blocks, each containing about 340 households. Other commonly used marketing units are census tracts (about 1,270 households each) and zip codes (about 2,320 households each).

THE PRIZM ZOOM LENS

America	Atlanta	De Kalb	Decatur
By Markets	By Counties	By Zips	By Block Groups

SOURCE: Claritas Corp., 1987.

and depth. On assignment for the Office of Economic Opportunity, he mined the wealth of federal studies to draw a computer-based profile of every county in the country—culminating in a massive 187,000-page report that characterized every jurisdiction's housing, educational level, health problems, even poverty index.

In 1971, Robbin launched Claritas (Latin for "clarity") Corporation to build a cluster system of U.S. neighborhoods for marketing applications. He began with the 1930s theories of University of Chicago sociologists who described city neighborhoods as prime examples of "social clustering," where people tend to congregate among people like themselves. Then he programmed Claritas computers to analyze each zip code according to hundreds of characteristics in five groupings: social rank, mobility, ethnicity, family life cycle and housing style. From the morass of census results—which included such data as the number of Samoans with indoor plumbing—Robbin identified thirty-four key factors that account, statistically speaking, for 87 percent of the variation among U.S. neighborhoods. Finally, he instructed a computer to rate each zip code on the thirty-four factors simultaneously in order to assign it to one of forty clusters.

Why forty? In fact, Claritas analysts tested more than three dozen experimental models, some involving one hundred neighborhood types.

But the forty-cluster system proved the ideal compromise between manageability and discriminating power. "There's a greater latitude for error when the cookie cutter is so small and the number of unclassifiable types becomes quite large," explains Robbin, from an office cluttered with computer printouts and statistical texts. "With more clusters, you could pinpoint a monastery or prison, but that's hardly meaningful in a marketing sense."

In 1974, Robbin and his colleagues announced the Claritas Cluster System—with its forty "lifestyle segments" ranked along a pecking order of affluence called a Zip Quality (ZQ) scale—from Blue Blood Estates (with a ZQ rating of 1) to Public Assistance (ZQ40). Marketers liked the manageability of forty consumer groups that ranged in size from 0.5 to 6 percent of all American households. Magazines such as *Time, Newsweek* and *McCall's* were among the first clients, sorting their

THE ZQ LADDER: HOW THE CLUSTERS RANK

ZQ	Cluster	Median Income	Median Home Value	Percent College Grads
1	Blue Blood Estates	$70,307	$200,000+*	50.7%
2	Money & Brains	45,798	150,755	45.5
3	Furs & Station Wagons	50,086	132,725	38.1
4	Urban Gold Coast	36,838	200,000+*	50.5
5	Pools & Patios	35,895	99,702	28.2
6	Two More Rungs	31,263	117,012	28.3
7	Young Influentials	30,398	106,332	36.0
8	Young Suburbia	38,582	93,281	23.8
9	God's Country	36,728	99,418	25.8
10	Blue-Chip Blues	32,218	72,563	13.1
11	Bohemian Mix	21,916	110,668	38.8
12	Levittown, U.S.A.	28,742	70,728	15.7
13	Gray Power	25,259	83,630	18.3
14	Black Enterprise	33,149	68,713	16.0
15	New Beginnings	24,847	75,364	19.3
16	Blue-Collar Nursery	30,077	67,281	10.2
17	New Homesteaders	25,909	67,221	15.9
18	New Melting Pot	22,142	113,616	19.1
19	Towns & Gowns	17,862	60,891	27.5
20	Rank & File	26,283	59,363	9.2
21	Middle America	24,431	55,605	10.7
22	Old Yankee Rows	24,808	76,406	11.0
23	Coalburg & Corntown	23,994	51,604	10.4

subscriber lists by cluster in order to publish upscale editions with ads hawking high-priced luxury cars and furs for the residents of Blue Blood Estates and Money & Brains. When Colgate-Palmolive wanted to test-market a new detergent for young families, it sent miniboxes to Blue-Collar Nursery, characterized by starter-home neighborhoods teeming with young families. Although no neighborhood is strictly homogenous in all respects, the system works because the differences among the neighborhoods are more significant than the differences among households in the neighborhoods. "People are all different," says Robbin, "but clustering predicts where you can find more of one kind."

Like many statistical concepts that prove effective, Robbin's geodemography is based on a handful of simple principles. The key one is the old saw, "Birds of a feather flock together." "Basically, people seek out neighborhoods that are most congenial to them," he says. "At each

ZQ	Cluster	Median Income	Median Home Value	Percent College Grads
24	Shotguns & Pickups	$24,291	$53,222	9.1%
25	Golden Ponds	20,140	51,537	12.8
26	Agri-Business	21,363	49,012	11.5
27	Emergent Minorities	22,029	45,187	10.7
28	Single City Blues	17,926	62,351	18.6
29	Mines & Mills	21,537	46,325	8.7
30	Back-Country Folks	19,843	41,030	8.1
31	Norma Rae-Ville	18,559	36,556	9.6
32	Smalltown Downtown	17,206	42,225	10.0
33	Grain Belt	21,698	45,852	8.4
34	Heavy Industry	18,325	39,537	6.5
35	Share Croppers	16,854	33,917	7.1
36	Downtown Dixie-Style	15,204	35,301	10.7
37	Hispanic Mix	16,270	49,533	6.8
38	Tobacco Roads	13,227	27,143	7.3
39	Hard Scrabble	12,874	27,651	6.5
40	Public Assistance	10,804	28,340	6.3
	National Median	**$24,269**	**$64,182**	**16.2%**

ZQ, or Zip Quality, is a socioeconomic ranking based on income, home value, education and occupation—a kind of pecking order of affluence. Although jobs have no social status per se, they're rated in a complex weighting system on the basis of how much education and training they require. Source: PRIZM (Census Demography), Claritas Corp., 1987.

*Because the upper census limit for home values is $200,000+, the figures for Blue Blood Estates and Urban Gold Coast are estimates.

stage in their life cycle, people tend to join their peers in appropriate communities, whether it's in high-rise city apartments or single homes out in suburbia." A directly related insight is that demographically similar neighborhoods tend to share the same consumer patterns, no matter what the geographic location. As Robbin puts it, "You can go to sleep in Fairfield, Connecticut, and wake up in Pasadena, California, but except for the palm trees, you're really in the same place."

To cluster analysts, it's a chicken-and-egg argument about which comes first: Do people create a neighborhood lifestyle? Or does a neighborhood environment (housing, schools and businesses) influence how residents live? The cluster system simply holds that neighborhoods are remarkably stable. Despite folks moving in and out, the community lifestyle remains basically the same. "Over time, any resident of the same Blue Blood Estates neighborhood will still belong to the same country club, drive the Mercedes and travel to London," Robbin explains. "When you compare the scene today and the way it was ten years ago, it's really quite similar."

News of geodemography received wide circulation among consumer researchers and demographers—those people who count noses and plot the direction they're headed in. With forty clusters, they could draw a startlingly detailed picture of U.S. consumers. We leave a lengthy paper trail of how we behave, through subscription lists, mail orders and warranty cards—records that can be converted into clustered addresses. In 1978, Claritas launched PRIZM—Potential Rating Index by Zip Markets—which further linked the clusters to dozens of media, product and opinion surveys. Among them: the list of new-car buyers from R. L. Polk, the TV viewing diaries of A. C. Nielsen and the consumer buying polls of Mediamark Research Inc. and Simmons Market Research Bureau. High-tech computers now could accurately measure consumption patterns for thousands of different products, services and media. Knowing only a community's cluster classification, a marketer could predict the lifestyle of residents with startling accuracy—from the brands of bread likely to be found in the pantry to the political bent of magazines on the coffee table. In the neighborhoods where people read *The New Republic,* for instance, they tend to eat croissants rather than white bread.

Such knowledge is power for merchandisers customizing their products and sales efforts to reach specialized audiences. In the last decade, businesses have employed the clusters to market everything from credit cards to frozen corn-on-the-cob. Ringling Bros. and Barnum & Bailey Circus used the clusters to find out which kinds of communities have the most circus fans (Young Suburbia and Blue-Chip Blues) for developing promotion campaigns. When Buick downsized its ritzy Electra in 1985, cluster maps charted a shift in buyers, from Money & Brains to Young Influentials, as the company shifted its commercials from the nightly news to "St. Elsewhere." Another cluster project involved finding out where Atlanta's present and potential tequila drinkers lived—the results to determine where an outdoor advertising firm put up its billboards.

"Location, location and location" have long been called the three most important factors in a successful business. With clusters, a firm can analyze small demographic areas to pinpoint precise locations for improving the odds of finding prospective consumers. Hertz, for instance, has relied on cluster maps to decide where to open its used-car outlets and which models to display given the tastes of nearby consumers. When Young Influentials dominate, sporty compacts and convertibles are out front, enticing the young and affluent singles. In Two More Rungs communities, typified by upper-middle-class retirees, the lot features large, roomy sedans.

By reversing the process and clustering sales records, marketers can discover who their typical customer is and how to find more of them. When the National Symphony Orchestra in Washington, D.C., profiled its 10,000 subscribers in 1985, it learned that four times more residents in Money & Brains neighborhoods attended concerts than in Furs & Station Wagons. The major difference between the two clusters is that the former is composed of cosmopolitan singles and couples while the latter consists of affluent suburban families. "As soon as kids enter the picture," says NSO marketing director JoAnn Stellar, "we lose them." As a result, the NSO's 1986 telemarketing campaign focused on cultivating hitherto ignored neighborhoods like Capitol Hill, where childless Bohemian Mixers reside. In some of the targeted areas, subscription sales jumped 25 percent.

But clusters do more than create cash transactions; they pigeonhole people according to their attitudes and aspirations. When Defense Department recruiters were low on qualified troops for the all-volunteer army in 1980, cluster analysts resurrected G.I. records for the previous three years to pinpoint the neighborhood types that supplied the best male soldiers. In contrast to the urban minority areas that were the Marines' best hunting grounds, the army found that its top recruits hailed from rural and small-town clusters: Shotguns & Pickups, Mines & Mills, Blue-Collar Nursery and Coalburg & Corntown. The results told the army where to build additional recruiting centers to reach more

MCCLUSTERS: WHO EATS AT MCDONALD'S?

Cluster targeting can help marketers pinpoint where their likely consumers live, aiding in selecting sites for new restaurants. In McDonald's case, customers tend to come from small-town America, but not too small: the clusters with the fewest McDonald's fans live in the nation's most isolated communities.

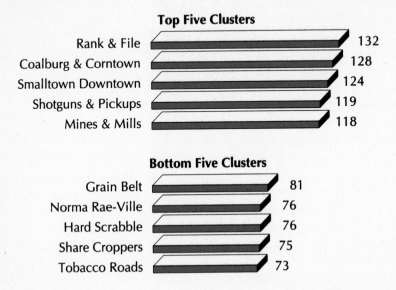

Top Five Clusters

Cluster	Index
Rank & File	132
Coalburg & Corntown	128
Smalltown Downtown	124
Shotguns & Pickups	119
Mines & Mills	118

Bottom Five Clusters

Cluster	Index
Grain Belt	81
Norma Rae-Ville	76
Hard Scrabble	76
Share Croppers	75
Tobacco Roads	73

Numbers indicate percentages of people who frequent McDonald's, indexed against the national average. An index of 100 equals the U.S. average: 36.2%. An index of 132 means a cluster has 1.32 times the national average, or 47.8%. Source: MRI Doublebase 1986, Claritas Corp., 1987.

promising recruits. And a cluster analysis of their reading habits revealed the recruits' favorite magazines—the logical publications in which to advertise. As it turns out, the men who want to "be all they can be" read *Field & Stream, Sports Afield, Outdoor Life* and *Mechanix Illustrated.*

To be sure, any student of popular culture may come up with roughly the same results. You needn't be a Rhodes Scholar to figure out that day-care centers don't hold much promise in the retirement resorts of Golden Ponds, or that a tattoo parlor won't make it big in Palm Beach, Florida. But people and their preferences frequently belie stereotypes.

Several years ago, the publishers of the Adam & Eve catalogue of erotic novelties wanted to find out precisely who was buying their

G.I. JOES: WHO JOINS UP

The U.S. Army's best recruits are high-school graduates from America's rural and small-town clusters. To lure them into joining up through print advertising, army officials discovered that their favorite magazines include *Field & Stream* and *Mechanix Illustrated.*

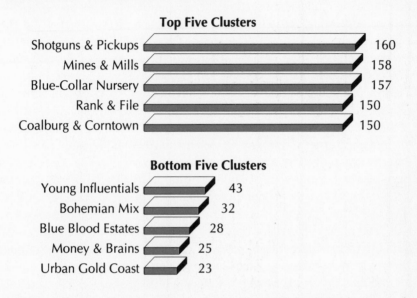

Top Five Clusters

Shotguns & Pickups	160
Mines & Mills	158
Blue-Collar Nursery	157
Rank & File	150
Coalburg & Corntown	150

Bottom Five Clusters

Young Influentials	43
Bohemian Mix	32
Blue Blood Estates	28
Money & Brains	25
Urban Gold Coast	23

Numbers indicate percentages of recruits indexed against the national average. An index of 100 equals the U.S. average: .67%. An index of 160 means a cluster has 1.60 times the national average, or 1.1%. Source: Claritas Corp., 1980.

offbeat wares. Cluster analysts presumed that the lacy lingerie and sex toys were purchased by those kinky residents of Bohemian Mix. But they were wrong. Money & Brains emerged as the dominant cluster in Adam & Eve's mailing list, a cluster only one step below Blue Blood Estates on the ladder of affluence. A typical Money & Brains neighborhood, the Coral Gables section of Miami is home to lawyers, doctors and corporate executives in swank stucco ranch houses. Cluster surveys showed these professionals to be sophisticated consumers of adult luxuries—whether they be speedboats or strawberry love oil.

From such profiles, America's consumer society reveals itself. In this land where you're pegged by what you wear, eat, drive and read, America's clusters illustrate that the ultimate yardstick for status and style is your neighborhood type. Is it any wonder that the second most common question in casual conversation after "What's your name?" is "Where are you from?" Answering that question reveals a great deal about "where you're coming from"—literally and figuratively.

Flavor boundaries, for instance, criss-cross the cluster map, reflecting the same factors of ethnicity, social rank and household composition that define neighborhood settlement. A kind of soft drink line splits the nation, separating the lemon-lime soda lovers of the north from the sweet fruit drink mavens to the south. Thus the heaviest consumers of lemon-lime sodas live in Grain Belt, the rural cluster of Scandinavian descendants with a taste for spicy foods, while Back-Country Folks, of English extraction, prefer sweet, fruity flavors to complement their relatively bland foods. In Atlanta, the citrus brands of Mountain Dew and Mellow Yellow are not big sellers among the city's blacks and transplanted northerners. But they do well in the surrounding mountain areas where many of the city's workers of English extraction live. You can see their bottles littering the roadsides of Interstate 75 leading into Atlanta.

Naturally, certain products find markets in all clusters, among all ages and ethnic groups. Consumers in all forty neighborhood types buy milk, toothpaste and toilet paper at similar rates. And dieters can be found in similar percentages in most clusters, although more Rotation Dieters may be found in Blue-Collar Nursery while Scarsdale Dieters may abound in Furs & Station Wagons. Not long ago, a cluster analysis of those who responded to a medical encyclopedia mail promotion produced a flat graph, prompting one Claritas executive to observe, "There are paranoid hypochondriacs everywhere."

Still, the cluster you call home will influence whether you want to be the first on the block to own a compact disc player or a Ronko potato peeler. Consumer surveys show that as a product ages, its appeal generally slides down the ZQ ladder. Thus, hi-fis, invented in the 1940s for classical music audiophiles of Blue Blood Estates, survive in the '80s as the boom boxes of Public Assistance projects. (Compact-disc players have moved into Blue Blood Estates.) And digital watches, the timepieces of Money & Brains in the '60s when their price tags hovered around $200, became the watches of Coalburg & Corntown in the '80s as prices dropped below $10. Today you find them in the five-and-dimes in the center of Columbia City, Indiana, a Coalburg & Corntown community of 5,502 that's been likened to "a real-life Mayberry." In a town with three stoplights, no movie theater and Old Glory waving down at the courthouse, residents take pride in tradition.

"You won't see a lot of Sony Walkmans around here," says Joseph Zickgraf, Columbia City's affable 59-year-old mayor. "Let other people

COLA WARS: COKE VS. PEPSI

Because of historic distribution patterns, Coke drinkers are more heavily concentrated in the South, while Pepsi drinkers are better represented in midwestern industrial cities. Even though more people buy Pepsi-Cola, Coca-Cola sells more, because Coke consumers drink more of their brand.

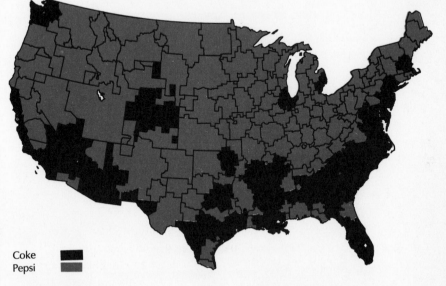

Coke
Pepsi

Top Five Clusters: Coca-Cola		Top Five Clusters: Pepsi-Cola	
Hard Scrabble	174	Hard Scrabble	162
Tobacco Roads	133	Norma Rae-Ville	124
Downtown Dixie-Style	119	Blue-Collar Nursery	120
Smalltown Downtown	117	Mines & Mills	117
Share Croppers	116	Coalburg & Corntown	116

Numbers indicate percentages of Coke and Pepsi drinkers indexed against the national average; data do not include diet brands. An index of 100 equals the U.S. average for each: 37.6% for Coca-Cola, 38.1% for Pepsi-Cola. An index of 200 means a cluster has twice the national average. Source: SMRB 1984/85, Claritas Corp., 1987.

try out new products and gadgets. We like to look things over before we accept them."

But popular culture doesn't always travel in a downward spiral. Who would have predicted that pro wrestling, long the sport of poor, rural

AMERICA'S SHOPPERS: SEARS VS. K-MART

Not all businesses aim for consumers in the wealthiest neighborhoods. Sears, for example, does booming business with the residents of middle- and upper-middle-class suburbs. K-mart, in contrast, appeals to shoppers from more downscale blue-collar towns.

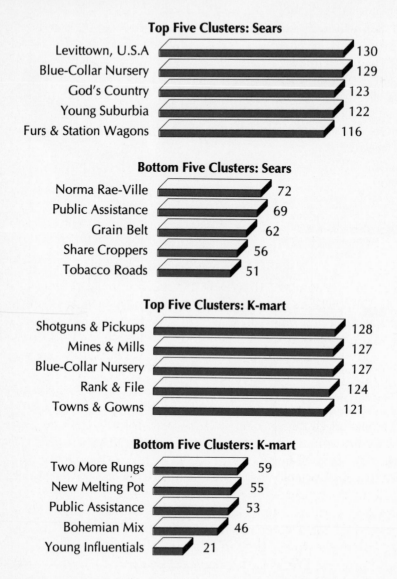

Top Five Clusters: Sears

Cluster	Index
Levittown, U.S.A	130
Blue-Collar Nursery	129
God's Country	123
Young Suburbia	122
Furs & Station Wagons	116

Bottom Five Clusters: Sears

Cluster	Index
Norma Rae-Ville	72
Public Assistance	69
Grain Belt	62
Share Croppers	56
Tobacco Roads	51

Top Five Clusters: K-mart

Cluster	Index
Shotguns & Pickups	128
Mines & Mills	127
Blue-Collar Nursery	127
Rank & File	124
Towns & Gowns	121

Bottom Five Clusters: K-mart

Cluster	Index
Two More Rungs	59
New Melting Pot	55
Public Assistance	53
Bohemian Mix	46
Young Influentials	21

Numbers indicate percentages of people who shop at Sears or K-mart, indexed against the national average. An index of 100 equals the U.S. average: 33.2% for Sears, 43.2% for K-mart. An index of 130 means a cluster has 1.3 times the national average, or 56.2% in the case of Sears. Source: SMRB 1985/86, Claritas Corp., 1987.

clusters like Norma Rae-Ville and Tobacco Roads, in the early '80s would become the darling of upscale rock'n'roll fans whose highest concentration is in Urban Gold Coast? Cluster analysts maintain that such cultural chasm-jumping is usually a sign of a fad—not a long-term trend. Recall the CB radio, a popular item among rural truck drivers that, in the early '70s, became the in thing for the wine-and-brie set commuting on congested freeways. Eventually, discouraging legislative statutes and new electronic gadgets put a damper on CB sales. By 1987, CB radios, like pro wrestling, had reverted to their origins in Norma Rae-Ville and Tobacco Roads, and the hip Urban Gold Coasters had moved on to the next symbols of reverse chic: plastic pink flamingos and "white trash" cooking.

In America's consumer jungle, sometimes there's just no accounting for taste.

CLUSTERS AND POLITICS

With their success in the marketplace, clusters moved into the political arena and the forefront of a revolution in American campaigning. In the late '70s, pollsters were tracking the declining influence of political parties at the same time consumer researchers were lamenting the breakup of the mass market. A new breed of volatile voter was going to the polls, ignoring party loyalties and traditional endorsements by unions, pastors and ethnic leaders. Ticket-splitting and single-issue voting began controlling elections as editorial writers dubbed these new voters "Demicans" and "Republicrats"—or just plain "Independents."

For political strategists, the clusters offered a way to reach these nontraditional voters where they lived. By merging opinion polls with the clusters, political marketers could "package" their candidates and issues to neighborhood voters with a degree of selectivity hitherto unimagined. In 1978, in the first political use of clusters, a Missouri labor organization killed an anti-union referendum by targeting pro-labor neighborhoods for a voter registration drive. Against all odds—two weeks before the vote, Missouri Senator Thomas Eagleton, a union backer, remarked, "We're going to get slaughtered"—the cluster campaign beat the referendum by a two-to-one margin.

Two years later, clusters figured in the re-election bid of West Virginia governor Jay Rockefeller by identifying the "fence-sitters" during the campaign—and what message would sway their vote. Polls showed that coal was the number-one issue in West Virginia, but it meant different things in different neighborhoods. Coal meant jobs to the working class residents of Mines & Mills towns like Beckley, and energy independence to the Towns & Gowns academics of Morgantown. Wherever Rockefeller appeared on the campaign trail, he tailored his coal speech to the appropriate clusters in his audience. And it worked. He was re-elected with 54 percent of the vote in the 1980 general election.

Nationwide, political surveys confirm that people living in the same cluster make similar choices—whether they're seeking a new liquor or a new leader. The threat of a Nicaraguan invasion, for instance, is feared more by the conservative, upscale suburbanites from Furs & Station Wagons than by the middle-class moderates of Levittown, U.S.A. According to nationwide surveys, Furs & Station Wagons voters see Central America as a potential Vietnam—a horrifying notion given so many teenage sons so close to draft age. In Levittown, U.S.A., which has one of the lowest concentrations of children in America, Nicaragua is seen as less of a threat to American peace and prosperity. Republican Furs & Station Wagons support aid to the contra-rebels. Moderate Levittowners donate money to political candidates advocating a hands-off policy in Central America.

Meanwhile, the newly arrived Asian immigrants of New Melting Pot are hardly aware of the contras. These generally apathetic citizens believe they have little impact on the political process, and many have never voted in a national election. They're concerned with establishing themselves in their new land, not with what happens to some rebel forces thousands of miles away. In surveys, they confuse the contras with the Sandinistas. Nicaragua might as well be Neptune.

William Hamilton, a Democratic pollster who's used the clusters in a dozen political and lobbying campaigns, sees their value in analyzing voter trends. As he explains, "Political strategists no longer have to say, 'Young people are going Republican.' They're able to say, 'Blue-Collar Nursery voters are going Republican but their upscale cousins in Young Influentials aren't.' They don't have to throw up their hands and shout, 'They're all over the place. How can I find them?' The clusters let them know that Young Influentials live in a little piece of Orlando, Florida, and two more pieces of Long Island. And polling them to find out their attitudes will let strategists craft a message to reach all of the cluster's voters."

With their ability to identify the political hot buttons of different voters, the clusters have gained acceptance in grass-roots lobbying and political fundraising campaigns. When the Reagan administration attacked Social Security as a drain on the budget in 1981, the Democratic

PROS AND CONTRAS

The threat of being drawn into a war in Central America is feared more by the conservative residents of Furs & Station Wagons, who support contra aid, than by the moderates of Levittown, U.S.A., who are dovish on any Central American involvement. The recently arrived immigrants of New Melting Pot are generally apathetic about the contra conflict—as well as most other political issues.

Cluster	Central American Doves	Dominant Ideology	Apathy Index
Levittown, U.S.A.	124	Moderate Republican	124
New Melting Pot	116	Independent	164
Furs & Station Wagons	72	Conservative Republican	78

Results are based on a survey of 5,500 Americans. Numbers indicate percentages of people who expressed specific ideologies or beliefs, indexed against the overall sampling. "Central American Doves" represents those opposing U.S. involvement in Central America; an index of 100 equals the sample average: 43%. The "Apathy Index" is based on several factors related to voting behavior and political participation. Source: Targeting Systems, Inc., 1985.

National Committee used the clusters for a direct-mail appeal to rarely tapped moderate-income Democrats for support to reinstate the proposed cuts. After sending its appeal to the subscription list of *Prevention* magazine, whose readership includes many over-55 Americans, the DNC discovered that the pitch worked best in clusters like Public Assistance (whose poor residents rely on Social Security as a subsistence income), Golden Ponds (where issues affecting the elderly hit close to home) and Young Influentials (where residents sympathized with the plight of older Americans).

A second DNC mailing, concentrating only on *Prevention* subscribers in the best-performing clusters, saw the response rate increase from 0.9 percent to 1.2 percent—a 33-percent improvement. Over the next two years, the DNC mailed some 15 million fundraising appeals to voters in the clusters sensitive to the Social Security issue, ultimately prompting 150,000 doners to ante up $15 to $20 apiece. The ground swell of support not only helped halt the cutbacks, it also illustrated the depth of concern among well-off young people in Young Influentials, who could afford to ignore the less fortunate elderly.

Young Influentials, which comprises 2.9 percent of America's households, is only one part of the most sought-after voting group: baby boomers, the largest segment of the populace, 70 million strong, now aged roughly 25 to 40. At least six neighborhood types are home to the boomers, each with a different lifestyle and political leaning. As a short-hand way of referring to the middle-class members with service-industry jobs, political consultants have dubbed them "new-collar voters." Numbering 25 million, they represent the nation's nonaligned populists: the voters who put Ronald Reagan in the White House while supporting Democratic congressional candidates. Unlike the yuppies of Young Influentials, new collars are more concerned about single-digit home mortgages, day-care centers for working mothers and clean air and water. Clearly, the two groups will never be confused.

"You tell a new-collar voter about $600 toilet seats at the Defense Department and he'll want to fire the people involved," says Ralph Whitehead, Jr., a University of Massachusetts professor who coined the new-collar term. "You tell a yuppie about one and he'll want to know what colors they come in."

Ultimately, the political strength of the cluster system lies in its ability to discriminate between two ideologically similar clusters. Knowing a neighborhood's political attitudes allows strategists to craft appeals using different voices to reach the distinct clusters. Analysts used to consider Urban Gold Coast and Bohemian Mix as cluster twins for their concentration of urban liberals with heavily Democratic registration; after all, these are the neighborhoods where the most popular TV show is "Late Night with David Letterman." But when Congress proposed legislation early in 1986 that would have doubled the 16-cents-a-pack federal excise tax on cigarettes, manufacturers mounted a write-your-representative campaign that demonstrated just how politically different the two clusters are.

Take Bohemian Mix, that political haven for what Tom Hayden has termed "frumpies—formerly radical, upwardly mobile professionals." Politically, they're anti-government leftists whose idea of nostaligia is talking about the last time they were gassed at a demonstration. The pro-cigarette campaign pitch cleverly appealed to their abhorrence of government intrusion into their private lives. Under a Marvel Comics–style portrait of an aging hippie titled "The Regulated American," the mailer listed a dozen areas of governmental control: PG-rated records, cyclamate bans and drug urinalysis, among others. "The message is tough but funny," recalls the campaign's creator, Lynn Pounian, president of Targeting Systems, Inc. (TSI). "Is life going to be one endless urine sample after another?"

To reach Bohemian Mixers' upper-class soul mates in the high-rise Urban Gold Coast, Pounian recognized a more serious, intellectual approach was needed. "This is where the American Civil Liberties Union is headquartered, and these people think smokers should be locked up," says Pounian, a reformed smoker herself. Accordingly, TSI's mailing to Urban Gold Coast was as dry as an annual report. "To Smoke or Not to Smoke—That Is Not the Question," the brochure began. "What Government Should Regulate—That Is the Question." The effectiveness of the opposition campaign was proved in part when, in late 1986, Congress defeated the cigarette tax increase. Although there are no records of how many letters were prompted by the targeted effort, TSI credits activism among Bohemian Mix and Urban Gold Coast residents for helping to defeat the measure. But each needed very different messages to light their political fires.

■ POTENTIAL FOR ABUSE

The victory for cigarette manufacturers raises ethical questions that have quietly dogged the cluster system since its invention. Should we worry about a computerized creation that plays to our subconscious? How vulnerable are we to these increasingly refined sales pitches?

Most Americans have a healthy paranoia about computerized files that can be manipulated to predict behavior—and for good reason. Computerized data bases are proliferating fast. Together, the top five credit-rating companies have records on more than 150 million Americans. And federal data bases contain some 288 million records on 114 million people, with 15 agencies mixing and matching data. Advances in technology are making it possible to cross-match information almost at the touch of a button to create detailed portraits of individuals and their expressed needs. As *American Demographics* editor Martha Richey observes, "The latest generation of marketers wants to get into that black box that is the mind of the individual."

To civil libertarians, these billions of bits of stored information about the private lives of Americans hold an alarming potential for abuse. "Companies are at the point where they can create a national data base on each person," claims Jan Goldman, staff attorney of the privacy project for the American Civil Liberties Union. "And we're very concerned whether private companies should have records of what people buy without their permission. Some information, like records of who's bought birth-control pills or X-rated cable shows, can hurt people."

For now, few laws govern the use of commercial data bases. In recent years, the ACLU has lobbied for an amendment to the Privacy Act of 1974 that would limit computer-matching capabilities among federal government agencies. But private companies are regulated at the state level and, in many states, the laws are often murky and contradictory.

Most marketers insist that their computer-based technology will never become Big Brother's bible. At Claritas, executives note that their cluster creation provides information about neighborhoods, not individuals; their smallest unit is the block group, averaging 340 households. Besides, they argue, target-marketing is still an incredibly inexact science. A successful direct-mail campaign using clusters may increase the response rate by a percentage point, from 2 percent to 3 percent—and be considered phenomenally successful because of the 50-percent improvement. But that still means that the system failed to motivate 97 percent of the targeted audience.

Despite such assurances, critics remain suspicious of the cluster technology, noting that "segmentation" sounds an awful lot like "segregation." Already, a West Coast bank has employed the clusters to decide whether to offer residents of certain neighborhoods a charge card with a credit line of $500, $1,000 or nothing at all—depending on each neighborhood's collective credit history. An East Coast developer now uses the clusters to decide where to locate new shopping malls and whether to seek as tenants Penney's or Bloomingdale's. Politicians who've used cluster polls to identify the undecideds in the electorate generally ignore the 50 percent of the population who don't vote, prompting charges that they're perpetuating low voter participation. Are clusters just another way for the rich to keep getting richer?

This question isn't irrelevant so much as misleading. Like it or not, computers—and their applications—are a fact of modern life. Just as the ancients saw patterns in the night sky and devised stories to explain the universe, we now look to computers to explain our world, to recognize patterns in our lives. The cluster system arrived at a time when both the mass market and the two-party political system were breaking down. It offered a new way to understand the behavior of huge segments of the populace. The prospect of returning to an era when communicators used only one broad channel to reach every American could mean a return to the time when advertisers addressed all women as housewives. Today, an advertiser simply can't ignore the vast majority of women who work in offices and factories and pursue a liberating variety of interests, careers and lifestyles.

As privacy laws eventually catch up with technology, the fear of abuses may be tempered by the benefits the clusters provide for our targeted, fragmented society. Instead of common-denominator TV programming, we can choose public or cable TV—"narrowcasted" to suit our interests and intellects. Merchandisers take chances on specialty products like taco chips, frozen croissants and granola bars, broadening our epicurean horizons. Soda machines, as RC Cola has spoofed in its commercials, thankfully serve more than just Coke or Pepsi. "The clusters help a big company think small," observes Coca-Cola vice president Pat Garner, who keeps one of two office computers loaded with cluster software. "They have a big impact on identifying niches in the marketplace and how to reach the targeted consumers. So a wine cooler is created for that niche between a soft drink and an alcoholic beverage."

John Wanamaker, founder of the Philadelphia department store chain that bears his name, once observed that half of all advertising dollars were wasted; he just didn't know which half. The clusters can now highlight the wasted half, with computer-drawn, color-coded maps. Although your zip code classification is one reason your daily mail is cluttered with brochures from Sears rather than The Sharper Image, the cluster system is also responsible for tons of junk mail your neighborhood never receives. The clusters keep businesses from sending their messages to the wrong people.

And the increasing sophisticiation of technology promises to produce only more cluster applications in the future. In 1986, *Reader's Digest* began planning for the day when it would become a completely clustered publication, printing forty editions each month to target-market their advertising. While the readers in Blue-Collar Nursery will be seeing ads for canned spaghetti, those in Young Influentials will be reading blurbs about health spas and espresso makers. It doesn't take a great leap of imagination to foresee *Digest* editors one day tailoring articles for each edition, sending a business profile to Young Influentials and a sports story to Blue-Collar Nursery.

In the political arena, the clusters are slowly entering the consciousness of pollsters and candidates alike. In *Power,* the 1983 Richard Gere film about campaign operatives, a discussion of how a candidate could reach "Pools & Patios" seemed only natural. On the 1988 campaign trail, the clusters have defined voters' concerns for the Democratic Party's attempt to recapture the White House. The results of one nationwide cluster poll became part of the 1986 report "New Choices in a Changing America," written by the Democratic Policy Committee, whose members include Delaware Senator Joseph Biden, Massachusetts Governor

Michael Dukakis and Missouri Congressman Richard Gephardt—at one time, all 1988 Democratic presidential candidates. Today's stump speeches are designed to appeal to coalitions of clusters with enough votes to win in November.

Whoever is in the White House, clusters will play an increasing role in American society. As the marketplace of ideas and goods becomes more competitive and crowded—nowadays, 60 percent of all new products fail within the first year—merchandisers and politicians will turn to clusters to reach their varied constituencies. Besides Claritas, several dozen marketing firms sell census data on floppy discs, and three advertise their own lifestyle cluster systems: C.A.C.I. of Arlington, Virginia; Donnelley Marketing Information Services in Stamford, Connecticut; and National Decision Systems of Encinitas, California. In addition, advances in technology are allowing businesses to merge such PRIZM-like cluster systems with other target-marketing tools, like SRI International's Values and Lifestyles (VALS), which divides Americans into nine categories based on introverted and extroverted personalities. And with each marriage of data bases, we take a step closer to understanding the tangle of reasoning and emotion that causes us to behave the way we do.

Where all this is going surely would have unnerved Benjamin Disraeli, the nineteenth-century British statesman who observed, "There are three kinds of lies: lies, damned lies and statistics." But even as we nod our heads in agreement, we remain obsessed with learning more about who we are and how we measure up. At its core, *The Clustering of America* reflects this long-standing love affair with numbers. The statistically based portraits of American lifestyles let us keep score of what we do, how we rate and whether we fit in—increasingly one of the great American pastimes. Does your convertible gain status points in downtown Dubuque or should you invest in halogen lamps in suburban Schenectady? Is your neighborhood the kind where partying means Gallo wine and Cheese Whiz or imported Scotch and Planter's honey-coated nuts? And why does reading this book probably place you among the communities of college-educated, white-collar, affluent Americans?

Of course, statistics don't tell the whole story. Walk through a Philadelphia ghetto, visit an Indiana town fair, listen to what's said at Sunday brunch in Queens, New York, watch singles socialize in Dallas. From these experiences, the flesh and blood of American life begins to emerge. And in the chapters that follow, we'll see the numbers come to life in the neighborhoods of all forty clusters throughout the country.

2

CLUSTER CLIMBING

"It's amazing. My grandparents lived in what was called a tenement. My parents lived in what was called an apartment house. I live in what is called a luxury condominium. What's so amazing about that, you might ask. It's all the same building."

—humorist Bob Orben

On the morning of December 11, 1983, an orange U-Haul van pulled into the driveway of a beige, Spanish-style ranch house in Paradise Valley, a suburb northeast of Phoenix. As a dry wind whipped up from the south, a carload of young men and women began hauling into the house boxes of books and racks of clothes, many from Brooks Brothers and Saks Fifth Avenue. They strained from the weight, moving with deliberation to avoid tracking any of the recently paved asphalt onto the front yard landscaped with river rock and crushed granite. On the driveway, two carpet-layers feverishly cut bolts of beige plush-pile that would grace much of the house.

Throughout Ryan Estates, a classic Furs & Station Wagons subdivision filled with roomy, contemporary ranch houses, this scene would be repeated countless times over the months and years to come. Located on the edge of one of the nation's fastest growing cities—Phoenix's population increased by 70 percent during the 1970s to 765,000—Ryan Estates has a reputation as a haven for "new money" and upwardly mobile executives. Many of its residents are entrepreneurs and high-tech engineers who relish their job titles, country club memberships and

29

backyard swimming pools. Nationwide, Furs & Station Wagons consumers are more than twice as likely as average Americans to play tennis, travel abroad, attend the theater and subscribe to *Architectural Digest.* In Phoenix society, living on one of Ryan Estates' third-of-an-acre lots means you've arrived.

Dave and Kathy Bost, a couple in their early 30s, are like many of their upwardly striving neighbors in this Furs & Station Wagons community. Raised in upper-middle-class suburbs of Pittsburgh, they both attended Michigan State University and married soon after graduation in 1977. Their 20s were a succession of cramped residences in run-down Single City Blues neighborhoods. In 1982, a year after the birth of their daughter, Laura, they borrowed most of the $180,000 needed to build a lace-stucco dream house in an area "suitable for bringing up a child," Kathy says. They planted cacti in the front yard and added a modular cedar playground out back. In a corner of the backyard, Dave transformed the Bermuda grass into a putting green—a place to entertain his bosses and stay on the fast track. And the track was fast indeed: in his seven years as a marketing manager with Morrison-Knudson, a construction consulting company, his salary had tripled—from $19,000 to $60,000.

But the Bosts, like many of their Paradise Valley neighbors, weren't putting down permanent roots in Ryan Estates. "Even as we were building this house, we were already talking about how we wanted the next one to look," says Dave, a tall and earnest man whose crisply pressed suit amazingly stands up to the withering Arizona heat. "Most people around here stay two or three years and then move up," adds Kathy, a part-time insurance claims adjustor with dark, gently tossed hair. "Our neighbors are always trying to better themselves through the size of their homes," she continues. "They're constantly saying, 'We have 2,400 square feet but we really need 3,200.'"

Ryan Estates represents the Bosts' fourth move in seven years, a typical American pattern. Almost a fifth of us relocate every year (not as frequently as an Arab nomad but much more footloose than the typical Japanese or English householder). Major life events—marriage, children, a job change, divorce—send us packing more often than the wish to acquire more square footage. Author and scholar Michael Novak likens moving to one of America's fundamental freedoms: the pursuit of happiness. "In a free society," he's observed, "there is no one story that people have to live. During one period, a person might be backwoodsy and rural, testing the simple life, and in another take on the fast-paced challenge of a city."

Why someone chooses a new neighborhood isn't easy to explain. A 1984 survey by the MIT–Harvard University Joint Center for Housing Studies found that people are drawn to neighborhoods because of a current, pressing need. To those in their 20s, the prime consideration in selecting a home is its suitability for raising young children. Those in their 30s are more concerned with the quality of local schools. From 40 to 55, ease in commuting is important. Older folks want safety from crime.

But overriding these basic considerations is the powerful clustering principle: people seek compatible neighbors who share their family status, income, employment patterns and values. When comparing 5,000 households that moved between 1978 and 1983, a nationwide study found that nearly half remained in the same cluster, moving, for instance, from a Bohemian Mix neighborhood in Chicago to a Bohemian Mix neighborhood in Boston. In addition, a significant portion stayed within a half-dozen rungs on the Zip Quality ladder of socioeconomic status, moving from, say, one small-town neighborhood type like Coalburg & Corntown to another slightly larger and more prosperous small-town cluster, Middle America. Every new home choice, according to the data, reflected the sum total of each household's upbringing, aspirations and achievements. Consciously or not, the movers understood where they fit in.

Traditionally, the American Dream is a steady progression up the ZQ ladder. A middle-class child of the baby boom generation starts as a college student living in Towns & Gowns, that cluster of college towns like Bloomington, Indiana, typically plopped down in the countryside. The graduate moves into the work force and an apartment complex in a Young Influentials haven, say, Redondo Beach, California, filled with health clubs and singles bars. After marriage and the first child, the new family settles into a split-level home in a Young Suburbia subdivision near good schools and crime-free parks—places like Lilburn in Atlanta or Smithtown on Long Island. As income and family size increase, it's into the moving van and on to homes in Furs & Station Wagons–type surroundings until, with retirement, a final move to a Gray Power retirement community like Sun City Center, Florida, surrounded by golf courses, social clubs and dependable medical services.

The ideal upwardly mobile climb, however, does not always coincide with reality. Where upward mobility for the middle class was once a given, midscale Americans now find themselves moving both up and down the economic ladder. A 1987 Gallup poll reported an all-time high in the percentage of Americans who expected their standard of living to

MOBILE AMERICANS

This map shows concentrations of neighborhoods whose residents have moved within the last year. The most active neighborhood types are those containing predominantly young, single people living in clusters like Young Influentials, Bohemian Mix and New Beginnings. A wide range of businesses—financial institutions, moving companies and builders, for example—use such maps to plot business expansion or marketing efforts.

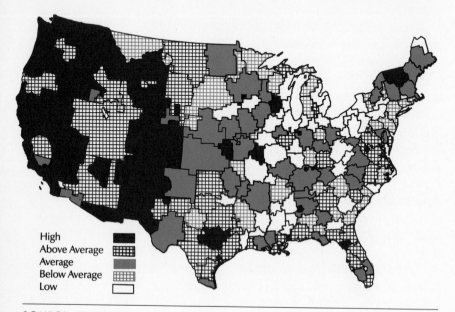

High
Above Average
Average
Below Average
Low

SOURCE: PRIZM (Census Demography), Claritas Corp., 1987.

improve during the next year. At the same time, a near-record number believed their living standard would decline.

This socioeconomic turbulence has even engulfed those who remain in their houses and apartments year after year. In the Back Bay area of Boston, a gentrifying district of Victorian brownstones, a wave of homesteading renovators in the '80s has helped push up local housing values 30 percent annually. Some longtime residents make more money going to sleep each night than heading for work each day. Locals have achieved a new level of affluence—and a higher ZQ level as their cluster designation jumped from Bohemian Mix to Money & Brains—just by sitting tight and cashing in on the inflationary spiral of their old homesteads.

Traditionally, education has opened the door to upward mobility. The nation's wealthiest neighborhoods in Blue Blood Estates, communities like Bloomfield Hills, Michigan, lead all the clusters in educational attainment—51 percent of residents have completed college. Conversely, a lack of education can keep even the most ambitious on the lower socioeconomic rung. That's typical in Hard Scrabble, the rural cluster that has the highest concentration of undereducated Americans—59 percent of its 2 million residents never completed high school. In these poor, remote settlements of several hundred residents—outposts such as Boonville, Kentucky, Pineville, Tennessee, and New Milton, West Virginia—the median household income, $12,874, is not much greater than the U.S. poverty line, and the highest-rated consumer items including chewing tobacco, CB radios, hunting magazines and powdered soft drinks. Of the Hard Scrabble children who go to college—less than 7 percent throughout the cluster—not surprisingly, most will not return there to live. They, like generations before, will head for opportunities in bigger cities. Without local jobs to improve their lot, many Hard Scrabble teenagers look to the U.S. Army as a ticket to higher social status.

Although small-town America as a whole grew by more than 15 percent in the decade from 1970 to 1980, Hard Scrabble represents those towns with fewer than 500 residents that have lost 3 percent of their population—mostly ambitious young people. That's what happened in New Milton, a Hard Scrabble community of 242 households located in the northwestern mountains of West Virginia. A gas and lumber center of 1,200 at the turn of the century, New Milton began to fade in the 1940s when the railroad ceased stopping in town, and the last bit of commerce, a general store, disappeared in a 1950 flood. Today, there's little more to New Milton than a two-room post office, a handful of churches and its characteristic "block houses," dwellings made of cinderblock with corrugated metal roofs, clutching the sides of twisting mountain roads. Grocery stores, medical clinics and even gas stations are a dozen miles away in the county seat of West Union. Postmistress Creola Nicholson estimates that half the households on her rural mail route are on welfare, and many others commute 100 miles a day for employment. "There's just nothing here in the way of work," says Nicholson, a no-nonsense woman who greets customers in a folksy mountain drawl. "You have to leave here if you want a job."

For the residents of New Milton's isolated "hollers," attending school has never been easy. Fern Cumpston, a 67-year-old native with thick glasses, unruly white hair and a strength that belies her age, never completed ninth grade, though not for lack of interest. "I lived way up in the holler and had to walk 3 miles to catch a bus that then had to travel 16 miles to school," she says from the living room of her block house decorated with ceramic owls and lace doilies on worn armchairs. "Every day I'd start before daylight and get in after dark. And when it rained, sometimes the mud would be up to my waist." After dropping out of school, Cumpston helped out on the family farm until her twenty-first birthday when she married a neighboring farm boy who only went as far as the eighth grade.

Today Fern and Rex Cumpston live on 234 rocky acres his father farmed, getting by on $272 monthly Social Security checks. They have a satellite dish that brings in televangelists and country singers from Nashville. But that's their only link to the global village. Rex, a laconic 73-year-old whose passion is racoon hunting by moonlight, has never flown in an airplane or driven more than an hour from their mountain hollow. Fern, who's visited out-of-state relatives, admits their lives are sheltered and wonders how they would have turned out "if we'd have lived closer to school." But she doesn't often dwell on might-have-beens. After finishing the household chores, she spends any free time reading the Bible, her horizon extending only as far as the top of the next ridge and the Union Mission Church, a white clapboard building with a freshly painted outhouse in back.

At all rungs on the ZQ ladder, Americans face obstacles when trying to upgrade their lifestyles. Some twenty-five years after the birth of the civil-rights movement, segregation in housing has hung on more tenaciously than any other aspect of racially divided American life. A decade ago the residents in South Boston, a working-class Old Yankee Rows community, greeted black schoolchildren bused in from the Public Assistance ghetto of Roxbury with demonstrations and physical abuse. Although the courts ordered busing to desegregate the schools, they couldn't crack the social barriers that resisted integration in white, old ethnic neighborhoods.

The same racial attitudes persist in Revere, Massachusetts, an Old Yankee Rows town of 37,500 predominantly Irish and Italian residents north of Boston. Intermarriage and low mobility have made relatives of many residents. "There are lots of Murphys on the roster of the Sons of Italy club," one local columnist observed. Both ethnic groups alternate in supplying the town's police force and political leaders—not to mention defendants ensnared in regular corruption trials that ultimately boil down to nepotism. Other ethnic groups, especially Asians, are slowly making inroads. Along Revere's main drag, you can stop for dinner at the China Roma Restaurant, owned by two locals—one Italian and the other Chinese.

While it may work on the menu, such mingling doesn't cross housing lines; Revere remains 99.2 percent white. When asked why his town had so few minorities yet was so close to the black neighborhoods of Boston, Revere Mayor George Colela, an old-fashioned pol with slicked-back hair, bushy sideburns and a wide tie, simply shrugged: "I just don't know."

However, in his appliance dealership down the street, Revere native William "Peco" Myers speaks with greater insight when he observes, "This is a close-knit community and people keep to themselves. Most of the homes for sale never get on the market." A stout figure with a ruddy Irish complexion and a puckish grin, Myers puts his feet up on his cluttered desk and breathes out a swirl of cigarette smoke. "First a house is offered to members of the family, and that means distant cousins," he explains. "If no member of the family wants it, it's offered to the other families on the block and all their relatives, and then to the families in the neighborhood. You rarely hear of a house being sold to an outsider—and this is the way it's been done since the 1940s." Leaning forward, he pauses to stamp out his cigarette butt before concluding: "If there's any sin here, it's that people watch out for their own."

For the poor, the stiffest resistance to bettering their lives typically comes from residents who only recently graduated from poverty themselves. In Anacostia, an Emergent Minorities district dominated by lower-middle-class blacks in Southeast Washington, D.C., the increase in Asian-American businesses has led to battles over economic integration. In one incident, a heated argument over an order of chicken wings between a dissatisfied black customer and a weary Korean carryout owner escalated into verbal abuse, vandalism and a weeks-long boycott that shattered the capital's black-Asian relations. Blacks charged that Asian-American newcomers had taken local businesses and some jobs away from blacks. The Asian-American store owners responded that blacks were jealous of their enterprise and unwilling to work hard themselves. The undercurrent of frustration that erupts in periodic violence is typical in Emergent Minorities communities, where the real enemy is the economic system that forces competition for the same scarce resources, jobs and housing.

"These blacks feel their sense of status in jeopardy by outsiders," says Dr. Elijah Anderson, an urban sociologist at the University of Pennsylvania, who's conducted landmark studies on race relations in

Philadelphia's gentrifying neighborhoods. "They've carved out their own niche and believe that any mixing threatens their group position. Working-class people tend to be xenophobic."

But it's not just working-class people. In most neighborhoods, residents resist whenever the government announces plans to build subsidized housing or a developer issues a press release for a high-density project out of character with the prevailing housing stock. In Beverly Hills, California, one of the oldest Blue Blood Estate enclaves, homeowners once considered building a wall around their exclusive area to keep out the riffraff of surrounding Los Angeles. Some residents of Potomac, Maryland, one of the newer Blue Blood Estates communities outside Washington, D.C., zealously guard their zoning restrictions, which prohibit building on plots of less than 2 acres, effectively barring new subdivisions. And whenever developers attempt to chop up a farm for a new split-level subdivision, locals protest the move on the grounds that the homes might obstruct the rights-of-way for fox hunts.

Although income restrictions frequently limit freedom of choice among neighborhoods, wealth does not automatically overcome community barriers. Both former President Richard Nixon and rock star Madonna discovered unwritten cluster restrictions when each was apartment-hunting among New York City's cooperatives in 1985; co-op owners repeatedly rejected their attempts to buy into high-rent buildings. The co-op residents, many recent settlers themselves, said they feared the disruption caused by these sometimes controversial public figures.

In areas wealthy or just-getting-by, residents guard their neighborhood's character, resisting outsiders who may bring change and uncertainty. Throughout America, a kind of social glue maintains the feeling and culture of a specific neighborhood. "To move into a neighborhood is to say, 'I'm as good as you are,'" says sociologist Anderson. "Well, longtime residents don't always believe that. And that makes upward mobility difficult."

THE CLUSTER LIFE CYCLE

At every age, Americans choose to move—or stay put—with people who share similar circumstances. Yet values, circumstances and economics carry people down different lifestyle paths, with many different stops along the way. Each move is an adventure, a chance to experience untried housing styles, consumption patterns and attitudes about art, politics, even love. From college town to retirement community, our cluster choices represent lifestyle way stations just as the developmental phases of Gail Sheehy's *Passages* mark our journey through life.

▤ APPRENTICE YEARS: 18–30

At what cluster level you begin life on your own greatly influences how you'll climb the social ladder, but many factors will sweep you in various directions. Children from the same family with similar educations time and again pursue entirely different lives, be it computer programmer or construction worker. Family experiences, teachers and socioeconomic conditions all influence a person's decision on where to settle down and what style of living to adopt. But simple demographics —what one's peers are doing at the same time—have the greatest effect on one's cluster options.

Since 1970, the biggest growth in entry-level households has involved the baby-boom generation. They grew up in a time of unprecedented affluence, raised on the belief that they'd live better than their parents. But theirs is the first generation of Americans for whom the Dream may not come true. Through sheer force of numbers, it was inevitable that many baby boomers would suffer overcrowding in the job and housing market. In 1986, the typical 30-year-old spent 44 percent of his or her monthly gross income on shelter, compared to 21 percent ten years before. In the '70s, home ownership experienced its first major decline in forty years.

The declining standard of living for baby boomers helped create the lower-middle-class Single City Blues cluster. Scattered throughout the nation's downscale urban areas, typically near city colleges, Single City Blues is home to the largest segment of people under 35 and earning less than $20,000 a year—places like Times Square in Manhattan, Mt. Rainier, Maryland, and Southeast Portland, Oregon. More than two-thirds of the residents are renters. Compared to the general population, they tend to buy cheap processed foods like canned chicken and macaroni, to travel by bus or discount tour packages and to listen to jazz and classical music albums. To visitors, Single City Blues is a poor man's bohemia.

While higher education usually means better wages and standards of living, that's not the case in Single City Blues communities. Nearly a third of the residents have gone to college, but half of all households earn under $15,000 annually. In essence, neighborhood status is measured not in take-home pay but in the intellectual awareness expressed by high subscription rates to magazines like *Harper's, Atlantic Monthly* and *Town & Country*—surprisingly, more than twice the frequency of the general population. A greater than average number of residents also belong to environmental groups and publish magazine articles.

Mary Jean Riehl, a resident of the Sunnyside section of Southeast Portland, is typical of the Single City Blues activists. A trim woman with thick red hair, she holds a bachelor's degree in geography from nearby Portland State University and once turned down a job as a stockbroker because "I didn't think it was important." Today, she works as a $21,000-a-year community organizer, trying to improve her neighborhood beset by high crime, a large transient population and the occasional residence overtaken by prostitutes and drug dealers. Hardly a trendy area, Sunnyside features more drive-ins than sushi bars, and the record stores tend to deal in used discs from the '60s—just Riehl's speed. "I don't like disco music, I don't drink Perrier and my friends aren't yuppies," she says, walking along streets lined with run-down apartments and rusted subcompacts. "I don't care that I don't have a BMW as long as I have a car that runs."

In Sunnyside, Riehl owns an unrenovated Queen Anne bungalow with slightly peeling blue paint and a shaggy yard littered with toy trucks. A divorced mother of two young boys, she's converted the front parlor into a playroom and doubled up the kids in a bedroom that can barely contain their building blocks. She'd like to move to a suburban home, but the $35,000 she could get for her house won't go far in the Portland market. "I'd just like to find a neighborhood where I wouldn't have to see all the problems I'm confronted with every day," she says. "But no one's running to move into this neighborhood. And no matter how much people fix up their homes around here, they'll never be perfect."

For Riehl and many Single City Blues residents, life in this lower-middle-class cluster leaves much to be desired. According to consumer surveys, cluster residents rarely purchase any goods at rates above the national average. They can't afford country clubs, backyard swimming pools and electric grills. And their prospects for moving up in lifestyle and neighborhood are dim. "The aspirations of these people are being frustrated," says George Tresnak, an economist with the National Association of Realtors. "Home ownership is still the preferred lifestyle. But it's becoming increasingly difficult for many baby boomers to find affordable housing."

Although it has almost 3 million U.S. households, Single City Blues is one of the least visible clusters in the nation. The media are far more fascinated with the acquisitive exploits of this group's more

THE APPRENTICE YEARS

Young people begin adulthood at many different socioeconomic entry levels, cluster starting points that can determine their future. Compared to their counterparts in Young Influentials neighborhoods, for example, young people in Single City Blues are twenty-five times more likely to join the armed forces and about one-sixth as likely to have annual incomes over $50,000.

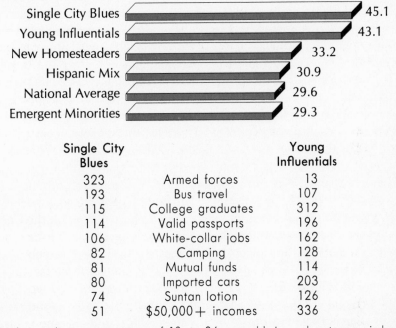

Single City Blues		45.1
Young Influentials		43.1
New Homesteaders		33.2
Hispanic Mix		30.9
National Average		29.6
Emergent Minorities		29.3

Single City Blues		Young Influentials
323	Armed forces	13
193	Bus travel	107
115	College graduates	312
114	Valid passports	196
106	White-collar jobs	162
82	Camping	128
81	Mutual funds	114
80	Imported cars	203
74	Suntan lotion	126
51	$50,000+ incomes	336

Numbers indicate percentages of 18- to 34-year-olds in each category, indexed against the national average. An index of 100 equals the U.S. average for that category. An index of 200 means a cluster has twice the national average for that category. Source: PRIZM (Census Demography), Claritas Corp., 1987.

glamorous peers, the yuppies—those young urban professionals who personify upward mobility. There are 4 million of them—Americans between the ages of 25 and 39 who make $40,000 or more from a professional or managerial job. And over the last decade, many have flocked to Young Influentials—cluster communities such as Atlanta's North Side, Pittsburgh's Shadyside section and Denver's Glendale suburb, featuring townhouse condominiums and singles apartments close to the urban action. Compared to the national average, twice as many Young Influentials residents have finished college, earn over $50,000 a year and work as white-collar professionals. Glendale resident Michelle Berg recently took stock: "I'm 34, unmarried and I already own two condos. That sort of lifestyle never would have occurred to my parents at this age."

On the streets of Glendale, a classic Young Influentials haven bordering Denver, the clichéd expressions of yuppie status hurry by: women professionals in running shoes on their way to work; men riding mopeds rather than motorcycles; everyone wired to Sony Walkmans and carrying squash rackets tucked into Gucci bags. Corner shopping plazas are sprinkled with Häagen-Dazs ice cream stores and Porsche repair shops. Locals will tell you that the center of community life is not the church or the club lodge as it is in Hard Scrabble and Coalburg & Corntown but the Sporting Club fitness center. On weekday afternoons, when most American adults are slogging away at their desks and assembly lines, the people of Glendale are "going for the burn" at this contemporary monument to financial and physical health. "Status around here," says Arienne Lahana, an aide to the Glendale City Council, "is owning a BMW, a 12-speed bike and membership in the Sporting Club."

Opened in 1978, the Sporting Club has become Glendale's social center for its commitment to keeping pace with the needs of its Young Influentials clientele—70 percent in the 35-to-44 age range. The twenty-one courts initially were devoted to racquetball, the rage of the '70s, but they've since been transformed: two courts became an aerobics studio, two converted into squash courts, two for a golfing practice area and two more house exercycles where riders watch their progress charted across a big screen. Steve Autrey, the fit and blow-dried director of the Sporting Club, notes that organized contests in all sports—with trophies for the winners—have become the center's most popular activities. "These people want the recognition for doing well," says Autrey, the ends of his blond mustache curling up as he smiles. "Not everyone becomes fit here, but after a sweaty workout and a drink in the club bar, everyone will feel better about themselves."

That sentiment could be a motto for all Young Influentials, who feign little embarrassment over their acquisitive, pleasure-seeking lifestyles. Surveys show they are more than twice as likely to possess Alfa Romeos, Acuras and BMWs as the general population. In their living rooms, they're twice as likely to cover their coffee tables with consumption guides like *Gourmet, Architectural Digest* and *Sea & Pacific Skipper.* At cocktail parties, which they attend twice as often as average Americans, conversation regularly turns to mutual funds, vintage wine, foreign travel and investment properties. They make up the prime yuppie market for sports cars, home computers, convenience appliances and gourmet foods. "These people have to have," notes social psychologist Richard Evans of the University of Houston, adding that many equate quality of life with quality of belongings. "They must be able to show some of the trappings of their success."

This yuppie way of life did not spontaneously spring into being in Young Influentials communities. While many cluster residents came from well-to-do families, others were middle-class children who joined the '60s counterculture. Like the characters in the movie *The Big Chill,* in the '80s they decided that "owning property is no longer a crime." And they own it with a vengeance, many feeling compelled to put their own stamp on that property, as evidenced by the current yuppie obsession with remodeling—from simple redecorating to lavish additions. Orange-crate bookshelves have been chucked in favor of Roche-Bobois wall systems.

This shift in attitude was not lost on the editors of *Apartment Life,* an alternative home furnishings magazine for the Woodstock generation. In 1981, they decided to redirect their magazine at the baby-boom generation that had entered young adulthood with two-income households and cosmopolitan tastes. *Apartment Life* evolved into *Metropolitan Home,* as its editors began to focus on high-style expressions of the good life for affluent suburban and city consumers. "We had characterized ourselves as the lifestyle magazine of the new generation," recalls Dorothy Kalins, the longtime editor who oversaw the metamorphosis. "But in the late '70s, we discovered that 60 percent of our readers owned their own place. And they were no longer into, 'I'm not going to buy it but rather make it or filch it.' All of a sudden, the need to be anti-materialistic evaporated."

With its new format, *Metropolitan Home* dropped its sports and music features to concentrate on interior design. Gone was the "Wizard of Amp," a column comprised of reader questions about audio equipment. In its place came "Ask Dr. Swatch," which highlights collectibles for yuppie tastes (classic Bob Dylan posters are featured rather than, say, Ming vases). To Kalins, a woman whose breezy editorials ripple with personal anecdotes about her coffee tables and salt shakers, the makeover was less of substance than of style. "Remember that the kids occupying the dean's office at Harvard or Columbia were wearing good leather boots and sturdy cotton jeans," she says. "The sense of quality never left them. Their icons simply changed. Instead of sneakers, it's high-priced running shoes. Instead of Pepsi, it's Perrier. Why are they all driving around in BMWs? I think it was bred in them. They just didn't

APARTMENT LIFE VS. *METROPOLITAN HOME*

In 1981, the editors of *Apartment Life* decided to turn their magazine into *Metropolitan Home*, upgrading their alternative home-furnishings focus to highlight high-style expressions of the good life. As a result, they gained subscribers in such upscale neighborhoods as Money & Brains and Blue Blood Estates, and lost readers in downscale Heavy Industry, Single City Blues and Downtown Dixie-Style.

Top Ten Clusters: *Apartment Life*

Cluster	Index
Urban Gold Coast	298
New Melting Pot	240
Two More Rungs	220
Downtown Dixie-Style	220
New Beginnings	192
Heavy Industry	175
Bohemian Mix	171
Young Influentials	169
Public Assistance	160
Single City Blues	160

Top Ten Clusters: *Metropolitan Home*

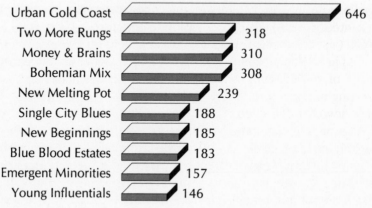

Cluster	Index
Urban Gold Coast	646
Two More Rungs	318
Money & Brains	310
Bohemian Mix	308
New Melting Pot	239
Single City Blues	188
New Beginnings	185
Blue Blood Estates	183
Emergent Minorities	157
Young Influentials	146

Numbers indicate percentages of people who read each magazine, indexed against the national average. An index of 100 equals the U.S. average: 0.81%. An index of 298 means a cluster has 2.98 times the national average, or 2.41%. Source: Claritas Corp., 1984. Proprietary database used with permission.

fall far from the tree. The baby boom is the most educated group of Americans to exist. And these people are smart consumers."

To test the impact of the magazine's makeover, *Metropolitan Home* publishers commissioned a cluster profile in 1981 to track the changing circulation patterns. Whereas *Apartment Life* was read in funky city neighborhoods and midscale suburban clusters, the new subscribers to *Metropolitan Home* came from the upper ranks of city and suburban clusters. Its biggest subscription gains came in Money & Brains, Blue Blood Estates and Urban Gold Coast clusters; its biggest losses were in Single City Blues, Heavy Industry and Downtown Dixie-Style areas. "Frankly, we lost the downscale carpenters with the degrees in nuclear physics who still wanted to build things," says Kalins. "But we went with a more affluent, settled group. There's a flashy edge to them." Not to mention a maturity: in 1986, the median age of *Metropolitan Home* readers was 40, up a decade compared to devotees of *Apartment Life* in the late '70s.

ACHIEVEMENT YEARS: 30–45

A generation ago, in 1955, a young family settling into a suburban home with a two-car garage on a half-acre lot personified the American Dream. To a nation that saw its cities begin to decay in the Depression, suburbia offered a liberating vision with its orderly rows of cozy habitats and private yards. Returning World War II veterans spurred a massive suburban building boom, fueled by mass-produced homes and federally guaranteed mortgages. Ex-G.I.s needed only the smallest of down payments (and sometimes none at all) to acquire cute Cape Cods or ranch houses in bedroom suburbs rimming smoky, gray cities. Faced with the choice of rehabilitating a cramped downtown rowhouse or owning a spanking-new rambler in the suburbs with modern appliances, Americans moved out of town.

The new suburbanites prized their communities of identical lots, similarly styled houses and like-minded neighbors. Believing their fortunes to be on the rise, they hoped one day to sell out and move up, perhaps, to a spacious split-level in what's now called a Pools & Patios neighborhood. But a funny thing happened to those postwar suburban parents as their children grew up. Like contemporary Willy Lomans, many didn't keep cluster-climbing to the top. Between 1970 and 1980, census data showed many suburban neighborhoods undergoing a phenomenon known as empty-nesting—the children grown and gone, their parents staying put. Remaining in the neighborhood became preferable to facing the high interest rates and steep housing costs associated with a move to a retirement condo or an apartment in town, as was the custom for childless households in the past. To find a house of equal size and convenience might triple their monthly payments and knock them down a couple of pegs in terms of space, convenience and image.

With these graying couples clinging to their homes, young families have had to scramble for increasingly scarce and costly housing far beyond the bedroom suburbs. Today the American Dream survives in the exurbs well outside major cities or suburbs. But that once-formidable institution, the nuclear family—consisting of a Dad, nonworking Mom and two school-aged kids—today accounts for only 4 percent of the population and is found mostly in Young Suburbia neighborhoods on the edge of the urban sprawl. One of the nation's most widespread clusters—consisting of communities like San Bruno outside of San Francisco, Lilburn near Atlanta and Eagan, Minnesota, just south of St. Paul —Young Suburbia is filled with white-collar breadwinners, elementary-school–aged children and recently built homes with two or more cars in the driveway. Along carefully planned streets, young children play in front of cookie-cutter houses in a portrait of a perhaps impersonal, yet undeniably comfortable world.

This picture comes to life in Eagan, an outer-ring suburb of new housing subdivisions for 25,000 people only a short commute from the Minneapolis–St. Paul business district. Located on what was prairie country just twenty-five years ago, Eagan has since been developed into one of the state's fast-growing suburbs. When Paul and Lynda Burkel bought their $90,000 split-level in 1983, it was the only house on the block. Three years later, there are ten families with preschoolers in the neighborhood. So many yards are still being sodded and planted with trees that many residents simply stretch out on chaise longues in their driveways to sunbathe in the summer.

"In this area, status is having a nicely landscaped yard, a good-looking fence around it and lots of flowers," says chunky, 30-year-old Paul Burkel, who works as a maintenance supervisor for Northwest Airlines. Neighborhood parties are laid-back affairs revolving around a couple of steaks thrown on the backyard Weber grill, a six-pack of Bartles and Jaymes wine coolers and a stereo playing old Rolling Stones records. Though a freeway's drive from the restaurants and theaters of downtown St. Paul, Burkel and his neighbors seem content with their earth-toned development, their Harvest Gold refrigerators filled with Juicy Juice and patios of jelly-stained plastic lounge chairs. "For our first house, we couldn't be much happier," says Burkel, who's proudly decorated his garage door with a foot-high Gothic letter *B*. "But it's still our first house and we won't be here forever."

The Americans who settle in Young Suburbia neighborhoods typically share solidly middle-class lifestyles. More than half of all households report incomes above $35,000, and despite being strapped by hefty mortgages, they manage to splurge a little when furnishing their homes. They buy stereos, personal computers and movie cameras 70 percent more often than the general population. They also buy high-performance cars like Corvettes, Datsun 280ZXs and Pontiac Firebirds at twice the national average. Still vulnerable to economic worries, Young Suburbanites will redeem cents-off grocery-store coupons while dropping more than $100 a week at the checkout counter. Their idea of a vacation is a trip to a theme park; a typical night on the town consists of taking the kids to a Friendly's ice cream parlor.

The residents of Young Suburbia comprise less than 6 percent of the population, but they nonetheless exert a strong influence on the American psyche. Although the cluster system includes nearly a dozen other neighborhood types that are home to midscale, child-rearing families, the images of Young Suburbia prevail. Pop culture—from Walt Disney to Whoppers to Rambo dolls—has always been geared to these middle-class families, with Hollywood scriptwriters celebrating their lifestyle in shows like "Leave It to Beaver" and movies like *E.T.* They're the loyal viewers in Johnny Carson's audience night after night; it's their funny bone he's trying to tickle.

But unlike June Cleaver, Young Suburbia mothers today must work to maintain the outward appearance of comfortable middle-class lives. And they're the prime market for tanning products, jogging suits, hair shampoos and conditioners. When Helene Curtis wanted to find out the best message for promoting its Suave brand of shampoo, it surveyed the Young Suburbia neighborhoods with high concentrations of working women. The result: Suave ads promising that the inexpensive shampoo would make their hair look like a million.

Just as double incomes have raised the standard of living for the white middle class, education has provided the socioeconomic lift for black Americans. During the '70s, the rise in level of schooling for blacks doubled the national average; more than a million blacks are enrolled in college today compared to 522,000 in 1970. At the same time, one of the most striking demographic changes has been the emergence of upper-middle-class black neighborhoods, dubbed Black Enterprise. Suburbs, once described as "a white noose" around U.S. cities, have begun to resemble what social critic Ben Wattenberg has called "a polka dot scarf." While the number of whites living in the 'burbs increased by 28 percent in the last decade, black residents in this traditional home of the American success story rose by 72 percent.

In Black Enterprise communities such as Capitol Heights outside of Washington, D.C., Morningside in Los Angeles and Atlanta's South Decatur suburb, educated and upscale black professionals—teachers, civil servants, lawyers—live in a mainstream ambience. The cluster is racially mixed (two-thirds of the households are black), well educated (one-third have gone to college) and solidly set in the upper-middle class (one-half earn over $35,000 annually). In contrast to the dismal life of Public Assistance areas, where a third of the residents rely on welfare for survival, the homeowners of Black Enterprise have made it through a combination of hard work, persistence and the courage to integrate what were typically all-white neighborhoods. As recently as 1978, a Harris poll found that one-third of all white Americans claimed to be upset if blacks moved next door. "These blacks believe in the system and meritocracy," says Elijah Anderson of America's black upper-middle class. "They're into pluralism."

The birth of the Black Enterprise cluster was not without social labor pains. In many cities, the appearance of black, middle-class homeowners resulted in "white flight"—the exodus of white residents who wanted no part of integrated neighborhoods. Porter Sanford, a burly salt-and-pepper-haired 45-year-old realtor from the Atlanta suburb of Decatur, remembers the uproar he caused when, in 1972, he moved into Decatur's Spring Valley community. Paying $60,000 for a four-bedroom home, Sanford recalls how a meeting with the seller was interrupted by a white neighbor who declared to both, "The people in this community will not forgive you for what you have done." For six months after he moved in, local vandals shot out his windows with BBs and drove their cars over his front yard. But he and his family remained and forged a comfortable lifestyle, putting a pool in the backyard and cutting trails through their 2-acre lot so the kids could ride minibikes. And acceptance by his white neighbors slowly followed—a pattern confirmed by nation-wide polls.

Between 1970 and 1980, Sanford watched South Decatur's racial composition shift from 99 percent white to 67 percent black. In some neighborhoods, the number of FOR SALE signs would jump from a hand-ful to a hundred in the course of a month. To Sanford, the racially motivated exodus was puzzling. "It made no sense," he protests, driving past the carefully landscaped Spring Valley lawns. "The lifestyles are the same between whites and blacks. We've all got big investments in our homes. Everyone here has concerns about schools, who gets elected and what happens to property values. And no matter who you are, you aren't driving a car unless it's a Mercedes."

Nationwide, the lifestyle profile of Black Enterprise is similar to predominantly white clusters of the same socioeconomic rank when it comes to drinking imported brandy, collecting stamps, owning a personal computer and reading *Esquire* and *Working Woman*. Compared to the national average, Black Enterprisers are twice as likely to join

---

THE ACHIEVEMENT YEARS

From predominantly white Young Suburbia to minority-filled Black Enterprise, the upper-middle-class neighborhoods share many lifestyle habits. A major factor influencing taste is a neighborhood's proximity to the city—whether it is urban (Black Enterprise) or suburban (Young Suburbia).

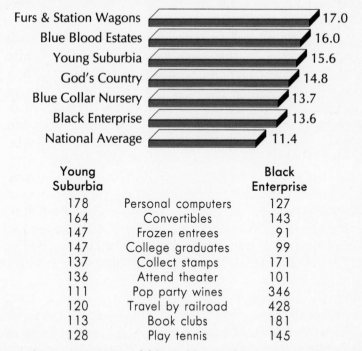

	Furs & Station Wagons	17.0
	Blue Blood Estates	16.0
	Young Suburbia	15.6
	God's Country	14.8
	Blue Collar Nursery	13.7
	Black Enterprise	13.6
	National Average	11.4

Young Suburbia		Black Enterprise
178	Personal computers	127
164	Convertibles	143
147	Frozen entrees	91
147	College graduates	99
137	Collect stamps	171
136	Attend theater	101
111	Pop party wines	346
120	Travel by railroad	428
113	Book clubs	181
128	Play tennis	145

Numbers indicate percentages of 35- to 44-year-olds in each category, indexed against the national average. An index of 100 equals the U.S. average for that category. An index of 200 means a cluster has twice the national average for that category. Source: SMRB and MRI data bases, Claritas Corp., 1987.

WHERE BLACKS LIVE

Black Americans are concentrated in only a handful of neighborhood types, typically in metropolitan areas. This pattern reflects the migration of blacks from the rural South in the first half of the century—as well as decades of entrenched prejudice.

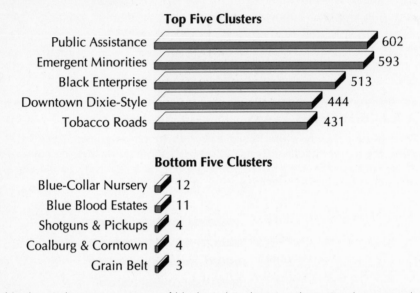

Top Five Clusters

Public Assistance	602
Emergent Minorities	593
Black Enterprise	513
Downtown Dixie-Style	444
Tobacco Roads	431

Bottom Five Clusters

Blue-Collar Nursery	12
Blue Blood Estates	11
Shotguns & Pickups	4
Coalburg & Corntown	4
Grain Belt	3

Numbers indicate percentages of blacks, indexed against the national average. An index of 100 equals the U.S. average: 11%. An index of 602 means a cluster has 6.02 times the national average, or about 66%. Source: PRIZM (Census Demography), Claritas Corp., 1987.

book clubs, buy disco records, drink malt liquor and drive convertibles. But like the general population, they mirror prevailing tastes in theater, golf, health food and European travel. In a 1985 TV survey, residents were just as likely to watch the exploits of a white detective in "Magnum, P.I." as they are to watch the black housekeeper in "Gimme a Break."

Although 11 percent of the U.S. population, blacks are concentrated in only a few clusters, none of which fall into America's top socioeconomic quarter. Entrenched prejudice by white homeowners undoubtedly contributes to this phenomenon. In 1985, the Justice Department's Community Relations Service counted more than sixty racially motivated attacks in housing cases—including the fire-bombing of black families in Chicago and Tacoma, Washington. Racial resistance is partly blamed for the fact that most blacks live in just 15 of the 200 or so suburban neighborhoods that ring Chicago.

But this sort of segregation also results from changes in attitudes. Integration itself faded as a primary housing goal for many blacks in the '80s. "The issue isn't integration versus nonintegration anymore—it's here-now things like jobs," reports Selwyn Cudjoe, professor of Afro-American studies at Harvard University. As integration has gained acceptance among whites, its importance has lessened among many blacks, maintains University of Michigan political science professor Ali Mazrui. "When whites began saying, 'Let's have it,' some blacks replied, 'Who says we want it any more?' "

Freedom to be ourselves among people like ourselves is at the heart of the cluster impulse. But with the exception of Black Enterprise neighborhoods, upper-middle-class blacks feel more comfortable living as a racial majority than fighting the battles at the forefront of social change.

▤ HARVEST YEARS: 45–65

"Nothing succeeds like address," satirist Fran Lebowitz has written. And nothing whets the appetite of those in pursuit of higher status more than a prestigious neighborhood address. Throughout America, there exist communities of homes valued far beyond their brick, mortar and square footage, simply because the demand for the neighborhood outstrips its housing stock. Such enclaves become home to the monied, the powerful and the elite who seek exclusivity. In these communities, if you have to ask how much a house costs, you probably can't afford it.

The drive to succeed—and success itself—are what define Americans who settle in the cluster designated Money & Brains. The nation's wealthiest in-town neighborhoods, Money & Brains is where middle-aged couples move when, after years of accumulating assets and home equity, after raising children and seeing them off to college, they want to play a little. Unlike those with inherited wealth who settle in Blue Blood Estates, these residents have risen to the upper status-sphere the old-fashioned way, as Smith-Barney commercials proclaim: "They earned it." Money & Brains citizens place a premium on education (46 percent hold college diplomas), not to mention a cosmopolitan taste in arts and entertainment. As consumers, they purchase sailboats, diamond jewelry, theater subscriptions and investment property at rates far above those of their fellow Americans. To protect their assets, they install burglar alarms at twice the national average. It's no coincidence that some of the nation's most sought-after addresses fall into this cluster category: Georgetown in Washington, D.C., Coral Gables in Miami, Menlo Park in San Francisco and Park Cities in Dallas.

Exclusivity thrives in Park Cities, a cluster haven for 35,000 comprising the adjoining communities of Highland Park and University Park, where the average home value in 1985 was $187,163. Available homes are so limited here that in order to enter the community, newcomers typically will buy a "tear-down"—an older cottage that will be razed and rebuilt. Along the shady, curving streets, nannies push baby carriages in the afternoon and middle-aged homemakers stop off at the Highland Park Library to check out books on travel, investing and fashion. At Highland Park Village, the oldest suburban shopping center in Texas, the well-to-do flock to so many rarefied boutiques—Hermes, Giorgio's and Ralph Lauren among them—that valet parking attendants must untangle the Porsches, Mercedes and BMWs from daily traffic jams. When nearby Park Cities Baptist Church needed funds for a new addition, congregation members pledged $4.5 million—all at one service. It is this kind of generosity that keeps neighboring Southern Methodist University well endowed and enables precocious high-school students to take college courses in math, science and music.

"Around here, we grow up ambitious," says lifelong Park Cities resident Doris Sosnowski, a fiftyish homemaker with a round face under a cap of curly, blond hair. "People call this area 'Camelot.'"

Park Cities has remained Dallas's most prestigious address for its ability to continually attract millionaires who like to show off their wealth as well as give some of it back to the community. When Doris married Walter Sosnowski, a Dartmouth-educated commercial real estate broker, they settled in Park Cities because, as he recalls, "It seemed like a large country club"—an observation that hasn't changed during the last three decades. A product of modest Jersey City, New Jersey, Walter is still struck by the community spirit "that goes first class": wealthy CEOs donate money to build indoor racquetball courts for the local high school or take time to plant shrubbery on the traffic islands. Every Christmas, some of his neighbors on Armstrong Avenue spend $10,000 on outdoor lighting displays, perhaps so the stream of admiring outsiders from other Dallas communities won't be disappointed. To entertain neighbors inside their homes, residents collect all manner of objets d'art, from rare Lichtenstein stamps to Roy Lichtenstein prints; the Sosnowskis, for instance, have amassed in their living room a small fortune in silver napkin rings.

But that's typical in this neighborhood type, where residents own thirteen times as many Jaguars as the U.S. norm. Walter Sosnowski notes that, if New York's greatest symbol is the Statue of Liberty, Park Cities' is the Jaguar. Arriving once for a concert at his daughter's elementary school, Sosnowski and his wife were startled to see four Jaguars of different colors parked in a row. "So we thought we'd be different," says Walter. "We parked our Jag across the street."

To be sure, not all upscale Americans lead such high-profile lives of luxury—or want to. In the affluent cluster of Two More Rungs—consisting of communities like Skokie, Illinois, Rancho Park, California, and Flushing, New York—residents shun the extravagant trappings of success. With its high concentration of Jewish, Irish, Italian and Slavic stock, this cluster is filled with professionals who dedicated their lives to sending their kids to college. Today they're comfortably settled in a paid-for condominium or split-level. Two More Rungs is filled with success stories of first-generation Americans living near the port cities to which their parents emigrated. Residents report that nearly half have gone to college, and one-quarter of their households earn more than $50,000 annually. But they're still two steps (and six ZQ levels) from the top of the socioeconomic ladder—one rung down in social class and another in affluence—with little interest in climbing higher.

The consuming patterns in Two More Rungs are hardly déclassé. Residents may not have chauffeured limousines, but their garages are filled with big-ticket cars: they buy Alfa Romeos and Jaguars at three times the national average. They often spend more than $100 weekly on groceries, although their shopping carts reflect Old World tastes—rye bread, corned beef hash and spaghetti sauce. They frequently travel to their ancestral homelands in Europe, but they tend to take discounted chartered plane trips or cruises. At home, Two More Rungs residents read *Scientific American* and *Atlantic Monthly* twice as often as the general populace, and they would rather host a family dinner than a cocktail party. In this tradition-bound neighborhood type, status is still a son who grows up to be a doctor, lawyer or college professor—junior-high teachers don't cut it.

Kew Gardens in the New York City borough of Queens is like many Two More Rungs communities, with a large Jewish populace and pockets of blacks and Orientals. The area is dotted with synagogues and Hebrew-speaking schools called yeshivas, and locals have street celebrations on Jewish holidays like Purim and on Israeli Independence Day. Those who cling to their roots can go to Italian delis, Hebrew book shops and jewelry stores where clerks speak several languages. Some of the borough's best libraries and senior centers serve the aging, educated populace, which tends to live in high-rise co-ops, townhouse condos or garden apartments—also aging but well kept. "There's usually a doorman, but it's not Catskills Mountains–style living by any means," observes Rabbi Stephen Steingel, leader of the area's Hillcrest Jewish Center. "These people could afford to retire to Florida but they'd just as soon stay put. They like to say, 'We're just hard-working, middle-class people.'"

As a nesting ground for the children of Eastern European immigrants, Two More Rungs communities typically were settled after World War II in the march to the suburbs. When Phyllis and Arthur Talmadge moved into a 130-unit apartment in Kew Gardens thirty years ago, many of their neighbors were schoolteachers and civil servants who commuted to jobs in Manhattan. Like other first-generation American Jews, they felt at home among neighbors who sent their children to yeshivas and saved their money for trips to Israel. And they found success as white-collar professionals: she's a film director for Hadassah, the Zionist women's organization; he works as a labor mediator. Although they're both nearing 60 years old, the Talmadges don't talk of retirement. "Who says people have to stop working at a certain age?" asks Phyllis, a handsome woman with owlish glasses and short-cropped hair.

Today the Talmadge household's income approaches six figures, but they've never forgotten the difficult financial times faced by their parents, who never owned a car and sometimes didn't have enough money to put food on the table. When she goes shopping, Phyllis still passes up the nearby Bloomingdale's to search for bargains at a distant Loehmann's and among the cut-rate merchants on the Lower East Side. Like other Two More Rung apartment dwellers, the Talmadges display little of the flash that characterizes Money & Brains residents. "Everyone spends money on nice vacations but you don't see a lot of furs or jewelry around here," says Phyllis.

With two grown children, the Talmadges have discussed moving into a midtown Manhattan apartment, perhaps a Money & Brains kind of neighborhood. But the idea never gets past the idle talking stage. "I just couldn't see investing a minimum of a half-million dollars to buy a very small apartment in an unsafe area," she says. "I'd want the freedom to do other things." She pauses, eyeing the apartment where she's spent the majority of her life. "Here, we read a lot, we travel a lot—this year we went twice to Europe—and we go to a lot of lectures. We're no different from anyone else around here."

If the clusters prove anything, it's that neighborhood choice reflects

THE HARVEST YEARS

In their peak earning years, the residents of Money & Brains have high-profile, flashy lifestyles compared to their socioeconomic cousins in Two More Rungs, who shun extravagance and would rather host a family dinner than a cocktail party.

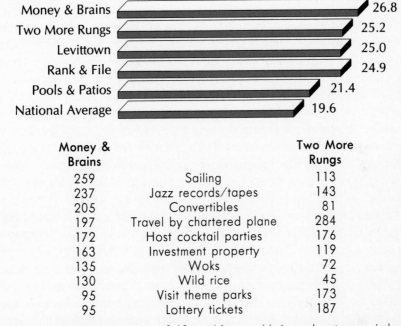

Money & Brains		26.8
Two More Rungs		25.2
Levittown		25.0
Rank & File		24.9
Pools & Patios		21.4
National Average		19.6

Money & Brains		Two More Rungs
259	Sailing	113
237	Jazz records/tapes	143
205	Convertibles	81
197	Travel by chartered plane	284
172	Host cocktail parties	176
163	Investment property	119
135	Woks	72
130	Wild rice	45
95	Visit theme parks	173
95	Lottery tickets	187

Numbers indicate percentages of 45- to 64-year-olds in each category, indexed against the national average. An index of 100 equals the U.S. average for that category. An index of 200 means a cluster has twice the national average for that category. Source: SMRB and MRI data bases, Claritas Corp., 1987.

a singular mind-set evident in everything from the make of car to the brand of humor one prefers. Kutscher's Country Club, a Two More Rungs retreat in New York's Catskill Mountains, regularly showcases rising comedians as part of the nightly entertainment. One recent spring weekend, it featured two comics with strikingly different styles. The first, a 62-year-old Shecky Green lookalike from Queens, was a master of low-brow schtick, complaining of denture problems, cemetery plot salesmen and his cronies who'd started wearing gold chains around their necks ("the only fashion statement created by a dog"). The second, a Seattle-based 40-year-old wearing the preppy uniform of a navy sports jacket, club tie and loafers, attacked the usual liberal elite targets: the National Rifle Association, televangelists and the hassles of driving an ancient, rusted Volkswagen Beetle. "You wouldn't believe the difficulties trying to make whoopee in that car," he began one bit.

And he was right. About a third of the audience walked out before Mr. Prep had completed his act. Many of the Jewish residents of Two More Rungs who vacation in the Catskills have vivid memories of the Holocaust and found it distasteful just to hear mention of a German-built car. By contrast, the Shecky Green wiseacre earned a standing ovation. His audience understood where he was coming from.

■ RETIREMENT YEARS: 65+

Before World War II, few retirees moved away from their neighborhoods to live out their remaining years. Many simply couldn't afford to leave their families because of their financial and physical health. In 1900, the average life expectancy for children born in the United States was 47.3 years. As recently as 1959, 35 percent of America's over-65-year-olds were classified as poor, according to the Census Bureau.

But these bleak numbers changed over the last generation with the improved health and higher standard of living that overtook America's growing senior population. For the first time in U.S. history, there are more people over 65 than teenagers. In 1980, the average life expectancy was 73.6 years, and the rate of elderly poor had dropped by two-thirds to 14 percent. With Social Security, pension benefits and accumulated savings, fewer than ever senior citizens need rely on their children for support. This steadily increasing number of mature, financially independent Americans has resulted in the emergence of two new neighborhood clusters, Gray Power and Golden Ponds. Like the residents of Two More Rungs, those in Gray Power and Golden Ponds communities have ended their climb to the top. But in these two clusters, older residents have chosen to leave the old neighborhood behind to live out their years.

Gray Power represents the nation's planned retirement communities —including Leisure World, California, Sun City Center, Florida, and Sun City, Arizona—and is home to more than a million upscale senior citizens. Tracing its origins in part to the demographic shift to the Sunbelt, Gray Power is a cluster of self-contained communities where affluent seniors maintain a lifestyle based on the concept of active retirement. A Gray Power community like Sun City, for example, offers enough daily activities to make a cruise ship social director envious: crafts clubs, sports events, dance classes, gardening groups, and on and on. Indeed,

GRAY-HAIRED CLUSTERS

Since World War II, an increasing number of the elderly have chosen to live out their years among other retirees in Gray Power and Golden Ponds communities. For the first time in U.S. history, many child-filled households in clusters like Young Suburbia and Blue-Collar Nursery lack live-in grandparents.

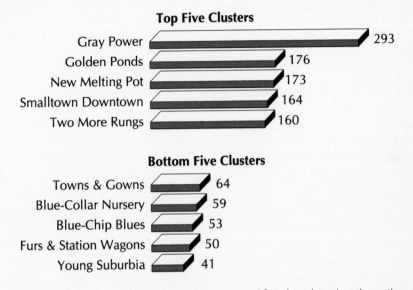

Top Five Clusters

Gray Power — 293
Golden Ponds — 176
New Melting Pot — 173
Smalltown Downtown — 164
Two More Rungs — 160

Bottom Five Clusters

Towns & Gowns — 64
Blue-Collar Nursery — 59
Blue-Chip Blues — 53
Furs & Station Wagons — 50
Young Suburbia — 41

Numbers indicate percentages of people over age 65, indexed against the national average. An index of 100 equals the U.S. average: 5.5%. An index of 293 means a cluster has 2.93 times the national average, or 16.1%. Source: PRIZM (Census Demography), Claritas Corp., 1987.

living in Sun City can resemble a round-the-world voyage aboard a luxury liner, with its endless roster of youthful leisure and hobby programs.

But as one of the oldest communities in America, Sun City can scarcely hide its wrinkles. With a median age of 69 (more than a third of its 47,000 citizens are over 75), Sun City is typical of America's Gray Power communities. When developer Del Webb founded it in 1960 on 8,900 acres of cotton fields, he envisioned an economically diverse and age-homogeneous village; to purchase a home in Sun City, at least one household resident must be 50 or older. But Webb probably never imagined that his senior Sun Citizens would become considerably wealthier than other older Americans. With a median income of $22,000 for households of two persons or more—a level roughly 30 percent higher than the national average for senior citizens—most residents pay cash for their homes, which sell for $50,000 to $275,000. More than $2 billion is on deposit in the area's fifty-six banks and savings and loan institutions, and one local Merrill Lynch office reported that the average customer has a stock portfolio worth $50,000. "Around here, you see more banks than gas stations," says Ken Plonski, public affairs manager for Del Webb.

In contrast to this affluence, Sun City's stucco ranch houses appear modest, sausaged together on circular streets with gently banked curbs for wheelchairs. Actually, there's less congestion on the roadways than on the eighteen golf courses where, in 1984, residents played a million rounds of golf. Away from the links, life in Sun City revolves around the sprawling recreation centers with their 400 sports and hobby clubs offering activities in everything from woodworking to needlepoint to lawn bowling. One sign of the vitality of Sun City's seniors: by signing up for a "riding club," one may be paired with a horse, bicycle or Harley-Davidson motorcycle. "If you like clubs, Sun City is paradise," says Herman Mandell, a 65-year-old former army colonel whose current title is vice president of the 600-member lapidary club. "There's an activity from 7 in the morning to whenever you want to go to sleep."

This active lifestyle is typical in all Gray Power communities. Cluster residents read *Tennis, Boating* and *Golf Digest* at twice the national average. They travel abroad, join health clubs, go bowling and ride bicycles all at rates above that of the general population. More than a few have even given up their cars for local travel by golf carts, and in Gray Power towns like Sun City, street signs urge caution not for people at work but golfers at play.

The Gray Power lifestyle, with its orderly streets and cluttered calendar of meetings, dances and games, is not nirvana for all retirees, however. Alcoholism is a persistent problem. In Sun City, a recently closed Safeway supermarket was replaced by a liquor store, and doctors at local Boswell Memorial Hospital tell of elderly patients who suffer alcohol withdrawal symptoms while undergoing treatment for other ailments. Some residents miss seeing young people around, and emotional problems stemming from retirement, isolation from loved ones or the death of spouses are common complaints. A recent health study uncovered cases of elder abuse at the hands of greedy bankers, lawyers and local businessmen. And as the community ages—its earliest settlers are now in their eighties—residents have difficulty coming to terms with their deteriorating health and faculties.

"People are always preparing for a rainy day," says Sylvia Cartsonis, a Sun City social worker. "But some elderly people have to be convinced that the rainy day is here and now. They can afford nursing homes, but they just don't want to give up their independence." In Gray Power communities, checking into a nursing home is like dropping out of society—which is why Sun City, until recently, had no nursing homes or cemeteries.

Still, newcomers from all over the country continue to flock to Sun City, keeping alive the town's Fountain-of-Youth allure. Johnnie and Connie Kroll, 70-year-old retirees from Detroit, arrived in 1971, "because we wanted to be active rather than sit on the back porch, rocking our lives away," says Johnnie, a former Chrysler personnel director. "Where in Michigan could I play golf all year round?" A husky man with a golf course tan and a basso profundo voice (he spent his early years as a radio broadcaster), Johnnie relishes chronicling his and Connie's weekly itinerary: Hawaiian dancing, lawn bowling, poker, nightclubbing. He calls bingo games several nights a week. She belongs to an acrobatic performing troup, the Sun City Pom Poms, a silver-haired version of the Dallas Cowgirls. "She goes her way and I go mine during the day," says Johnnie. "But at night we get together for activities."

No one would suspect that Johnnie Kroll recently suffered a heart attack—and he boasts of that, too. He shows no signs of slowing his active pace, which he claims is the best therapy. "Sometimes I wonder if we'd both still be alive if we had stayed in Michigan, where the hospital is miles and miles away," says Connie, whose bright eye makeup and slender figure recall the days when she was crowned Miss Michigan of 1934. "Here, we were in the hospital in 20 minutes and he's been fine since he got out." With children and grandchildren living in distant cities, the Krolls look to fellow retirees to supply the warmth that once emanated from family. And if they get homesick, they can always look to the future. In 1986, their 46-year-old son came for a visit with his wife to check out housing prices; he plans to take early retirement in a few years.

While Gray Power communities allow retirees to escape to age-segregated societies, the Golden Ponds cluster reflects another segment of the American populace who seek to retire within mainstream society. In these cottage communities named for the 1981 film *On Golden Pond,* senior citizens live in the chaos of resort towns with their short-term vacationers and longtime rural townsfolk. Cluster towns are usually near water and include hundreds of rustic spots along coastal beaches, mountain streams and wooded lakes—places like Cape May,

New Jersey, Hudson, New York, and Needles, California. Neither as affluent nor as aged as Gray Power, Golden Ponds nevertheless offers residents ample leisure pursuits appropriate to their middle-class (ZQ25) status. They spend more time in the garden than on the golf course. Rather than buy boats, they build them in bottles.

Befitting its hodge-podge populace, Golden Ponds is the nation's only cluster where residents purchase both *Scientific American* and *The National Enquirer* at rates 25 percent above the national average. (What surveys don't show, however, is whether the seekers of scientific understanding are the same "inquiring minds" curious about the possibility of sex after death.)

For two centuries, Cape May has offered the Golden Ponds pleasures of a beach community for vacationers and retirees alike. Billing itself as the nation's oldest seashore resort, Cape May features hundreds of restored Victorian homes and inns that have earned it a rare, townwide designation as a national landmark. Its 5,500 year-round residents (the population explodes to 40,000 during the summer tourist season) include a high percentage of retirees and slightly younger dropouts from corporate America who arrived in Cape May to launch a restaurant or a bed-and-breakfast inn. "Many of the people who came here to retire had vacationed here in their youth and liked the lifestyle," explains Fred Coldron, the town's city manager. "Others just liked the peace of mind that comes with looking out at the ocean."

Unlike the age-segregated clubs of Sun City, organizations like Cape May's Mid-Atlantic Cultural Center draw both retirees and younger people. Members offer guided tours of the Victorian homes, maintain community gardens and show old movies throughout the summer. One-third of the city employees are retirees, executives from Fortune 500 companies who now work with younger professionals as zoning secretaries and land management advisors. In the early 1970s, town officials flirted with the idea of becoming a retirement community and passed laws that discouraged young people from visiting Cape May. One regulation prohibited lifeguards from having mustaches and beards. But as the town's fiscal health began to wane, residents joined a reform movement to revitalize the town as a Victorian resort, attracting a new wave of young entrepreneurs and craftspeople. Today Cape May is a thriving year-round community with its inns booked months in advance and its two-bedroom duplexes listing for $80,000. As innkeeper John Dunwoody puts it, "Cape May is not a retirement town. It's a resort town with a lot of retirees living here."

Cape May's Village Green community gives credence to Dun-

THE RETIREMENT YEARS

The upper-middle-class residents of Gray Power lead more active lives than their middle-class brethren in Golden Ponds. While Gray Power residents go sailing, those in Golden Ponds are more likely to stay home and build ships in bottles.

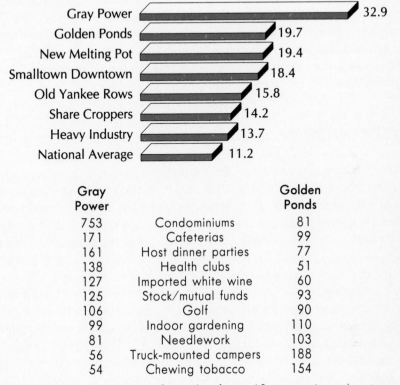

Gray Power		Golden Ponds
753	Condominiums	81
171	Cafeterias	99
161	Host dinner parties	77
138	Health clubs	51
127	Imported white wine	60
125	Stock/mutual funds	93
106	Golf	90
99	Indoor gardening	110
81	Needlework	103
56	Truck-mounted campers	188
54	Chewing tobacco	154

Numbers indicate percentages of people of age 65 or over in each category, indexed against the national average. An index of 100 equals the U.S. average for that category. An index of 200 means a cluster has twice the national average for that category. Source: SMRB & MRI data bases, Claritas Corp., 1987.

woody's subtle distinction. Initially opened as a retirement area in the 1960s, before the renovation fervor took hold, this flat, checkerboard subdivision of single-story duplex and fourplex homes bears a striking resemblance to the ranch-house neighborhoods of Sun City. But whereas the initial residents were retirees, today more than half the homes are owned by out-of-town professionals who use the residences as summer cottages. Year-round homeowners like Doc Jardin, a 70-year-old Philadelphian who moved with his wife to Village Green in 1981, have come out of retirement to take part-time jobs. Jardin, avuncular with wavy gray hair and bushy eyebrows, works several days a week as an advertising sales manager for the *Cape May Times*. After spending his professional life as a marketer in Philadelphia, he never seriously considered moving to a Sunbelt retirement community cloistered from mainstream society. "A typical Saturday in Cape May includes a surfing competition for young people, a restored auto show for the middle-aged, a big band concert for the older folks and the Kiwanis Pet Parade for everybody," says Jardin. "This is not the kind of community where people play golf and worship the sun all day long."

LIFE AT THE TOP

No matter what stage of life or strata of society, Americans constantly compare themselves with those at the top. Our curiosity is piqued by darkened limousine windows, glimpses into private homes in *Town & Country* and the lurid tales of excess detailed on TV's "Lifestyles of the Rich and Famous." It's been this way since the 1930s when, as sociologist Vance Packard observed, the Great Depression frightened the conspicuous consumers among the rich into becoming "discreet, almost reticent, in exhibiting their wealth." Old monied families left their in-town mansions for exclusive hideaways in the greenbelt suburbs of major cities, keeping their attendants and extravagances out of sight of envious commoners and prying journalists. Their lifestyle never changed, only the ethic of not showing it off except behind electronic fences and peek-a-boo shrubbery.

"The very rich are different from you and me," wrote F. Scott Fitzgerald, and nowhere is that more evident than along the avenues of Blue Blood Estates. The most affluent cluster of neighborhoods represents that pinnacle of achievement to which most Americans traditionally aspire: an address in Beverly Hills, California, Palm Beach, Florida, Scarsdale, New York, or McLean, Virginia. Home to one in ten of America's millionaires, Blue Blood Estates communities are often filled with luxurious center hall colonials, stately English Tudor manses and overwrought replicas of San Simeon.

Many Americans immediately think of the super-rich as idle and decadent, like the late Lord Alington, a British blueblood who was so bored one rainy day that he bet 3,000 pounds on which drop of water would reach the bottom of the windowsill first. But only a scant 5 percent of America's millionaires inherited their family fortunes. The vast majority are the nation's corporate kingpins and the upper-crustiest whitest-collared professionals like heart surgeons and entertainment lawyers. They come from middle- or working-class families and made their fortunes the traditional way—as workaholics for years at a stretch. Of America's million millionaires in 1985, the average age was 63. The road to Blue Blood Estates is paved with 16-hour days, seven days a week.

Although the residents of Blue Blood Estates comprise only 1.1 percent of the U.S. population, by dint of wealth alone, their influence is felt far beyond their numbers. They hold one-third of the nation's private wealth, 60 percent of America's corporate stocks, 30 percent of all interest-bearing assets and nearly a tenth of the country's real estate. According to Thomas Stanley, a Georgia State University marketing professor who's spent over a decade studying the ways of the very rich, saving, not spending, is the ticket to Easy Street. Stanley has reported that most millionaires spend less than 10 percent of their net worth annually, though that's still enough for them to lead lives of 24-karat luxury. Compared to the general population, they buy twenty-three times as many Rolls Royces, take eight times as many international business trips and spend four times as many hours playing tennis. They like to host dinner parties, as shown by their frequent trips to gourmet shops and liquor stores, where they tend to buy French champagne and Irish whiskey. But Stanley describes millionaires as one of the most "undershopped" groups in America, able to distance themselves from mainstream marketers and society.

With high-priced private schools facing a shrinking student population, luring Blue Blood Estates' high-school graduates has become a necessary challenge. Virginia Intermont College, a small liberal arts school in Bristol, Virginia, set about attracting such upscale students by analyzing its current enrollment lists to discover which neighborhoods provided most of its students. An overwhelming number called Blue Blood Estates home. Accordingly, recruiters went after these communities—some as far away as Detroit and Dallas—with brochures that emphasized what many cluster teenagers could appreciate: a major in equestrian studies, a strong business program, the new horse stables and other "good life" activities on campus. "For the small liberal arts school, this kind of recruiting is a matter of survival," explains Mills Kelly, vice president of the Washington, D.C.–based Consultants for Educational Resources and Research. For Blue Blood Estates residents, it means passing on aristocratic values to the next generation.

LIFE AT THE TOP: BLUE BLOOD ESTATES

Residents of the nation's richest neighborhoods may have golden nest eggs, but they don't just sit on their money. They travel, attend the theater, give to charities and buy a wide range of luxury items. They can afford to take care of themselves, attending health clubs and drinking bottled water at well above average rates.

	National Average	Blue Blood Estates	Cluster Index
Air travel credit cards	1.5%	7.9%	530
U.S. Treasury notes	0.7	3.6	521
Irish whiskey	1.5	6.0	401
Rental cars	4.9	19.5	398
Imported cheese	6.9	26.1	379
Downhill skiing	4.2	13.6	322
Personal computers	7.0	20.2	288
Valid passports	10.2	29.3	287
Men's business suits	8.0	20.9	261
Bottled water	9.3	23.6	253
Health clubs	6.1	14.6	238
Book clubs	8.9	19.9	224
Croissants	12.3	26.4	215
Country clubs	1.2	2.5	207
Attend live theater	15.4	29.9	194

Numbers indicate percentages of people in each category and indexed against the national average. An index of 100 equals the U.S. average for that category. An index of 200 means a cluster has twice the national average for that category. Source: SMRB & MRI data bases, Claritas Corp., 1987.

Preserving a lifestyle that celebrates exclusivity is no easy task in a nation built on democracy. But few Blue Blood Estates communities are more successful at it than Gibson Island, Maryland, a 960-acre island lying along the upper western shore of the Chesapeake Bay. Developed in 1921 as a golf course and country club by three prominent Baltimoreans tired of waiting to tee off at city courses, the picturesque island was later divvied up by club members who wanted vacation homes to escape the steamy summers of Baltimore and Washington, D.C. Nowadays, Gibson Island is a year-round residential community of quaint Cape Cods and storybook cottages, painted in pastels and framed with flowering shrubs. The scarcity of the 178 houses means bayfront properties list for $500,000 to $1.5 million, making the island a paradise few outsiders can afford. Locals further maintain their distance thanks to a causeway that limits access between the mainland and the island. Guards at a stone gatehouse must check in any guests who wish to drive over the island's private bridge, in much the way medieval knights let down the drawbridge over a castle's moat.

To maintain the quiet natural beauty—two-thirds of the island is a bird sanctuary—Gibson Islanders have resisted welcoming celebrities to their ranks. Many real estate deals are contingent on prospective homeowners gaining admittance to the Gibson Island Club, whose members can blackball candidates in secret ballots. Applicants who have succeeded, according to the club's heavy-set, phlegmatic president, Jack Morgan, are a "mishmash" of successful doctors, lawyers and businesspeople who've tired of bustling city life. On weekends, they hike the island's woodlands or prune their gardens, with cordless telephones attached to their belts. Morgan can't remember the last time the community met to deal with a civic concern, and islanders rarely bring politics —much less politicians—across the causeway. An overture from former President Dwight Eisenhower to move onto the island was once rebuffed by residents who feared disruptions by his attendant security force and press corps. "You can imagine what that would have meant to the way of life here," says Morgan, shaking his head. "No one wanted a bunch of reporters sitting off our bow full time."

Like water-based Blue Blood Estates communities on Martha's Vineyard and Newport, sporting life dominates Gibson Island. With so many residents retired or free to work when they choose, the club's swimming pool and golf course are busy every day, and traffic is brisk among sailboats in the harbor and canoes in Otter Pond. An old saying around Gibson Island holds that boats are more important than people, and one glance at the $100,000 yachts in the inner harbor confirms the notion. To celebrate the Fourth of July, residents watch a fireworks display while bobbing atop vessels christened Fantasy, Love Boat and Cookie Monster. And though grocery stores and restaurants are banned from the island, residents do allow one commercial enterprise: a boat repair yard. School-aged children must journey to the mainland to study math and science but never have to leave the island to take classes in boat handling and water safety. The only church on the island, the Protestant Episcopal Church of St. Christopher-by-the-Sea, is named after the patron saint of seafarers.

"Gibson Island is like a dream world in some ways," says Sally Henderson, 61, a lifelong resident, retired teacher and granddaughter of one of the founders. "You can walk in the gorgeous woods around here and never worry about someone jumping out and mugging you. You can sit outside day after day and enjoy the peace and quiet. In our household we talk a lot about boats and gardening but only occasionally about what the hell the president is doing."

Like other residents of Blue Blood Estates communities, Henderson downplays the exclusivity of her lifestyle. A petite woman with black hair cut like Prince Valiant, she's usually dressed in blue jeans and a worn smock. She lives with her husband, nautical author Richard Henderson, in a yellow bayfront home only a short bike ride away from their 38-foot sailboat, Kelpie, moored in the harbor. She knows neighbors who may underwrite philanthropic or environmental causes but typically do it anonymously. Unlike the glitzy social scene that's part of some wealthy enclaves, quiet dinner parties are more the island style. "And you won't see a lot of furs or Cadillacs around here," says Henderson. "Status around here is not being concerned with status. People have money but it's inconspicuous money."

Geographically, not all the well-heeled gravitate to neighborhoods of like-minded millionaires. The Census Bureau found that some 15,000 U.S. households with annual incomes exceeding $75,000 reside in mobile homes. Although the rich can live virtually anywhere, about one-fifth of the very affluent choose not to reside with their own kind. A good example is Sam Walton, 69, America's richest man and owner of Wal-Mart, the nationwide discount chain worth $6 billion. Since opening his first Wal-Mart in 1945, he's launched 823 stores in the Ozarks and in twenty-two states in the Sunbelt and Midwest, mostly in the small towns of America's outback. Though he could dwell in a Tara-sized mansion with a Rolls Royce for every day of the week, he chooses to live in the remote Ozark hamlet of Bentonville, Arkansas (pop. 9,920), a middle-class Golden Ponds community. At his ranch house surrounded by woods, an old pickup sits in the garage, the furniture has been described by visitors as "early Holiday Inn," and muddy bird dogs stroll through the house where one might expect servants. When his previous house burned down a few years back—lightning struck his roofing shingles—he was content to live in a double-wide trailer on the property until wife Helen protested.

Despite the reputations of the great dynasties—the Fords, Cabots and Rockefellers—fortunes in the United States rarely survive beyond two or three generations. The typically male-dominated household among the very rich is one reason why, maintains marketing expert Thomas Stanley. Because many millionaires are secretive about how they control their money, their deaths frequently leave rich, ill-informed widows ripe for bad advice. "It's not uncommon for half an estate to be lost within a few years after the widow takes over," says Stanley. "A great fortune that's taken decades to amass can be lost in a relative instant." Nevertheless, census data have shown that the concentration of wealth in this country has changed little since 1945; the number of rich, middle-class and poor Americans has remained roughly the same. Thus, while the upwardly striving are building their fortunes, an equal number are on the downward slide, each group taking up its appropriate station on the ZQ ladder. As the cluster system shows, America is truly a nation of churning riches and changing values.

3

THE MYTH OF
THE AVERAGE AMERICAN

> *"Strictly speaking, the 'average American' is*
> *a 29-year-old hermaphrodite (slightly more*
> *female than male)."*
> —Barry Tarshis, *The 'Average*
> *American' Book*

More than a century ago, Alexis de Tocqueville observed that "Americans become assimilated" as they mingle. And from
that legendary melting pot, a mold emerged of John and Jane Doe, Mr.
and Mrs. John Q. Public and a mythical family of relatives distinguished
only by their ordinariness. It's safe to say that nothing has ever been
so measured, tracked, probed and studied by survey industry researchers as the Average American. Every day more than 55,000 Americans
are surveyed about how they live, what they eat, how they spend their
money and what's on their minds in hopes of fleshing out our composite
portrait. Those survey questions aren't always discreet, either. Is
premarital sex wrong? asks the Roper Organization. Are you concerned
about your health? General Mills wants to know. Are you romantic?
Which sport is truly America's national pastime? How's the President
doing?

From the avalanche of answers, merchandisers attempt to capture
the ever-changing essence of the buying public. In the corporate world,
knowledge of national averages has meant money and power. By offering a single product to a huge mainstream audience, companies can
lower their advertising and distribution costs—and increase their prof-

its. Henry Ford's assembly line produced both cookie-cutter cars and handsome profits as thousands of Americans found they could own a Model T in any color as long as it was black. The 1950s became the era of mass-marketing, with consumers shopping at the same chain stores, watching the same network TV shows and reading all-things-to-all-people magazines like *Look, Life* and *Saturday Evening Post.* Americans could travel across the country and find similarly styled shopping centers, subdivisions and drive-ins. The Average American ruled the marketplace.

But no more. In the last generation, American culture has become increasingly fragmented in a megatrend process that John Naisbitt calls "decentralization." The mass market has split apart, shattered by such shifting demographics as double incomes and divorce rates. These changes blur the line between upper and lower classes. New service occupations such as paralegals and data-processing-equipment repairers erode differences between blue and white collars. Large-circulation, general-purpose magazines have disappeared while publishers have launched more than 13,000 special-interest publications. Whether you're into Barbie doll memorabilia or Nordic folkdancing esoterica, there's a journal for you. And for every subscription list, there's a direct-mail marketer eager to lay hands on it. According to Standard Rate and Data Service, the number of direct-mail address lists has steadily increased to 55,000, identifying the fans of country records as well as conservative Republicans.

In the electronic media, meanwhile, the number of television channels in most areas has jumped from four to more than a dozen in the last twenty-five years. At the same time, network television's grip weakens—the audience share is expected to dip to 70 percent by 1990—as viewers switch to video cassettes, syndicated stations and cable TV's specialized audience programming. "Broadcasting" has evolved into "narrowcasting."

Despite this decentralization, one fact remains: the unshakable dominance of the Average American in marketing research. Developers of new products continue to introduce their brands in cities selected as having an age and income mix near the national average. If a new laundry detergent plays in Peoria, so the thinking goes, a company can be reasonably sure it will also move in Modesto and win in Wilmington. Dancer Fitzgerald Sample, a prominent Manhattan advertising agency, listed forty-two of the favorite test markets in 1986. Among the guinea-pig locales: Cleveland, Indianapolis, Albany, Chattanooga, Des Moines and Minneapolis. From 1983 to 1985, Minneapolis alone served as the test market for 110 products. Its popularity, noted one DFS executive, was based on the fact that its citizenry are "demographically close to the average."

But what's "average"? The traditional image of the nuclear family —Dad, nonworking Mom and two kids—long ago went the way of Ozzie and Harriet: in 1985, 63 percent of all U.S. households had no children; married couples with children made up only 29 percent. Statistically speaking, the "average household" (determined by dividing the census totals for income, home value, etc., by the number of Americans) consisted of a married couple and one child. Dad, age 30, worked as a blue-collar laborer in durable manufacturing; Mom held a job as a white-collar clerk. Both were of West European ancestry, high-school graduates and had a combined salary of a little over $22,000. Their house, a $57,800 three-bedroom with TV, air conditioning, a dish washer and clothes washer, was located in the suburbs of a midwestern city.

Yet this mathematical composite, while rooted in census data, has a major flaw: it bears no connection with reality. To be sure, millions of households throughout the midwestern suburbs fit this portrait. But in their effort to reduce the nation to an Average American household, market researchers have whittled away the variables that truly define the American character. For example, 34 percent of the populace own one car while 35 percent own two cars. So what's "average"—a one-car or two-car family? In Manhattan, very few people own any car. In other words, the statistical average is often a vacant place in space.

On a cluster map, the search for Average Americanhood loses all meaning. The population isn't distributed evenly across the nation but unevenly among the forty neighborhood types, with distinct socioeconomic levels, family life cycles and ethnic makeups. Black Americans comprise about 11 percent of the population nationwide, meaning that on the Average American street, the odds are nine in ten that you'll bump into someone who isn't black. On the other hand, if you walk through Washington, D.C., Atlanta or other cities with heavy concentrations of Black Enterprise and Emergent Minorities communities, the odds change considerably. Seven out of ten residents in these clusters are black. The fact is, there's no place to find the Average American.

Minneapolis, for all its virtues as a city with demographic figures near the national average, is anything but representative of the nation's neighborhoods. According to a cluster analysis, Minneapolis boasts more than four times the national average of rural Grain Belt neighborhoods, nearly three times the average of Bohemian Mix areas, and better than twice the average of Agri-Business, Young Suburbia and Single City Blues zip codes. In contrast, there are ten clusters that lack representation entirely in Minneapolis, among them Black Enterprise, Urban Gold Coast, Gray Power and Hispanic Mix. The largest concentrations of neighborhoods are rural and middle-class. What the city lacks are ethnic enclaves, havens for the super-rich, ghettos of underclass residents and pockets of highrise-living sophisticates. Overall, the kinds of neighborhoods that one-quarter of all Americans call home simply aren't present.

In midtown Minneapolis, beneath the IDS Center's tower of glass and steel, this cluster analysis comes alive. At noon on a spring weekday, the cars whizzing along 8th Street are Ranger Jeeps, Chevy Corvettes and Olds Toronados, not the Mercedes 380s or Jaguar XKEs that you'd see in an Urban Gold Coast. Across the busy plaza, vendors hawk hot dogs and croissant sandwiches, not the tamales and "bar-

TESTING THE TEST MARKETS

Two popular test markets, the Minneapolis and Peoria metropolitan areas, are by no means a reflection of the country as a whole. Each lacks ethnic, urban neighborhoods and has an abundance of agriculturally based communities. Only in the singles-filled New Beginnings cluster do both come close to the national average.

Cluster (% of U.S. Pop.)	Minneapolis	Peoria
Urban Gold Coast (0.5%)	0	0
Black Enterprise (0.8%)	0	0
Hispanic Mix (1.9%)	0	0
Tobacco Roads (1.2%)	0	0
God's Country (2.7%)	40	169
New Beginnings (4.3%)	112	100
Blue-Collar Nursery (2.2%)	145	422
Coalburg & Corntown (2.0%)	209	400
Bohemian Mix (1.1%)	264	0
Grain Belt (1.3%)	468	126

Numbers indicate percentages of people living in each cluster, indexed against the national average. An index of 100 equals the U.S. average for that cluster. An index of 200 means a cluster has twice the national average. Source: PRIZM (Census Demography), Claritas Corp., 1987.

bacao" you find in cities with a large Hispanic Mix district. Most people you see—a clutch of tellers emerging from the Midwest Federal Bank, two jobbers in Walkmans from Loring Park, a crowd of Control Data Corporation techies strolling down Nicollet Mall—are all fresh-faced, nattily dressed and Caucasian. Any one might have been an Ivory Snow baby model.

Cultural stereotyping? Not if you're looking for a city that represents America-in-miniature. At the neighborhood level there is no one archetypical city but dozens of common city profiles with distinctive cluster profiles. So it is that the best market for chain saws is Sioux Falls, South Dakota (heavy in Grain Belt clusters), and the prime town for selling hand-crafted $150 shoes is Helena, Montana (overrun with God's Country communities). If the perfect test market is a city whose population mirrors nationwide percentages of rich, poor, black, white, blue-collar, white-collar, urban and rural, no such place exists. And not one of the nation's 300 major TV markets even barely conforms to the cluster representation of the entire nation.

■ CITY THUMBPRINTS

Every American community has a unique cluster makeup—and its own lifestyle thumbprint. A walking tour through any city can reveal its pattern—whether the driveways are cluttered with Porsches and sailboats or Toyota vans and tricycles. But the cluster system quantifies these and other behavioral characteristics by correlating a community's neighborhood types with its consumer purchases, devising an accurate portrait without benefit of first-hand observation. Consider a handful of big-city markets as viewed through a lifestyle lens:

■ New York City. If there's one neighborhood type that dominates the Big Apple skyline, it's urban Gold Coast. This cluster of dense, high-rise neighborhoods is eleven times more prevalent here than in the typical American city. But metropolitan New York also reflects its historical role as the entry point for immigrants with its polyglot society of New Melting Pot, Hispanic Mix and Two More Rungs communities. Together, these neighborhoods are home to a high concentration of single apartment-dwellers engaged in lower-level white-collar jobs in business and the financial industries—a postindustrial service economy. As consumers, New Yorkers show a strong preference for movies,

THE CLUSTERS OF NEW YORK

The Big Apple skyline is dominated by high-rise Urban Gold Coast neighborhoods—eleven times more prevalent there than in the typical American city. Its cluster profile also represents the city's historical role as an entry point for immigrants. The relative affluence of residents allows them to travel abroad—and to live well at home.

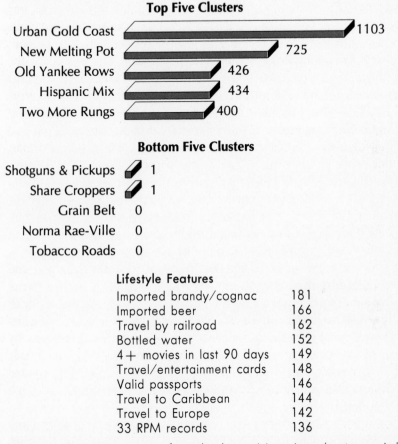

Top Five Clusters

Cluster	Value
Urban Gold Coast	1103
New Melting Pot	725
Old Yankee Rows	426
Hispanic Mix	434
Two More Rungs	400

Bottom Five Clusters

Cluster	Value
Shotguns & Pickups	1
Share Croppers	1
Grain Belt	0
Norma Rae-Ville	0
Tobacco Roads	0

Lifestyle Features

Feature	Index
Imported brandy/cognac	181
Imported beer	166
Travel by railroad	162
Bottled water	152
4+ movies in last 90 days	149
Travel/entertainment cards	148
Valid passports	146
Travel to Caribbean	144
Travel to Europe	142
33 RPM records	136

Numbers indicate percentages of people who participate in each category, indexed against the national average. An index of 100 equals the U.S. average for that category. An index of 200 means a cluster has twice the national average for that category. Source: SMRB and MRI data bases, Claritas Corp., 1987.

European travel, imported brandy, winter suits, sangria, jazz and black disco music. On the other hand, New Yorkers obviously don't live in Tobacco Roads, Norma Rae-Ville and Grain Belt communities. And it's unlikely that many are pickup-owning hunters who listen to country music while chewing tobacco.

■ Los Angeles. This sprawling city, another ethnic haven of Hispanic Mix and New Melting Pot clusters, is more upscale than New York as shown by the widespread presence of Blue Blood Estates and Money & Brains neighborhoods. The concentration of young, college-educated singles contributes to a significant percentage of household incomes in the $50,000–$75,000 range—not to mention a real-estate wonderland where the median home value tops $200,000. Los Angelenos are more likely than the general population to own a convertible, belong to a health club, have a brokerage account, enjoy sailing, attend the theater and drink imported wine at dinner. On the other hand, L.A. surveys reflect little interest in woodworking, owning a utility vehicle, buying from catalogues or installing mufflers on their cars. "Los Angeles," observes writer Ben Stein, "is playground, lotus land, energy center and center of the universe. L.A. worships movement." And woodworkers need not apply.

■ Washington, D.C. More than any other metropolitan area, the nation's capital is filled with upper-class suburban and urban neighborhoods: a mix of Blue Blood Estates, Money & Brains, Bohemian Mix and Black Enterprise clusters found four times more often here than the national average. About 10 percent of Washington's 3 million residents live below the poverty line, but they exhibit little economic impact on the metro area compared to the more affluent majority. What these neighborhood types have in common are residents with college educations, homes worth over $200,000, household incomes pushing $100,000 and jobs in business, education and public administration. According to lifestyle surveys, Washingtonians tend to read books, lis listen to classical music, own personal computers, watch tennis, buy 35-mm cameras, contribute to public television, attend health clubs, drink imported beer and visit Europe and the Caribbean. Without Heavy Industry, Gray Power, Rank & File and Public Assistance clusters in the capital, Washingtonians exhibit little interest in drinking powdered soft drinks, smoking cigarettes, ordering records through TV offers, frequenting K-mart or hosting Tupperware parties. If, as Richard Nixon once observed, Washington is filled with "pointy-headed, briefcase-toting bureaucrats," their standard of living is nothing to sneer at.

■ Dallas. Unlike the nation's older metropolitan areas, Dallas epitomizes the New American City—a place without tenement neighborhoods or a crumbling infrastructure. Its predominant clusters—Money

THE CLUSTERS OF LOS ANGELES

Sprawling Los Angeles is home to large concentrations of both downscale and upscale neighborhoods but completely lacks high-rise communities and rural areas. Its consumption patterns reflect all the trappings of the good life: imported wine and cars, exotic travel and entertainment.

Top Five Clusters

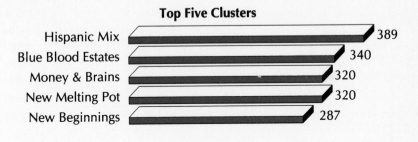

Hispanic Mix	389
Blue Blood Estates	340
Money & Brains	320
New Melting Pot	320
New Beginnings	287

Bottom Clusters

Urban Gold Coast	0
Grain Belt	0
Mines & Mills	0
Tobacco Roads	0

Lifestyle Features

European luxury cars	146
Travel to Hawaii	145
Convertibles	142
Jazz records/tapes	142
Valid passports	142
Travel/entertainment cards	137
Sailing	136
Imported white wine	135
Health clubs	132
Brokerage accounts	131

Numbers indicate percentages of people in each category, indexed against the national average. An index of 100 equals the U.S. average for that category. An index of 200 means a cluster has twice the national average for that category. Source: SMRB and MRI data bases, Claritas Corp., 1987.

& Brains, New Beginnings, Furs & Station Wagons and Young Influentials—reflect a populace of young up-and-comers who came to town during the Sunbelt boom. They're big beer drinkers, college basketball fans, racquetball players, European travelers, personal computer owners, book readers, convertible owners and gospel music lovers. Con-

THE CLUSTERS OF WASHINGTON, D.C.

More than any other city, the nation's capital is dominated by neighborhoods of the affluent and the educated, of black and white achievers. Compared to the nation as a whole, theirs is an elite lifestyle, complete with a fondness for imported cognac, classical music and public TV.

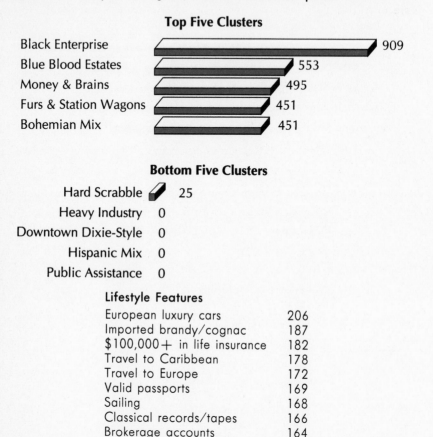

Top Five Clusters

Black Enterprise	909
Blue Blood Estates	553
Money & Brains	495
Furs & Station Wagons	451
Bohemian Mix	451

Bottom Five Clusters

Hard Scrabble	25
Heavy Industry	0
Downtown Dixie-Style	0
Hispanic Mix	0
Public Assistance	0

Lifestyle Features

European luxury cars	206
Imported brandy/cognac	187
$100,000+ in life insurance	182
Travel to Caribbean	178
Travel to Europe	172
Valid passports	169
Sailing	168
Classical records/tapes	166
Brokerage accounts	164
Contribute to public TV	156

Numbers indicate percentages of people in each category, indexed against the national average. An index of 100 equals the U.S. average for that category. An index of 200 means a cluster has twice the national average for that category. Source: SMRB and MRI data bases, Claritas Corp., 1987.

trary to the image presented at South Fork on TV's "Dallas," there are few communities of super-wealth—the number of Blue Blood Estates zip codes is zero. Neither is there much of a "ranch" presence in clusters like Grain Belt and Agri-Business. Indeed, lifestyle features ranking low in Dallas are a fondness for chewing tobacco, hunting,

THE CLUSTERS OF DALLAS–FT. WORTH

TV soap images notwithstanding, Dallas lacks the affluence of Blue Blood Estates and the concentration of Ewing-style ranches found in Agri-Business. Indeed, this city's lifestyle, reflected in a population of young up-and-comers who arrived during the Sunbelt boom, is characterized by a high rate of health club members, sports-car owners and active vacationers.

Top Five Clusters

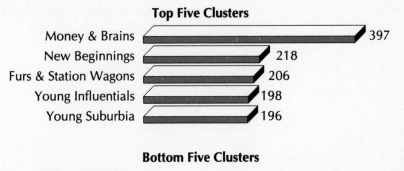

Cluster	
Money & Brains	397
New Beginnings	218
Furs & Station Wagons	206
Young Influentials	198
Young Suburbia	196

Bottom Five Clusters

Cluster	
Blue Blood Estates	0
Two More Rungs	0
Urban Gold Coast	0
Rank & File	0
New Melting Pot	0

Lifestyle Features

Convertibles	131
Sailing	128
Travel to Mexico	127
Two or more foreign trips	125
Burglar alarms	124
Imported white wine	124
Downhill skiing	123
Health clubs	123
Racquetball	120
Imported cars	120

Numbers indicate percentages of people in each category, indexed against the national average. An index of 100 equals the U.S. average for that category. An index of 200 means a cluster has twice the national average for that category. Source: SMRB and MRI data bases, Claritas Corp., 1987.

THE CLUSTERS OF CHICAGO

Chicago truly is a toddlin' town, as indicated by residents' high consumption of alcohol. As befits one of the nation's venerable cities, its demographic landscape is filled with working-class, wealthy and ethnic neighborhoods.

Top Five Clusters

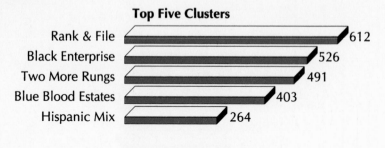

Rank & File	612
Black Enterprise	526
Two More Rungs	491
Blue Blood Estates	403
Hispanic Mix	264

Bottom Five Clusters

Back-Country Folks	1
Downtown Dixie-Style	1
Norma Rae-Ville	0
Smalltown Downtown	0
Hard Scrabble	0

Lifestyle Features

Imported brandy/cognac	149
Scotch whisky	139
Gin	137
Imported wine	137
Travel to Eastern Europe/Middle East	134
Brokerage accounts	132
Jazz records/tapes	132
Contribute to public TV	131
Convertibles	130
Two or more foreign trips	128

Numbers indicate percentages of people in each category, indexed against the national average. An index of 100 equals the U.S. average for that category. An index of 200 means a cluster has twice the national average for that category. Source: SMRB and MRI data bases, Claritas Corp., 1987.

THE CLUSTERS OF CLEVELAND

Cleveland's profile is that of a factory town: blue-collar, ethnic, black and working-class. Compared to their counterparts in, say, Dallas and Washington, residents' consumption habits reflect more conservative, less adventuresome tastes.

Top Five Clusters

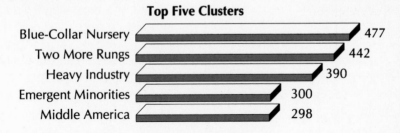

Blue-Collar Nursery	477
Two More Rungs	442
Heavy Industry	390
Emergent Minorities	300
Middle America	298

Bottom Ten Clusters

Young Influentials	0
Urban Gold Coast	0
Bohemian Mix	0
New Melting Pot	0
Golden Ponds	0
Norma Rae-Ville	0
Tobacco Roads	0
Hard Scrabble	0
Downtown Dixie-Style	0
Hispanic Mix	0

Lifestyle Features

Watch/listen to/attend tennis matches	125
Rental cars	125
Burglar alarms	124
Gin	122
Unions	121
Foreign tour packages	120
Pancake/donut restaurants	119
Health clubs	118
Bottled water	118
4+ movies in last 90 days	116
Folk records	116

Numbers indicate percentages of people in each category, indexed against the national average. An index of 100 equals the U.S. average for that category. An index of 200 means a cluster has twice the national average for that category. Source: SMRB and MRI data bases, Claritas Corp., 1987.

horse-racing and pickup trucks. J. R. Ewing notwithstanding, Dallas's ten-gallon-hat lifestyle has faded into the sunset.

■ Chicago. One of the nation's great established cities, Chicago has dense housing, a big ethnic population and a conglomeration of wealthy, working-class and poor neighborhoods. The city's most populous clusters are Rank & File, Blue Blood Estates, Black Enterprise and Two More Rungs. Demographically, those neighborhood types feature households with recent immigrants and second-generation Eastern Europeans, high-rise apartments and $100,000–$150,000 homes and lower-level white-collar workers involved in the service industries of business, wholesale trade and finance. As the song goes, Chicago is still a "toddlin' town": its top four lifestyle characteristics are consumption of table wine, gin, imported brandy and Scotch. But it is also a worldly city where a significant percentage of its residents attend plays, shop at health food stores, enjoy movies, listen to jazz and travel to Europe. In cluster terms, Chicago is testament to Old World sophistication.

■ Cleveland. The quintessential factory town—blue-collar, ethnic, black and working class—Cleveland is built of clusters such as Heavy Industry, Two More Rungs, Blue-Collar Nursery and Emergent Minorities. Its residents have Eastern European roots, its households are occupied by double-wage-earners making $35,000–$50,000 annually, and its neighborhoods are old and stable with a significant portion of the populace living in the same homes for more than twenty years. In contrast to the more upscale residents of Dallas and Washington, Cleveland's citizens prefer to go bowling, drive domestic cars, belong to a union, watch golf, install their own vinyl flooring, use cents-off coupons and travel with a tour group to Europe. While other cities have shifted from manufacturing to service economies—resulting in the formation of Young Influentials, Bohemian Mix and New Beginnings communities— Cleveland remains a center of aging industrial neighborhoods, a city arrested in time.

LIFE IN "AVERAGE AMERICA"

Traveling through the clusters demonstrates the diversity of America's lifestyles and, in particular, its vast extremes—from the Palm Beaches of Blue Blood Estates to the Bedford-Stuyvesants of Public Assistance. But what of life in the middle, where folks eat, drive, read and watch TV at rates close to the national average? Theoretically, no single Average American cluster exists, because neighborhood settlement reflects a blend of influences: race, ethnicity and urbanization, among others. But it is possible to discern an "average" cluster by using the ZQ scale of social rank.

If you went in search of America's socioeconomic midpoint, to explore a lifestyle halfway between Blue Blood Estates and Public Assistance, you'd end up in a cluster appropriately called Middle America. Composed of towns like Oshkosh, Wisconsin, Sandusky, Ohio, and Marshall, Michigan, Middle America exists at the nation's demographic crossroads: close to the U.S. average on most measures of age, ethnicity, household composition and lifestyle. Advice columnist Ann Landers has written that everyone wants to be normal but no one wants to be average, yet in Middle America being average can be a cause for celebration.

Take Marshall, a classic Middle America community of 7,702, in the center of Michigan's flat, agricultural plain. Far removed from the urban sprawl—an hour west of Detroit—Marshall mirrors the nation's average profile (median age—31, median household income—$24,209, median education—12.6 years). Its pace is slow, its crime rate low and its economic base modest but solid. There's just enough employment at the State Farm Insurance division office and several nearby factories to keep residents off the dole and living comfortably in century-old houses along wide, shady streets. In Marshall, there is no "other side of the tracks." With its three stoplights, one movie theater and a renovated stable for a city hall, Marshall is a slice of Americana most city dwellers believe went the way of the plough horse.

"This is the kind of town where people say good morning to you on the street even if they don't know you," says Marshall's mayor, J. Allen Bassage, a native New Yorker who favors polyester slacks, Wallabees and T-shirts advertising the latest community event. "They're proud of their houses and active in their churches. And they take the time to care for the flowers in the parks."

That pride of place is characteristic of Middle America, with its high number of residents who belong to civic, fraternal and service clubs. Marshall benefits from thirty such groups, which have taken on projects like building a barrier-free elevator for the handicapped in City Hall and sending local kids to music camp. Residents are considered "well connected" if they belong to more than three voluntary organizations. Bassage himself owes his position to one such group, the Executive Club, composed of several dozen retirees who meet over coffee every morning at Yesteryear's Restaurant and proudly boast of "a thousand years of collective service to the community." Says Bassage: "The only rule for joining is that you have to send a postcard to the group when you take a trip." In 1982, club members drafted him to run for mayor even though he had no platform and wanted no part of the job's responsibilities, which included performing marriage ceremonies for townspeople. He still shrugs when asked how he beat his two opponents. "There weren't any issues to speak of," he says somewhat sheepishly. "Even now, people only call me when their garbage isn't picked up or a city tree is swaying too close to someone's house."

Maintaining the homestead is important in Middle America communities, especially in Marshall, where 1,300 homes predate the turn of the century. Founded in 1831 as a stagecoach stopover between Detroit and Chicago, Marshall later became known as a manufacturing center for patent medicines, hernia trusses and folding bathtubs (popular at the turn of the century). Today the mix of blue- and white-collar workers spend their off-time renovating their homes, purchasing table saws, power drills and electric sanders at above-average rates. In Marshall, status is having your restored gingerbread house included on the annual Historic Home Tour.

Sally Bulgarelli, a 34-year-old mother of two, is one reason renovation chic survives in Middle America. A chatty hospital secretary with an earth-mother's appeal, she and her husband fled Detroit's inner city in 1979 and moved to Marshall after falling in love with the town on a weekend holiday. Swept up by local renovation fever, they paid $75,000 for an 1871 Victorian two-story beauty, sank $10,000 into building materials and a lot more in sweat equity and began devoting weekends to reconnoitering antique shops and reading books on Victoriana. Soon their living room sported period loveseats, an 1850 fainting couch and walls painted an authentic shade of dusty rose. "Sometimes we feel like we're owned by this house," says Bulgarelli, eyeing an end-table stack of *Family Handyman,* one of Middle America's most popular magazines. "We get to feeling guilty whenever we take a trip, thinking, 'We should have remodeled this room instead.' "

True to their midscale demographics, consumers in Middle America buy most products—cars, periodicals and groceries—at average rates. Middle Americans would rather join Christmas clubs than country clubs, watch college basketball than soccer, buy canned corn than exotic fresh varieties. No one comes to a Middle America town to dine in trendy restaurants, shop for imports or pick up a baguette. If you want to strut your stuff in Marshall, you've got to leave town to find a dance floor.

Along Marshall's single commercial strip, Mom & Pop shopkeepers try to compete with out-of-town malls by offering "old-fashioned person-

HOW MIDDLE IS MIDDLE AMERICA?

In Middle America, there are few extremes to life. Little is eaten, driven or purchased at rates far from the national average.

	National Average	Middle America	Cluster Index
Convertibles	1.0%	1.1%	105
Filter cigarettes	35.5	37.3	105
Mouthwash	60.6	63.0	104
Hunting	9.3	9.7	104
Headache remedies	86.3	88.9	103
Swimming	29.0	29.9	103
Life insurance	64.1	66.0	103
Home baking	23.0	23.5	102
Aftershave	34.7	35.4	102
Cola drinks	63.0	63.6	101
Shampoo	92.5	92.5	100
Compact cars	11.1	11.1	100
Deodorant	92.9	92.9	100
Cold/sinus remedies	48.0	48.0	100
Vinyl flooring	4.1	4.1	100
Home sewing	13.1	13.0	99
Domestic travel	59.5	58.3	98
Watch/attend/listen to pro football	31.4	30.5	97
Digital watches	9.3	8.9	95
Music/dance concerts	15.3	14.5	95
Books and magazines	49.9	46.9	94

Numbers indicate percentages of people in each category and indexed against the national average. An index of 100 equals the U.S. average for that category. An index of 200 means a cluster has twice the national average for that category. Source: SMRB and MRI data bases, Claritas Corp., 1987.

alized service," says Gladys Bailey, the spry, 78-year-old owner of the Vogue Shop for women. Toward that end, there are flower boxes outside her shop, a nativity painting on the back wall and a table in the center with crayons and coloring books to occupy youngsters while their mothers try on clothes. In summarizing the tastes of her customers, she confesses there's little interest in Calvin Klein, Ann Taylor or other designer labels. "What works in city fashions won't do too well here," says Bailey, whose credo is "Never tell a woman a dress looks beautiful on her if it looks like the devil." "In Marshall, people like traditional basics, the kind of clothes advertised in *Better Homes & Gardens,* not *Women's Wear Daily.*"

Despite having catered to Marshall's middling preferences and pock-etbooks for over twenty-five years, Bailey expresses no interest in retiring. Two years ago, a shop next door caught fire and all the area merchants pitched in to save her stock—and her livelihood—from ir-reparable smoke damage. "Some business friends once told me, 'Mar-shall never hits the peak but it never scrapes the bottom either,' " says Bailey in what might be a fitting summation of life in Middle America. "You'll never get rich here, but you'll never suffer either."

It's easy to imagine that everyone in Middle America has stepped rosy cheeked out of a Norman Rockwell illustration. And there's little evidence in Marshall to the contrary. Every Thursday in July, for in-stance, about 200 Marshallites gather in Carver Park for a performance by the Rotary Club Band. Unfolding aluminum chairs in jagged rows, townsfolk fan themselves with mimeographed programs as band mem-bers tune their instruments, two dozen volunteers sporting yellow T-shirts and varying degrees of musical expertise. Several yards away, high schoolers in hopped-up pickup trucks and motorcycles compete noisily for attention along Michigan Avenue, the town's main drag. But no one in Carver Park seems to mind. With the wind whipping up an American flag and purple Rotary Club banner, the band launches into a Sousa march, and everyone taps along with the energetic, if unsteady, brass section. Along the edge of the crowd, the youngest children wave balloons and turn cartwheels in the grass, just as their parents and grandparents did before them.

The small-town values of Marshall—and most Middle America com-munities—translate to centrist views at the polls. With a nearly equal split of Democrats and Republicans, Middle Americans are the nation's swing voters. They gave Reagan 63 percent of their votes in 1984, but divided their numbers between the parties' congressional candidates in 1986—voting primarily according to local economy issues. According to a 1985 political survey, the cluster's middle-class residents tend to fear "the power of both the top dog and the underdog groups within the two-party system." Marshallite James Sobel, a 27-year-old college drop-out who earns $9.25 an hour at an auto parts plant, understands those suspicions, having been laid off twice for several months in the last five years—"though that's not such a bad record," he allows. In fact, Sobel voted for President Reagan in 1984 because the town has remained prosperous enough to keep its shopkeepers along Michigan Avenue in business at a time when nearby communities are in decline. Administra-tion policies that don't directly touch Marshall are, in Sobel's view, ignored. "At work most people don't talk politics, because they think it's a lot of crap," declares Sobel, usually found in T-shirt, jeans and jogging shoes. "There really aren't a lot of big problems out here and that's the way people try to keep it."

At Yesteryear's, Marshall's elder statesmen would agree with Sobel's analysis, as they try to maintain their community's viability and fend off any signs of deterioration. Mayor Bassage, for one, worries that his town's aging population may scare off younger transplants. "Too many gray heads," he scowled as he surveyed the crowd at a July band concert. He knows about the traffic jams that occur behind the Michigan Avenue bank on the third of every month—when the town's Social Security checks arrive. But he and other city officials found cause for celebration recently when two school bond issues were passed, a sign that even the empty-nested residents are willing to support the education of their neighbors' children. "Living here is real safe and cozy," says Bassage. "And we just hope that doesn't change too much." Residents know too well that the balance that characterizes Middle America is more precious than the breeze of a cool July night.

AMERICA'S MOST POPULAR LIFESTYLE

Middle America by no means represents a majority of Americans. In 1987, it was home to only 3.2 percent of the nation's households and was fairly typical in size compared to the other clusters. If you went in search of the most populous cluster—and the most "popular" lifestyle in America—you'd head for Blue-Chip Blues, a collection of the nation's most affluent blue-collar communities, like Ronkonkoma, New York, Hillview, California, Mesquite, Texas, and Coon Rapids, Minnesota. Peppering big cities all over the country, Blue-Chip Blues communities contain 6.0 percent of U.S. households—about the size of the Los Angeles metro area. Hardly a significant number in terms of the total population, Blue-Chip Blues still accounts for three times the population of the Money & Brains, Urban Gold Coast and Black Enterprise clusters combined. While the predominant neighborhood type in another culture might be rural villages filled with peasants, in this country, it's a suburban community filled with middle-class workers.

The fact that more U.S. citizens live in Blue-Chip Blues neighborhoods than any other single cluster says much about America's pluralistic society in the 1980s. Through initiative, ability and luck, residents have parlayed high-school educations and skilled-labor jobs into a real measure of suburban comfort for their large families. The cluster ranks tenth on the ZQ scale, with a median income of $32,218 and median home value of $72,563—slightly above the nation's average. Thanks to the preponderance of double-wage-earning households, residents have enough discretionary cash in their jeans to lead active leisure lives. Surveys show they're heavy consumers of campers, above-ground swimming pools, boats and recreational vehicles. They read hobby and recreational magazines at rates far above the general population—publications like *Popular Photography, 4 Wheel & Off Road* and *Golf.* These are the people who relentlessly pursue recreation when the workday is done. The "Miller time" crowd.

Coon Rapids, Minnesota, a suburb northeast of Minneapolis, typifies this Blue-Chip Blues way of life. Bordered by a crooked stretch of raccoon-populated riverbank, Coon Rapids for most of this century was a rural hamlet where settlers farmed to make a living and fished in the state's northern lakes to relax. But all that changed in the late 1950s when Twin Cities developer Orrin Thompson started building tract subdivisions for the young families of the baby boom. For under $15,000, they could buy a three-bedroom rambler with eat-in kitchen, living room, basement and garage. The homes came in 960- and 1,100-square-foot models; though, like the "ticky-tacky little boxes" Malvina Reynolds sang about, the homes all looked the same inside and out. "You could walk into any of these houses with your eyes closed and find your way around," says Lee Starr, Coon Rapids planning director for the last five years.

But rubber-stamp styling hardly dissuaded the flood of Coon Rapids settlers, many of them blue-collar workers who labored in local factories making shotgun shells, electrical devices and soda dispensers. By the mid-'80s, the community boasted 43,000 residents, including an increasing number of white-collar techies who commuted to Honeywell, Control Data Corporation and some of the smaller regional computer firms. The town has flowered with dozens of parks, a creditable school system and a handful of shopping centers that offer the latest amenities: drive-through fast-food, video supermarts, a tanning studio, even a couple of sprawling car dealerships—Detroit models only, thank you. "No one around here sells Japanese subcompacts, European luxury cars or Rolls Royces," says Starr, a lean and soft-spoken man. "This isn't Beverly Hills, you know."

Few visitors would think it is. Along the flat, straight blocks of Coon Rapids, sprinklers twirl in the backyards, American flags flap in the front, and driveways are filled with pickups and vans painted with names like "Trickie Dick." Community life centers on family, work and self-reliance, according to locals. That last fact is confirmed by surveys portraying Blue-Chip Blues residents as do-it-yourselfers who buy hand-powered drills and gas-powered mowers at many times the national average. In Coon Rapids, the handyman spirit has customized the tract ramblers with a rainbow of colors, trims and angled additions. "It's nothing for people around here to finish their basements, expand their garages and put in underground irrigation systems," says city manager Robert Thistle, a stocky, balding Detroit transplant. "They believe in the work ethic at home."

Like a lot of her neighbors in Coon Rapids—and in Blue-Chip Blues neighborhoods everywhere—Sharon Pennie defines the community's lifestyle in unpretentious terms. "People are happy if they have a nice family car, a deck in the backyard and can go out to supper once in a while," she says from the kitchen of an original Orrin Thompson home bought eight years ago for $48,000. A matter-of-fact 37-year-old housewife with a preference for brightly flowered blouses and faded jeans, Pennie used to work part time at a deli to add to her husband's $20,000-a-year income as a roofer. But the hours cut into her homemaking routine, which includes volunteering at area schools and watching the afternoon TV soaps. Many evenings are spent shuttling her two teenagers to softball and hockey games. Typical of Blue-Chip Blues homemakers, she shops for clothes at discount department stores, buys canned goods in bulk at the supermarket and likes to go bowling for recreation. Once a year, she and husband Daryl may take off for a Las Vegas getaway, but more often they'll take the kids and their aging speedboat to one of the state's northern lakes for an inexpensive weekend campout. "We know the value of a dollar around here," Pennie says, fingering a stack of discount grocery coupons. "We don't live in the lap of luxury, but we're comfortable."

Coon Rapids residents take pride in their homogeneous community —a place without Oriental or black enclaves, a place where most everyone is either Catholic or Lutheran, a place where the biggest complaint is the lack of quarrelsome issues that engulf most communities. "The city can be a little bland here at times," concedes Peter Bodley, managing editor of the *Coon Rapids Herald.* "As a journalist, there aren't many controversial issues to sink your teeth into." At one time, during the height of the '60s civil rights movement, a referendum proposed changing the name of Coon Rapids, because it was considered a slur against blacks. The referendum failed, partly because the voters, 99 percent white, were fond of the city's link to the masked creatures that inhabit the area lakes and partly because they had no idea what to change the name to. "Someone proposed calling us, 'Place of the Next Three Exits,' " chuckles Lee Starr.

Politically, Blue-Chip Blues communities across the country tend to mirror national voting trends: 28 percent describe themselves as liberals, 29 percent as conservatives and 41 percent as middle-of-the-road. Cluster voters gave Ronald Reagan a sweeping majority of 26 percentage points in 1984 but for Congress turned to Democrats who supported federal aid to the working class. In Coon Rapids, where voter turnout is unusually high (92 percent in 1984), residents are said to be liberal on economic issues but conservative on moral ones. "Many people are pro-life but even more would just as soon avoid the whole abortion issue," says Bodley. The last time anyone can remember a demonstration was in early 1986 over banning *Playboy* and *Penthouse* at the area 7-Eleven stores. "People around here don't get over-excited about national issues," says Bodley. "They're more interested in leisure activities than politics."

With so many residents working 9-to-5 shifts in Blue-Chip Blues, families place a premium on togetherness in their after-work hours. Rick Packer, a Coon Rapids resident since 1979, comes home most nights to find neighbors relaxing in lawn chairs, beers in hand, keeping an eye on their youngsters riding bikes in the street. Watching TV with the family is a common pastime, and surveys reflect the popularity of prime-time sitcoms. "When I was a kid, the whole family would watch Sunday night television with 'Walt Disney World' and 'My Favorite Martian,' " says Packer, a 32-year-old landscape architect, married with two toddlers. "Now, the four of us sit around to watch the Thursday night lineup of 'Cosby,' 'Family Ties' and 'Cheers.' " As in other Blue-Chip Blues suburbs, locals disdain the chablis-sipping downtown scene in favor of family restaurants tucked inside the shopping centers along Coon Rapids Boulevard—restaurants with signs out front that read Have A Nice Day. "We're White Castle kind of people," says Lee Starr, referring to the hamburger carryout as much as the community state of mind.

Not that Coon Rapids citizens don't have fun. Every summer, the town throws a Carp Festival to honor one of the more maligned species of fish, a scavenger, that's typically thrown back by anglers who happen to snare one. Partly tongue-in-cheek, but mostly as an excuse to hold a community celebration, the festival treats visitors to contests of carp-catching, carp-eating and even dressing up the captured fish in pinafores and party hats. Some of the more artistic residents paint the fish and print T-shirts from their scaly bodies. One big seller: T-shirts reading "Minnesota carp—not just for breakfast anymore."

AMERICA'S BIGGEST CLUSTER: BLUE-CHIP BLUES

The lifestyle habits of America's biggest cluster reflect its top-of-the-line blue-collar salaries. Life, for them, is a modest version of the American Dream: residents have parlayed high-school educations and skilled-labor jobs into suburban comfort and active leisure lives.

	National Average	Blue-Chip Blues	Cluster Index
Camper/trailers	.9%	1.8%	202
Above-ground swimming pools	2.6	5.1	197
Preferred stock in own company	1.8	3.1	173
Hedge trimmers	5.1	7.8	153
Second mortgages	.7	1.1	153
Dipilatories	1.0	1.5	150
Automatic garage door openers	2.1	3.1	149
Racquetball	6.3	9.1	145
Desk-top calculators	2.4	3.3	137
Vans	4.8	6.5	136
Salt-water fishing	5.9	7.9	134
Push power mowers	6.7	8.8	132
Compact cars	11.1	14.7	132
Diet pills	6.7	8.6	129
Bowling	19.2	24.5	128

Numbers indicate percentages of people in each category and indexed against the national average. An index of 100 equals the U.S. average for that category. An index of 200 means a cluster has twice the national average for that category. Source: SMRB and MRI data bases, Claritas Corp., 1987.

With *Playboy* boycotts and carp-dressing among the most diverting community activities, it's no wonder Coon Rapids is booming. Across the country, better-off white-collar families are moving into such Blue-Chip Blues neighborhoods, threatening the homogeneous flavor of the tract neighborhoods with upscale split-levels and multi-unit condominiums. Coon Rapids city manager Thistle talks of the transformation of his community from a farm village to a bedroom suburb of Minneapolis to its own suburban metropolis along with attendant problems of density and development. But as he cruises around the community in a city van, pointing out the parks and pools, the new duplexes and Pennsylvania Dutch homes, there's only pride in his voice. "If more people live in this kind of community than any other, it says a heck of a lot about the lifestyles of the nation," he says. "The quality of life here is more than enviable."

Although they may be "average" on the ZQ scale and "popular" among many Americans, the Middle American and Blue-Chip Blues lifestyles are far from typical. In 1987, the two clusters represented only 9.19 percent of the nation's households—slightly more than all the residents of New York City and its surrounding suburbs. Without significant numbers of ethnic groups, retired couples and young singles, these clusters require the other thirty-eight clusters to complete the American portrait, a portrait that lays to rest once and for all the notion of an Average American.

4

THE WAY WE WORK

"My great-grandmother used to keep a little diary with one-line entries. And the day her husband died, she wrote, 'George died today. Hard work. Short life. Not much to show.' Well, for all the hard work we've done, we have plenty to show for it."
—David Passmore, State College, Pennsylvania (Towns & Gowns)

Thirty miles south of Nashville, amid pastures of grazing Jerseys and Holsteins bordering Highway 31, lies drowsy Spring Hill, Tennessee (pop. 1,100). Like many southern hamlets overrun with antebellum farmhouses and highway markers commemorating the Confederacy, Spring Hill seems lost in the past. For a half century, the town's major industry has been Early's Honey Stand, a touristy roadside attraction that sells country hams, honey and twenty kinds of preserves. The Spring Hill town fathers oversee two stoplights, one elementary school and a part-time judge. And the highlight of Spring Hill's social calendar is Mule Day, when farmers celebrate their faithful friend with a parade, mule auction and liar's contest, usually won by a preacher or policeman.

Spring Hill in the '80s represents the rural southern backwater town typical of the Back-Country Folks cluster. Poorly educated, lower-middle-class and dotting the Ozarks and Appalachia, Back-Country Folks communities are the most White Anglo-Saxon Protestant enclaves in the nation. They have the highest concentration of residents of English ancestry, some of whom are descendants of colonial settlers and still speak with a British inflection. A Back-Country Folks town almost always has no movie theater or shopping center, though it usually has a diner where grits are featured on the breakfast menu. Cluster residents are only a third as likely as other Americans to belong to health clubs, travel abroad, attend the theater and buy gin or Irish whiskey. This is a world of country music and compact pickups, barbecue and RC Cola. In Spring Hill, which is deep in Tennessee's Bible Belt (its six churches are predominantly Baptist or Pentecostal), liquor wasn't even sold by the bottle until the 1970s.

"When you go to the bank in Spring Hill, you don't run in and out but expect to spend time talking with all the old ladies," observes local editor Wallace Hebert, three years transplanted from New Orleans. "Around here, the phones won't even dial fast."

But on July 31, 1985, Spring Hill's pace skipped a beat when General Motors chose it as the site of its $3.5 billion Saturn project, a state-of-the-art subcompact factory geared to compete with the Japanese. In all, thirty-eight states representing more than a thousand communities had tried to snare the billion-dollar project. On land where corn grows as high as the tops of John Deere tractors, GM plans to build the largest auto plant in the world: a 6-million-square-foot manufacturing and assembly facility, 150 acres under one roof. When up to speed in 1990, according to GM projections, the plant will employ 3,000 people and create three times that number of jobs for parts suppliers in nearby communities. All told, the Saturn project represents one of the largest single industrial investments in American history.

But the blueprint to transform Spring Hill into a megafactory town also promises to change irrevocably the Back-Country Folks way of life, where the strategy of local Civil War skirmishes is still hotly debated. One developer predicted that Spring Hill would become a metropolis of 50,000, with acres of rolling cropland ploughed under to erect townhouse subdivisions. Other folks worried that GM's pledge to hire laid-off United Auto Workers from other factories meant a new labor force would move in—a labor force that's northern, black and pro-union. On the night of the GM announcement, seventy area residents met at a community center to voice their concerns with a mixture of anger and sadness. "As far as I'm concerned, Spring Hill has just died," declared John Campbell, a wiry dairy farmer with a face creased and freckled from the sun. "It'll never be the same. We feel like the people of Appalachia whose government has said, 'Your way of life's not good enough. We're going to change it to something different.' "

What's happened to Spring Hill since that landmark day in 1985 illustrates how important work and development are to a community—and how quickly a change in the employment base can transform a town's way of life. Within hours of GM's announcement, a real estate frenzy pushed up the price of farmland from $1,000 an acre to more than $10,000 an acre. At the Interstate 65 interchange that many believed would be the future cloverleaf for the Saturn plant, land that initially listed for $200,000 went for $1.5 million. "Prices are going up by the hour," said Norman Dean, a local real-estate broker then in the midst of the fray. "And in most cases, two and three people are standing in line to buy the same property." Dean, a portly teetotaler who favors wide ties and Stetson hats, tried to keep track of the skyrocketing prices beside a constantly ringing phone and a paper avalanche of legal contracts and buyers' bids. "I'll tell you," he said with a twang, "the California gold rush couldn't have compared to this."

At the town hall (which doubles as a fire station), local officials admitted to being ill prepared for an industrial revolution. The town had no one resembling an urban planner on staff. Questions about Saturn's long-term impact were thrust upon George Jones, Spring Hill's unflappable mayor and town lumber merchant. In May 1985, he won election to his second four-year term, campaigning on a platform promoting progress, development and industry. "It looks like I forgot to turn the spigot off," he said sheepishly after GM's announcement. Jones is a high-school graduate—seven out of the eight town council members did not go beyond the ninth grade—but he knew what to do. He quickly met with state planning officials to talk about constructing two schools, a jail, fire department, courtroom and, oh yes, a new city hall complex. Called the "Dimple of the Universe" by early settlers for its rich farmland and plentiful game, Spring Hill was about to undergo plastic surgery.

Well aware of the decline in farming and smokestack industries, Spring Hill's residents could appreciate Saturn's economic benefits. Like other Back-Country Folks towns, Spring Hill had a long history of workers fleeing the economically depressed area for better opportunities up North. After GM selected Spring Hill for its auto plant, Tennessee Governor Lamar Alexander observed that GM's decision meant that the children of Tennessee's workers, exiled in the past, "were coming home."

"There's no doubt we can use the jobs around here," said Peter Jenkins, a local author *(A Walk Across America)* and perhaps Spring Hill's most famous resident. "But we just don't want GM to run over us." Jenkins, a lanky 35-year-old with red hair and a bushy beard, found special irony in GM's choice of sites. Only three years before, after gaining first-hand knowledge of the whole country by researching his book, he chose to settle down in Spring Hill. "My friends thought I was moving to a backward redneck land," he recalls. "But I really wanted a slower lifestyle away from a frantic megalopolis. Now, the big questions is how much of the small-town atmosphere we'll lose."

For the residents of Spring Hill, that question won't be answered for several years. But a hint of what's to come may be seen 40 miles away in Smyrna, Tennessee, once a rural hamlet of 8,900 that became home to Nissan Motors' $660 million truck assembly plant. The same industrial amenities that now attracted GM—extensive highways, low-cost electrical power and an abundance of water—had also lured Nissan in 1982. Within three years, the Nissan factory brought Smyrna 3,000 new jobs, a sixfold increase in the monthly sales-tax revenues to $190,000 and an urban cast to the bucolic setting. The local work force, once agrarian-based, shifted with the influx of new factory workers, small businesspeople and "yurpies" (young rural professionals). Smyrna's main street sprouted two new shopping centers complete with a tanning spa, a fiberglass-swimming-pool dealership and the town's first Catholic church. In cluster terms, Smyrna's classification jumped fourteen rungs up the ZQ ladder, changing from Back-Country Folks to Blue-Collar Nursery, characterized by middle-class, child-rearing towns. In Blue-Collar Nursery, residents are twice as likely as average Americans to own campers, buy savings bonds, go power boating and subscribe to *Mother Earth News*.

But changing gears in Smyrna has had its drawbacks. The town's streets now experience rush hours when the Nissan plant changes shifts at 7:30 A.M. and 3:30 P.M. In 1985, temporary classrooms had to be hauled to the junior high to handle the crush of adolescent-age students. The police force has doubled—to ten officers—to handle the increase in auto theft, larceny and the passing of bad checks. And locals are still leery of the small army of developers who, as one police officer observed, "are building apartments out the ying-yang." Despite these new community concerns, there's plenty of consolation in Nissan's $90 million annual payroll: factory workers who once made $12,000 now report $25,000 salaries. "People around here own more boats, drive newer cars and have more money they can spend on entertainment in Nashville," says Sylvia Watkins, a 30-year-old Smyrna native and Nissan assembly-line manager. "A lot of people worried we were going to turn into a Little Detroit. But it hasn't happened at all." Adds Sam Ridley, who retired in 1986 after forty years as Smyrna's mayor, "Nissan hasn't changed our lifestyle, only upgraded our income."

To Smyrna's populace, Nissan didn't despoil a rural way of life. The auto plant just altered the lifestyle, creating a middle-class community with the attendant frustrations of too much traffic and crime, balanced by the joys of a year-round tan and backyard pools. For the residents of Spring Hill, understanding that trade-off may smooth Saturn's landing in a Back-Country Folks culture.

A NATION OF WORKERS

The American Dream—a decent home, a car and money enough to educate the kids—begins with a job. But like almost every other aspect of American life, the nation's labor force is changing dramatically—and changing the way we live. New patterns of supply and demand for labor have drawn millions of women out of the house and millions of immigrants, legal and illegal, across the borders. Beyond suburbia in the low-density fields of exurban God's Country, high-tech firms are spreading. That trend has created one of the most diffuse and decentralized economies in the industrial world. Less happily, it is also leaving behind unemployed steelworkers in Mines & Mills, bankrupt farmers in Grain Belt and an urban underclass in Public Assistance. In the United States, working is not merely a state of employment but a way of life.

On the cluster map, what you do for a living is critical to where you settle and how you live. And the converse is also true: where you live is a good indicator of the kind of work you do. It's no coincidence that Towns & Gowns, the nation's cluster of college communities, boasts the highest percentage of residents who work in education—at three times the national average. In the marketplace, that fact helps explain their campus-bred tendency to buy books, running shoes and magazines like *Natural History* and *Scientific American* at many times the rate of the general population. On the other hand, in Black Enterprise, the middle-class black cluster, residents lead the nation in the concentration of public administration and protective service workers—at rates nearly double the national average. Just as such public sector

WHO DOES WHAT: WORK IN AMERICA

Americans live close to people with similar pay, education and status—and far from people who don't share those characteristics. White-collar workers are concentrated in America's wealthiest metropolitan neighborhoods, while relatively few are found in poor rural and agricultural areas. Service workers, representing everything from fast-food cooks to janitors, typically hail from neighborhoods filled with poor urban blacks and young single whites, including many students working their way through college at minimum-wage jobs. Blue-collar workers live in a variety of lower-middle-class communities, ranging from mountainside coal-mining towns to inner-city industrial districts. Agricultural workers, reflecting the nation's farm crisis, are found in some of the nation's most isolated and poorest areas.

White-Collar Workers

Top Five Clusters

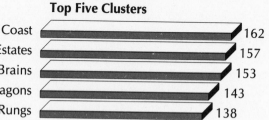

Urban Gold Coast	162
Blue Blood Estates	157
Money & Brains	153
Furs & Station Wagons	143
Two More Rungs	138

Service Workers

Top Five Clusters

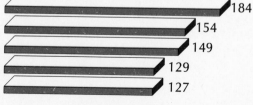

Public Assistance	184
Downtown Dixie-Style	154
Emergent Minorities	149
Single City Blues	129
Towns & Gowns	127

White-Collar Workers	Index	Service Workers	Index
Most		**Most**	
Urban Gold Coast	162	Public Assistance	184
Blue Blood Estates	157	Downtown Dixie-Style	154
Money & Brains	153	Emergent Minorities	149
Furs & Station Wagons	143	Single City Blues	129
Two More Rungs	138	Towns & Gowns	127
Least		**Least**	
Shotguns & Pickups	70	Two More Rungs	76
Share Croppers	66	Money & Brains	64
Hard Scrabble	63	Furs & Station Wagons	64
Tobacco Roads	62	Urban Gold Coast	63
Grain Belt	55	Blue Blood Estates	54

Blue-Collar Workers

Top Five Clusters

Mines & Mills	146
Back-Country Folks	145
Share Croppers	142
Hispanic Mix	140
Heavy Industry	140

Agricultural Workers

Top Five Clusters

Grain Belt	1111
Hard Scrabble	397
Agri-Business	379
Tobacco Roads	357
Share Croppers	284

Blue-Collar Workers	Index	Agricultural Workers	Index
Most		**Most**	
Mines & Mills	146	Grain Belt	1111
Back-Country Folks	145	Hard Scrabble	397
Share Croppers	142	Agri-Business	379
Hispanic Mix	140	Tobacco Roads	357
Heavy Industry	140	Share Croppers	284
Least		**Least**	
Furs & Station Wagons	48	Bohemian Mix	17
Bohemian Mix	42	Two More Rungs	16
Money & Brains	32	New Melting Pot	16
Blue Blood Estates	29	Old Yankee Rows	16
Urban Gold Coast	19	Urban Gold Coast	5

Numbers indicate percentages of people employed in each job sector, indexed against the national average. An index of 100 equals the U.S. average: 53% for white-collar, 12.9% for service, 31.2% for blue-collar, and 2.9% for agricultural workers. An index of 162 means a cluster has 1.62 times the national average for that job sector. Source: PRIZM (Census Demography), Claritas Corp., 1987.

jobs offered Italian and Irish immigrants a route to the economic mainstream, so too have these jobs provided the way out of poverty for blacks.

Employment patterns have always influenced Americans in their choice of neighborhoods. According to the clustering principle, people like to live not only among those who hold jobs of similar pay and status, but away from those whose occupations are foreign to their educational attainment and values. For instance, neighborhoods at the top end of the ZQ scale show a strong correlation between residents who make over $75,000 in income, own homes worth over $250,000 and hold jobs as executives and managers. In other words, the families of wealthy corporate leaders tend to live together in the enclaves of Blue Blood Estates and Furs & Station Wagons. No surprise here.

But who's excluded from such neighborhoods? It's natural to assume that such communities also have the lowest percentage of poor, unemployed people in broken homes—the antithesis of the super-rich. In fact, the most exclusive enclaves have the lowest concentration of families headed by middle-income, skilled blue-collar workers—laborers who live in clusters like Norma Rae-Ville and Heavy Industry. While the poor may live near the rich and serve as maids and gardeners, after a century of American labor disputes you just won't find the brass living next door to the workers. There's a natural mutual antipathy between these people: One went to college, the other may not have finished high school. One wears black socks, the other wears white. They have different values, consumption patterns and lifestyles.

These distinctions help explain the formation of neighborhoods in a milltown like Dalton, Georgia, which produces carpets and textiles in the northwest corner of the state. The mill workers, $4-an-hour, nonunion laborers, live in run-down cinderblock-and-wood bungalows surrounding the carpet mills in a Norma Rae-Ville district. The managers, mill owners and executives reside in $300,000 slate-and-glass Shangri-las on the Furs & Station Wagons side of Rocky Face Mountain, with a spectacular view of the town and countryside. The two groups rarely meet socially; they join different clubs, send their kids to different schools, vote differently at the ballot box. "You've got your snobs and people just existing," one longtime resident indelicately put it.

But shifting demographics, technology and global competition can change the job opportunities that influence where people live. And in the last decade, most of the job and neighborhood growth has occurred on the fringes of the large metropolises, leaving the old downtowns as specialized centers for finance, tourism, conventions and cultural services. While these developments bode well for upscale clusters like Urban Gold Coast and God's Country, they're ominous for the less affluent Mines & Mills and Grain Belt clusters. More than the cold numbers provided by the Bureau of Labor Statistics,

the forty clusters bring alive the shocks and trends of American enterprise.

■■■■■■■ **A WHITE-COLLAR WONDERLAND**

In the high-tech, service-oriented world that's taking shape, America's predominant collar color has changed from blue to white. The
professional and service sectors—providing everything from financial
advice to fast foods—accounted for 87 percent of all employment
growth during the '70s, and between 1970 and 1985, the ratio of white-
collar-to-blue-collar workers shifted from 99-to-100 to 169-to-100. At the
same time, ripples from that labor redistribution have altered community settlement patterns throughout the nation.

Nowhere is the growth of service-based jobs more apparent than in
Urban Gold Coast, which leads all clusters in the concentration of white-
collar professionals—89 percent of its work force—and in-town wealth.
These high-rise neighborhoods are limited to only a few big cities where
urban sprawl has gone up and not out—predominantly New York, Chicago and Washington, D.C. Because the high cost of real estate limits
the presence of blue-collar factories, Urban Gold Coast has evolved into
a service-based society working at postindustrial jobs. The cluster ranks
first in the percentage of workers engaged in finance, insurance and
business services like advertising and public relations—at rates more
than twice the U.S. average. And they have the substantial salaries
(median household income is $36,838) to afford the luxury of an eight-
room condo twelve floors above a cosmopolitan core. Urban Gold Coast
leads the nation in residents who read two daily newspapers, drink
imported wine and shop at gourmet food stores. It is also the home of
all three network news anchormen—Dan Rather, Tom Brokaw and
Peter Jennings—whose lofty perspectives no doubt color their reading
of current affairs.

On the Upper East Side of Manhattan, the heart of the Urban Gold
Coast, life is a bowl of raspberries—at $6 a pint in the dead of winter.
Thirty-story buildings rise into the sky like redwoods, and no one flin-
ches at advertisements for new two-bedroom condos that cost $350,000
—without parking. Perhaps only the workaholic populace can truly appreciate the development ethic that creates such towers: in dense city
centers, tall buildings offer more rentable space per site, and Urban Gold
Coast is the most densely populated cluster in the nation. To live in the
skyscraper forest of the Upper East Side, says resident Gail Belsky,

URBAN GOLD COAST: THE WHITEST COLLARS

During their leisure time, the upscale sophisticates of Urban Gold Coast generally don't stay cooped up in their high-rises. They travel three times as often as the national average and are active in a wide range of participatory sports. The concentration of older retirees living next door to young professionals helps explain residents' fondness for knitting and flower-arranging.

	National Average	Urban Gold Coast	Cluster Index
Travel by railroad	0.9%	13.5%	1504
Travel by cruise ship	1.5	8.8	584
Travel by commercial airline	10.5	51.7	492
Travel by commercial bus	1.5	7.2	483
Tennis rackets	2.8	10.9	388
Sailing	3.4	10.2	301
Ice-skating	4.1	11.8	287
Watch/listen to/attend horse races	2.0	5.1	253
Adult-education courses	11.4	25.8	226
Backpacking/hiking	4.8	8.8	184
Knitting	6.2	11.0	177
Flower arranging	5.0	8.3	167

Numbers indicate percentages of people in each category and indexed against the national average. An index of 100 equals the U.S. average for that category. An index of 200 means a cluster has twice the national average for that category. Source: SMRB and MRI data bases, Claritas Corp., 1987.

"takes a devotion to work. Status around here is the big three: money, power and fame—preferably all at once."

Belsky, a 25-year-old writer for *Adweek,* is the kind of hard-charging professional who thrives in this congested environment. A slight, animated woman who favors mod miniskirts and go-go boots, she gets home at the dinner hour maybe three times a month and generally socializes only with colleagues—for meals, movies or late nights at an East Village club. As a result, she knows the names of no neighbors in the six-story co-op where she's lived for three years, a fact that would appall the chummy residents of Coalburg & Corntown neighborhoods but is hardly noticed among Urban Gold Coasters. "My neighbors are into their own jobs and schedules," says Belsky, shaking her dark-haired shag. "We just don't seem to cross paths."

Like many other back-to-the-city settlers in Urban Gold Coast,

Belsky is the product of a middle-class suburban upbringing. She fled to the city when she was 22 to escape what she saw as a cultural wasteland in Ridgewood, New Jersey. In 1984, she decided to put up $158,000 to buy a compact, two-bedroom co-op on the Upper East Side because "the neighborhood (a) was safer than Brooklyn, (b) had loads of coffee shops and (c) was closer to my midtown job than most anywhere else. My feeling is that if you're going to live in Manhattan and pay ridiculous prices, then you should find a place with access to every other place in Manhattan," Belsky says. Indeed, her stove is rarely turned on, most of her meals are eaten outside of her apartment, and breakfast typically means a quick sprint to a corner diner for coffee and a pack of cigarettes. "I was hoping to find a place that felt homey," she says, looking around at her sparsely decorated apartment, "but this has really just become a place to sleep. It took me a year to finish unpacking."

Although Urban Gold Coast is one of the smallest neighborhood types—representing only 0.5 percent of the nation's population—its economic presence as the most affluent urban cluster (with a ZQ rating of 4) cannot be ignored. As home to heavy-hitting consumers, its residents are five times as likely as average Americans to travel abroad, four times as likely to acquire U.S. Treasury notes and money-market funds and three times as likely to buy stocks and mutual funds. These are the people who keep up with the chic life through their subscriptions to *Metropolitan Home, Atlantic Monthly* and *New York*—at more than seventeen times the national average.

Local businesses do their best to satisfy the varied interests and hectic lifestyles of their clientele. For instance, along a single block in New York City—Lexington Avenue between 70th and 71st streets—shoppers can visit the Dietz Market, Donohue Cafe, La Cuisinaire (kitchenware), Baby Arnold Toy Store, Artist Materials & Stationers, Lenox Court Antiques, Yook Wah Lai Chinese Laundry, The Uncommon Basket (dry floral bouquets), Hennor Jewelers & Clockmakers, Erika Cleaners & Tailors, Nail Salon, Lexington Shoe Salon, Salon Guy & Friends (beauticians), Healthy Candle (health food store) and T&K Travel.

And that's just on one side of the street. Entire counties in the Hard Scrabble countryside of West Virginia have fewer businesses.

THE CORPORATE PLAYGROUND

But most Americans don't expect to live and work downtown anymore. In the '70s, America's fastest-growing communities were midsized Sunbelt towns like those found in New Homesteaders. During the '80s, the most promising communities have been the exurban boom-towns of God's Country surrounding high-tech corridors such as Massa-chusetts' Route 128 and North Carolina's Research Triangle. Typically located near prestigious universities, God's Country has become a major source of innovative jobs in areas where locals used to earn their wages employing centuries-old farming techniques.

Take the God's Country town of Plainsboro, New Jersey, not far from Princeton University and, by some calculations, destined to be-come the core of the state's largest city by the mid-'90s. Already a visitor can watch a plexiglass model of the future metropolis come to life inside a gleaming glass-and-concrete office building in Plainsboro. As the overhead lights dim, tiny color-coded bulbs light up the building blocks on the model that's as big as a car. "Blue is for university research," a somber architect intones, "yellow for residential housing, red for commercial space—shops, restaurants, a health club, day care center. . . ." With a wave of his hand, he points out the building that houses this very model—now glowing inside as well as outside—just one piece of a city that by 1995 will have an estimated 15 million square feet of office space, surpassing downtown Milwaukee in scope.

The model and lecture are courtesy of K. S. Sweet Associates, project manager for the Princeton Forrestal Center, a 3-square-mile scientific and corporate research park located on a flat stretch of Route 1 in Plainsboro. Once the town was home to the largest dairy in the world, Walker Gordon Farms, and the birthplace of Elsie the Cow. But these days Elsie wouldn't recognize her old pastures. Rising from the verdant landscape are fifty boxlike buildings girdled by walls of glass. In 1987, Plainsboro's crop of industrial giants already included RCA, IBM, Mobil, Prudential and Xerox. Merrill Lynch's corporate training center alone is the size of one of New York's World Trade towers.

"What we're making here," says Sweet marketing director Eugene Biddle Jr., "are products of the late 1980s, products based on the silicon technology developed in the '70s. Communications. Computer software. Bioengineering. Energy research." Biddle, a preppie Stanford M.B.A., offers driving tours of the area in his Mercedes, mud-streaked from construction sites, making sure to stop at the experimental nuclear fusion plant as well as the new townhouse subdivisions going up around the center. Thanks to the Princeton Forrestal Center, says Biddle, Plainsboro has become an intellectual boom town for 11,000—an eight-fold population increase since 1970. Fifty-nine percent of its residents have attended graduate school—quadruple the national average—and

GOD'S COUNTRY: CITY TASTES, COUNTRY LIVING

God's Country contains the nation's most affluent neighborhoods outside the major metropolitan sprawl. These predominantly white-collar workers have migrated from the city, bringing a lot of their urban tastes to their rural climes.

	National Average	God's County	Cluster Index
Investment property	.7%	4.7%	675
Microwave ovens	.7	2.9	410
Automatic dishwashers	3.9	9.3	239
Hard contact lenses	3.9	8.5	217
Desktop calculators	2.4	4.0	168
Jogging	11.6	18.9	163
Travel/entertainment cards	3.3	5.3	161
Electric organs	5.6	8.4	150
VCRs	8.7	11.5	132

Numbers indicate percentages of people in each category and indexed against the national average. An index of 100 equals the U.S. average for that category. An index of 200 means a cluster has twice the national average for that category. Source: SMRB and MRI data bases, Claritas Corp., 1987.

almost as high a percentage of 25- to 44-year-olds earn over $40,000. "I lived in California's Silicon Valley before it exploded the way it did," says Biddle, adjusting his tortoiseshell horn-rims. "And what I see going on here is just what I saw going on there in the mid-'70s."

The story of Plainsboro reflects one of the employment megatrends of the last quarter-century. Rather than follow the familiar postwar pattern of suburban sprawl, businesses are coalescing into "urban villages" in low-density exurban regions, attracting workers for the scenic beauty as often as the new, high-tech jobs. God's Country communities contain the nation's most affluent white-collar neighborhoods outside the metropolitan sprawl. Their quirky, exurban mindset—athletic, intellectual, epicurean—is best reflected in some of their favorite magazines: *Ski, Science, Food & Wine* and *National Lampoon.* Having only recently left the city, however, God's Country consumers still share many of the tastes of upscale urbanites—from health food to Subarus. They lead all clusters in purchasing woks, for instance; but unlike their city cousins, they also rank first in installing their own shock absorbers.

In Plainsboro, 31-year-old Ken Moch typifies this new breed of God's Country settler. Reared in New York's affluent Westchester County and a graduate of Princeton and Stanford Business School, he moved to Plainsboro in 1982 to be near his job as vice president of the Liposome Company, a recently formed biotech firm that markets time-release pharmaceuticals. Mannerly and self-assured with thick black hair framing boyish features, Moch is Liposome's youngest exec, besides being one of the least countrified. Though he lives in a $150,000 townhouse condominium in a singles-filled development, Princeton Meadows, he still maintains an active social life in New York City. He makes the hour-long train commute several nights a week to attend the theater or meet friends for dinner. "If I'm going to see a play in the city, I'll work until 7 o'clock, hop on the train and work for an hour more, spend a few hours in New York and then put in another hour on the train ride home," says Moch, who likes to wear conservative, pin-striped suits and club ties to appear older in his dealings with other corporate chiefs. To quash any sense of isolation in God's Country, Moch has even installed a New York City phone number at his home. "I know it's psychological," he concedes. "But I don't want my friends in New York to have a block about dialing three extra digits if they want to call me at 5 o'clock to go out for a drink at 7:30. It's hard to get people out to the boonies to play."

As in other burgeoning God's Country communities with young, highly educated workers, Plainsboro's planners are grappling with how to create a style of life that will keep them down on what used to be a farm. There's still not so much as a neon disco or sushi restaurant in town, so many residents seek their nighttime entertainment in New York City or Philadelphia, also about an hour's train ride away. "One of the biggest problems we've faced," says township clerk Patricia Hullfish, "is congestion from joggers on the roads. That's about all there is locally."

To help remedy the situation, Princeton University several years ago leased land to a developer who began building a massive, $100 million shopping complex near the research park. Among the one hundred businesses soon to open: a 70,000-square-foot health club (larger than any in Manhattan), a day-care center to tend to the children of dual-income households, and ten full-size and "boutique" restaurants catering to palates accustomed to everything from goat cheese pizza to gourmet ice cream. Perhaps as a nod to the area's once down-home style, the mall's main thoroughfare has been quaintly named Main Street —like something out of Disneyland. "It will have everything but a history," says Biddle as he points out the skeleton of the health club surrounded by bulldozers. "The history will start when it opens."

For the old families of Plainsboro, coping with the greening of their piece of God's Country has taken some adjustment. Those who didn't have property to sell to developers grumble about the invasion of town-houses and the increase in traffic tie-ups among Porsches and Nissan "Z" cars. Others lament the high-tech mentality that's replaced the old-fashioned sentiments behind Elsie the Cow. When builders reno-vated an old black barn to become Plainsboro's new town hall, many of the aging farmers shook their heads in wonderment as a kitschy, wrought-iron-cow weather vane was placed on top. The yuppies, how-ever, loved it.

■ WOMEN'S WORK

The most dramatic change in the labor force during the past genera-tion has been the increase of women in the workplace. The 1980 census reported for the first time that slightly more than half of all women work outside the home. And that statistic represents not only young women just out of school, in clusters like urban Bohemian Mix, but older women who've taken jobs after their children have grown, in suburban Two More Rungs. The feminist movement, access to college educations, postponement of children, economics—all have contributed to this working-woman revolution. In the affluent suburbs of Furs & Station Wagons (ZQ3), fully half of all couples now draw two paychecks to maintain their comfortable lifestyle. So many women now work in the cluster community of Columbia, Maryland, that those homemakers left behind have organized therapy groups to cope with their loss of self-esteem as housewives. As one group member put it, "We weren't raised, even those of us from traditional families, to think we'd stay at home."

That view is echoed in Young Suburbia, which leads all clusters in two-income households. In these suburban, family-oriented neighbor-hoods, working women are necessary to help maintain a standard of living that, a generation ago, could be well maintained by a single bread-winner. In the Young Suburbia community of Eagan, Minnesota, 29-year-old Lynda Burkel knows the dilemma well. From 8 to 4 on week-days, she's a cooly efficient, $24,000-a-year secretary for Northwest Airlines. But every other moment she's the harried mommy of 10-month-old Nicole, who's dropped off at a Kindercare day-care center during working hours. Lynda can't spend more time at home because, frankly, the Burkels need the second income. They carry an $850-a-month mortgage on their three-bedroom split-level and are still paying off loans on an '85 Buick Century and an '82 GMC four-wheel-drive truck.

Like many Young Suburbia couples just starting out, the Burkels have a long wish-list: finish the basement, landscape the yard, launch a college fund for Nicole. "You get used to a lifestyle and don't want to have to cut back on things," says Burkel, talking as she feeds a bottle to Nicole in their cathedral-ceiling living room, "Right now, we can buy things immediately, like a new VCR camera, that we'd have had to save for if I didn't have a job. And I don't want to have to ask my husband, 'Paul, can I have five dollars today to go out to lunch.' I want to be able to have my own checking account so I don't have to hesitate about buying a toy for Nicole."

In the great march to equality, women have yet to achieve wage or occupational parity in many fields. In 1985, women still averaged only 64 cents for every dollar men were paid. Even in clusters with the highest ZQ levels, female professionals make only 72 percent as much as their male colleagues. Women have made strides in positions once thought to be the domain of men: in the last decade, the number of female clergy doubled, women judges and lawyers tripled and female radio and television announcers increased sixfold. But despite these numerical gains, obstacles to advancement remain in lower-echelon white- and blue-collar professions—and clusters. In 1987, nearly four out of five women workers remain in "pink-collar" occupations such as clerk and secretary.

Take Emergent Minorities, the cluster with the highest concentration of female workers. In these predominantly black, lower-middle-class city neighborhoods, more residents are employed in health services than in any other field—46 percent above the national average. But they are not prestigious doctors or even head nurses. In Emergent Minorities communities such as Anacostia in Washington, D.C., South Park in Houston and Rimpau in Los Angeles, it's more likely these residents are employed as orderlies, nursing aides and hospital cafeteria workers. Cluster-wide, salaries are low (one-third of all households earn under $15,000 annually) and college graduates are rare (41 percent never completed high school). Compared to average consumers, residents are only half as likely to belong to health clubs, frequent white-table-cloth restaurants or attend the theater. They're more likely to smoke cigarettes, eat at cafeterias and spend their entertainment dollars on jazz and disco records.

WHERE WOMEN WORK

Economics, education and the feminist movement—all contribute to the megatrend of four in ten American women now in the workforce. Except for Urban Gold Coast, which contains many young white professionals, the neighborhoods with the most working women also contain significant proportions of minorities. Areas where women don't work for pay include starter-home neighborhoods, enclaves of wealthy traditionalists and communities where jobs are hard to come by.

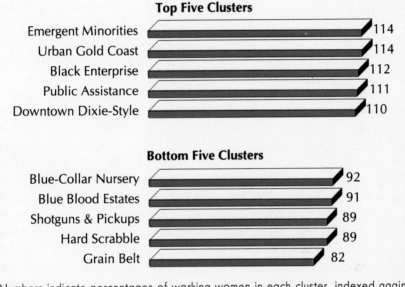

Top Five Clusters

Cluster	Index
Emergent Minorities	114
Urban Gold Coast	114
Black Enterprise	112
Public Assistance	111
Downtown Dixie-Style	110

Bottom Five Clusters

Cluster	Index
Blue-Collar Nursery	92
Blue Blood Estates	91
Shotguns & Pickups	89
Hard Scrabble	89
Grain Belt	82

Numbers indicate percentages of working women in each cluster, indexed against the national average. An index of 100 equals the U.S. average: 42.6%. An index of 114 means a cluster has 1.14 times the national average, or about 49%. Source: PRIZM (Census Demography), Claritas Corp., 1987.

Located in Southeast Washington, Anacostia is typical of Emergent Minorities communities. Only minutes from the U.S. Capitol, this home to 106,000 people crammed into 11 square miles is separated from the rest of the city by its namesake river—a narrow channel that represents an enormous socioeconomic gulf. Anacostia claims the city's highest number of welfare recipients, and in 1984 46 percent of the families were headed by women. Laverne Plater, a single mother of an 8-year-old girl, has lived in the midst of Anacostia's housing projects for most of her 28 years. As a psychiatric nursing assistant at nearby St. Elizabeths Hospital, Plater has tried to keep her life on an upward course since she first began working at the hospital fresh out of high school. Today, she earns $20,000 a year helping mentally ill patients prepare for life in community halfway houses—"good money for this area," she points out. "A lot of people do nothing else but lie in bed all the time."

Plater, a trim woman with bold, bright eyes, high cheekbones and a quick smile, puts in long days, working a 3-to-11 P.M. shift and, during dinner breaks, walking home to feed daughter Natasha and help her with homework. In the morning, Plater attends classes at the University of the District of Columbia, studying to become a registered nurse. "I'm always busy, but you have to be to survive," she says from her narrow brick duplex filled with family photos and her graduation diplomas from high school and junior high. Some days, she says, drug dealers crowd her off the sidewalks, and on a few nights shootings can be heard outside her window. "These are my roots," she says, offering no apologies for her community's boarded-up apartments and graffiti-scrawled schools. "I like my life here." Despite two more years of classes before she can qualify for her R.N. degree, Plater has already begun considering new job opportunities with more challenges and better pay. Moving to a new neighborhood, however, is not yet on her agenda.

Although the presence of women in the work force is a national trend, it is by no means a universal cluster phenomenon. Male bread-winners are still the norm in a handful of neighborhood types, identified by their physical locations and cultural predilections. In the poor black farm communities of Tobacco Roads, there simply are no jobs to be had for women—and precious few for men. In Blue Blood Estates, on the other hand, where the male earners typically earn more than enough for two workers, women aren't expected to hold down jobs, at least not paying ones. Many capitalize on their economic independence by contributing time—often, long, hard, unpaid hours—to cultural and public service organizations. As *Preppy Handbook*'s Lisa Birnbach has observed, "The same dictum that teaches modesty about financial status also insists on generosity, if only out of guilt for a lifetime of debutante seasons."

Then there are the clusters steeped in the old-fashioned family tradition, like Blue-Collar Nursery, with its starter-home subdivisions where women believe there's no nobler occupation than caring for their home and family—usually a large family. Blue-Collar Nursery leads all the clusters in the concentration of households with three children or more —not to mention the purchase of board games, ownership of campers and use of cents-off coupons. Judy McDougal, a 44-year-old housewife and mother of seven (ages 11 to 19) has never considered working outside her home in the cluster community of West Jordan, Utah. "It's a full-time job trying to keep up with my family," says McDougal, a statuesque, dark-haired woman whose laugh is hearty and long. She spends her days chauffeuring the kids between basketball practice and Brownie troop meetings, music lessons and slumber parties. She can usually tell the season by whether she's cheering on her teenage sons at football games or wrestling matches.

Asked if she feels she's missed out on not having a professional career, she shakes her head slowly and replies, "My family is too important to leave for someone else to care for. If I failed with my family it wouldn't matter if I did something great in the world." But wouldn't the extra money supplement her husband's salary as credit manager at a turkey marketing company? "If it's a question of having more money or making a home he feels good about," she says, "well, we can do without some things."

The differences between working and nonworking women are understood by magazine publishers seeking to attract readership among either group. By identifying the clusters where they live, the magazines can determine their distinct interests and buying patterns—and whether advertisers are addressing those needs. Consider the readership profiles of two women's magazines: *Better Homes & Gardens,* where the ratio of working to nonworking women subscribers is about even, and *Working Woman,* where readers in the labor force outnumber homemakers by four to one. *Better Homes & Gardens* subscribers tend to be high-school educated, married with teenage children, have a household income of $35,000–$50,000 and live in clusters like Furs & Station Wagons and Coalburg & Corntown. As consumers, they show strong preferences for gardening and golf, owning 35-mm cameras and life insurance policies, visiting theme parks and shopping by mail-order catalogues. In contrast, *Working Woman* readers are typically single, with some college education, have household incomes of $50,000–

WORKING WOMEN VS. HOMEMAKERS

In many ways, the readers of *Working Woman* are similar to those of *Better Homes & Gardens*—middle-class women, 25 to 44 years old. But there is one major difference: *Working Woman*'s audience contains 31 percent more women who hold full-time jobs. That lone fact translates into sharply different neighborhoods and lifestyles.

Top Five Clusters: *Working Woman*

Cluster	Index
Bohemian Mix	279
Two More Rungs	261
Gray Power	199
Black Enterprise	197
Emergent Minorities	174

Top Five Clusters: *Better Homes & Gardens*

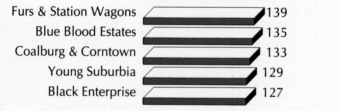

Cluster	Index
Furs & Station Wagons	139
Blue Blood Estates	135
Coalburg & Corntown	133
Young Suburbia	129
Black Enterprise	127

Lifestyle Characteristics

Working Woman	*Better Homes & Gardens*
Racquetball	Outdoor gardening
Jazz records/tapes	Car camping
Imported beer	Cents-off coupons
Contribute to public TV	35-mm cameras
Health clubs	Veterans clubs
Imported cars	Domestic cars

Numbers indicate percentages of people who read each magazine, indexed against the average for all households. An index of 100 equals the U.S. average: 1.83% for *Working Woman,* 19.53% for *Better Homes & Gardens.* An index of 279 means a cluster has 2.79 times the national average. Source: SMRB 1984/85, Claritas Corp., 1987.

$75,000 and are concentrated in Bohemian Mix and Two More Rungs. Away from work, they play racquetball and watch movies, own personal computers and subcompact hatchbacks, travel to Europe and shop through the Yellow Pages. Armed with such profiles, today's women's magazine editors know whether to fill their pages with ads about cameras or computers, gardening or racquetball.

■ HANGING ON BY A THREAD

For most Americans, the shift from a manufacturing to a service economy has meant new jobs opening up in fields such as computer electronics, engineering, medicine and financial services. Not so for the residents of the nation's factory towns and industrial suburbs. Global competition and low-cost imports have wrought havoc in communities where employment is keyed to nondurable manufacturing products like textiles, shoes and clothing. Between 1985 and 1995, economists predict that the apparel industry will lose 350,000 jobs. While Congress continues its perennial debate over trade protectionist legislation, a mood of desperation has descended over hundreds of small towns where factories rest on a fragile and vulnerable economic base.

This worldwide industrial battle is being played out in Norma Rae-Ville, that cluster of southern milltowns with the highest concentration of workers engaged in nondurable manufacturing—a rate two-and-a-half times the national average. Composed of small towns like Dalton, Georgia, Childersburg, Alabama, and Tarboro, North Carolina, Norma Rae-Ville has little affluence (the median income, $18,559 annually, is 23 percent below average) and a big problem with illiteracy (49 percent of all residents never finished high school). The cluster's reading tastes are geared toward low-brow publications such as the *National Enquirer* and *Soap Opera Digest.* In Dalton, a town of 22,000 that calls itself the carpet capital of the world, fully half the 1980 work force had never finished high school. Typically, teenagers go right from high school into the mills —with or without their degrees—put a down payment on a $30,000 woodframe house and settle into working-class lives. "You don't see a lot of people trying to better themselves. They do what everybody did before them," says Robin Sponberger, a Dalton aide to Democratic congressman Ed Jenkins. "A lot of people believe it doesn't matter whether you finish high school; you'll end up in a carpet mill anyway."

As in most Norma Rae-Ville communities, Dalton's life revolves around its dozens of mills. Radio newscasters feature nightly reports on the carpet industry. In the summer, teams of mill employees compete in softball leagues, the scores receiving prominent play in the local *Daily Citizen-News.* Many of the town's mills provide staff and financial support for the Chamber of Commerce, Boy Scouts, Big Brothers and Big

NORMA RAE-VILLE: LIFE ON THE LINE

With their lower-middle-class incomes, the textile workers who predominate in Norma Rae-Ville neighborhoods opt for self-treating remedies, home beauty aids and cheap, packaged, filler foods. Even their eggs are imitation.

	National Average	Norma Rae-Ville	Cluster Index
Egg substitutes	2.8%	7.1%	255
Canned stews	5.6	13.9	248
Feminine hygiene deodorants	6.3	12.3	196
Frozen corn-on-the-cob	19.9	37.0	186
Laxatives	22.5	41.8	186
Asthma relief remedies	2.1	3.8	180
Chewing/smokeless tobacco	4.5	7.9	175
Watch/listen to/attend pro wrestling	7.1	12.4	175
Sleeping tablets	3.3	5.1	154
Canned corned-beef hash	5.6	8.6	152
Electric hair-styling combs	5.2	7.6	146
Compact pick-up trucks	8.8	12.0	136
Pizza mixes	13.3	17.8	134
Diarrhea remedies	16.4	21.8	133
White rice	46.1	59.5	129

Numbers indicate percentages of people in each category and indexed against the national average. An index of 100 equals the U.S. average for that category. An index of 200 means a cluster has twice the national average for that category. Source: SMRB and MRI data bases, Claritas Corp., 1987.

Sisters. But most of all, the giant looms and dye vats provide jobs in Dalton—56 percent of employment here is related to textile manufacturing. With the town's location in the hilly pinewoods of northeast Georgia, its mills attract workers from a 100-mile radius—typically outlying Hard Scrabble areas where there's no work to compete with the $3.35-an-hour minimum wage offered in the nonunion mills. "Dalton is a real hotspot for out-of-work out-of-towners," says Moody Connell, city editor of the *Daily Citizen-News.* "A lot of people just rent here with their families, work for a time and then go home. That's their whole lives —just making a living."

For Dalton's workers, who can tick off the names of mills that have shut down in neighboring communities, a minimum wage beats the alternative—unemployment and a comatose community. Winston Palmer, a 53-year-old master weaver for the Beaulieau plant, considers himself lucky to be a mill worker, however fragile the economic security. His father, mother, brother and daughter all earned paychecks by working the clanging, dusty carpet looms. After thirty-six years in the mills, he can't complain about his $20,000-a-year salary, enviable wages in Dalton. Along with his wife, who makes $13,000 as a binding operator, Palmer maintains that their household income makes for a comfortable lifestyle. "You don't get rich, but you can get a modest living out of it," he says in a syrupy southern drawl. "Besides, it's not how much you have but what you do with it." And Palmer, an amiable man with slicked-back gray hair and a passing resemblance to Art Linkletter, has done plenty. The three-bedroom farmhouse he bought for $15,000 ten years ago is paid for, and he figures it's now worth $60,000. When he's not working, Palmer likes to garden in the backyard vegetable patch, pitch horseshoes with cronies or watch one of the TV stations his satellite dish brings in. A typical night out involves dinner at the local Town & Country Restaurant, where the bill for a big platter of fried chicken, two vegetables and a salad comes to $3.95.

The downscale economics of Norma Rae-Ville communities like Dalton encourage the purchase of basic necessities rather than luxury items. Cluster residents are more likely than the general population to buy canned stews and home permanents, to treat themselves with laxatives and cough syrups when ill rather than go to the doctor, to frequent Hardee's and K-mart's. Reflecting their low ZQ ranking of 31, they rarely travel abroad, drink imported wines, ski or acquire mutual funds. "Status around here is getting a month ahead on your bills," says Robin Sponberger.

Palmer stashes $50 away every week just in case, remembering the two plants he's worked for that have shut down due to foreign competition. Walking past the racks of polypropylene thread leading to one of Beaulieau's looms, Palmer reaches up to lovingly caress a 9-by-12-foot floral-patterned carpet that will sell for $300. "We make the most beautiful carpet in the world and at an inexpensive price," he says. "Now why would anyone want an imported one that costs ten times as much?" Palmer's recent choice in automobiles, a 1986 Chrysler New Yorker, stemmed from his empathy for another industry facing competition from abroad. "I won't buy anything that's not American—if I can help it," he remarks. "I work to produce quality, grade-A carpets. And that gentleman's working in Detroit to produce a quality automobile. Now, if I don't buy his automobile, how can he buy my carpet?" If nothing else, that pride has kept Norma Rae-Ville towns like Dalton hanging on by a thread.

■■■■■■■■■■■■■■■ **WHEN THE LIGHTS GO OUT**

To the people of Monessen, Pennsylvania, 35 miles south of Pittsburgh, that buy-American ethic has lost its promise. Here, where America's industrial age was forged, the once-bright optimism of the townspeople has become as tarnished as the soot-stained hills of the Monongahela Valley.

Picture a fall night in 1986: Monessen's downtown streets are empty except for the parking lot outside the union hall of steelworkers Local 1229. Inside, about a hundred members have gathered in the cavernous hall, still decorated with streamers and bunting from an earlier dance. But on this occasion the mood is subdued. Wheeling-Pittsburgh Steel, the town's economic lifeblood for most of this century, filed for bankruptcy in mid-1985 and eventually laid off most of its work force. Now, more than a year later, these steelworkers have come, stone-faced men with broad backs and thick hands, to listen to their leaders assess the admittedly bleak situation. Yes, their pension fund is in jeopardy. No, company executives have said nothing about reopening the Monessen plant. Maybe the steelworkers should look into job prospects at other steel mills in other cities.

"But who in the hell's going to give you a job if you're 62 years old?" lashes out one blast-furnace operator.

"The company's written off Monessen, so we've got to get the politicians on our side to get this place going," offers another, noting the upcoming congressional elections.

"We've got to find a way to help us here in Monessen," adds a third, though he doesn't need to look far to illustrate the sorry state of the local. The union hall where they speak is up for sale to raise money for laid-off workers and their families.

Monessen is a model for what happens to a Mines & Mills steeltown when the factory shuts down. An industrial boom town at the turn of the century, Monessen attracted a massive migratory movement of blacks and immigrants—from Italy, Greece, Syria and Russia—to its smoky plants, which produced steel, railroad tracks, nails and wire. Union wages brought prosperity to the businesses along Monessen's riverfront, and locals describe the Saturday night streetlife, with its

UNION CARDS

Union membership has dropped from a high of 33 percent of the U.S. work force in the 1950s to 11 percent in the 1980s. It's still popular in a variety of small towns located near factories, mines and mills.

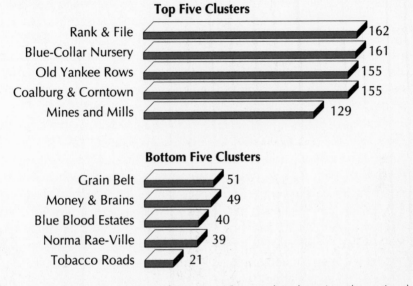

Top Five Clusters

Rank & File	162
Blue-Collar Nursery	161
Old Yankee Rows	155
Coalburg & Corntown	155
Mines and Mills	129

Bottom Five Clusters

Grain Belt	51
Money & Brains	49
Blue Blood Estates	40
Norma Rae-Ville	39
Tobacco Roads	21

Numbers indicate percentages of union members, indexed against the national average. An index of 100 equals the U.S. average: 10.9%. An index of 162 means a cluster has 1.62 times the national average, or about 18%. Source: SMRB 1983/84, Claritas Corp., 1987.

crowded bars and dancehalls, as "Little Pittsburgh." Which is to say, so jammed with hearty partyers that children would have to walk in the street to avoid being trampled on the sidewalks.

But factory strikes and shutdowns in the late '70s sounded the death-knell for a once-vibrant town. In moribund Monessen today, downtown restaurants are empty and clothing stores have locked their doors. The 3-mile-long Wheeling-Pittsburgh Steel factory that borders the town lies rusting in a field of weeds, a cruel and everpresent reminder of how far King Coal and Big Steel have fallen. With several thousand Monessen residents dropped from Wheeling-Pittsburgh's payroll, there are more downtown storefronts displaying CLOSED signs than are open for business, and city services have been cut back. "Everyone's begun to curb their expectations," says Monessen mayor James

Sepesky, the son of a steelworker, who teaches high school social studies. "People are still maintaining their homes but they're down to buying essentials at the supermarkets. About all they have left is their pride."

For most of this century, Monessen has mirrored the ups and downs of Mines & Mills, the nation's cluster of mining villages and steeltowns concentrated in the rust bowl, from New England to Lake Michigan. Half a century ago, Mines & Mills towns like Monessen, La Salle, Illinois, and Athol, Massachusetts, thrived as their factories churned out steel rails and automobiles. During the good years, blue-collar workers settled into modest ramblers, raised families and lived comfortably on secure union wages—in 1983, steelworkers were paid an average $26,500.

But the struggle against overseas rivals subsidized by their governments and the cost of modernizing outdated equipment have devastated America's smokestack industries and forced Mines & Mills residents to cope with a lifestyle in decline. Home values are dropping, half the cluster's households report an annual household income of less than $21,537 and, as young people flee to jobs elsewhere, a quarter of the residents are over 55 years old. "In five years, Monessen could be a ghost town," predicts 60-year-old Russ Bergstedt, a lifelong resident and steelworkers union official. "There will be more old people, more decaying buildings, fewer schools and more people needing welfare. And every year it will get worse." Indeed, between 1985 and 1986, the number of needy families applying to the church-sponsored Food Bank tripled to 180. At the Keystone Bakery, a handwritten sign informs customers that no welfare checks are accepted for purchases under 50 cents.

For the steelworkers of Monessen, living in a fading company town has taken its toll, financially and emotionally. Buzzy Byron, a 34-year-old pipefitter who went to work for Wheeling-Pittsburgh in 1974, has watched his monthly income plummet from $2,000 paychecks to $200 welfare checks. Now he and his wife outfit their two boys with hand-me-downs, and hamburger has replaced steak at the dinner table. They've cut out vacations altogether, dipped into savings to make the mortgage payments on their $15,500 home and limited use of their Sears and Montgomery Wards credit cards to the occasional sale. "When the plant was going strong, you wouldn't think anything of buying a new car, redoing your kitchen or going on vacation," says Byron, a third-generation steelworker who sports a thick mustache and long hair peeking from beneath a Pittsburgh Steelers cap. "Now, no one's spending money. We're all holding tight." Byron earns a little money in a sideline

MINES & MILLS: BLUE-COLLAR LIVING

Mines & Mills, the nation's steel and coal towns, is a blue-collar society: cigar-smoking factory workers and their young families, who treat themselves to large stereos and video games. Factory shut-downs have lowered their culinary tastes: the food bought most often is canned stew.

	National Average	Mines & Mills	Cluster Index
Travel by railroad	.9%	2.3%	261
Cigars	5.6	13.0	232
Ale	6.1	12.1	199
Watch/listen to/attend pro wrestling	3.5	6.9	197
Archery	3.0	5.6	186
Stereo consoles	5.5	10.1	183
Install own mufflers	4.3	7.3	170
Disposable diapers	12.8	20.5	160
Electric drills	5.2	8.2	158
Video games	5.5	8.3	151
Compact pickup trucks	8.8	12.8	146
Canned stew	5.6	7.8	140

Numbers indicate percentages of people in each category and indexed against the national average. An index of 100 equals the U.S. average for that category. An index of 200 means a cluster has twice the national average for that category. Source: SMRB and MRI data bases, Claritas Corp., 1987.

remodeling business, but it's not enough to stave off the anxiety attacks that have struck many of Monessen's laid-off workers. "Stress pills are the most popular pills at the pharmacy," Byron notes. "I have friends whose marriages have fallen apart since the plant shut down. Basically, the rhythm of life has changed."

Nationwide, the economic hard times that have befallen Mines & Mills communities like Monessen are reflected in the lifestyle patterns. As people have quit buying more than the basics, supermarkets have shut down while convenience stores are surviving on small-quantity products like canned stews, packaged starches and jarred vegetables. Car dealers are hanging on with stripped-down American subcompacts like the Dodge Omni and the AMC Eagle; cluster-wide, eighteen of the twenty poorest-selling cars are luxury imports. Politicians have charted the crumbling of Mines & Mills' once-solid Democratic bloc; in 1984, Walter Mondale could muster only 25 percent of the cluster's votes. Analysts trace the disappearing liberalism to the loss of union jobs and the declining influence of the local shop.

In Monessen, town leaders now spend a lot of time trying to convince residents to fight off their depression and develop a postindustrial economy and attitude. Four business groups are trying to recruit firms to thirty-two communities in the Monongahela Valley, and state representatives are lobbying to expand the Pittsburgh highway to turn towns like Monessen into bedroom communities. But there's still resistance among Monessen townsfolk to admitting that their steeltown is a thing of the past. "We've got to come up with new ideas for survival," says Bob Leone, a gas-station owner and local promoter. "If it's plastics, let's go with plastics. If it's high-tech, let's do that. We have good people. We have a good work force. We have to get off that old thinking that the strength of this town is tied to the steel mill."

▬▬▬▬▬▬▬ PULLING UP ROOTS

For the residents of small farm towns across the nation's heartland, the choice offered by a shifting economic base is frequently no choice at all. With families rooted in agriculture for generations, there's often no alternative but to abandon their homesteads—or be forced out. In 1985, an American farmer went bust every 6 minutes, and real per capita income in farm counties dropped to 76 percent that of metropolitan counties.

Those sad statistics are all too well known in Grain Belt, the cluster that leads the nation in agricultural workers—eight and a half times the national average. Residents of these rural communities scattered throughout the Great Plains and Mountain states are typically lower-middle-class (47 percent earn under $20,000 annually), poorly educated (78 percent never went beyond high school) and elderly (26 percent are over 55 years old). Each year, cluster residents watch the annual migration of newly minted graduates to brighter futures out of town. And in the grim economic climate that reduced the number of U.S. farmworkers by 12 percent during the '70s, Grain Belt communities are dying: their farmers bankrupt, their train lines shut down, their businesses closed up. America's Grain Belt may be more aptly called the Drain Belt.

Consider Early, Iowa, a Grain Belt outpost of 600, hit hard by the farm crisis. Its sole commercial strip has begun to resemble a decayed inner-city block, with boarded-up shops next to grafitti-covered storefronts. In the last five years, Early has lost a supermarket, two gas stations, a beauty salon and the Payless Cashway lumber and supply yard—part of a chain that had been founded in town and at one time was its leading employer. Perhaps the biggest blow came in July 1986, when the bank collapsed and a new one opened up, minus a loan officer and investment funds to revive the community. "It was like the crash of the stock market," recalls Rev. Gary Byrd, minister of the United Methodist Church. "It destroyed any feeling of self-worth among the people."

Citizens have been steadily fleeing Early—10 percent of the population has left in the last four years. And the United Methodist Church, which was built for 500 members in the early 1960s, can claim barely half that membership today. In fact, about all that's left to Early are its three churches, which now sponsor potluck dinners as well as crisis workshops. "There's really not much else here," concedes Rev. Byrd, a gentle man with a mustache and goatee. "A lot of the older people say this is the way it was during the Depression."

Like many Grain Belt communities, Early is caught in the financial squeeze between falling prices for corn and soybeans and rising costs for seed, fertilizer and machinery. Land that went for $2,800 an acre several years ago isn't worth $1,000 these days. And farmers who expanded in the flush years of what's been termed "the go-go '70s"

GRAIN BELT: LIFE DOWN ON THE FARM

The financially strapped residents of Grain Belt rely on a self-sufficient pioneer spirit to provide for their families, typically purchasing such do-it-yourself products as chain saws and canning jars. Their high ownership of cats reflects the invasion of mice on grain farms.

	National Average	Grain Belt	Cluster Index
Second mortgages	2.0%	5.1%	256
Standard pickup trucks	16.0	36.0	225
Gas chain saws	3.0	6.3	210
Motorcycles	9.2	18.1	197
Cats	21.9	37.7	172
Watch/listen to/attend rodeos	2.3	3.9	171
Canning jars and lids	4.8	8.0	166
Factory-loaded ammunition	5.8	9.3	161
Home freezers	4.1	6.5	159
Canned stews	5.6	8.3	148
Powdered breakfast drinks	22.6	29.4	130

Numbers indicate percentages of people in each category, and indexed against the national average. An index of 100 equals the U.S. average for that category. An index of 200 means a cluster has twice the national average for that category.
Source: SMRB and MRI data bases, Claritas Corp., 1987.

suddenly found themselves doing a slow dance and heading for insolvency: in 1985, one-third of all Iowa's farmers faced foreclosure. Neil Mason, a fifth-generation farmer who raises 750 acres of corn and soybeans on land his father tilled, gave up 140 acres to pay off his debts that year. He blames the loss of foreign grain markets for his loss of $25,000 on a million-dollar farm operation. "We just got hit with too many grain embargoes," complains Mason, a 40-year-old father of three with sandy hair, sunburnt skin and an aw-shucks manner. Though some of his neighbors have sold out, he and his wife, Anita, have no plans to leave their land. "There's no easy way to get out of farming," says Anita, noting that the "closeness of the people" keeps the Early community alive. "We grew up here and this is all we've ever known."

Instead, the Masons are belt-tightening their middle-class lifestyle: Gone are the family vacations and the cars traded in after five years. Now there's an occasional trip to relatives and their eight-year-old Buick is pushing 80,000 miles. The family will drive out of town on Sunday for an after-church dinner, but otherwise most meals come off the farm, from the hogs they raise to the vegetables they grow. "Some people have left out of embarrassment of what's happened to them, but farmers don't cash you out easily," says Neil. "And we're all in the same fix. We just hope that we'll be more secure in a few years and able to provide a start for our kids."

It's an irony in American society that the farther we live from our neighbors, the more we seem to care about them. Grain Belt, the nation's most sparsely settled cluster, has high rates of residents who work as volunteers, join fraternal clubs and get involved in local civic issues. In Early, where many families live a quarter-mile from their closest neighbors, residents leave their houses unlocked during winter blizzards in case someone's car breaks down and the homeowners can't hear their knock. Whenever a fire engine passes, neighbors watch to see where it's headed and if their help is needed. Not long ago, townspeople learned of a local woman who had hemorrhaged during childbirth and "was as close to dying as a person could be," in the words of Joyce Landgraf, a 27-year-old farm wife and reporter for a local newspaper. Landgraf and her neighbors responded by organizing a "prayer chain" to request divine intervention on the woman's behalf. "She's home now and the baby's fine," says Landgraf, shaking her head at the memory. The mother of a 4-year-old son herself, she adds: "People are so close to God around here because they see so much nature every day. Farming isn't a 9-to-5 job but a way of life. People become a part of the fabric of nature."

Throughout America's Grain Belt, hard-working families are learning to coexist with the farm crisis. Consumer surveys show they've given up on most luxury items in favor of tools for survival: chain saws, electric drills, canning jars and home freezers are all bought at above-average rates. Grain Belt leads all the clusters in the concentration of residents who shop at discount stores—67 percent of all households. Like other rural communities, they occasionally indulge in country pleasures like rodeos, hunting trips and horseback riding. But in towns like Early, where the convenience store cash registers are now equipped with buttons to indicate food stamp purchases, townsfolk are cutting back. In the fall of 1986, a three-bedroom rambler on a half-acre plot sold at auction for $6,200. All that's left in the way of local entertainment is Virgil's Cafe, where a foursome of elderly men in overalls and brimmed caps can usually be found sipping Stroh's draft and playing rummy—albeit, as the hours pass, more playing than sipping.

Virgil's is a favorite spot for Alan Mattice, an insurance salesman and president of the Early Promoters Group. A self-assured 32-year-old who came to Early five years ago after marrying a local girl, he describes a big date as "a cheeseburger at the local truck stop." And yet even Mattice admits there's excitement to living in a Grain Belt town where community survival is at stake. In the two years since becoming the town's chief promoter, he's managed to lure only a physician's assistant to the town's deserted Main Street. "We see so many things on a TV show like 'Falcon Crest,' where the high and mighty drink wine at the race track, and we wonder if we're missing out in life," muses Mattice. "But our life isn't dull. Every day, we're just trying to keep Early around."

▄▄▄▄▄▄▄ WHERE OPPORTUNITY RARELY KNOCKS

The decline in many industrial and farm-based industries has had a ripple-down impact on the clusters at the bottom of the ZQ ladder. One out of seven Americans in the 1980s lived below the official poverty line. And many people thrown out of work due to manufacturing plant closings are joining the ranks of untrained and poorly educated workers ill prepared for a job market that requires more skills than it did ten years ago. In Public Assistance, home of the nation's urban ghettos, residents have the dubious distinction of reporting America's highest unemployment rate—79 percent above the U.S. norm. Almost a third of all households—nine times the U.S. average—survive on government programs such as subsidized housing and food stamps. And those who do work are forced to commute outside their inner-city neighborhoods for the lowest-paying jobs, as domestics, cooks and unskilled laborers.

Overwhelmingly black, poorly educated and without local employment opportunities, Public Assistance communities are the result of decades of complete segregation from mainstream America's economy. Residents rarely break the poverty cycle from one generation to the next. In the twenty years since riots engulfed sixty-one American cities, the number of blacks living in inner-city poverty has actually increased by 65 percent. Now, with more than half the households headed by women, communities such as the South Bronx, West Philadelphia and West Newark, New Jersey, reflect what has come to be called the

WELFARE NEIGHBORHOODS

There's an inverse correlation between educational achievement and being on the dole. The communities with the highest concentrations of welfare recipients also have the lowest concentrations of college graduates.

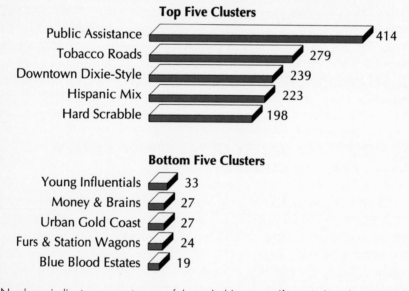

Top Five Clusters

Public Assistance	414
Tobacco Roads	279
Downtown Dixie-Style	239
Hispanic Mix	223
Hard Scrabble	198

Bottom Five Clusters

Young Influentials	33
Money & Brains	27
Urban Gold Coast	27
Furs & Station Wagons	24
Blue Blood Estates	19

Numbers indicate percentages of households on welfare, indexed against the national average. An index of 100 equals the U.S. average: 7.85%. An index of 414 means a cluster has 4.14 times the national average, or about 32%. Source: PRIZM (Census Demography), Claritas Corp., 1987.

"feminization of poverty." At a West Newark housing project, single mothers with kids in tow gather on the first day of each month at the project's mail room, waiting for their welfare checks. Locals have termed this monthly ritual "Mother's Day."

In Clairmont Village, a government-subsidized project housing 18,000 in the Morrisania section of the South Bronx, twenty teenage girls become pregnant every month. Located in one of the poorest Congressional districts in the country, Clairmont Village watched as arsonists in the '70s torched 100,000 housing units, transforming entire blocks into grimy rubble. Then, in the early '80s, the drug pushers moved in. "Crack devastated this area like a hurricane," says Vincent Gray, a Clairmont Village manager. Today, newspapers report the first signs of recovery in the form of renovated, moderately priced apartments and homes sprouting amid the rubble-strewn lots—"rock gardens," as some city officials call them. But long-time residents remain skeptical of the impact this recovery will have for the one in three households subsisting on welfare.

"To poor people, moderate-income housing is for the rich," says Blanca Ramirez, a 28-year-old community organizer and lifelong resident of the South Bronx. "Life here is tough for a parent on public assistance whose kids aren't keeping up in school, who has to walk by drug dealers on the street, who has to shop in markets that don't provide the freshest foods and who has to use a hospital emergency room where people wait for hours for care." Even the best-intentioned developers, says Ramirez, are eyed with distrust by the underprivileged.

"There's an absence of hope among these people," says Sister Falaka Fattah, a dashiki-clad former journalist who operates the House of Umoja, a home for disadvantaged black youth in Carroll Park, one of the most blighted areas of West Philadelphia. "Their biggest concern is just trying to take care of themselves from day to day. Their kids talk about making it the easy way, the illegitimate way. But most of the people in the poor community never move away. It usually takes blasting powder to get them out."

The problem of unemployment in Carroll Park has been compounding for years. Block after block of graffiti-scrawled homes and litter-strewn lots support virtually no legitimate business activity. Locals estimate that 25 percent of black teenagers earn income through crime. Like the bottom-of-the-rung poor in rural Hard Scrabble settlements, many teens join the army or the marines to get out of the ghettos. Of those left behind, some drift into the netherworld of unemployment, welfare and drugs from which there is often no escape. "How can you get a job if you're so high that you can't even think?" asks Charles Shaw, a 24-year-old counselor at the House of Umoja. "You won't even be able to understand what the man is saying to you."

Shaw, a short intense man with a scraggly beard, scarred face and welterweight's physique, has lived in Carroll Park all his life. One of six children who grew up in a two-bedroom rowhouse, he recalls a childhood spent on the city's mean streets, "when you'd have to fight someone every day on your way to school." As a teenager he became a leader of the Moon Gang, which at one time boasted 300 members along a ten-block stretch between Market and Landsdowne streets. During the early 1970s, when gangs in Philadelphia reached their peak, violence killed 40 people and left 150 paraplegics each year. The appalling statistics frightened everyone but the gang members, typically the products of broken homes and neglect, who saw the groups as substitute family units. "The gangs offered security and trust," says Shaw. "Many kids were closer to the gang than they were to their parents."

Much of the gang violence subsided in 1974 when Sister Falaka brought 500 of the city's toughest youths together to settle the street wars, much as foreign ministers tackle Third World debt. After the conference, Sister Falaka set out to find a more permanent solution to helping outcast teens through local community development. Thus was born the House of Umoja (Swahili for "Unity of the Family"), a collection of rehabbed houses where gang members can take high-school equivalency and training classes, learning skills in cooking and construction among others. Dozens of former gang members have been trained as unarmed security guards. Today they may protect the same 7-Elevens and Burger Kings they once robbed.

But the prospects for an economic recovery in such Public Assistance neighborhoods are dim. Near the House of Umoja, graffiti and grates cover the picture windows of the corner markets and beauty salons, and bags of cocaine and PCP are sold openly in alleyways. A visitor passing by the boarded-up Utopia Bar is startled to learn that it's open, as patrons stumble out into the glaring sunlight. Nationwide, Public Assistance supports a convenience-store economy; residents purchase cigarettes, orange juice and packaged cold cuts at rates above the national average. And they're five times as likely as average Americans to read *Ebony, Jet* and *Essence,* which preach self-help for blacks. Without movie theaters and nightclubs, locals have to make their own parties and are big purchasers of alcohol—malt liquor, rum and pop wines—as well as records—soul, jazz, disco and Latin. "Music helps you cool out," says Shaw, who earns $4 an hour at his counseling job. "After a tough day, I can come out with a brand new positive attitude."

New attitudes—not to mention job training—are just what's needed in Public Assistance communities, where too many young people look to crime as a career. After a decade of House of Umoja efforts to offer local youth the job skills to provide a future, Shaw sees only minimal improvement in his neighborhood. "The older people still don't come out after dark," he says, nodding toward a group of derelicts passing a bottle around an ashcan fire, "even though we're making progress showing youth the right way to make money." Shaw can point to some personal success: in early 1986, he took title to a roofless rowhouse shell that he hopes to renovate with neighborhood help. "I plan to live my whole life here," he says. "This neighborhood, despite its drawbacks, is a part of me." In Carroll Park and other Public Assistance communities, the need for jobs is not simply an economic issue but a matter of hope for an underclass society. The American Dream begins with a job.

5

WHERE THE MONEY GOES

"We think we're typical. We're loyal to our brands."
—Alan Mattice, Early, Iowa (Grain Belt)

Traveling salesmen have known it all along: where people live offers one of the best clues to what they buy. But today's computer-assisted marketers don't even need to set foot in a neighborhood to discover local tastes. With the punch of a lap-top PC, they can determine what magazines residents read, what cars they drive, whether they're more likely to buy calculators or computers, whiskey or wine, turkey roast or tuna extender. By correlating product sales and local addresses, it's possible to predict how a cluster's lifestyle will affect a local market, documenting how one block in Manhattan prefers Wheaties while another favors Wheat Chex.

Consider the lifestyle portrait of a single Manhattan zip code, Radio City's 10019, which encompasses West 59th to West 48th streets, from 12th Avenue to Rockefeller Plaza. More than 30,000 people live in this heterogeneous district, classified as Bohemian Mix on a zip code level but comprising eight different neighborhood types when analyzed by square blocks: Gray Power, Single City Blues, Urban Gold Coast, Downtown Dixie-Style, Public Assistance, Hispanic Mix, New Melting Pot and Bohemian Mix. Travelling west on 57th Street across 10th Avenue, the architecture changes from renovated co-op apartment buildings to run-down urban renewal projects; the cluster designation shifts from Bohemian Mix to Downtown Dixie-Style. And as the scenery changes, so do the tastes. TV viewing turns from "At the Movies" and "Late Night with

A SLICE OF MIDTOWN

More than 30,000 people live in midtown Manhattan zip code 10019, a heterogeneous community comprising eight different neighborhood types. Such information could help a grocer determine where to mail promotional coupons: to Gray Power residences for a sale on oatmeal, to Bohemian Mix blocks to introduce a new granola.

Urban Gold Coast		Hispanic Mix	
Single City Blues		Downtown Dixie-Style	
Bohemian Mix		Public Assistance	
Gray Power		New Melting Pot	

SOURCE: Claritas Corp., 1987.

David Letterman" to "Dynasty" and "Falcon Crest." Continuing south toward the crumbling brownstones of Hell's Kitchen below West 54th Street, the cluster changes again, to Single City Blues, where the residents tend to watch "Dance Fever" and "Friday Night Videos." In this sense, the cluster system becomes a marketer's zoom lens, moving down from a single nation to 36,000 zip codes to 254,000 block groups.

Despite the detail with which the cluster system can depict what people do with their time and money, determining why they do it is a trickier business. While personal attitudes and opinions determine one's tastes, a neighborhood of like-minded people exerts a powerful influence on each individual's consuming patterns. Moreover, the same factors that define neighborhood settlement also determine a cluster's buying patterns: social rank, household composition, ethnicity, urbanization and mobility. Understanding that connection can explain why, for instance, the residents of Two More Rungs are big consumers of pumpernickel bread and tea (ethnicity: many are children of Eastern European immigrants with Old World tastes) but rarely buy children's vitamins (household composition: a majority are close to retirement age with grown children). Often without our even being aware of it, these five geodemographic factors influence nearly every purchase we make.

WHY WE BUY

SOCIAL RANK

Up and down the ZQ ladder, affluence is an obvious determinant of what people buy. It's no coincidence that the residents of Money & Brains own ten times as many Rolls Royces and Jaguars as the U.S. norm. The residents of such success-oriented communities devote a great part of their incomes to status purchases and leisure pursuits. Money & Brains consumers purchase luxury imports, rare wines, stocks, gold jewelry and country club memberships at rates far above those of their fellow Americans. Indeed, one might conclude that Money & Brains residents are almost cult-oriented toward conspicuous consumption. There's a certain community pressure that leads them to consume specific high-ticket items, a kind of rich people's "keeping up with the Joneses."

For the vast majority of less well-heeled Americans, consumer behavior is governed by whatever's affordable. For every Blue Blood Estates resident who collects exotic stamps, there's a Share Croppers counterpart sending away for Franklin Mint commemorative plates. In that cluster of poor rural hamlets concentrated in the South, status can be a $2.50 bottle of Vidal Sassoon shampoo rather than the generic store brand. Such a purchase, sociologist C. Wright Mills explained, allows one "to buy the feeling, if only for a short time, of higher status." Share Croppers residents, who own mobile homes at two-and-a-half times the rate of the population at large, are able to emulate the well-to-do with prefab luxury options in their trailer. Most mobile home sales lots feaure at least one model whose interior is adorned with woodgrain veneer walls, polyester shag carpets, plastic Tiffany lamps and neo-Mediterranean furnishings—but for the wheels, a downscale copy of an upscale home's decor. A favorite joke going around the Share Croppers town of Plains, Georgia (where Billy Carter once sold mobile homes) has a farmer complaining to a dealer that he can't find a two-story mobile home to purchase. "A man with the means shouldn't be denied luxury," he huffs.

Yet money alone doesn't determine high-status purchasing; educa-

WOK OWNERS

It doesn't necessarily take money to have status. Some products, like woks, reflect consumers' worldliness, education and desire to be trendy. Those who rarely own woks include the least-educated and -traveled Americans.

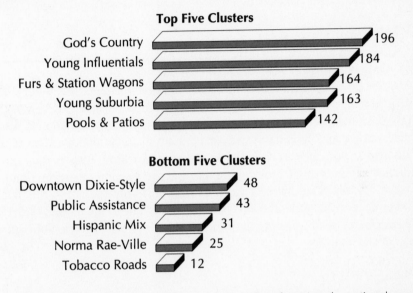

Top Five Clusters

God's Country — 196
Young Influentials — 184
Furs & Station Wagons — 164
Young Suburbia — 163
Pools & Patios — 142

Bottom Five Clusters

Downtown Dixie-Style — 48
Public Assistance — 43
Hispanic Mix — 31
Norma Rae-Ville — 25
Tobacco Roads — 12

Numbers indicate percentages of wok owners, indexed against the national average. An index of 100 equals the U.S. average: 6.74%. An index of 196 means a cluster has 1.96 times the national average, or about 13%. Source: SMRB 1984/85, Claritas Corp., 1987.

tion also figures into social rank. Although most people can afford to buy a wok, the appliance's popularity among the yuppie clusters of Young Influentials and God's Country is a sure sign of their trend-conscious worldliness, cultivated with education and broadened by travel. The consumers in these clusters own woks at twice the national average and at approximately ten times the rate of someone living in remote Norma Rae-Ville or rural Tobacco Roads. It's a fitting reminder of sociologist Russell Lyons's claim that class has less to do with money than with taste, knowledge and perceptiveness.

■ HOUSEHOLD COMPOSITION

Family status is another factor that affects neighborhood purchasing patterns. An analysis of college-educated households with at least

$35,000 in annual income and heads of households aged 25 to 40, reveals a range of dissimilar purchasing preferences between the childless couples and those with children. The childless ones read *Metropolitan Home, GQ* and *Food and Wine.* The with-children households subscribe to *Golf Digest, Country Living* and *Popular Mechanics.* Without kids means jazz records, answering machines, cruises and ski vacations. With kids means Christmas-club accounts, Tupperware parties, movie cameras and theme park visits.

Columnist Bob Garfield observed these parallel universes in a February 1986 *Washington Post Magazine* article about the lifestyle chasm between his single, urban friends and his family-oriented neighbors in the Young Suburbia community of Burke Centre, Virginia. "They lead state-of-the-art urban lives," he wrote of his childless friends. In suburbia, however, "you have two small children, drink domestic beer in cans and never once have eaten in a marvelous little Thai restaurant. You have a house full of coloring books, but not a single Dolby anything. You're choosy about your peanut butter, but you haven't been to a movie in months. And the last movie you did see, not counting *101 Dalmatians,* wasn't playing at some chichi downtown revival house. It was at the mall."

■ ETHNICITY

Ethnic background affects the consumption habits of many clusters —and not simply in the obvious tendency of some Hispanic Americans to favor tacos, beans and rice. Hispanic Mix residents, 80 percent of whom trace their ancestry to Central America, exhibit a more subtle cultural bias in their preference for products ranging from cigarillos to rum to bottled water (a likely carryover from the unsanitary plumbing facilities they left behind). They spend more on food than other Americans—$20 more a week—and are more likely to buy home remedies. During their assimilation, Hispanic Mix residents also influence mainstream America's tastes. As the nation's Hispanic population grew by 20 percent between 1980 and 1985, to 17.6 million residents, ethnic staples like tortillas and burritos spread north from Mexico to Safeways across the country. Today, you can find Mexican restaurants in the God's Country settlements of Vermont.

The national popularity of many ethnic foods notwithstanding, "flavor boundaries" divide much of America. A kind of "mayonnaise line" splits the heartland from coast to coast according to the salad dressing preferences of consumers. In clusters like Old Yankee Rows and Rank & File, composed of rowhouse neighborhoods in cities north of the line,

FLAVOR BOUNDARIES

Flavor boundaries criss-cross the nation, reflecting the same factors of ethnicity, social rank and household composition that define neighborhood settlement. A kind of "mayonnaise line" separates the creamy Hellman's mayonnaise buyers to the South from the tart Kraft Miracle Whip salad dressing lovers to the North. A marketer of a spicy new dressing would know not to dip below the Mason-Dixon Line to market its product.

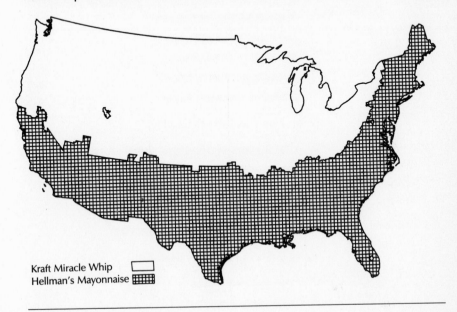

Kraft Miracle Whip
Hellman's Mayonnaise

SOURCE: Claritas Corp., 1987.

the residents are of Central European extraction and prefer tart salad dressings for their sandwiches and slaws. To the south, in Hard Scrabble and Back-Country Folks communities settled by the English and Irish, consumers prefer creamy dressings and cole slaw. The Mayonnaise Line divides the creamy Hellman's buyers in the South and Northeast from the tart Kraft Miracle Whip lovers in the Midwest and Northwest.

■ URBANIZATION

Whether you live in the shadow of a skyscraper or a grain elevator, your geography affects your buying habits. Residents of Agri-Business, the cluster of middle-class farm towns centered in the Great Plains states, are weak consumers of many foodstuffs because they typically raise their own meat and vegetables. They're also among the nation's

WHO LISTENS TO WHAT

What you listen to has a lot to do with what live music is available in your area. Jazz remains an urban phenomenon due largely to the prevalence of city clubs, just as country music is listened to in rural America. Classical music lovers tend to live in upscale areas in and around big cities that have symphonies and classical radio stations. As for heavy metal, its listeners come primarily from upscale family suburbs filled with rebellious teens.

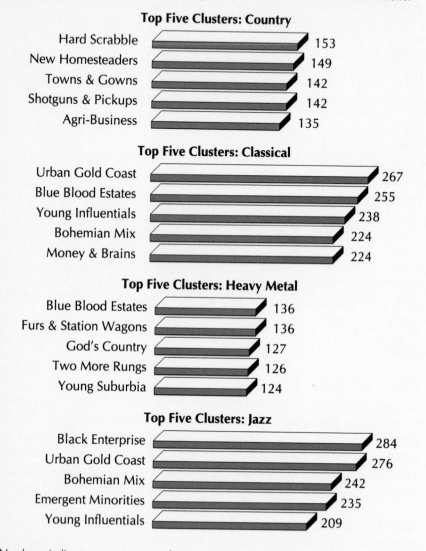

Top Five Clusters: Country

Cluster	Index
Hard Scrabble	153
New Homesteaders	149
Towns & Gowns	142
Shotguns & Pickups	142
Agri-Business	135

Top Five Clusters: Classical

Cluster	Index
Urban Gold Coast	267
Blue Blood Estates	255
Young Influentials	238
Bohemian Mix	224
Money & Brains	224

Top Five Clusters: Heavy Metal

Cluster	Index
Blue Blood Estates	136
Furs & Station Wagons	136
God's Country	127
Two More Rungs	126
Young Suburbia	124

Top Five Clusters: Jazz

Cluster	Index
Black Enterprise	284
Urban Gold Coast	276
Bohemian Mix	242
Emergent Minorities	235
Young Influentials	209

Numbers indicate percentages of record and tape buyers, indexed against the national average for each music type. An index of 100 equals the U.S. average for each: 10.96% for country, 3.04% for classical, 5.62% for heavy metal, and 2.47% for jazz. An index of 200 means a cluster has twice the national average. Source: SMRB 1985/86, Claritas Corp., 1987.

leading owners of deep freezers so they can store their harvests. With movie theaters and concert halls sometimes long drives away, Agri-Business residents are the nation's top consumers of woodworking and needlepoint material and the leading members of record and tape clubs. Although many point to their TV sets and satellite dishes as links to mainstream America, there's no denying occasional feelings of isolation. "We're in the middle of nowhere," admits Bruce Bierma, the 34-year-old town manager of Clarion, Iowa, an Agri-Business town about 100 miles north of Des Moines. "There's no place to go if you get a Big Mac attack. If you want to go window shopping in a mall, it's a 2-hour drive to Des Moines." When Clarion's movie house burned down, residents chipped in to reopen it, even though most of the movies shown there arrive eighteen months after their New York debuts—and sometimes well after appearing on cable TV.

The ubiquity of television can sometimes lead to cluster clashes. One reason those late-night TV offers hawking $9.95 Veg-O-Matics and K-Tel Record Selectors offend so many normally acquisitive yuppies is that the ads are not aimed at them. The residents of Hard Scrabble, who live in some of the nation's most sparsely settled areas, respond to TV offers at twice the national average and four times as often as Bohemian Mixers. Living far from shopping centers, consumers in Appalachia have been buying by direct mail since the advent of the Sears catalogue a century ago. The proliferation of home-shopping TV programs testifies to contemporary television's role as the latest in-home department store. For isolated communities, it's often their only accessible market-place.

■ MOBILITY

Many of the nation's trends originate in Young Influentials and Bohemian Mix, clusters located near urban colleges, where residents move often and turn their avant-garde ideas into national crazes. In fact, one reason so many banks have begun charging higher fees for overdrafts and automatic teller machine transactions is that young customers in these two clusters stay in the area less than a year and carry their assets with them. Wherever they go, these trendsetters lead active intellectual lives. Bohemian Mixers lead all clusters in subscriptions to *Atlantic Monthly,* in membership of book clubs and in writing letters to newspaper editors. Young Influentials helped spur the '70s natural foods revolution that made big business of yogurt, granola, Perrier and whole-grain bread—items they consume at rates at least 50 percent above that of the general population. With their high indices for travel as well as mobility, these twin clusters represent the prime launching ground for everything from Trivial Pursuit to Tofutti.

Take SoHo, the Bohemian Mix haven for art galleries and fashion boutiques in lower Manhattan, south of Houston Street—hence the name. There, locals are used to the constant turnover of storefront shops on Sullivan and Thompson Streets. "The biggest concern people have in SoHo is being creative," says Pat Kery, director of a gallery of contemporary art. "They don't worry that their avant-garde ideas are pleasing a big audience. Some stores last three months and disappear." Then there are the success stories, like the tiny jewelry shop that was "discovered" by the New York press, moved to a larger, two-story space, and began selling its objets d'art to boutiques around the country. Kery claims a similar SoHo diaspora accounts for current yuppie demands nationwide for such items as handmade paper, wall pottery and smoked mozarella. "This area," says Kery, a flamboyant brunette encircled by multicolored bangles, "is like a living museum in Europe."

Moving down the ZQ ladder, mobility further influences how people maintain their homes. The residents of Single-City Blues communities devote little time and money to fix-up work; they're often renting duplex flats or apartments in transient neighborhoods. Grain Belt communities, however, have the nation's lowest mobility rate and tend to live on the same property for decades. Thus, they lead most clusters in the purchase of hand tools, vinyl flooring and push-power lawn mowers. They're self-reliant farmers who add on bedrooms, fix tractors and have workshops that rival big-city gas stations. The high-rise residents of Urban Gold Coast, by contrast, engage in the same activities a fraction of the time. When it comes to home maintenance, they'd just as soon call a contractor.

THE LIFE AND DEATH OF AN AMERICAN PRODUCT

Like people, products have a life cycle, and their age will typically attract different cluster consumers. As a rule, the older the product, the greater its popularity in downscale neighborhoods, a process Paul Fussell describes in his sardonic book *Class* as "prole drift": "the tendency in advanced industrialized societies for everything to become proletarianized. Prole drift seems an inevitable attendant of mass production, mass selling, mass communication and mass education, and some of its symptoms are best-seller lists, films that must appeal to everyone (except the intelligent, sensitive and subtle), shopping malls and the lemming flight to the intellectual and cultural emptiness of the Sun Belt." Although some products enjoy long life cycles—Spam, after fifty years, is still going strong—many disappear in a matter of months. In the competitive marketplace of the '80s, 60 percent of all new products fail within the first year.

Computer video games are a classic example of a product with an eye-blink life span. In late 1981, during the heyday of Pong, Pac-Man and Donkey Kong, game buffs from suburban upscale clusters—Money & Brains, Blue Blood Estates and Furs & Station Wagons—were snapping up the leading models at nearly four times the rate of the farm and small-town residents of Back-Country Folks, Share Croppers and Tobacco Roads. But during the next two years, as prices dipped and the market became glutted with other games and cartridges, the profile shifted. By 1983, suburban sophisticates were buying the early models at rates 25 percent below the national average while the folks from the sticks were taking them home at a rate 25 percent above the norm. And shortly thereafter, the games nearly disappeared from the map—not to mention their manufacturer, which reorganized to fend off bankruptcy —as consumer fascination shifted from game machines to home computers.

Although rural clusters are slower to adopt new products, they're also more reluctant to give up those that finally make it to their market basket. Cream deodorants, eclipsed by roll-ons and sprays during the 1970s, are still popular in rural clusters, surviving without advertising or new, improved variations. Headache powder remains another drugstore favorite among the loyal consumers from Back-Country Folks and Tobacco Roads communities. Long before aspirin arrived in tablets and capsules, headache medication came in loose powder tucked into a square of wax paper. And it still does, predominantly in southern states. A lot of northern urbanites were no doubt taken aback the first time they tuned in to Ted Turner's Atlanta WTBS cable TV station and heard race-car driver Richard Petty promoting Goody's Headache Powder— the kind of product dinosaur sold in small farm towns before the Depression.

Some specialty products can appeal equally to consumers in demographically dissimilar neighborhoods. Owners of high-quality binoculars fall into two groups clearly at cross-purposes: nature lovers, who use the binoculars to admire birds and other woodland beasts, and hunters, who use the glasses to line up said wildlife in their rifles' sights. Not surprisingly, correlations of other purchasing behaviors showed the two binocular-buying groups to have completely different personalities. The nature lovers, who rank high in Urban Gold Coast, Money & Brains and Blue Blood Estates communities, tend to take a lot of foreign trips, listen to classical music, enjoy skiing and host monthly cocktail parties. The hunters, who typically live in towns and rural clusters like Grain Belt, New Homesteaders and Agri-Business, travel by bus, listen to country music, enjoy fresh-water fishing and belong to veterans clubs. In fact, one of the few material possessions that both groups share is that pair of binoculars.

CARS: (LIFE)STYLE ON WHEELS

In 1986, 130 million passenger cars rolled down the road reflecting a staggering array of sizes and designs—as well as cluster values—on wheels. Today, more than 175 designs produced by thirty automakers vie for the attention of a car-hungry public. Next to purchasing a house, buying an automobile is the largest investment many people make in their lives. And despite the persuasive powers of showroom salesrepresentatives—an aggressive breed in any cluster—consumers choose Nissan pickups or Ford wagons based on the same complex factors that determine neighborhood settlement. A class car in one neighborhood may be a clunker in another.

Wealth still separates clusters filled with chauffeurs from those with driveway mechanics. The nation's most affluent neighborhood types remain the prime audience for the world's elite cars—the Porsches, Ferraris and Silver Clouds—varying only slightly in their rates of purchase. In Gray Power communities, where residents value tasteful consumption rather than ostentation the status car of choice is a Cadillac. The cluster's upscale seniors buy nearly three times as many DeVilles, Sevilles and Fleetwoods as the national average. "There's no better way to show you're well off than to have a Cadillac parked in your garage," explains Johnnie Kroll, a retiree from Gray Power's Sun City, Arizona. Meanwhile, in the downscale neighborhoods of Hispanic Mix, where few cars are bought new, one of the most popular models is a used Chevy pickup. Thanks to the auto parts stores that proliferate in the West Side barrio of San Antonio, most motorists can keep their aging trucks running despite crumbled streets. "If you drove a Cadillac in this neighborhood," longtime resident Frank Ramos says matter-of-factly, "you wouldn't live here."

WHICH STATUS CARS HAVE THE MOST STATUS

After decades of debate over which car confers the most status, this table provides the definitive ranking, based on the concentration of owners in the nation's six wealthiest neighborhood types.

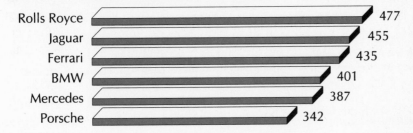

Rolls Royce	477
Jaguar	455
Ferrari	435
BMW	401
Mercedes	387
Porsche	342

Numbers indicate percentages of car buyers in the six clusters, indexed against the national average for each make. An index of 100 equals the average U.S. market penetration for 1985. An index of 200 means the make has twice the national average penetration in the six wealthiest clusters. Source: R. L. Polk, 1985 model year, Claritas Corp., 1987.

While stiff housing costs and restrictions prohibit upward mobility among socioeconomic groups, low interest rates and plentiful car loans allow many clusters to share the status of luxury cars. "People will buy above their economic status," automotive consultant Thomas O'Grady has observed, "like 'dressing for success' in a car." Indeed, among the top ten clusters that consistently buy the Lincoln Town Car are both Blue Blood Estates and Share Croppers—thirty-four ZQ rungs apart. These two groups of buyers read different messages in the elegant Town Car: For the upscale motorists, it's sturdy family transportation. In less affluent farm communities, it represents a moving taste of the good life.

Betty Lou Hagerson, a 58-year-old homemaker from the Share Croppers town of Concord, Georgia, recalls the day in 1979 when she and her husband took home their Town Car. "When we bought it, I thought I'd have to duck my head whenever we drove into town," chuckles Hagerson, brushing a gray curl behind designer glasses. "I figured people would think we were trying to be bigger than we should be." Gradually, the car became part of the family, hauling wedding cakes for Hagerson's home catering business and carting the kids to vacations in Ohio and Florida. By 1986, their Town Car had 130,000 miles on it, and the Hagersons began talking about trading it in—reluctantly. "Now that we've gotten so accustomed to it, we don't want to get rid of it."

In style and substance, automotive status can be fleeting. Because of the steady evolution of automobile technology, the look of a car—not to mention its buyer profile—can shift over time. When GM introduced the Chevrolet Chevette in 1975, the front-engine, rear-drive compact found an audience among the children of suburbia. But as the years passed and more and more upscale drivers turned to front-wheel-drive cars and imports, the Chevette became the darling of middle- and lower-class car buyers. Between 1981 and 1984, Chevette's buyers in Money & Brains communities dropped by 50 percent. Meanwhile, its buyers in Tobacco Roads jumped by the same percentage. A before-and-after map would show the geographic turnaround, the concentration of buyers shifting from midwestern cities to the rural South.

Left to their own devices, automakers can also alter the profile of their customers by redesigning their cars and targeting their advertising to different markets. In 1985, the Buick Riviera rolled out of the factory as a heavy, rear-wheel-drive luxury car that attracted two distinct buyer

---

WHO'D RATHER HAVE A BUICK

Between 1983 and 1986, General Motors shifted the styling of its Buick Electra from a boxy, rear-wheel-drive design to a sleeker front-wheel-drive machine. As a result, the Elektra's appeal moved upscale, from midscale farm and factory towns to more affluent suburban neighborhoods.

Cluster	1983	1986
Blue Blood Estates	149	320
Furs & Station Wagons	148	222
Grain Belt	146	106
Money & Brains	103	209
Norma Rae-Ville	149	107
Share Croppers	149	70
Back-Country Folks	140	82
Pools & Patios	106	158
Two More Rungs	78	132

Numbers indicate percentages of Buick buyers indexed against the national average for sales of domestic cars. An index of 100 equals the U.S. average for each: 1.3% for 1983, 1.2% for 1986. An index of 200 means a cluster has twice the national average. Source: Claritas Corp., General Motors Corp. proprietary data base, 1987. Used with permission.

groups: affluent suburbanites in clusters like Money & Brains and Pools & Patios and middle-class town residents in Coalburg & Corntown and Blue-Collar Nursery. But the downsizing of the Riviera in 1986, resulting in a lighter, sleeker and more cosmopolitan design, also completely altered the car's customer profile. Its sales rate fell by half among the midscale, small-town clusters where residents spend their leisure time bowling, gardening, hunting and visiting theme parks. In their place appeared a new group of buyers—the more urbane residents of Young Influentials and New Beginnings—who buy computers, go sailing and attend plays. "The new buyers are basically leading a more exciting lifestyle," says Paula Travenia, Buick's supervisor of marketing research. "They have a stronger correlation between higher incomes, home values, education and upscale occupations."

To cultivate this lucrative market, Buick devised a new advertising strategy. In 1986, Buick's ad agency, McCann Erickson, dropped the traditional visuals of a Riviera zipping around curves between fishermen casting lines and families washing cars. In one ad, "Touches You Revisited," the viewer scarcely sees the car's exterior. The entire commercial, bathed in a Tron-like neon glow, focuses on the Riviera's touch-sensitive dashboard with enough colorful graphics to titillate the most discerning computer hacker. The Buick catch-phrase, "Wouldn't you really rather have a—," appears in digital letters as background music recalls the theme from *Close Encounters of the Third Kind.* To make sure the new, yuppie motorists caught the updated message, Buick even chose to run the ads on TV shows where it hadn't traditionally bought commercial time: "St. Elsewhere," "Hill Street Blues" and "Mac-Guyver." "Image is very difficult to change," says Buick's Travenia. "So we're constantly trying to develop strategies to find more of these new types of people."

Whether Buick succeeded in landing these younger car buyers is difficult to say. In the fall of 1986, following lagging sales and a dip in Buick's share of the domestic market (from 10.6 percent in 1985 to 9.5 percent), GM vice president William Hoglund declared that Buick's image had become "a little schizophrenic." Accordingly, for the 1987 model year, GM executives decided to reposition Buick as the car of choice for the gray-temple set. Out went ad copy buzzwords like "youth" and "excitement." In their place, Hal Holbrook presided as Buick's spokesman, a rock-solid personality to regain stability for the Buick nameplate. New car, old audience.

Like soft-drink consumption, regional biases in car purchases can be affected by the location of an automaker's dealers. After World War II,

WHEELS: DOMESTICS VS. IMPORTS

This comparison of two similar types of cars reveals much about Americans' car-buying habits. Escort buyers are predominantly blue-collar workers centered mainly in the country's Rust Belt, whose affinity with U.S. autoworkers leads them to "buy American." The Tercel buyers, in contrast, are largely white-collar suburbanites who live near port cities. The Blue-Collar Nursery-ites in the Salt Lake City area buy both cars in high numbers.

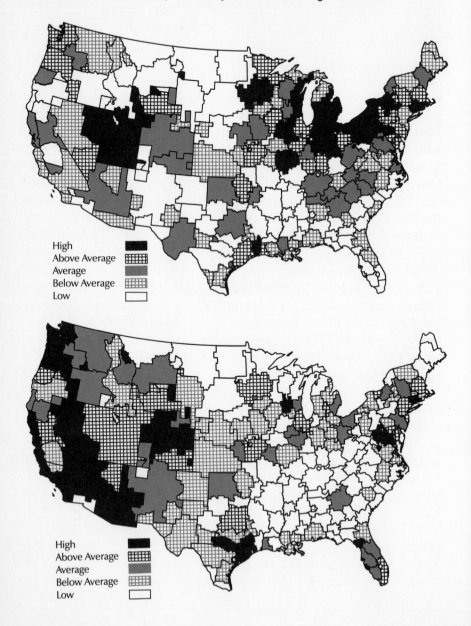

Ford Escort *(top)*	Index	Toyota Tercel *(bottom)*	Index
Blue-Collar Nursery	194	Young Influentials	210
Blue-Chip Blues	149	Furs & Station Wagons	200
Rank & File	140	Blue Blood Estates	191
Young Suburbia	137	Money & Brains	182
Shotguns & Pickups	137	God's Country	180

Numbers indicate percentages of car buyers in each cluster indexed against the national average for the 1984 model year of all cars sold. An index of 100 equals the national average: 4.0% for Escort, 1.0% for Tercel. An index of 200 means a cluster has twice the national average. Source: R. L. Polk, 1985 model year; SMRB 1985/86; Claritas Corp., 1987.

General Motors made a marketing decision to follow consumers to the suburbs, concentrating its dealers accordingly. Meanwhile, Chrysler-Plymouth carved out its turf in communities of Midwest blue-collar workers—Jean Shepherd's "My Old Man and the Plymouth" country. In rural areas, Ford opened dealerships to cater to America's farm towns. One result is that brand loyalty among these Big Three's customers has made it difficult for foreign automakers to reach buyers beyond the big-city markets.

Neighborhood lifestyle further affects a consumer's choice of a car made in Japan or America. Take the 1984 Toyota Tercel and Ford Escort, similar subcompacts in terms of cost, size, styling and handling. The Tercel found its prime audience among the affluent white-collar suburbanites living in Young Influentials and Furs & Station Wagons. The Escort, on the other hand, became a big seller in heartland America, among the middle-class families of Blue-Chip Blues and Blue-Collar Nursery. The customer split was a question of racquetball-playing, VCR-owning computer users vs. bowling, coupon-redeeming, gardening types. For years it's been fashionable for the young and college educated to buy imported cars. Middle-class blue-color motorists, however, stayed with cars "made in the U.S.A."

That rural-urban split among America's car buyers became evident to Steve Lashbrook, pastor of the Congregational United Church of Christ in Clarion, Iowa. In the summer of '86, he performed the wedding of a 35-year-old local woman who'd left the Agri-Business community for the brighter lights of Kansas City and a job with Universal Studios. The guest list included the woman's old and new friends, and as Lashbrook stood on the steps of the 114-year-old church, he surveyed the dichotomy of driving tastes among the wedding guests. "It wasn't so much country bumpkin versus city slicker," recalls Lashbrook, a chunky

30-year-old with thinning hair. "I found myself aware of two distinct lifestyles: those who drove Volvos, Toyotas and BMWs and the ones who came in the Buicks, Chevys and Plymouths. Two different worlds: imports and domestics." Not surprisingly, Clarion's four dealerships sell only American-made cars.

■■■■■■■■■ YOU ARE WHAT YOUR NEIGHBORS EAT

Even the cut of your bread says much about your cluster's values. In the aftermath of the natural foods insurgency of the '70s, the elite residents of Urban Gold Coast and Blue Blood Estates buy whole-wheat and rye bread and croissants at three times the national average. At supermarkets, they pick up white bread about as often as they wear polyester leisure suits. Wonder Bread, that all-American white bread hawked by Howdy Doody and wrapped in balloon-covered packages, is found predominantly in the pantries of small-town clusters like Back-Country Folks and Middle America. Compared to the wheat-bread eaters, these consumers tend to have lower incomes, eat more often at fast-food restaurants and not worry much about exercise. Appropriately, they're also among the nation's biggest purchasers of packaged luncheon meats.

Not all white-bread lovers live in the hinterlands beyond big cities, however. In a major market like Washington, D.C., a kind of Wonder Bread Line slices through the city's central Rock Creek Park, defining distinctive cluster tastes. The white-bread shoppers live to the east, in the lower-middle-class Emergent Minorities neighborhoods of the city, as well as in the middle-income Young Suburbia subdivisions of Maryland and Virginia. The whole-grain buyers hail from the Money & Brains enclaves of the city's northwest section, the Bohemian Mix areas of Old Town Alexandria, Virginia, and the more affluent Pools & Patios developments of Montgomery County, Maryland. In the whole-grain strongholds, residents also fill their carts with wild-berry frozen yogurt and orange-flavored Perrier—the quintessential portrait of the upscale gourmet.

Nationwide, the tendency to buy fancy foods is strongest among the sophisticated Money & Brains and Bohemian Mix residents, who act as if food has become fashion. Compared to average Americans, they're nearly four times more likely to subscribe to *Gourmet* and *Bon Appetit*

WHOLE WHEAT OR WHITE?

Sometimes a region's residents can be divided geographically according to their preference for a particular product. In the Washington, D.C., area, a kind of "white bread line" divides the poor, who buy white bread (blue area), from the affluent, who favor whole-wheat bread (black area).

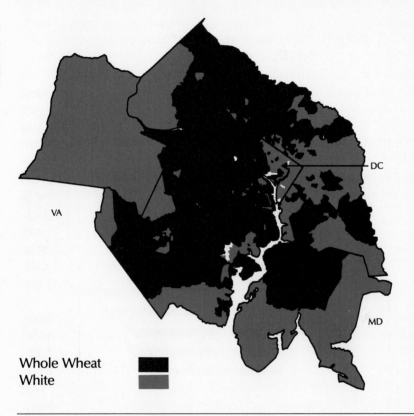

Whole Wheat
White

SOURCE: Claritas Corp., 1987.

magazines and three times more likely to shop at health-food and gourmet shops. Like car owners who trade in their vehicles every few years to stay stylish, these fickle eaters are always embracing some new cuisine or kitchen device to demonstrate culinary currency. Ethiopian food is replaced by Hunan Chinese, raw tuna by blackened redfish, crock pots by Cuisinarts. Prole Drift is carrying the cooking craze throughout America's neighborhoods: market researchers estimate that 10 percent of the nation's households now boast recreational cooks—a fivefold increase over the last decade.

In Philadelphia's Bohemian Mix neighborhood of Queen Village, entrepreneur Michael Silverberg opened Chef's Market in 1985 to cater to the locals' epicurean tastes. Lining the shelves of his 4,000-square-foot store are 160 kinds of cheese, 25 types of bread and 30 brands of mustard. For a Friday night dinner party, two young attorneys recently filled a shopping bag with Scottish salmon, Middle Eastern tabouleh, fresh Japanese shiitaki mushrooms, Greek goat cheese, Italian bread, French butter and American fresh fruit tarts—a veritable United Nations of cuisine. "We get a young urban crowd who think nothing of

CROISSANTS VS. TOASTER PASTRIES

People who buy toaster pastries like Kellogg's Pop-Tarts tend to believe they're wholesome and nutritious, a sharp contrast to the upscale, educated consumers who consider these highly processed products to be junk foods. While the Pop-Tart buyers want to belong to the masses, croissant eaters want to distinguish themselves from the masses.

Top Five Clusters: Croissants

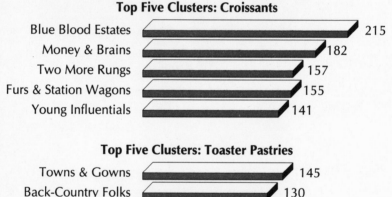

Cluster	Index
Blue Blood Estates	215
Money & Brains	182
Two More Rungs	157
Furs & Station Wagons	155
Young Influentials	141

Top Five Clusters: Toaster Pastries

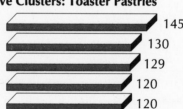

Cluster	Index
Towns & Gowns	145
Back-Country Folks	130
Rank & File	129
Blue-Collar Nursery	120
Mines & Mills	120

Numbers indicate percentages of product buyers, indexed against the national average. An index of 100 equals the U.S. average: 21.49% for croissants, 29.23% for toaster pastries. An index of 200 means a cluster has twice the national average. Source: SMRB 1985/86, Claritas Corp., 1987.

spending $100 for a gourmet meal," says Silverberg, a reedy New York transplant with a background in commercial renovation. "Many of our shoppers have traveled around the world and cultivated tastes for exotic foods. When they come back from a trip to Italy, they don't want to sit down to boring meat and potatoes."

Such worldly tastes clash with the values of many family-oriented suburban clusters like Blue-Chip Blues, where foreign travel is uncommon, chauffeuring children after school is de rigueur and food is sometimes an afterthought. "For us, dinner is whatever we can slam on the plate before the kids get restless," says Rick Packer of Coon Rapids, Minnesota, the father of two toddlers. "Sometimes it's peanut butter and jelly or a tuna salad sandwich." Cluster residents are typical of the

FROZEN BAKED ENTREES VS. FROZEN BOILED ENTREES

Price separates the upscale Lean Cuisine baked-salmon fan from the middle-class Banquet creamed-chipped-beef buyer. Other factors are work and children: the baked entrees appeal mostly to white-collar and childless singles and couples, who tend to buy newer, trendier foods.

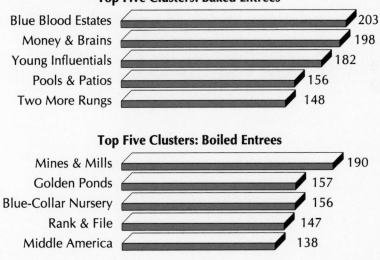

Top Five Clusters: Baked Entrees

Cluster	Index
Blue Blood Estates	203
Money & Brains	198
Young Influentials	182
Pools & Patios	156
Two More Rungs	148

Top Five Clusters: Boiled Entrees

Cluster	Index
Mines & Mills	190
Golden Ponds	157
Blue-Collar Nursery	156
Rank & File	147
Middle America	138

Numbers indicate percentages of product buyers, indexed against the national average. An index of 100 equals the U.S. average: 12.15% for baked entrees, 6.95% for boiled entrees. An index of 200 means a cluster has twice the national average. Source: SMRB 1985/86, Claritas Corp., 1987.

one in ten Americans who each day buy take-out food—mostly of the burgers-and-fries variety. Little wonder that Blue-Chip Blues families have one of the nation's highest rates for patronizing fast-food restaurants. "We don't like to go to restaurants where you have to wear a coat and tie, where the waitresses introduce themselves and dinner costs $20 a person," Packer explains. "That's not us."

More than what we eat, what we drink reflects the sharp distinctions among cluster tastes. Urban Gold Coast residents are the most prominent purchasers of imported wines, at four times the national average. Beer drinkers can be found in most clusters, though "light" beer drinkers tend to come from the ranks of health-conscious Young Influentials,

DIETERS

More than one in three Americans are dieting at any one time, the highest concentrations found in a mix of upscale metro areas and outlying boomtowns. The fewest dieters live in communities of poor immigrants and minorities, where basic nutrition is of more concern.

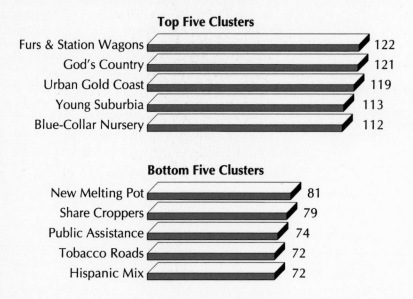

Top Five Clusters

Furs & Station Wagons	122
God's Country	121
Urban Gold Coast	119
Young Suburbia	113
Blue-Collar Nursery	112

Bottom Five Clusters

New Melting Pot	81
Share Croppers	79
Public Assistance	74
Tobacco Roads	72
Hispanic Mix	72

Numbers indicate percentages of household members on a diet, indexed against the national average. An index of 100 equals the U.S. average: 36.5%. An index of 122 means a cluster has 1.22 times the national average, or about 45%. Source: SMRB 1984/85, Claritas Corp., 1987.

a cluster that also consumes natural spring and mineral water at high rates. And when it comes to pop and party wines, the nation's heaviest consumers come from two distinct lifestyle types: middle-class blacks who live in Black Enterprise and Emergent Minorities communities and the students and recent graduates who live in the campus communities of Towns & Gowns and the downtowns of Bohemian Mix. Social observer Paul Fussell has developed a formula for determining one's class standing: "If the locution 'a Seven and Seven' is strange to you, if your nose wrinkles a bit at the idea of drinking a shot of Seagram's Seven Crown mixed with Seven-Up, you are safely at or near the top, or at least

CENTS-OFF COUPONS

Coupon clippers transcend geography and social status, from America's childless suburban couples to its smalltown families. Those who don't clip range from downscale rural consumers, whose local papers rarely contain coupons, to ritzy Urban Gold Coasters, who buy ready-to-eat foods from delis and greengrocers for which coupons simply don't exist.

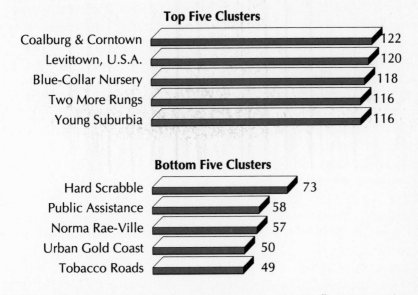

Top Five Clusters

Coalburg & Corntown	122
Levittown, U.S.A.	120
Blue-Collar Nursery	118
Two More Rungs	116
Young Suburbia	116

Bottom Five Clusters

Hard Scrabble	73
Public Assistance	58
Norma Rae-Ville	57
Urban Gold Coast	50
Tobacco Roads	49

Numbers indicate percentages of households that use cents-off coupons, indexed against the national average. An index of 100 equals the U.S. average: 63.7%. An index of 122 means a cluster has 1.22 times the national average, or about 78%. Source: SMRB 1983/84, Claritas Corp., 1987.

not deeply compromised by the sugar fixation at the bottom. To a startling degree, prole America is about sweet."

■■■■■■■■■■ MEDIA MORES

Since 1975, advertising researchers have divided most Americans into two broad groups: those visually oriented consumers who receive their information through the printed word of magazines and newspapers, and those consumers with an aural bent who tune into television and radio to keep abreast of the news. Readers and viewers. The split is sharpest along the extremes of the ZQ index. Residents in Money & Brains, for instance, are heavy readers and light viewers. They subscribe to periodicals like *The New Yorker, Atlantic Monthly* and *Barron's* at many times the national average and only occasionally turn on the TV, and then usually to the Public Broadcasting Service. In many such homes, the TV is even hidden away in an oak bookcase or tinted glass "wall system."

Twenty-eight rungs down the ZQ ladder, the residents of Back-Country Folks are light readers and heavy viewers. They watch prime-time TV shows like "Dallas" and "Knots Landing" at above-average rates and have a low index for subscribing to magazines. The magazines they do read tend to be related to leisure rather than intellectual pursuits, such as *Popular Hot Rodding* and *Field & Stream.* If they want intellectual stimulation, as one resident of Spring Hill, Tennessee, explained, they'll turn on "Jeopardy" or "Wheel of Fortune."

This distinction in how Americans use the media—and what they choose to watch and read—speaks volumes about how they live when they're not engrossed in their magazines or TV shows. Readers of *The Dial* (now defunct), a monthly once distributed to public television contributors, were known by demographic studies to be college educated and have incomes over $50,000. On the cluster map, 75 percent of those readers lived in the top four neighborhood types, and their statistics zoomed off the charts when it came to sophisticated purchases. Though they represented only 15 percent of all adults, they held 57 percent of the travel-and-entertainment cards, took 63 percent of all trips to Europe and Israel and 53 percent of all international cruises. They comprised nearly half of America's stockholders, bought over three-fifths of all European luxury cars and consumed more fifths of Scotch whisky than all other clusters combined. They were the core of what sociologist C. Wright Mills dubbed The Power Elite.

GIRLIE MAGS

While readers of both magazines are overwhelmingly urban males, *Penthouse* has more working-class readers and a higher percentage of minorities compared to *Playboy*'s better-educated, white-collar buyers.

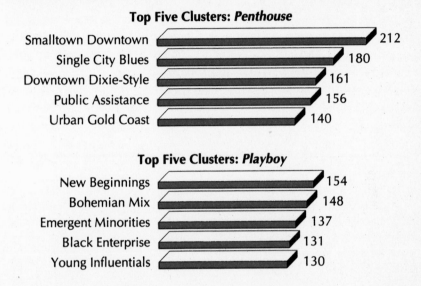

Top Five Clusters: *Penthouse*

Cluster	Index
Smalltown Downtown	212
Single City Blues	180
Downtown Dixie-Style	161
Public Assistance	156
Urban Gold Coast	140

Top Five Clusters: *Playboy*

Cluster	Index
New Beginnings	154
Bohemian Mix	148
Emergent Minorities	137
Black Enterprise	131
Young Influentials	130

Numbers indicate percentages of households subscribing to each magazine, indexed against the national average. An index of 100 equals the U.S. average: 3.05% for *Penthouse*, 7.04% for *Playboy*. An index of 200 means a cluster has twice the national average. Source: SMRB 1984/85, Claritas Corp., 1987.

With the explosion of special-interest magazines, it's possible to see how even similarly focused publications reach different kinds of people. While the readers of *Playboy* and *Penthouse* have similar demographics —single men, 18 to 34 years old—the cluster system shows that not all men's magazines are alike and neither are their subscribers. The heaviest concentration of *Playboy* readers resides in clusters like New Beginnings, Bohemian Mix and Black Enterprise, mostly upscale urban areas with a high percentage of college-educated singles and couples pursuing cosmopolitan lifestyles. By comparison, the chief fans of *Penthouse* live in neighborhood types like Single City Blues, Downtown Dixie-Style and Smalltown Downtown, typically characterized by working-class districts in small cities, with less education, less affluence and a higher minority concentration than *Playboy*'s audience. "The urban elite drop off the map," says political analyst Charles Welsh, who recently conducted a cluster analysis of magazine readers. "It seems that the more Middle American the reader, the more they buy a men's magazine for the pictures and not the words."

Not all publications appeal to only a handful of neighborhood types. *Reader's Digest,* one of the nation's most popular magazines, with a circulation of 16 million copies every month, penetrates at least 20 percent of every community type in the nation. Although the heaviest concentration of subscribers is in rural, small-town clusters like Shotguns & Pickups, Grain Belt and Agri-Business, the magazine's flat readership profile runs contrary to the image of *Digest* readers as "little old ladies in tennis shoes sitting on their porch rocking chairs," in the words

---

WOMEN'S MAGAZINES

As with their male counterparts, not all women's magazines are alike—nor are their readers. While both *Redbook* and *Cosmopolitan* are targeted to the same age group—18- to 34-year-olds—they have very different readerships. *Redbook*'s readers are mostly middle-class, high school-educated homemakers in small towns, while *Cosmo* women tend to be urban, white-collar and college educated.

Top Five Clusters: *Redbook*

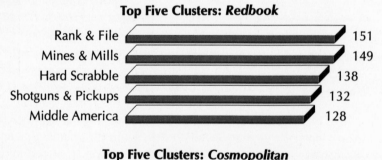

Rank & File	151
Mines & Mills	149
Hard Scrabble	138
Shotguns & Pickups	132
Middle America	128

Top Five Clusters: *Cosmopolitan*

Young Influentials	162
Bohemian Mix	158
Urban Gold Coast	152
Two More Rungs	147
Blue Blood Estates	141

Numbers indicate percentages of households subscribing to each magazine, indexed against the national average. An index of 100 equals the U.S. average: 5.72% for *Redbook,* 6.15% for *Cosmopolitan.* An index of 200 means a cluster has twice the national average. Source: SMRB 1984/85, Claritas Corp., 1987.

of Paula Byrne, the magazine's sales development director. "We know that our subscribers are also the guys working on an oil pipeline in Shotguns & Pickups or the newly married couples in Young Suburbia." Compared to the national average, *Reader's Digest* subscribers are married with children, of Northern European ancestry, high-school educated, earn a $28,988 median income and live in single-family homes. As consumers, they're the people who buy "an awful lot of bread and peanut butter, Cheerios and domestic cars," notes Byrne, "products typically appealing to a heartland audience."

But the large percentage of *Digest* readers in all the clusters makes the publication alluring to merchandisers of upscale, high-tech products. When Columbia Record and Tape Club decided to launch a Compact Disc Club, consumer surveys showed that CD players were owned by less than 1 percent of the U.S. population—mostly in large metropolitan areas. But Columbia bought ad space in *Reader's Digest*'s regional editions to San Francisco, Dallas and Denver because of the magazine's hefty circulation throughout those cities—about a quarter of all households. Among those readers are tomorrow's CD audiophiles.

Like magazines, television has evolved from mass-audience appeal into a specialized medium reaching audiences as different as David Letterman is from Punky Brewster. Letterman, for example, plays well to the metropolitan sophisticates of Urban Gold Coast and Bohemian Mix, runs neck-and-neck with Johnny Carson in the outlying suburbs of Furs & Station Wagons and Two More Rungs, but comes in dead last among the elderly traditionalists in Golden Ponds. Perky Punky Brewster, with her modern-day Orphan Annie exploits, has always fared better in the rural downscale clusters of Hard Scrabble and Tobacco Roads. In these isolated settlements without the big city newspapers and movie theaters that provide fodder for Letterman's monologues and guest lists, viewers don't need to be "with it" to enjoy an 8-year-old's heartwarming adventures.

Many Americans favor TV programs whose characters reflect their neighborhood's values and demographic profile. For instance, in 1985 the yuppie viewers of Young Influentials gave the yuppie doctors of "St. Elsewhere" their top rating, while the predominantly black Emergent Minorities cluster reported that "Benson," "Gimme a Break" and "Webster"—all featuring black leads—were their favorite shows. Prime time's long-lived number-one program, "The Cosby Show," crossed color and socioeconomic boundaries and, with 41 percent of America's TV sets tuned in, had a large number of viewers in every cluster.

WHO WATCHES TV

The heaviest commercial-TV viewers, who keep their sets on for an average of 35 hours a week, live in predominantly black neighborhoods. Among their top programs during the 1985 season: "Knots Landing," "Cagney & Lacey," "Facts of Life," "Miami Vice," and "Friday Night Videos." In contrast, upscale people are more selective in how they spend their leisure time; these are the nation's book and magazine readers. When they do turn on the tube, they tune in to public TV.

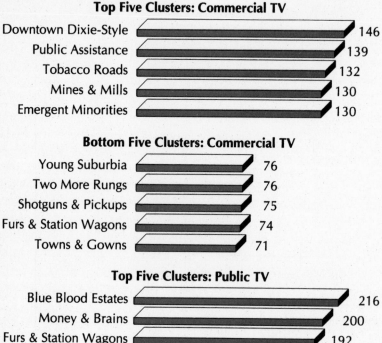

Top Five Clusters: Commercial TV

Cluster	Index
Downtown Dixie-Style	146
Public Assistance	139
Tobacco Roads	132
Mines & Mills	130
Emergent Minorities	130

Bottom Five Clusters: Commercial TV

Cluster	Index
Young Suburbia	76
Two More Rungs	76
Shotguns & Pickups	75
Furs & Station Wagons	74
Towns & Gowns	71

Top Five Clusters: Public TV

Cluster	Index
Blue Blood Estates	216
Money & Brains	200
Furs & Station Wagons	192
Two More Rungs	181
Pools & Patios	168

Bottom Five Clusters: Public TV

Cluster	Index
Back-Country Folks	50
Hispanic Mix	45
Tobacco Roads	34
Share Croppers	31
Hard Scrabble	23

Numbers indicate percentages of households in the top 20 percent of total TV viewing and the top 20 percent contributing to public TV stations, indexed against the national average. An index of 200 means a cluster has twice the national average of heavy viewers or subscribers. Source: SMRB 1985/86, Claritas Corp., 1987.

An audience's sensibility also determine the direction the TV dial is flipped. The young townies of New Homesteaders watch the mellow detective work of Angela Lansbury in "Murder, She Wrote" 25 percent more often than the violent pursuits of undercover cop Don Johnson in "Miami Vice." That show's insistent rock beat and nouveau visual flair appeal to an assortment of city clusters, the highest concentration of viewers living in the neighborhoods of Black Enterprise, Single City Blues and Hispanic Mix, where the show's drug- and crime-filled storylines hit close to home.

Still, we can't always be labeled by what we watch. The biggest fans of soap operas, whether daytime brands like "As the World Turns" and "Santa Barbara" or nighttime variations like "Falcon Crest" and "Dallas," tend to live in downscale rural and town clusters such as Norma Rae-Ville and Downtown Dixie-Style. There, downtrodden residents are drawn to the high melodrama, the exotic fashions and the risqué relationships for a brief peek at how the higher classes supposedly play. Among the perennial favorites of suburban sophisticates in Money & Brains are detective adventure shows like "Cagney & Lacey," "Murder, She Wrote" and "Magnum, P.I." Given their white-collar, workaholic schedules, an escapist romp in Hawaii with Tom Selleck may be just what the analyst ordered.

America's TV-news junkies can be found in a variety of clusters, mostly tied to the education levels of neighborhood residents. But a prime-time "info-tainment" show like "Donahue" draws high ratings even among the downscale working-class residents of Heavy Industry and Hispanic Mix. And the heaviest viewers of "Good Morning America" live in Gray Power and Towns & Gowns communities, places where educated retirees and college students needn't rush off to early morning jobs. Few TV programs are watched at above-average rates among the reading class of Blue Blood Estates. Two exceptions, "60 Minutes" and "20/20," supplement the information gleaned from *The New York Times* and *The Wall Street Journal,* which Blue Blood Estates residents read at the highest rates in the nation.

When it comes to armchair sports fans, there is an undeniable link between the games watched and the lifestyles of their fans. Towns & Gowns residents are the biggest TV viewers of college basketball, doubtless because of their proximity—in age and distance—to their campus teams. Yet the top cluster for watching college football is Tobacco Roads, whose rural black residents live a great distance from the professional sports stadiums of urban centers. They consider college teams like the Arkansas Razorbacks and the Michigan Wolverines their

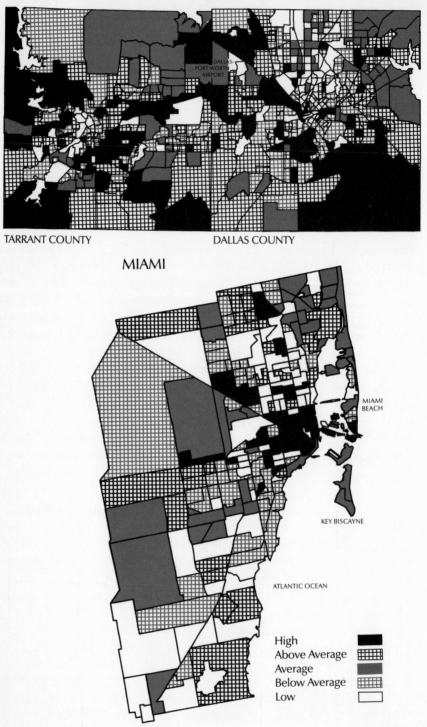

DALLAS

TARRANT COUNTY

DALLAS COUNTY

DALLAS-FORT WORTH AIRPORT

MIAMI

MIAMI BEACH

KEY BISCAYNE

ATLANTIC OCEAN

High

Above Average

Average

Below Average

Low

WHO WATCHES "DALLAS" IN DALLAS; WHO WATCHES "MIAMI VICE" IN MIAMI

In Dallas, J.R.'s biggest fans are nothing like the TV Ewings. They are mostly downscale minorities and farmers drawn to the high melodrama of the oily rich. In Miami, the highest concentration of Crocker and Tubbs viewers are the black and poor for whom, all too often, the story line hits too close to home. The city's elderly residents, in contrast, want no part of "Miami Vice"; too violent.

Dallas		Miami	
Most		**Most**	
Tobacco Roads	165	Public Assistance	130
Emergent Minorities	131	Tobacco Roads	127
Golden Ponds	129	Emergent Minorities	126
Grain Belt	122	Black Enterprise	125
Norma Rae-Ville	117	Golden Ponds	116
Least		**Least**	
Two More Rungs	83	Norma Rae-Ville	89
Young Suburbia	83	Shotguns & Pickups	86
Blue Blood Estates	79	Gray Power	86
Towns & Gowns	75	Agri-Business	76
Bohemian Mix	72	Grain Belt	55

Numbers indicate percentages of households viewing each show, indexed against the national average. An index of 100 equals the U.S. average: 23% for "Dallas," 17.25% for "Miami Vice." An index of 200 means a cluster has twice the national average. Source: SMRB 1985/86, Claritas Corp., 1987.

own. Professional baseball, mostly played in the stadiums of major-league cities, finds its highest concentration of viewers among the metropolitan clusters of Urban Gold Coast, Old Yankee Rows and Black Enterprise. As for professional basketball, the heaviest concentration of fans is found in the urban clusters of Black Enterprise, Emergent Minorities and Public Assistance. These three neighborhood types reflect a range of community affluence, but they share one feature: like the majority of the players, their hard-core TV fans are black.

LEISURE AND TRAVEL

In the great American rat race, true leisure for many wage earners is frequently a fiction. Though the 40-hour workweek has been pro-

A.M. TV

While both "Good Morning America" and "Today" are watched by approximately one in ten U.S. households, the longer-running "Today" show has more of a downscale, rural- and town-based audience. GMA's appeal is found in upscale suburbs as well.

Top Five Clusters: "Good Morning America"

Cluster	Index
Gray Power	194
Towns & Gowns	142
New Melting Pot	141
New Homesteaders	134
God's Country	131

Bottom Five Clusters: "Good Morning America"

Cluster	Index
Rank & File	74
Levittown, U.S.A.	70
Bohemian Mix	62
Urban Gold Coast	58
Hard Scrabble	56

Top Five Clusters: "Today"

Cluster	Index
Share Croppers	154
Smalltown Downtown	143
Golden Ponds	141
Coalburg & Corntown	139
Hard Scrabble	138

Bottom Five Clusters: "Today"

Cluster	Index
Urban Gold Coast	68
Hispanic Mix	64
New Melting Pot	64
Young Influentials	57
Grain Belt	56

Numbers indicate percentages of households viewing each show, indexed against the national average. An index of 100 equals the U.S. average: 9.2% for "Good Morning America," 10.94% for "Today." An index of 200 means a cluster has twice the national average. Source: SMRB 1985/86, Claritas Corp., 1987.

HOOPSTERS: PRO VS. COLLEGE FANS

Fans of professional basketball are concentrated in predominantly black urban and upscale white suburban areas. College ball fans also are found in affluent suburbs, indicating a high percentage of well-off alumni rooting for their alma maters.

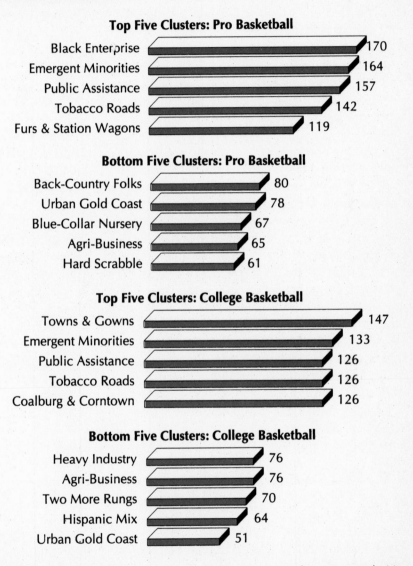

Top Five Clusters: Pro Basketball

Cluster	Index
Black Enterprise	170
Emergent Minorities	164
Public Assistance	157
Tobacco Roads	142
Furs & Station Wagons	119

Bottom Five Clusters: Pro Basketball

Cluster	Index
Back-Country Folks	80
Urban Gold Coast	78
Blue-Collar Nursery	67
Agri-Business	65
Hard Scrabble	61

Top Five Clusters: College Basketball

Cluster	Index
Towns & Gowns	147
Emergent Minorities	133
Public Assistance	126
Tobacco Roads	126
Coalburg & Corntown	126

Bottom Five Clusters: College Basketball

Cluster	Index
Heavy Industry	76
Agri-Business	76
Two More Rungs	70
Hispanic Mix	64
Urban Gold Coast	51

Numbers indicate percentages of households viewing each sport on television, indexed against the national average. An index of 100 equals the U.S. average: 10.73% for professional basketball, 10.77% for college basketball. An index of 200 means a cluster has twice the national average. Source: SMRB 1985/86, Claritas Corp., 1987.

tected by federal law since the '30s, pollster Lou Harris found that the average workweek in 1985 totalled nearly 49 hours, while the amount of leisure time afforded Americans has dropped by a third in the last dozen years to 17 hours weekly. Thus people must now consider carefully how to commit their scarce hours away from work—whether they bowl or play tennis, whether they collect guns or Chinese artifacts. And their decision says much about their community's values regarding time and how it should be spent.

The premium that Urban Gold Coast residents place on contemporary culture, for instance, can be seen in their buying twice as many books and movie tickets as the general population. The hard-driving residents of Young Influentials play squash at twice the national norm, partly because that sport takes less time than, say, baseball or golf. In more impoverished Public Assistance communities, entertainment tends to revolve around the home as residents buy dance records at three times the U.S. average. The super-rich leave Disney World to the Blue Collar Nursery crowd, preferring the slopes of St. Moritz and the steeplechase at Kensington-on-Stafford. As critic Paul Fussell states, high-class sports tend to be any that are "expensive, inconvenient and practiced only in distant places."

One virtue of blue-collar life is the clear line separating free time and work. In the professional world of Towns & Gowns, with its education-bound work force, college professors work around the clock at teaching and research positions, grabbing recreational moments on a catch-as-catch-can basis. Dave Passmore, a special-education professor at Penn State University in State College, Pennsylvania, describes his workday as 6 A.M. to 6 P.M., with 2 hours in the afternoon for jogging, racquetball or jumping rope. "You'll find faculty members in the rec hall at any time between 4 A.M. and midnight," says Passmore, a bearded 39-year-old who favors corduroy jackets with turtlenecks.

In contrast, workers in the Coalburg & Corntown community of Columbia City, Indiana, leave their jobs behind once the factory whistle blows. At the Little League field, as many as 1,500 townspeople play or watch baseball every summer night. "There are about eight different leagues, maybe sixty teams and people playing from 6 years old on up," says Duane Schuman, sports editor of the Columbia City Post & Mail. "The city's had to widen the parking lot just to accommodate all the players and parents who come to watch." In the winter, residents turn to bowling with the same relentless energy, their scores spilling onto

THE WAY WE PLAY: BOWLING

Attractive to neither the rich nor the poor, bowling finds its fans among blue-collar Americans. Rural people simply don't have access to lanes; neither do many city dwellers, where costly downtown land makes spacious bowling alleys unprofitable. Bowling's biggest fans live in middle-class, small-town America.

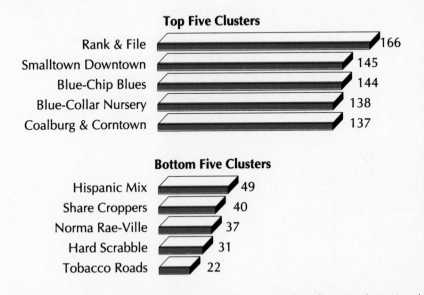

Top Five Clusters

Rank & File	166
Smalltown Downtown	145
Blue-Chip Blues	144
Blue-Collar Nursery	138
Coalburg & Corntown	137

Bottom Five Clusters

Hispanic Mix	49
Share Croppers	40
Norma Rae-Ville	37
Hard Scrabble	31
Tobacco Roads	22

Numbers indicate percentages of individuals who bowl, indexed against the national average. An index of 100 equals the U.S. average: 14%. An index of 166 means a cluster has 1.6 times the national average, or about 22%. Source: SMRB 1985/86, Claritas Corp., 1987.

the sports pages. When the sports editor of a neighboring Coalburg & Corntown community, Warsaw, suggested limiting coverage to only high-scoring 240+ games, townspeople threatened to boycott the paper. "He went back to reporting every score," smiles Schuman, a fresh-faced recent graduate from Purdue. "It takes him most of an afternoon just to type up all the numbers."

Of course, many leisure activities are popular in more than one cluster; the boom in camping illustrates how one pastime can be integrated into several different lifestyles. Surveys of God's Country communities show these back-to-the-land residents to be strong consumers of L. L. Bean fare like nylon tents and down sleeping bags, for rustic

THE WAY WE PLAY: RACQUETBALL

One reason for racquetball's rapid rise in popularity is that courts can fit into new health club complexes and downtown office buildings. Racquetball players are overwhelmingly urban, white-collar and upscale; court time, after all, isn't cheap.

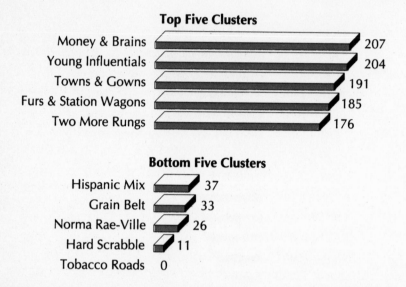

Top Five Clusters

Cluster	Index
Money & Brains	207
Young Influentials	204
Towns & Gowns	191
Furs & Station Wagons	185
Two More Rungs	176

Bottom Five Clusters

Cluster	Index
Hispanic Mix	37
Grain Belt	33
Norma Rae-Ville	26
Hard Scrabble	11
Tobacco Roads	0

Numbers indicate percentages of individuals who play racquetball, indexed against the national average. An index of 100 equals the U.S. average: 5.1%. An index of 207 means a cluster has 2.07 times the national average, or about 11%. Source: SMRB 1985/86, Claritas Corp., 1987.

weekend hikes through the mountains. The downscale residents of Back-Country Folks, however, approach their camping trips with a different style. As shown by consumer surveys, their idea of roughing it is to haul a sleeps-six camper to an overnight trailer park and hook it up to the water and sewer facilities. Some of their chosen campgrounds are more luxurious than their homes.

From yachting to creek-fishing, water attracts all cluster types. The small-town ranchers from Shotguns & Pickups and Agri-Business go fresh-water fishing at rates 40 percent above the national average, no doubt to serve the catch of the day at dinner. Meanwhile, the well-to-do of Blue Blood Estates and Urban Gold Coast enjoy sailing at twice the national average, for the fresh air and sporting challenge as well as the thrill that comes with financial extravagance. Sailing, according to *Preppy*

THE WAY WE PLAY: FRESH-WATER FISHING

Unlike salt-water anglers, who tend to live in big coastal cities, those who fish in rivers, lakes and streams generally live in nearby small towns, much in the spirit of Tom Sawyer. While fresh-water fish tend to end up on dinner tables, salt-water fish tend to end up on walls.

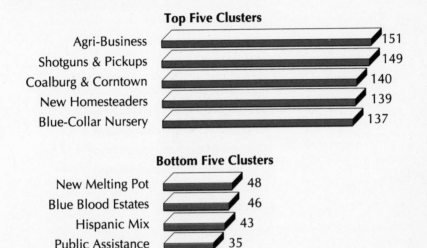

Top Five Clusters

Agri-Business	151
Shotguns & Pickups	149
Coalburg & Corntown	140
New Homesteaders	139
Blue-Collar Nursery	137

Bottom Five Clusters

New Melting Pot	48
Blue Blood Estates	46
Hispanic Mix	43
Public Assistance	35
Urban Gold Coast	17

Numbers indicate percentages of individuals who fresh-water fish, indexed against the national average. An index of 100 equals the U.S. average: 17.8%. An index of 151 means a cluster has 1.51 times the national average, or about 27%. Source: SMRB 1985/86, Claritas Corp., 1987.

Handbook's Lisa Birnbach, is like "standing in a cold shower tearing up $100 bills."

■■■ GAMBLING AND FINANCIAL MANAGEMENT

When it comes to the use of financial services, the higher a cluster's level of affluence, the longer its residents are prepared to wait for gratification. Thus, the super-rich of Blue Blood Estates invest in long-term stocks and real estate partnerships that may not yield a return for years. In contrast, the poorer residents of Single City Blues spend their money on lottery tickets that offer instant gratification—if they win.

THE WAY WE PLAY: CAMPING

Camping brings out a sort of reversal of class consciousness. The more upscale residents of God's Country, for example, face the elements with the bare necessities: a nylon tent, a down sleeping bag, a few pots and pans. The idea of "roughing it" for the more downscale residents of Shotguns & Pickups, in contrast, is to haul a camper to an overnight trailer park. Those least inclined to go camping are poor folk for whom life is already rough enough.

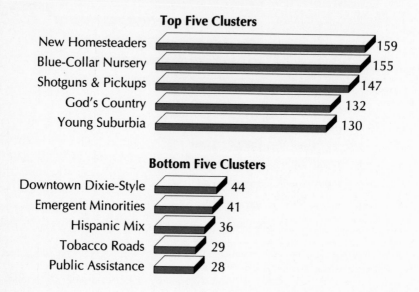

Top Five Clusters

New Homesteaders	159
Blue-Collar Nursery	155
Shotguns & Pickups	147
God's Country	132
Young Suburbia	130

Bottom Five Clusters

Downtown Dixie-Style	44
Emergent Minorities	41
Hispanic Mix	36
Tobacco Roads	29
Public Assistance	28

Numbers indicate percentages of individuals who camp, indexed against the national average. An index of 100 equals the U.S. average: 5.29%. An index of 159 means a cluster has 1.59 times the national average, or about 8%. Source: SMRB 1985/86, Claritas Corp., 1987.

Both are gamblers, with different rates—and waits—of return. When a Single-City Blues resident of Takoma Park, Maryland, was asked why he bought state lottery tickets every day, his answer said it all: "To get out of the rut."

Gambling is an American tradition: lottery revenues supported the Revolutionary War and helped build Harvard, Yale and Princeton. But they do not have universal cluster appeal. When the Massachusetts State Lottery decided to learn more about the best customers for its rub-off, instant ticket game, cluster profiles found that households in Blue-Collar Nursery had the highest concentration of players—57 per-

HOW WE TRAVEL: CRUISE SHIP

Cruising is big among a hodgepodge of passengers—from yuppies to retirees. But it's distinctly unpopular among poor, rural clusters where travel on water means only small powerboats.

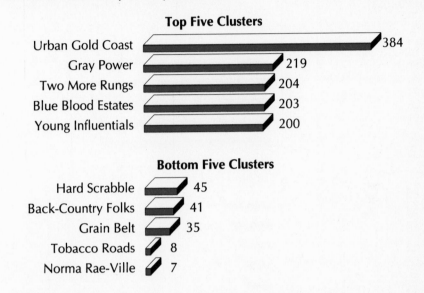

Top Five Clusters

Cluster	Index
Urban Gold Coast	384
Gray Power	219
Two More Rungs	204
Blue Blood Estates	203
Young Influentials	200

Bottom Five Clusters

Cluster	Index
Hard Scrabble	45
Back-Country Folks	41
Grain Belt	35
Tobacco Roads	8
Norma Rae-Ville	7

Numbers indicate percentages of residents who travel by cruise ship, indexed against the national average. An index of 100 equals the U.S. average: 3%. An index of 384 means a cluster has 3.84 times the national average, or about 12%. Source: SMRB 1985/86, Claritas Corp., 1987.

cent above the state's average. Not coincidentally, that same cluster also had the highest rate of winners: 2.35 percent. The worst lottery customers were the residents of Blue Blood Estates, with a market penetration 75 percent below the state average. (Nationally, because of their concentration in many lottery-free states, Blue-Collar Nursery residents rarely score high on lottery surveys.) For middle-class Americans, the appeal of the lottery ticket is that it's gambling camouflaged as a sporting activity. When you look at the ghettos of Public Assistance, people like to play the numbers—legally or illegally—because it's raw action, no disguises to it. It's just a roll of the dice.

Bingo operates on the same principle as the lottery ticket, a sporting gamble that proves to be popular in middle-class clusters like Blue-Chip Blues, Middle America and Coalburg & Corntown. In the Coalburg &

HOW WE TRAVEL: SCHEDULED AIRLINE

America's airline passengers tend to live in urban areas near major airports, have above-average incomes and travel mostly for business. The down-scale, rural residents of clusters like Hard Scrabble and Norma Rae-Ville rarely get off the ground.

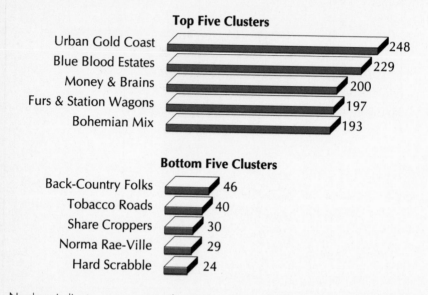

Top Five Clusters

Urban Gold Coast	248
Blue Blood Estates	229
Money & Brains	200
Furs & Station Wagons	197
Bohemian Mix	193

Bottom Five Clusters

Back-Country Folks	46
Tobacco Roads	40
Share Croppers	30
Norma Rae-Ville	29
Hard Scrabble	24

Numbers indicate percentages of residents who travel by scheduled airline, indexed against the national average. An index of 100 equals the U.S. average: 14%. An index of 248 means a cluster has 2.48 times the national average, or about 35%. Source: SMRB 1985/86, Claritas Corp., 1987.

Corntown community of Columbia City, Indiana, nearly 20 percent of the entire town's populace belongs to the American Legion—and one of the major reasons is bingo. Bingo games take place every night of the week, sponsored by local fraternal organizations like the Elks, Moose Lodge, American Legion and Veterans of Foreign Wars. In a community without nightclubs, dance halls and movie theaters, bingo offers a chance to socialize with friends, not to mention the possibility of a quick return on a small investment—25 cents a card, split the pot with the house.

No matter how low the stakes, not everyone enjoys gambling with their money. Gray Power, home to the richest senior citizens, is ranked thirteenth in terms of social status but ranks third in the purchase of investments—often fiscally conservative investments. Rather than stocks, Gray Power residents are prime consumers of low-risk, high-

HOW WE TRAVEL: BUS

The young residents of Urban Gold Coast take buses because they don't own cars. For the impoverished of Public Assistance, it is the only way to get around. Farmers of Tobacco Roads and Share Croppers don't ride because their towns can't support regular service.

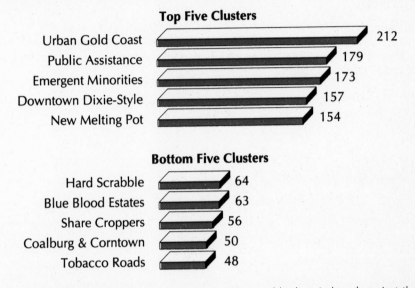

Top Five Clusters

Urban Gold Coast	212
Public Assistance	179
Emergent Minorities	173
Downtown Dixie-Style	157
New Melting Pot	154

Bottom Five Clusters

Hard Scrabble	64
Blue Blood Estates	63
Share Croppers	56
Coalburg & Corntown	50
Tobacco Roads	48

Numbers indicate percentages of residents who travel by bus, indexed against the national average. An index of 100 equals the U.S. average: 4%. An index of 212 means a cluster has 2.12 times the national average, or about 8%. Source: SMRB 1985/86, Claritas Corp., 1987.

yield investment alternatives such as Certificates of Deposit and money-market funds. They don't want to risk their retirement nest eggs on long shots, and they aren't interested in growth equity; they want a high return on a fixed amount of investment.

In contrast, the Blue Blood Estates and Money & Brains residents are heavily involved with brokerage services and investment planners. Of the corporate stock that's in private hands, 60 percent is owned by 1 percent of the people—about three-quarters of whom live in Blue Blood Estates, Money & Brains and Urban Gold Coast. Slightly younger residents who live in Young Influentials and Bohemian Mix areas are more prone to invest in funds that spread risk over a wide variety of stocks. Busy with their careers as they are, they give someone else free rein to make money with their money. Moving upscale into Two More

HOW WE TRAVEL: RAILROAD

Trains bridge the socioeconomic gap more because of geography than affluence. Blue Blood Estates, Public Assistance and others in the Northeast use the vast network of rail lines, but trains rarely stop anymore in America's isolated farm regions.

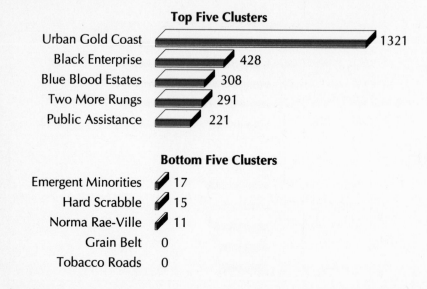

Top Five Clusters

Cluster	
Urban Gold Coast	1321
Black Enterprise	428
Blue Blood Estates	308
Two More Rungs	291
Public Assistance	221

Bottom Five Clusters

Cluster	
Emergent Minorities	17
Hard Scrabble	15
Norma Rae-Ville	11
Grain Belt	0
Tobacco Roads	0

Numbers indicate percentages of residents who travel by train, indexed against the national average. An index of 100 equals the U.S. average: 1%. An index of 1321 means a cluster has 13.21 times the national average, or about 13%. Source: SMRB 1985/86, Claritas Corp., 1987.

Rungs and Pools & Patios, many residents have their money tied up in mortgages—house-rich, cash-poor. They traditionally represent the supporters of any politician offering a tax break.

The clusters with young, child-rearing families like Blue-Chip Blues and Young Suburbia have little cash available after basic needs have been met. Perhaps as a function of their educational background and approach to long-term goals, the high-school-educated residents of Blue-Chip Blues often spend discretionary money on boats and campers while those in college-educated Young Suburbia are more prone to establish college funds for their children. For downscale rural and urban clusters, putting children through college isn't a concern, because after high school, teens are more likely to go into the army or land a blue-collar job.

MONEY MATTERS: LOTTERY TICKETS VS. BROKERAGE ACCOUNTS

Americans don't like to take risks with their money. But when they do, the wealthier investors are willing to wait—for a while, at least—before cashing in. More middle-class, blue-collar types are drawn to the quick pay-off of lottery tickets.

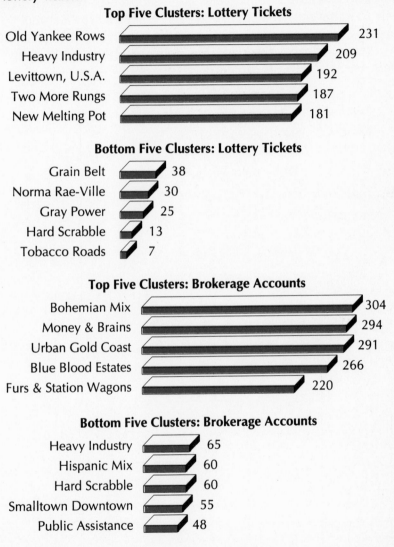

Top Five Clusters: Lottery Tickets

Cluster	Index
Old Yankee Rows	231
Heavy Industry	209
Levittown, U.S.A.	192
Two More Rungs	187
New Melting Pot	181

Bottom Five Clusters: Lottery Tickets

Cluster	Index
Grain Belt	38
Norma Rae-Ville	30
Gray Power	25
Hard Scrabble	13
Tobacco Roads	7

Top Five Clusters: Brokerage Accounts

Cluster	Index
Bohemian Mix	304
Money & Brains	294
Urban Gold Coast	291
Blue Blood Estates	266
Furs & Station Wagons	220

Bottom Five Clusters: Brokerage Accounts

Cluster	Index
Heavy Industry	65
Hispanic Mix	60
Hard Scrabble	60
Smalltown Downtown	55
Public Assistance	48

Numbers indicate percentages of residents who buy lottery tickets at least once a week or who have brokerage accounts, indexed against the national average. An index of 100 equals the U.S. average: 5.4% for lottery tickets, 6.4% for brokerage accounts. An index of 200 means a cluster has twice the national average. Source: SMRB 1985/86, Claritas Corp., 1987.

The influence of neighborhood settlement comes full circle when these young men and women establish their own households and adopt the same behaviors—from leisure to money management—that governed their parents' lives. But should any of the five major geodemographic factors change for these people—should they move to a big city or climb up several notches in social rank—they'd discover a whole new world of consumer goods and leisure activities. And they'd wonder how they ever got along without sun-dried tomatoes, turbo-power compacts or jet skis.

■ Who Drinks Tab?

In the winter of 1982, a handful of research and marketing specialists wandered the halls of Coca-Cola's Atlanta headquarters, pondering the future of Tab. The executives were about to launch a $50 million campaign for a new low-cal soda that people would drink "just for the taste of it." But they feared market self-cannibalization. Coca-Cola already boasted the top diet cola in the nation with Tab. And company executives worried that the emergence of a new diet soft drink would come at the expense of that one-crazy-calorie concoction. In 1982, Tab possessed 4.1 percent of the $21 billion soft-drink market, a slim 0.3 percent lead over its closest competitor, Diet Pepsi. Says Pat Garner, a Coca-Cola marketing executive who worked on the ultra-secret project team, "We didn't want to wreck a huge and extremely profitable business."

Still, launching a new low-cal cola, to be called Diet Coke, wasn't a hastily planned move. At a time when an increasing number of fitness buffs were drinking both sweet and sugar-free beverages, Coca-Cola chose to abandon its skinny-at-all-costs diet theme and stress cola taste and the Coke name. The inaugural splash would be ubiquitous, designed for every region, age bracket and socioeconomic group. "For the first time," says Garner, "we were trying to position a diet soft drink like a regular soft drink. It was going to be everywhere."

But where would that leave Tab? Since its introduction in 1963, the diet cola had proved to be a hearty competitor, weathering the cyclamate ban that flattened other diet soft drinks as well as stiff competition from the likes of Diet Rite, Diet Dr Pepper and Diet 7Up. Tab had built a loyal and thirsty following around such ad campaigns as "One Calorie Beautiful" and "Tab 1—Water 0." Demographic surveys showed the typical Tab drinker to be a figure-conscious woman, 18 to 49 years old, who drank copious quantities of the stuff, sometimes a six-pack a day. But Garner's group also realized that she represented a prime target for Diet Coke. Somehow, the company had to get the message to her not to abandon Tab in the hoopla surrounding Diet Coke.

"As a marketer, I could paint you a wonderful color portrait of the Tab drinker in terms of age, sex, income, education and even some lifestyle attitudes," says Garner, from an office strewn with colorful cans and bottles of test designs that never made it to the vending machine. "But how do you find her? How do you reach her? Mass advertising wasn't the only answer."

Having heard of Claritas's PRIZM cluster system through marketing magazines, Garner set out to find those Tab drinkers, using sales data provided by local supermarket outlets. By matching store addresses with the heaviest Tab consumption, analysts identified the standout clusters for Tab

TAB VS. DIET COKE

Four years after the introduction of Diet Coke, the soft drink is consumed by nearly five times as many households as Tab. Compared to Diet Coke drinkers, who tend to live in the suburbs, brand-loyal Tab drinkers can be found in cities, suburbs, towns and rural areas.

Top Ten Clusters: Tab

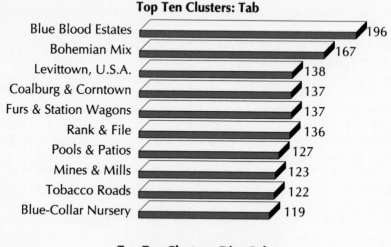

Cluster	Index
Blue Blood Estates	196
Bohemian Mix	167
Levittown, U.S.A.	138
Coalburg & Corntown	137
Furs & Station Wagons	137
Rank & File	136
Pools & Patios	127
Mines & Mills	123
Tobacco Roads	122
Blue-Collar Nursery	119

Top Ten Clusters: Diet Coke

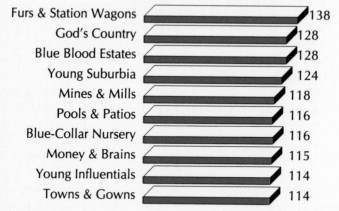

Cluster	Index
Furs & Station Wagons	138
God's Country	128
Blue Blood Estates	128
Young Suburbia	124
Mines & Mills	118
Pools & Patios	116
Blue-Collar Nursery	116
Money & Brains	115
Young Influentials	114
Towns & Gowns	114

Numbers indicate percentages of households that drink each beverage, indexed against the national average. An index of 100 equals the U.S. average: 4.06% for Tab, 17.36% for Diet Coke. An index of 200 means a cluster has twice the national average. Source: SMRB 1985/86, Claritas Corp., 1987.

drinkers. In state after state, the same kinds of neighborhoods appeared: Money & Brains, Furs & Station Wagons, Pools & Patios, Young Influentials, Black Enterprise and Young Suburbia. As Garner recalls, "The clusters that bought Tab in California were the same ones that bought Tab in Michigan and Ohio and Massachusetts."

Armed with the store addresses, Coca-Cola could target a keep-the-faith campaign to Tab drinkers while encouraging everyone else to try its new brand. In July 1982, as Diet Coke began blitzing the nation's radio and TV stations, local Coca-Cola bottlers joined in a direct-mail campaign sending Tab discount coupons to neighborhoods of Tab-aholics. "Call it an insurance policy," says Garner. "If I'm a Tab drinker and I go into a store and see lots of Diet Coke that I've never seen before, I'm less prone to switch out of the brand if I'm carrying a 50-cents-off Tab coupon."

Beverage analysts claim the protection policy met with mixed success. Between 1982 and 1986, Tab's share of the soft drink market dipped from 4.1 to 1.9 percent. Meanwhile, Diet Coke was setting sales records on its way to capturing 9 percent of the total market—some of it from Tab consumers—and becoming one of the industry's greatest success stories. "Diet Coke was like a baby jumping out of a crib and doing a mile in under 3 minutes," observes Jesse Meyers, editor of *Beverage Digest,* the industry biweekly newsletter. Although part of Diet Coke's gain was clearly rooted in Tab's loss, the two brands together have widened their lead over Diet Pepsi from 0.3 to 3 percent—a tenfold increase. As Meyers put it, "Victory is when the sum of the parts is larger this year than it was last year." And Tab loyalists, equipped with the latest diet book and copy of *Vogue,* still know where to get their six-packs.

6

LOVE, AMERICAN ZIP CODE STYLE

"My husband is always saying how much he likes to come home to a hot meal on the table. Well, I like to have dinner on the table when I get home, too. Let him cook. I'd rather manage people than make barbecue."
—Barbara Collins, Glendale, Colorado (Young Influentials)

Like the characters in yesterday's television sitcoms, the American family has radically changed with the times. Just thirty years ago, we all agreed that "Father Knows Best" and were more than glad to "Leave It to Beaver." In those '50s classics, Dad went off to work in the morning, Mom stayed home with the kids and the neighborhood remained pleasantly stable. It was a scene that accurately portrayed life in more than half of America's households—not to mention the dreams of many others. A 1959 survey found that three-quarters of all American couples wanted traditional families of three or more children.

Today, that consensus has given way to a myriad of family styles as a result of people living longer, marrying later, divorcing more often and changing mates to suit the seasons of their lives. Indeed, "American Family" now is a misnomer; better the plural, "American Families," to describe our current social structure. The TV Andersons are now outnumbered by the Huxtables, the two-career family of "The Cosby Show," and the Romanos, a single parent raising two daughters in "One

Day at a Time." In fact, households with a breadwinner father, stay-at-home mom and two kids under 18 years old account for only 4 percent of the nation.

As the traditional family has gone the way of the black-and-white TV, communities have evolved to deal with the tangle of nontraditional households: childless couples who flock to yuppie Young Influentials suburbs, large child-rearing families who settle in Blue-Collar Nursery towns and single-parent households characteristic of New Beginnings, fringe-city neighborhoods of bungalows and garden-style apartments.

These new family configurations reflect the increased freedom afforded individuals in our increasingly mobile society. Because we can satisfy our basic wants more easily than in the past, we are able to pursue unconventional paths. "When you look at the life course of people thirty years ago, you see only a handful of fairly predictable points of transition," says Census Bureau demographer Art Norton. "People got married at 21, finished child-bearing at 31, had a spouse die at 64 and lived alone after that." Now an individual may experiment with independent living, live as part of an unmarried couple, get married and divorced a couple of times and live with children but without a spouse. "People undergo wide experiences in today's world," says Norton. "There are many more transition points in the life course of an adult."

At each turning point, Americans move to different communities compatible with their needs for dating, mating or raising a family. Those choices create communities filled with young singles, middle-aged families or empty-nesting retirees—each with different ideas about what to serve for dinner, how holidays should be celebrated, whether premarital sex is acceptable or verboten. As more Americans head in different lifestyle directions, a sense of national mores—our collective notions about how people should manage their lives—has evaporated. In its place are a multitude of ideas and alternatives barely imagined by Wally and the Beav. The clusters allow us to examine these options and appreciate the trials and triumphs of meeting, settling down and raising families in the '80s.

■■■■ DATING—WHERE THE BOYS AND GIRLS ARE

More than work, politics or finances, romance is the central drama of life in many communities. As the average household size has declined steadily over the past decade, the number of people living alone has soared. More than 20 million Americans now live by themselves—a 90 percent jump in the last fifteen years. This horde of singles is not just the result of divorce and widowhood; couples are taking their marriage vows later than ever before, meaning that more and more adults are undergoing long periods of singlehood. In the process, they're redefining courtship in many of the nation's clusters.

Unlike married people, whose concerns may focus on food, shelter and clothing, dating singles must worry about another financial imperative: the cost of meeting people. Money must be spent on polishing an image that will catch the eye of the opposite sex. And the preferred bait changes according to community lifestyle. A 1985 survey of singles in affluent Westchester County, New York, and Fairfield County, Connecticut, found that men aged 30 to 50 looked for women who were young and beautiful, while women of that age range wanted men with money and social status. Accordingly, the single men tended to drive Ferraris instead of Thunderbirds, buy Rolexes rather than Timexes and read *Town & Country* rather than *True Story*. And the women were most deeply involved in fitness clubs and aerobics classes.

Pauline Thompson, a millionaire realtor from the Money & Brains community of Fairfax Circle, Virginia, observes that high-status possessions are a necessary form of self-expression that indicate "where I'm coming from." Like other Money & Brains residents, she balances a workaholic's schedule with frequent trips abroad and a social life spent attending the openings of cultural events she supports through charitable contributions. The 44-year-old divorcée typically arrives for a symphony concert in a Mercedes sport coupe, draped in an Adolpho gown and white mink. "It's my way of showing I belong to a circle of friends that go first-class," says Thompson, a blue-eyed platinum blond named one of the capital area's ten most eligible women in 1984 by *The Washingtonian* magazine. "Some of the men who approach me say I'm out of their league. But a man has to be confident enough in himself so he won't be intimidated by my lifestyle." Among the men who aren't intimidated, says Thompson: "Presidents of corporations, independent thinkers and self-made millionaires—people like me."

For younger singles just starting out, the courtship profile is decidedly less luxurious. Single residents in Towns & Gowns communities are often establishing their first households away from their parents—sometimes in group homes—and more of their budgets are devoted to activities that take place outside their temporary quarters. Their dates

SINGLE PEOPLE

All the top singles clusters have high concentrations of 18- to 24-year-olds. And, except for postgraduates still living in Towns & Gowns communities, most singles leave rural areas for cities and the chance to meet other singles.

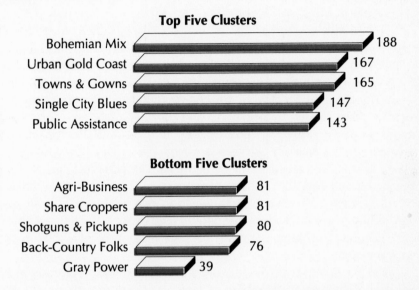

Top Five Clusters

Bohemian Mix	188
Urban Gold Coast	167
Towns & Gowns	165
Single City Blues	147
Public Assistance	143

Bottom Five Clusters

Agri-Business	81
Share Croppers	81
Shotguns & Pickups	80
Back-Country Folks	76
Gray Power	39

Numbers indicate percentages of singles, indexed against the national average. An index of 100 equals the U.S. average: 26%. An index of 188 means a cluster has 1.88 times the national average, or about 49%. Source: PRIZM (Census Demography), Claritas Corp., 1987.

typically involve athletics: they jog, play tennis and water ski nearly twice as often as the general population. In these communities, even the lowliest chores can take on the significance of a social mixer. A supermarket outside the Towns & Gowns community of State College, Pennsylvania, designates Wednesday nights "For Singles Only," to encourage the ripening of romance along with the imported cheeses. In the cluster town of College Park, Maryland, home of the University of Maryland, a local laundromat has become a hot pick-up spot with the addition of a pizza restaurant, two color TV sets and fourteen video games. The laundromat, named Soap's, allows students the chance to mingle while their dirty socks clean. In fact, the owner complains that people end up picking up dates and leaving their clothes behind.

For America's singles searching for Mr. or Ms. Right, clusters offer an easy-to-follow map. Bohemian Mix leads the nation in the concentration of single and divorced residents—at a level more than three times the national average. And the reputation of these funky urban areas as a swinging haven feeds on itself: singles move there, in part, because other singles already have moved there. Census data show that a high proportion of Bohemian Mix women come from isolated rural areas in search of mates and careers in the big city. Though the competition is stiff—single women generally outnumber men in inner cities—their chances for mating far outweigh the odds in a cluster like Grain Belt, with the nation's highest concentration of married couples.

In Bohemian Mix, daily life presses young people against each other as in no other cluster, in bars, parks and gourmet groceries—the "meet markets" of the '80s. With no family commitments, Bohemian Mixers are nearly twice as likely as average Americans to spend time attending plays, movies, lectures and public activities like anti-nuke rallies. Like the Left Bank residents whose society revolved around the Parisian cafes, Bohemian Mixers seek community in local bars. While single men and women in other clusters may attend church socials, Bohemian Mixers take dates to demonstrations to save historic buildings from the wrecker's ball.

Fred Wistow, a trim, 37-year-old attorney and writer, lives in Manhattan's Bohemian Mix district of Greenwich Village, partly for the "jumping atmosphere" that he likens to a carnival. "Every night there's a stream of people moving down the winding streets from one club to another," says Wistow, speaking in the staccato rhythm of a stand-up comic. "You feel like you're in the middle of a midway." Previously married and living in suburban Staten Island, he fled the 'burbs after his divorce in 1980 and returned to the Manhattan singles scene. He settled in a two-bedroom West Village co-op within steps of two supermarkets, dozens of restaurants and a handful of bars like the White Horse and Lion's Head "that still resemble those Beat coffee houses where you can schmooze for hours." The action is nonstop in the West Village, where people smoke pot on the streets, exchange business cards at the corner produce market and schedule romantic rendezvous for 2 A.M. at an all-night pasta parlor. "You'll bump into someone on the street and end up at a party in someone's loft," says Wistow. "There's a lot of cruising by gays and straights, which makes the scene always, uh, unpredictable."

Matrimony, of course, isn't always the goal of all this cruising. Nationwide, the 1980 census found 1.9 million households—3 percent of the total—made up of "persons of the opposite sex sharing living quarters" without benefit of wedlock—quadruple the rate since 1970. Bohemian Mix, as home to the highest concentration of unmarried singles living together—23 percent of the cluster—traditionally has been the nation's Babylon, where sexual mores are looser than anywhere else. In contrast to the rural residents of Share Croppers who, as one pointed out, "don't think very highly of premarital sex," Bohemian Mixers believe that sexual permissiveness comes with the territory. According to *American Couples,* a study of the lives of 6,000 U.S. couples, married couples engage in sex less frequently than unmarried couples. Especially homosexual couples. It's no surprise that many of the nation's gay communities are located in Bohemian Mix districts: Castro Street in San Francisco, Christopher Street in Greenwich Village, Dupont Circle in Washington, D.C. Here, unmarried couples make love, travel together, care for one another when sick and live under the same roof for years without ever tying the knot. Indeed, they seem to shun conventional commitments; these neighborhoods rank at the bottom of membership rates in civic and fraternal clubs.

Within the last few years, the AIDS epidemic has decreased the sexual rowdiness of Bohemian Mix—and all the clusters, for that matter. The owners of the Saint, an East Village club founded for a gay clientele, recently began welcoming heterosexuals two nights a week, linking the drop-off in gay patrons to the fear of AIDS. According to some social commentators, the Saint's new admissions policy is further evidence that America has passed through the Age of Liberation and into the Age of Restraint. "Is Sex Dead?" asked a 1982 *New York* magazine cover story that claimed the old singles-bar scene had fallen victim to fears of communicable diseases and a lifetime of unfulfilling one-night stands. A 1986 survey of 4,000 singles by New York research psychologist Srully Blotnick found that 9 percent of the women said they'd become "urban nuns," avoiding all new entanglements, while 4 percent of the men had opted for celibacy. As Blotnick put it, "The sexual merry-go-round has slowed down."

With the singles bar out of vogue in most communities, today's mate-seekers search for spouses through dating services, networking groups, open-university courses and receptions that focus on their lifestyles. Personal Profiles, a Chicago dating service that costs $1,250 a year, turns away blue-collar applicants. For $4,600, the service guarantees that affluent white-collar mate-seekers will be engaged or married in three years. The lonely hearts of Grain Belt and Agri-Business have their own personals listing service, a monthly newsletter published by the Minnesota-based Rural Singles of America. Page after page lists SRE's (single rural eligibles) in search of cigar-chomping bachelor sheep ranchers and "farmerettes" who enjoy fishing, canning and baking. In Washington, D.C., the capital's Open University even offers a course titled "For Geographically Desirable Singles Only," where students learn places to meet and lines to use on other singles "geographically close to you." (For openers, "What's your zip code?" has replaced "What's your sign?")

But dating in the '80s isn't restricted to the young and the restless. Widowhood and an increased life expectancy have created 13 million over-65 singles—an increasing number of whom are returning to the dating ranks in this later stage of life. In Gray Power communities nationwide, elderly singles are rewriting the rules of the dating game. Take 72-year-old Mary Ann Gurch, who found herself re-experiencing the first-date jitters as a recent widow in Sun City, Arizona. Her husband of forty-eight years had died of cancer in 1985, and she missed the companionship that came with marriage. One night in the winter of 1986, during choir practice at St. Clement's Catholic Church, she struck up a conversation with a handsome tenor, a retired university administrator who'd also recently been widowed. She felt no embarrassment about making the first move. "The older women around here are always eyeing the guys up and down," says Gurch, who favors a very contemporary blond hairdo, fashionably tattered blouse, peddle pushers and pumps. In an age group where older single women outnumber elderly single men by five to one, Gurch knew she had to move fast.

Soon, the two were showing up together at choir practice and church dances, stealing away for midday picnics in the mountains surrounding Sun City and spending afternoons lolling around a community swimming pool. Friends weren't surprised when, in the spring of 1986, the couple announced their engagement and Gurch decided to sell her three-bedroom home and move in with her fiance. "We never thought about living together first, because we're old-fashioned," says Gurch. "Besides, combining the furniture won't be a problem. Both of our houses are green."

Nor will there be any of the clash in values so common in modern marriages. After a small ceremony in which Gurch plans to wear white lace and take her fiance's last name, the couple will honeymoon in California and then begin their lives together. "The first time, we married for love," says Gurch. "Now it's for friendship and companionship. If we get one or five or ten years together, that'll be a blessing." For

The "meet markets" of the '80s—bars, open universities, even supermarkets—cater to the lifestyles of their singles clientele. This cartoon, which appeared in the *Hartford Courant,* satirizes the heightened awareness of "geographic desirability" among many mate-seekers for whom their cluster (in this case, Young Influentials) reveals much about their tastes—as well as their approach to the opposite sex.

"HI, THERE. I'M PHIL ROYCE, EAST SIDE, 02906. CAN I BUY YOU A YOGURT?"

© DON BOUSQUET

American couples of all ages, that optimism is borne out in a variety of marriage styles.

THE DUAL-CAREER COUPLE

In the Glendale, Colorado, townhouse of Tim and Barbara Collins, a vase of fresh white gladiolias sits in the middle of a living room dominated by an expansive chalet roof. Every few days the flowers are changed—spider mums, day lilies or tulips—just so long as they're fresh. When they married in October 1985, Tim and Barbara vowed to keep fresh flowers in the house, not so much as an extravagance but as an expression of the lifestyle to which they'd like to become accustomed. And through their carefully choreographed schedules of work, grocery shopping, morning runs and evening civic meetings, the ritual has survived.

As upwardly mobile residents of Young Influentials, the Collinses represent one of the biggest changes in the structure of society: the explosion of two-career marriages. In 1970, only 39 percent of all households reported dual incomes; by 1986, three out of five American couples brought home two paychecks. Most chose to face the joys and headaches of juggling two jobs and a home life to foster a stronger sense of equality between husband and wife and gain a higher standard of

TWO-INCOME HOUSEHOLDS

As a nation of working couples, America displays little variation in the concentration of two-income households. Neighborhoods at both ends of the scale are near the national average. With the exception of Young Influentials, clusters with the most working couples are also those with the most children.

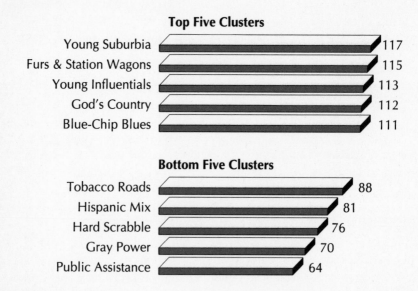

Top Five Clusters

Young Suburbia	117
Furs & Station Wagons	115
Young Influentials	113
God's Country	112
Blue-Chip Blues	111

Bottom Five Clusters

Tobacco Roads	88
Hispanic Mix	81
Hard Scrabble	76
Gray Power	70
Public Assistance	64

Numbers indicate percentages of households with two or more workers, indexed against the national average. An index of 100 equals the U.S. average: 54%. An index of 117 means a cluster has 1.17 times the national average, or about 63%. Source: PRIZM (Census Demography), Claritas Corp., 1987.

living. It is a lifestyle typified in the Young Influentials community of Glendale, a tiny Denver suburb of 3,100 residents, of which only 20 are school-aged children. With its high concentration of white-collar couples pursuing dual careers, cluster residents can afford to travel extensively, own investment property, collect vintage wines and devote more than a few hours each week to sports and shopping. On the bumper stickers of their BMWs, Porsches and Alfa Romeos, these yuppie motorists proudly proclaim "The one who dies with the most toys wins."

Indeed, relaxing on the overstuffed beige couch in the center of their townhouse living room, Tim and Barbara Collins cheerfully admit they're yuppies. Between their two jobs—he works as a construction engineer at a nuclear power plant and she oversees thirty paralegals at a law firm—their annual household income is $70,000. The two 30-year-olds eat out three nights a week, let the cleaners do their laundry and shop at the Town & Country Market, a gourmet store featuring specialty cuts of meat and fish. Their private motor pool includes a Datsun 280Z, a BMW 320i—"a Bimmer" in the yuppie lexicon—and a 1931 antique Chevrolet reserved for events like the annual polo match fundraiser for the Denver Symphony. To solve their biggest complaint—Glendale's lack of sophisticated clothing stores—the Collinses hop airplanes for shopping sprees in Chicago, San Francisco and New York. "That's what our lifestyle allows us to do," says Barbara. "If we see something we like, we don't give a second thought to how we're going to pay for it."

In Glendale, the Collinses aren't alone. Like other Young Influentials communities—Redondo Beach in Los Angeles and Parkfairfax outside Washington, to name two—Glendale features more than its share of singles apartments and condominium developments, never far from a swimming pool, disco bar or Mexican restaurant. At the corner of Dexter and Kentucky streets, garden-style apartments break the horizon in every direction—boxy buildings in stucco or pink brick, their balconies shadowed by hanging plants, their windowsills lined with Mateus bottles. Known for years as a bar district where area singles pub-crawled the weekend away, Glendale has slowly altered its image as two-career couples moved into the newly built townhouse condos, bringing their tastes for gourmet markets and fitness centers, video parlors and fashion boutiques. The newest nightclub in town, Neo's, enforces a dress code requiring patrons to attire themselves like the cast of "Miami Vice."

The Collinses are part of this new breed, two recent transplants who met while both were running for Glendale City Council in 1982. He was a city boy from Gary, Indiana, with short brown hair parted down the middle and the well-scrubbed look of a barbershop quartet singer. Barbara, a dark-haired beauty with piercing black eyes and a quick tongue, grew up in the tony North Shore of Chicago. They came to Glendale partly because of its reputation as a party town but also because young people could get involved in civic affairs and "make a difference." Nationally, Young Influentials residents show high rates of community activism, working as civic volunteers, joining environmentalist organizations and participating in political campaigns. Although Barbara eventually dropped out of the race—she feared a conflict of interest because of her job—Tim was elected to the city council and Barbara became Glendale's planning commissioner.

These days, their positions satisfy their community spirit, but their volunteerism is also a drain on their time. Like other Young Influentials couples, Barbara and Tim find that making their marriage a success has become a matter of logistics. With Glendale City Council meetings several nights a week, they usually come home at day's end exhausted. Household chores are left for the weekend, and negotiations over who'll clean the bathroom sometimes rival the SALT talks for length and diplomacy. "When you both have careers, you don't have time for yourself," says Barbara one evening over Brie and stone-ground wheat crackers. "On the odd night we don't have a meeting to attend, we're too exhausted to do anything but vegetate in front of the TV."

Like many of their cluster peers, the Collinses find their marriage a delicate balance between traditional and contemporary values. "To be an ordinary housewife is looked down upon around here," says Barbara. "And I want to be in there with the big honchos every day." But Barbara's new-woman aspirations sometimes conflict with Tim's traditional outlook. "It wouldn't faze me if she stopped working to spend time maintaining the house and putting food on the table," he says, pouring himself a Perrier.

"But what if that isn't the role I want?" Barbara interrupts. "I'd rather manage people than worry about the laundry." She pauses, then laughs with a sense of sudden realization. "The hardest part of our lives is that there's no one for us to follow. We have no role models. In our lifestyle, none of the roles are conventional."

The future for Young Influentials couples like the Collinses points to other clusters up the ZQ ladder. With two condos providing rental income, Tim and Barbara are now saving for a house in the suburbs with a garage big enough to stable their posh cars and a garden to supply them with fresh flowers. "We both agree that a Jaguar is what our car should be," says Tim. They already talk of having children in several years, but Barbara can't envision giving up her career for a traditional homemaking role. From her perspective in Young Influentials, life can be like that Michelob Light commercial, the one that says "You can have it all."

■■■■■ DONNA REED REDUX

Despite the ubiquity of dual-career marriages, the traditional family won't disappear. About a fifth of all married couples still opt for the old-style marriage in which the wife stays home to raise children while the husband works. And a majority of Americans cling tenaciously to conventional gender roles for housework and raising children—even when the wife holds down a job. With many baby boomers now having families—28 percent of all U.S. households have children under 18—the growing minority of women putting family ahead of career has led observers to proclaim a renaissance in the old-fashioned family.

This traditional approach to family is most evident in Blue-Collar Nursery, the cluster that ranks first in the concentration of married couples with children—communities like Detroit's Richmond, Houston's Magnolia and West Jordan outside Salt Lake City. In these middle-class industrial towns, most activities revolve around children and their qualify of life. Residents buy above-average numbers of campers, above-ground swimming pools, TV video games and pets (especially toy-sized dogs that won't scare toddlers). Parents are more likely to host a family barbecue than a cocktail party—it saves the cost of baby sitters. And Mom and Dad's idea of a night out is taking the kids bowling and then to Burger Chef; they've made that fast-food emporium their favorite.

West Jordan, a Blue-Collar Nursery town settled by Mormon pioneers in 1847, attests to the continued health of the traditional family. A rural community until 1970, West Jordan's population exploded from 4,200 to 41,000 during the following fifteen years, attracting legions of Salt Lake Citians in search of large but affordable housing for their expanding families. Mormons aren't forbidden to practice birth control, but the church encourages couples to have many children and women to adopt the homemaker role. As Craig Dearing, president of the West Jordan Chamber of Commerce, puts it, "Most women work for economic reasons rather than to feel accomplished. They're proud of taking care of their kids full time. Status around here is raising good kids, having a good home and being a good parent."

KID COMMUNITIES

America's child-filled communities are generally middle- to upper-middle-class and suburban, with high levels of homeowners and dual incomes. Childless clusters are generally filled with retirees, aging immigrants and upscale high-rise dwellers.

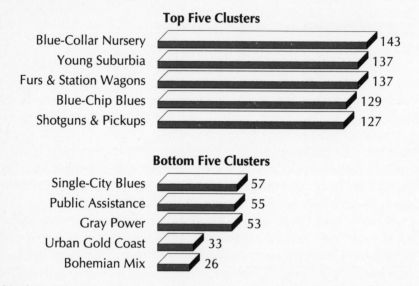

Top Five Clusters

Cluster	Index
Blue-Collar Nursery	143
Young Suburbia	137
Furs & Station Wagons	137
Blue-Chip Blues	129
Shotguns & Pickups	127

Bottom Five Clusters

Cluster	Index
Single-City Blues	57
Public Assistance	55
Gray Power	53
Urban Gold Coast	33
Bohemian Mix	26

Numbers indicate percentages of households with children, indexed against the national average. An index of 100 equals the U.S. average: 32.03%. An index of 143 means a cluster has 1.43 times the national average, or about 45%. Source: PRIZM (Census Demography), Claritas Corp., 1987.

James Peterson, the principal of West Jordan Elementary, knows first-hand what it means to live in a Blue-Collar Nursery community where the baby boom never went bust. From the front door of his school, with its low, beige brick exterior, he can see six more schools and churches surrounded by labyrinthine subdivisions, the steeples rising among new split-levels and colonials. In 1981, when Peterson's school was built, planners expected 732 students at most; four years later, 967 youngsters enrolled. Three portable classrooms were towed on to the playground, but that still couldn't relieve the stress on the school's facilities and student body. "At recess, there were always fights," recalls Peterson, a balding, genial man whose wife and three kids all went into teaching. "The playground simply wasn't big enough to accommodate the children."

In July 1986, West Jordan and several other school districts went on a year-round schedule to cope with the overcrowding. Nowadays, students attend classes for three months at a stretch, take a three-week break and repeat the schedule. Although it's too early to gauge the long-term academic impact of year-round classes, parents have registered their support. "The only alternative for us was to go on double shifts, and parents didn't want the kids showing up early in the morning and staying until late at night," says Peterson. "They like to have them home."

In Blue-Collar Nursery towns like West Jordan, the business community caters to child-filled subdivisions. At Bennett's Video, the window posters promote not the latest Stallone shoot-out but the newest Care Bears animation. On weekends, residents flock to discount stores like K-mart and the Safeway Super Saver, which specializes in bulk foods for bulk families. As homemaker Jody Smith puts it, "You don't find families paying $50 for a pair of Reeboks. They'll go to Pay-Less and buy five pairs of shoes at a time." Indeed, parents often look for entertainment deals, for example, theaters offering "$5 Specials" that let the whole family see a movie for a flat rate. "Anywhere you go, you see kids," says 28-year-old Smith, a Marie Osmond look-alike with a husky voice. "You have to be careful driving down the street because there are always kids on bikes. At a community ballgame, you'll see a mom with three kids, one in a dance uniform, another in jogging clothes and the third in

---

WEST JORDAN, UTAH: NOT ALL-AMERICAN

A traditional Blue-Collar Nursery community of 41,000, West Jordan is fast-growing, all-white and child-filled—a far cry, demographically, from the national average.

	National Average	West Jordan
Married couples with children	32%	70%
Households with 5+ persons	13%	37%
Median age (years)	30	19
Black population	12%	0%
Homeowners	65%	91%
Female labor force	43%	36%
White-/blue-collar index	169	98
Households 11+ years old	33%	10%
Housing under 5 years old	13%	52%

SOURCE: REZIDE (Census Demography), Claritas Corp., 1987.

diapers. And Mom's wearing aerobics stuff because she just got out of her class to grab the kids and go to a ballgame."

Smith doesn't find it at all unusual that she and her husband, a $24,000-a-year salesman, have four young children after ten years of marriage. On her street of twenty homes, Smith counts seventeen that are filled with large families. "It used to be that you had a big family because you needed it," says Smith. "But we love kids because they're exciting. They're a pain in the wazoo but they're fun." Married right out of high school to a man eleven years her senior, Smith describes herself as "a traditional mother who always wanted to be a homemaker. When I was in high school, I wrote an essay on what kind of mother I wanted to be when I grew up." And she takes her housewife's role seriously:

COUCH POTATOES

Video cassette recorders have not only redefined night life in suburbia to mean Chinese take-out in front of a tape of *The Terminator.* In the kid-filled communities of Furs & Station Wagons and Young Suburbia, the VCR has become a surrogate baby sitter, occupying countless tykes through weekends of Disney classics.

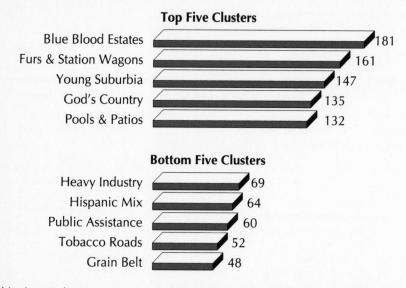

Top Five Clusters

Blue Blood Estates	181
Furs & Station Wagons	161
Young Suburbia	147
God's Country	135
Pools & Patios	132

Bottom Five Clusters

Heavy Industry	69
Hispanic Mix	64
Public Assistance	60
Tobacco Roads	52
Grain Belt	48

Numbers indicate percentages of households with video cassette recorders, indexed against the national average. An index of 100 equals the U.S. average: 22.4%. An index of 181 means a cluster has 1.81 times the national average, or about 41%. Source: SMRB 1984/85, Claritas Corp., 1987.

she sews many of her children's clothes, provides homemade cake and breakfast in bed on their birthdays, and carts them to dance classes, rodeos and baseball games. For dinner, she tries to prepare foods that, if not haute cuisine, are at least colorful enough to pique her children's interest.

"I'll throw in carrot sticks to provide color if there's just white potatoes, brown chicken and yellow corn," Smith says. "I have a friend who cooks Chinese twice a week and I'm impressed. My kids are lucky to get casseroles with a Jello salad."

In West Jordan homes like the Smiths', the family is a throwback to the past, a time before the arrival of such demographic trends as the shrinking household size and the rising number of women in the work force. Smith maintains a busy volunteering schedule, helping teachers on field trips, class parties and picture days. Like other cluster parents, her education stopped after high school, and she sometimes regrets she didn't go on—"just to set an example for my kids. I want to be able to answer their questions when they get older." Still, she expresses few misgivings about her decision to be a full-time homemaker. "My career now is my home, my family and my kids," she says, obviously taking pride in her job performance to date. "I very strongly believe in the family unit. And I feel like we're raising tomorrow's leaders today. If I can keep them on the straight and narrow, then the future will be okay."

THE ONE-PARENT FAMILY

For an increasing number of Americans, the concept of "family" is being redefined in households headed by single parents. Fifteen years ago, the solo-parent family was a relative novelty and represented only 15 percent of the nation's households. "Broken homes," they were called, with more than a hint of disapproval. But due to spiraling divorce rates and unwed parenthood, today one in four households is headed by a single parent—typically a woman who must balance the roles of wage earner and child caretaker. That change in the structure of the family has been profound: 60 percent of children born in 1984 can expect to live in a solo-parent family before they reach age 18. Sixty percent.

As the numbers continue to climb, more communities are adapting to these new-style households, catering to their single-income budgets and unrelenting parental pressures. Perhaps no cluster better reflects this growth in one-parent families than New Beginnings, a collection of suburban middle-class communities where young singles just starting

SINGLE PARENTS

Single parents are concentrated in urban black America, home to the nation's poorest minorities. Single parents are rarer in the high-rent Urban Gold Coast and farmtowns of Grain Belt—which, not surprisingly, has the highest percentage of married people.

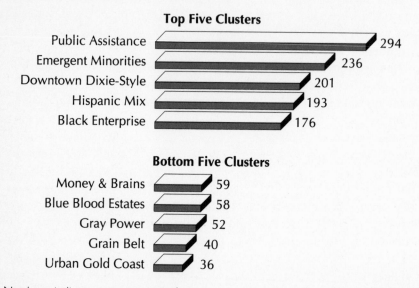

Top Five Clusters

Public Assistance	294
Emergent Minorities	236
Downtown Dixie-Style	201
Hispanic Mix	193
Black Enterprise	176

Bottom Five Clusters

Money & Brains	59
Blue Blood Estates	58
Gray Power	52
Grain Belt	40
Urban Gold Coast	36

Numbers indicate percentages of single parents, indexed against the national average. An index of 100 equals the U.S. average: 8%. An index of 294 means a cluster has 2.94 times the national average, or about 24%. Source: PRIZM (Census Demography), Claritas Corp., 1987.

out live alongside older divorced men and women—places like Reseda, north of Los Angeles, Edgewater, near Cleveland and Bloomington, Minnesota, south of the Twin Cities. Scattered from coast to coast and concentrated around most major cities, New Beginnings neighborhoods are characterized by one- and two-bedroom apartments and modest houses once filled with blue-collar nuclear families. The current residents—never-married and newly single—include a high percentage of people the SRI International research company calls "experientials," its Values and Lifestyles (VALS) classification for individuals with a zest for experiences to improve their minds and bodies. Experiential ads usually tell consumers to "go for the gusto," turning beer-drinking, say, into a spiritual quest.

And New Beginnings residents respond to such messages. In these neighborhoods, they belong to civic clubs, take adult education courses and work out at health clubs—all at rates 50 percent above national averages. At the grocery store, they're the ones who buy products that promote healthfulness, like whole-wheat bread, fresh fruit, skimmed milk and natural cheese. Many are among the 15 million Americans who belong to self-help groups searching for ways to cope with their circumstances as solo providers. In New Beginnings, residents regard support organizations as extended families.

The east side of Bloomington, Minnesota, is one New Beginnings nesting ground for single-parent families. Part of a greenbelt suburb of 84,000, the community blossomed after World War II to earn a reputation among realtors as "the city of a million ramblers." Baby-boom parents and, later, their children moved there, drawn to plentiful jobs at high-tech companies like Control Data. But the area also beckoned single-parent families—nearly 60 percent of the half-million adults in the Twin Cities are unmarried—thanks to a plethora of support groups for adults and organized athletic leagues for kids. These budget-conscious consumers are welcomed along the strips of fast-food franchises and bakery thrift outlets, at the tranquil parks and lush public gardens. For the divorced hoping to get back into circulation, Bloomington's chapters of Parents Without Partners and Singles All Together sponsor activities ranging from creative writing and photography courses to cribbage games and Bible study groups—most accompanied by a social hour. "They're a nice way to meet people because you can get to know them before going out with them," says divorcée Connie Schramm. "It's not like picking up a guy in a bar."

As with other single parents, economic needs influenced Schramm's decision to live in a New Beginnings community. Ten years ago, newly divorced Schramm found herself broke, unemployed and with four children to raise on her own. Her job skills rusty, she went back to college while working as a substitute teacher, earned an education degree and took a job as a $19,000-a-year financial officer for the local school system. At the same time, she joined the local chapter of Parents Without Partners, as much for the athletic leagues offered her teenage children as for the opportunities to meet other single parents like herself. "All my friends were married and I wasn't in sync with them any more," says Schramm, a slight, 49-year-old woman with green eyes and frosted hair. Although she avoided dates for the first five years after her divorce, gradually she began going out with men she met at Parents Without Partners card games and discussion groups. "At first, I'd meet someone for dinner outside the house because it was so stressful having a guy come up to the door," she recalls. "But finally I decided that, 'Hey, this is the way it's going to be.'"

Today in her Bloomington home, Schramm finds few liabilities in her single-parent lifestyle. One daughter is married and a son is in college on a Parents Without Partners scholarship. And, after years of counseling in family relations to deal with her role as a divorced mother and provider, Schramm now leads single-parent discussion groups, covering topics like "How to Relax at a Discussion Group." Money is still tight and, like other New Beginnings residents, who tend to buy cheap imported subcompacts, Schramm gets by in a 1978 VW Rabbit. "At least it's paid for," she shrugs. She recently vetoed a son's plea for a VCR on the grounds that saving for college tuitions took precedence. On Schramm's modest salary, her family can afford only free band concerts, 99-cent movie specials or nearby park picnics. "I have to be careful with a buck," she explains. "But it's probably brought our family closer together than a lot of two-parent households. Money's an issue we have to face together."

Single parenthood doesn't have to be a permanent family condition, however. In fact, the remarriage rate in America exceeds the first-marriage rate in most age groups. For the last year Schramm's been involved with a man she met through Parents Without Partners. It could turn into a long-term involvement but Schramm frankly is in no hurry to start contemplating marriage. "I wouldn't mind it," she says, "but only if I believed it would be a very, very good relationship." Like so many pioneers in single-parent households, Schramm knows it's tough to start a new family tradition.

IN SEARCH OF HOME, SWEET HOME

As household composition has changed, so have the traditions of the home itself. In America's pluralistic society, home-based rituals such as mealtimes, holidays and family gatherings differ vastly from community to community. Each cluster determines for itself the proper way to raise children and pass on parental values, whether it's okay to smoke cigarettes (or something stronger) and if birth control should be discussed in the schools. A surprising number of issues are decided by the same factors (income, education, household composition) that determine neighborhood settlement—issues over which children have little control. In America, having a Money & Brains mentality or Mines & Mills outlook may be simply a happenstance of birth—a geodemographic crap-shoot.

Take the children of Tobacco Roads, those tiny, predominantly black farm towns centered in the Mississippi Delta. Most youngsters grow up in a society that is poor (the median household income is $13,227), racially segregated and medically unsophisticated. Tobacco Roads leads the nation in homes without indoor plumbing and has the highest infant mortality rate. Cluster residents frequently can't afford private physicians and are America's top consumers of home remedies to treat their ailments. To grow up in Tobacco Roads is to know first-hand the standard of living in Tunica, Mississippi, where a raw sewage ditch runs alongside the shanties of black residents—a scene so squalid that Rev. Jesse Jackson and "60 Minutes" have paid visits to call attention to the Third World–like conditions. Infants born in Tunica in 1985 were more likely to die before their first birthday than children born in Jamaica, West Indies, a developing nation.

In Tunica and other Tobacco Roads towns like Mound Bayou and Belzoni, Mississippi, the children quickly learn that segregation is still an everyday fact of life. The cluster's black youth attend poorly funded public schools while most of their white peers enroll in private academies. The few students with higher educational goals—38 percent never complete high school—are urged to leave for better opportunities. Herbert Allen, a cotton farmer from Belzoni, only completed the ninth grade, but he sent seven of his nine kids to college. Four of them earned master's degrees. The two who only completed high school still live on the Allen farm, helping their father work 800 acres of cotton and soybeans. Allen wishes they had gone on to college and left this world defined by *Grit, Hot Rod* and *True Story*—magazines all purchased by Tobacco Roads residents at more than twice the U.S. average. "If you've got any kind of ambition, you leave this area," says the grizzled Allen as he sits beneath a cottonwood tree while chickens peck around him. "There's nothing here but farm work and segregated neighborhoods and trying to survive."

On the other hand, growing up in upscale neighborhoods can result in other pressures endemic to the obsessively ambitious. According to federal health statistics, the more successful and affluent a community's residents, the more likely they are to suffer from stress—a condition passed on to children. A few years ago, a wave of teen suicides rolled through several upscale bedroom suburbs, including Plano, Texas, Fairfax, Virginia, and White Plains, New York. All are classified as Furs &

Station Wagons, and all share a high divorce rate, problems with drug and alcohol abuse as well as the rootlessness associated with upwardly mobile families. Sixty percent of the cluster's adults have attended college, and their teens typically face enormous pressures to excel not only in class but at extracurricular activities that would spruce up college applications. Medical authorities, in trying to explain the suicides in these communities, pointed to the "over-programming" of young people. As Plano city manager Bob Woodruff explains, "This community is tremendously competitive, and the disappointment of not living up to expectations can be incredible." Sometimes the inability to cope with those pressures can be fatal.

Whatever the cluster, America's teens can't escape the varied pres-

THE ELECTRONIC CHURCH

The most devout followers of the Christian Broadcasting Network live in the small towns of rural America—a profile not unlike the nation's Methodists. The city dwellers who rarely tune in live in neighborhoods with comparatively high concentrations of Catholics and Jews.

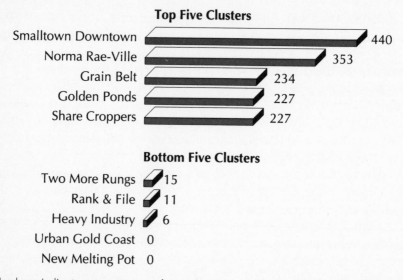

Top Five Clusters

Cluster	
Smalltown Downtown	440
Norma Rae-Ville	353
Grain Belt	234
Golden Ponds	227
Share Croppers	227

Bottom Five Clusters

Cluster	
Two More Rungs	15
Rank & File	11
Heavy Industry	6
Urban Gold Coast	0
New Melting Pot	0

Numbers indicate percentages of people who watch the Christian Broadcasting Network 5 or more hours a week, indexed against the national average. An index of 100 equals the U.S. average: 3.1%. An index of 440 means a cluster has 4.4 times the national average, or about 14%. Source: MRI Doublebase 1986, Claritas Corp., 1987.

sures of school, sex and illicit drugs. A 1985 nationwide poll found that four in ten teenagers regularly used marijuana, and drug abuse was cited as a local concern in virtually every neighborhood type. Of course, not every cluster considers drug use a problem, especially in Bohemian Mix, where one Greenwich Village resident boasted of "throwing pot parties for 200," or in the Urban Gold Coast of Manhattan's Upper West Side where a stockbroker linked his cocaine intake to the Dow Jones average. But in Smalltown Downtown, a cluster of working-class neighborhoods in aging factory towns throughout the Bible Belt, the Christian Broadcasting Network boasts its biggest audience and residents view drug use as immoral. Cluster voters consistently support anti-abortion efforts, harsher penalties for drug sellers and the presidential aspirations of Rev. Pat Robertson. Kathy Smith, a 21-year-old accounting clerk from Parkersburg, West Virginia, believes it a virtue that she's never smoked marijuana, rarely been inside a bar and still lives at home. "Most of my friends are Christian and know what I'll do and won't do," she says. "It's important to have a good relationship with God."

Although access to health information has never been greater, the cluster system explains why Americans are still among the world's biggest smokers, puffing away nearly 4,000 cigarettes per adult per year. True, the upscale residents of Blue Blood Estates, Young Influentials and Urban Gold Coast have heeded the Surgeon General's warning: these communities have the lowest rates for smoking nonfilter cigarettes as well as the highest rates for belonging to a health club. In stark contrast, the clusters with the most cigarette smokers include Tobacco Roads, Share Croppers and Hard Scrabble. These low-income, poorly educated residents are the same people who rarely belong to health clubs. The inverse relationship has obvious consequences: low-income blacks now suffer the highest rates of heart disease and lung cancer of any population group.

The marketing industry's understanding of its target audience makes any change in these grim statistics doubtful in the near future. In 1986, R. J. Reynolds began phasing out its ads in such upscale publications as *U.S. News & World Report* and *Vogue,* placing them instead in more blue-collar magazines like *Field & Stream* and *Jet.* Philip Morris has become one of the leading marketers to Hispanic Mix residents, with cigarette ads plastered on buses and subway trains used by low-income commuters. In the Mom & Pop stores of Public Assistance, cigarettes can be bought individually—and illegally—at a dime apiece, and they're freely sold to children. You've come a long way, baby.

The cluster factors also influence the nutritional content of the foods

HEALTH HABITS: CIGARETTES VS. HEALTH CLUBS

The message that smoking is hazardous to your health has gotten through to America's most educated communities, where one finds the fewest smokers and the most health-club members. The opposite is true in the nation's least-educated rural towns, communities with the worst access to the media's "no smoking" message.

Top Five Clusters: Nonfilter Cigarettes

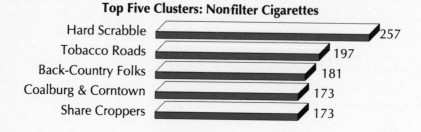

Hard Scrabble	257
Tobacco Roads	197
Back-Country Folks	181
Coalburg & Corntown	173
Share Croppers	173

Bottom Five Clusters: Nonfilter Cigarettes

Hispanic Mix	42
Blue-Collar Nursery	42
Young Influentials	36
Blue Blood Estates	12
Urban Gold Coast	0

Top Five Clusters: Health Clubs

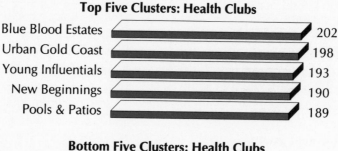

Blue Blood Estates	202
Urban Gold Coast	198
Young Influentials	193
New Beginnings	190
Pools & Patios	189

Bottom Five Clusters: Health Clubs

Agri-Business	31
Grain Belt	18
Share Croppers	18
Tobacco Roads	11
Hard Scrabble	0

Numbers indicate percentages of people who smoke nonfilter cigarettes or belong to a health club, indexed against the national average. An index of 100 equals the U.S. average: 3.56% for cigarette smokers, 5.4% for health-club members. An index of 200 means a cluster has twice the national average. Source: SMRB 1983/84 (cigarettes); MRI Doublebase 1985 (health clubs), Claritas Corp., 1987.

we eat, what time we eat and whether we're around a table or a TV set. In some neighborhood types, dinner comes from the garden; in others, from a gourmet take-out or the grocer's frozen food aisle. The growing aversion to slaving away in the kitchen has caused more than one in three Americans to eat out every day. That figure is even higher among the young white-collar singles of Urban Gold Coast. These residents are known in the food industry as "grazers" for their tendency to eat at odd hours or just nibble on appetizers and crudités—completely rejecting the home-cooked sit-down meal. They purchase only a handful of foods at rates greater than the national average—mostly breakfast items like orange juice, English muffins and skimmed milk.

Even when Urban Gold Coasters do eat dinner at home, their meals usually involve carry-out food from a local restaurant or gourmet deli —packaged food that can become forgotten leftovers. Jokes about hiding "old science projects" in the fridge are common among Urban Gold Coast residents of Manhattan's Upper East Side, where workaholic schedules make for irregular meals. David Singer, an Upper East Side attorney, has apparently come to terms with the uselessness of his apartment refrigerator: inside, he keeps nothing but the take-out menus from five nearby Chinese restaurants.

Residents of Share Croppers wouldn't call that behavior "eating." In these farm towns throughout the South, where residents labor from sunup to sundown, traditional values from a century past dictate what's on the table. These households are heavy consumers of starchy breakfast foods like pancakes and biscuits and cholesterol- and nitrate-laden meats like bacon and corned beef hash—all at rates far above the national average. Conversely, among the products with the lowest rates of consumption are frozen entrees, yogurt, instant rice and instant tea.

Share Croppers homemaker Betty Lou Hagerson of Concord, Georgia, prepares meals for her husband, sons and hired help on their 1,000-acre peanut farm. A tall, sturdy woman with neatly coiffed hair and an omnipresent apron, she fixes the main meal of the day at noontime, often consisting of ham or beef, two vegetables, salad, corn bread or biscuits and a dessert like a pie—all homemade. "We might be poor but we eat well," she says of the midday meal. "Riches aren't always in the bank account." Indeed, the bounty of the farm's garden and animal pens is stocked in the kitchen freezer and pantry. Hagerson generally prepares only sandwiches for the men when they come in after the evening chores, often at 8 P.M. At the supermarket, she fills her cart with the cluster staples her garden doesn't grow: flour, sugar, eggs, Crisco, paper products, milk, butter and fruits. "We don't do much shopping in the frozen foods bin," she smiles. "And we can do without TV dinners."

Supermarket freezers are terra incognita also for a Towns & Gowns professor like David Passmore, from State College, Pennsylvania. After academic posts at a half-dozen college towns, his contacts with foreign students and educators have influenced his family's fondness for exotic but healthful dishes like couscous, bulgur grain, tofu and stir-fried vegetables. He's one reason why a mass-market company like Campbell Soup has diversified its line of canned tomato and chicken soups to include Fresh Chef refrigerated salads and Gold Label Creamy Natural soups aimed at specialty market niches. Passmore recognizes that his family's fondness for less-homogenized fare is far different from the customs of

EATING OUT: FAST-FOOD RESTAURANTS

Everyone goes to fast-food restaurants, but those who go there most are blue-collar families and cost-conscious students. Urban singles and childless couples go less frequently due to their increased health-food consciousness—and because they can enjoy the potpourri of eateries most cities offer.

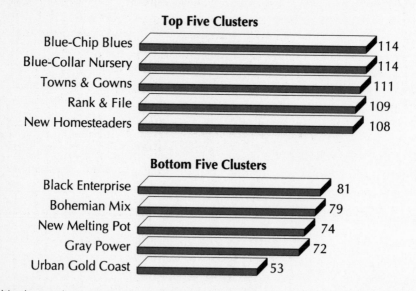

Top Five Clusters

Blue-Chip Blues	114
Blue-Collar Nursery	114
Towns & Gowns	111
Rank & File	109
New Homesteaders	108

Bottom Five Clusters

Black Enterprise	81
Bohemian Mix	79
New Melting Pot	74
Gray Power	72
Urban Gold Coast	53

Numbers indicate percentages of people who frequent fast-food restaurants, indexed against the national average. An index of 100 equals the U.S. average: 55.68%. An index of 114 means a cluster has 1.14 times the national average, or about 63%. Source: SMRB 1985/86, Claritas Corp., 1987.

his parents' poor, working-class generation. "We once took some relatives to the New Morning Cafe nearby and it took them a long time to order because they just hadn't seen dishes like lemon soup or pita bread sandwiches," he says. "They'd never been exposed to anything like it before."

Not surprisingly, a majority of Americans order "Mom's home-style cooking" when they eat at restaurants, preferring dishes they grew up with, like meat loaf, mashed potatoes and baked beans. Of course, Mom's menu is much less mundane in neighborhoods like Two More Rungs and Hispanic Mix, where nearly half the residents are immigrants or the children of immigrants. In Two More Rungs communities, the

EATING OUT: FAMILY RESTAURANTS

It's not just families who eat the fare at family restaurants, from HoJo's hamburgers to Mama Leone's meatballs. It's also a lot of rural Americans, who have no easy access to fast-food restaurants, and middle-class families who are watching their budgets. The surprising appearance of trend-conscious Young Influentials near the top of the list may simply be a result of their eating out more often than average Americans.

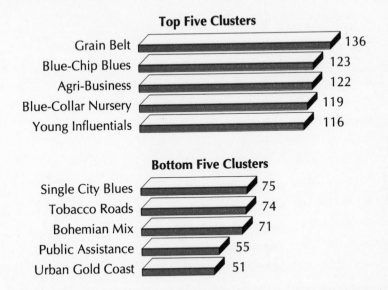

Top Five Clusters

Cluster	Index
Grain Belt	136
Blue-Chip Blues	123
Agri-Business	122
Blue-Collar Nursery	119
Young Influentials	116

Bottom Five Clusters

Cluster	Index
Single City Blues	75
Tobacco Roads	74
Bohemian Mix	71
Public Assistance	55
Urban Gold Coast	51

Numbers indicate percentages of people who frequent family restaurants, indexed against the national average. An index of 100 equals the U.S. average: 28.34%. An index of 136 means a cluster has 1.36 times the national average, or about 38%. Source: SMRB 1985/86, Claritas Corp., 1987.

most lavish meal of the week is often Sunday brunch, with many delicacies reflecting the residents' Eastern European, Jewish roots. Phyllis Talmadge of Kew Gardens in Queens, New York, describes her typical brunch as "Jewish soul food"—lox, cream cheese, bialis (salt rolls) and babka, a Russian coffee cake found at a specialty bakery. Daughter of Russian immigrants, she and her husband still drink hot tea out of glasses nestled in brass holders à la the Old Country. In the background, from 8:30 A.M. on, their radio's tuned to WEBG, a Yiddish station established by the *Jewish Daily Forward* newspaper. Like many of her neighbors, she has plenty of opportunities to preserve her culinary heritage in nearby bagel shops and kosher delicatessens. Not long ago, a Chinese kosher take-out opened nearby with the clever name, T'ain Li Chow ("ten lee," in Hebrew, means "give me").

Although most Two More Rungs residents speak English at home,

EATING OUT: "OTHER" RESTAURANTS

Urban singles top the list of those who frequent "other" restaurants, which range from white-tableclothed dining rooms to checker-tableclothed booths to ethnic eateries of all descriptions.

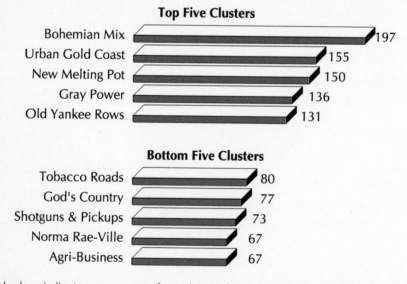

Top Five Clusters

Cluster	Index
Bohemian Mix	197
Urban Gold Coast	155
New Melting Pot	150
Gray Power	136
Old Yankee Rows	131

Bottom Five Clusters

Cluster	Index
Tobacco Roads	80
God's Country	77
Shotguns & Pickups	73
Norma Rae-Ville	67
Agri-Business	67

Numbers indicate percentages of people who frequent "other" restaurants, indexed against the national average. An index of 100 equals the U.S. average: 9.73%. An index of 197 means a cluster has 1.97 times the national average, or about 19%. Source: SMRB 1985/86, Claritas Corp., 1987.

HISPANIC COMMUNITIES

Most Hispanics settle in cities, from San Antonio's barrios to New York's ethnic pockets. Migrations of poor Mexicans to the rural Southwest have also created Hispanic communities in Hard Scrabble areas. But in the Midwest, their presence is negligible.

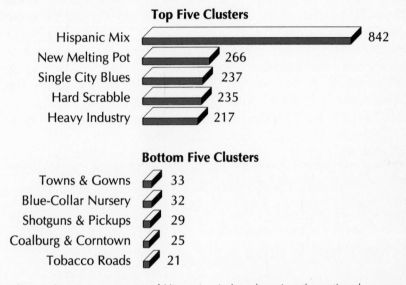

Top Five Clusters

Hispanic Mix	842
New Melting Pot	266
Single City Blues	237
Hard Scrabble	235
Heavy Industry	217

Bottom Five Clusters

Towns & Gowns	33
Blue-Collar Nursery	32
Shotguns & Pickups	29
Coalburg & Corntown	25
Tobacco Roads	21

Numbers indicate percentages of Hispanics, indexed against the national average. An index of 100 equals the U.S. average: 7%. An index of 842 means a cluster has 8.42 times the national average, or about 59%. Source: PRIZM (Census Demography), Claritas Corp., 1987.

Spanish is often the primary language in the homes of Hispanic Mix. In the cluster barrios of Miami and San Antonio, nearly 40 percent of the residents speak Spanish at home. On the streets of West San Antonio, local grocers sell barrels of baccalhau (dried cod) and cans of barbacao (barbecue); above them, billboards advertise "Es La Mejor Bud Light." To residents, preserving Spanish in the home is a matter of pride and politics; Hispanic Mixers oppose legislation to make English the nation's official language. "We don't believe in the melting pot concept. We don't want to melt," declares Maria Berriozabal, the city councilwoman who represents San Antonio's West Side barrio. "We like the notion of this country as a mosaic where people of different cultures live side by side, where the children know the difference between bananas and plantains."

For Frank and Emilia Ramos, two of Berriozabal's constituents,

America's cultural pluralism harmonizes in their daily meals. They serve a mix of American and Mexican dishes: eggs and potatoes for breakfast, meat and macaroni for lunch and enchiladas, beans and rice for dinner. "When you go to a friend's house, the first thing they ask you is if you want coffee and a tamale," says Frank, a husky and bespectacled 54-year-old who emigrated from Mexico thirty years ago. And though his eight children attend English-speaking public schools, Spanish remains the language of choice in the Ramos household. "In this community, everyone still speaks Spanish," he continues. "The priest speaks Spanish, the grocer speaks Spanish, my children watch the novellas—the Mexican soaps—in Spanish, too."

Still, Ramos fears that his children have become too Americanized and are forgetting their Mexican heritage. According to an old Mexican custom, he says, a husband serenades his wife on Mother's Day at 2 o'clock in the morning. "When that happened here," he recalls, "one of my kids woke up and said, 'Someone must be drunk again.'" Ramos chuckles for a moment and then turns serious. "Sometimes at the dinner table my youngest daughter says, 'I don't understand what you're saying.' And that upsets me. It's important to keep the old culture."

HOPE, HELP AND HOLIDAYS

Nothing better illustrates America's clustering phenomenon than those activities that bring neighbors together: Fourth of July parades, block parties and civic events that express local concerns. Social activism isn't characteristic of every community, but where it is present, it takes many forms. There are clusters whose residents tend to write letters to newspaper editors (Bohemian Mix and Money & Brains), visit public officials in person (Tobacco Roads and God's Country) and work for a political candidate (Blue Blood Estates and Gray Power). Generally, the more affluent the neighborhood, the more people participate in civic issues, their social rank affording them equal footing in dealing with school board officials and local utility administrators. But each cluster deals with social issues according to the prevailing values of its residents.

When Live Aid and Hands Across America shone national attention on the plight of the hungry in the mid-'80s, communities responded with a multitude of events that personalized the issue. In Agri-Business communities like Waynestown, Indiana, residents filled semis with grain and hay to help fellow farmers devastated by drought and depressed

CITIZEN ACTIVISTS AND CIVIC CLUB JOINERS

Unlike America's citizen activists, residents from a wide range of neighborhood types join civic clubs to organize charity fundraisers and improve the community. The poor and disenfranchised rarely belong to such groups. More upscale urbanites participate on their own in public events and demonstrations. Those in Blue Blood Estates—the wealthiest Americans —can afford to do both.

Top Five Clusters : Citizen Activists

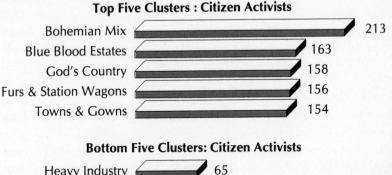

Bohemian Mix	213
Blue Blood Estates	163
God's Country	158
Furs & Station Wagons	156
Towns & Gowns	154

Bottom Five Clusters: Citizen Activists

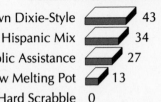

Heavy Industry	65
Hispanic Mix	60
Hard Scrabble	58
Smalltown Downtown	55
Public Assistance	48

Top Five Clusters: Civic Club Joiners

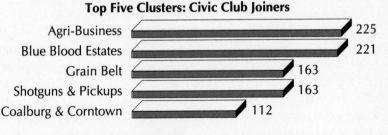

Agri-Business	225
Blue Blood Estates	221
Grain Belt	163
Shotguns & Pickups	163
Coalburg & Corntown	112

Bottom Five Clusters: Civic Club Joiners

Downtown Dixie-Style	43
Hispanic Mix	34
Public Assistance	27
New Melting Pot	13
Hard Scrabble	0

Numbers indicate percentages of people who participate in three or more public activities a year or belong to civic clubs, indexed against the national average. An index of 100 equals the U.S. average: 6.36% for public activities, 1.82% for civic clubs. An index of 200 means a cluster has twice the national average. Source: SMRB 1984/85, Claritas Corp., 1987.

prices. When the ailing steel industry forced layoffs in the Mines & Mills community of Monessen, Pennsylvania, locals organized a Food Bank to distribute canned goods to needy neighbors. And as unemployment benefits ran out, the donors became the recipients. Meanwhile, in the Pools & Patios community of Litchfield, Connecticut, the big concern was not hunger at home but starving children in Africa. Accordingly, Litchfield residents held a fundraising auction that offered, among other things, an Arabian stallion, dinner with a notable resident—local actress Susan St. James—and a vasectomy performed by a town urologist. "Nothing brings a community together better than a common cause," remarked St. James after the event, which raised $40,000. "This is more than just sending a check."

One powerful impetus for community action—regardless of economic status—is an environmental threat. A 1986 Lou Harris poll found that 93 percent of the public felt water pollution caused by toxic wastes was a serious national threat. But membership in environmental organizations illustrates how the clusters side in the debate if cleaning up the environment might cost factory jobs. Affluent communities like Money & Brains and Furs & Station Wagons, where people make their living in white-collar positions, have the highest concentration of environmental reformers. Those communities where residents earn their paychecks from factories, clusters like Mines & Mills and Rank & File, report the lowest percentage of environmentalists. Ironically, the deadliest toxic waste dumps and environmental threats are closest to those factory communities.

Ever since the Wheeling-Pittsburgh steel plant in Monessen, Pennsylvania, shut down, residents have been able to fish in the Monongahela River that borders the plant. "Ten years ago, you wouldn't know what you'd come up with, there were so many chemicals in the water," says Bob Leone, a local gas-station owner. "Now, the rivers are great for catching sunfish, bass and catfish." Leone is quick to point out, however, that there's hardly a citizen in Monessen who wouldn't trade the clean river and all its fish for the revival of the mill. Townsfolk believe the environmental regulations requiring that scrubbers be installed on furnace smokestacks were one reason their steel couldn't compete with the Japanese, forcing the plant to lay off thousands of workers.

Still environmental problems are galvanizing clusters not known for being upscale, anti-business or politically liberal. As the quantity of chemical pollutants has increased exponentially, residents of Golden Ponds communities have grown more concerned about the potential harm these toxics pose to their resorts. The middle-class residents of

Cape May, New Jersey, who vote overwhelmingly as conservative Republicans, become "flaming environmentalists," in the words of one, over the issue of toxic waste dumping in the Atlantic Ocean. Fearing damage to their beaches, this otherwise sedate Golden Ponds community has organized letter-writing campaigns, legislative lobbying at the Trenton statehouse, even a march in Washington. "Preserving the town has become our number-one concern," says Bruce Minnox, a former Cape May mayor. "People come out of the woodwork whenever their quality of life is at stake. They look at the seashore as their livelihood."

Trying to safeguard a community's natural beauty cuts across cluster demographics. On any weekday morning in the Blue Blood Estates world of Beverly Hills, you'll see more gardeners than homeowners on front lawns, dutifully manicuring the tall hedges and scraggly coconut palms that surround the mansions. But even in Public Assistance, which ranks dead last in the percentage of residents who garden, 6 percent of its citizenry cultivate plants in an effort to beautify otherwise bleak streets. Retiree Hilda Mae Bullock became so fed up with the devastation of her Public Assistance section of North Philadelphia that she took to planting flowers and vegetables in vacant lots. Neighbors soon joined in, and together they began transforming blighted streets into urban gardens they call Hope Springs. Colorfully painted tires recycled as geranium planters now sit before boarded-up rowhouses. Fenced-in lots once littered with broken bottles and rotted wood now bloom with rows of broccoli, corn, sweet potatoes and collard greens.

The makeshift gardens of Philadelphia reflect the heritage of local residents, from the Oriental vegetables grown along the streets of Chinatown to the collard and kale sprouting in black South Philadelphia. "We planted the gardens out of self-defense," says Bullock, a diminutive 65-year-old, who speaks with exuberant gestures. "If we didn't, the streets would have become garbage heaps."

Americans band together not only to fight hunger, pollution and blight but also to celebrate holidays, religious traditions and each other. Molalla, Oregon, a Shotguns & Pickups town in the foothills of the Cascade Mountains, doesn't worry about the over-commercialization of holidays like Washington's Birthday or Columbus Day. Its downtown is so economically depressed that thrift shops outnumber the clothing stores, and a bag full of clothes costs $1.50. Every year it's touch-and-go whether residents will pass a school levy to keep the local high school open one more year. But when deer-hunting season begins in the fall, the town comes to a standstill as residents pack up their 30:30 rifles and head for the hills. Even the lumber mills, the economic lifeblood of

Molalla, turn off their saws to give employees a week's freedom. "We'd have no one to work here if we didn't," concedes an Avison Mill executive.

In more urban, upscale communities, where news and information are the local currency, most holidays are duly noted by cocktail parties, chatty affairs that are an endless source of William Hamilton cartoons. You hear their voices in Money & Brains neighborhoods: professors and Foreign Service officers worrying over the decline in Soviet relations early in the evening and singing their Ivy League fight songs later on. The residents of the Georgetown section of Washington, D.C., can usually tell when such a soiree is taking place by the traffic jam of limos along the neighborhood's narrow streets. If the affair isn't catered, it's customary for the hostess to do her party shopping at one of the local French markets, leaving the cook at home and the chauffeur in the car.

Actually, "cocktail parties" has become a misnomer in Money & Brains, where residents really believe "You can never be too rich or too thin." In recent years, the thin-obsessed partyers have given up the hard stuff in favor of white wine and imported champagne; both are consumed at twice the national average in this cluster. Social observer Paul Fussell notes that so many former liquor drinkers have given it up that cocktail parties have created a new breed of "white-wine drunks who, because they are seen to be knocking back only something light and sensible, hope that their swayings and stammerings will pass unnoticed." One tradition hasn't changed: the residents of Money & Brains still consume more cocktail nuts than any other cluster.

Holidays are about tradition and passing on customs from one generation to the next. And the presence of children is one of the most powerful influences on how clusters celebrate holidays. In the Gray Power community of Sun City, Arizona, where children under 21 are banned as residents, the Fourth of July is just another sunshine-filled day, marked without fireworks or community parades. In the Single City Blues areas of Southeast Portland, the Christmas season is often a sad time, because residents have so few family ties. For years, police officials and psychiatrists have reported the increased incidence of suicides and domestic violence during Christmas. As Washington therapist Dr. Barton Kraff has observed, "For single and divorced people apart from their families and feeling out of sync with everyone else, Christmas can be a downer." To cope, Single City Blues residents join together for "orphans" dinners at holidays, taking comfort in their surrogate families.

A cluster map of religious preferences is a good predictor of how communities will observe religious holidays: Two More Rungs communities, filled with the children of Jewish immigrants, turn into ghost towns on Yom Kippur, a day of fasting and prayer; the Catholics of Old Yankee Rows towns decorate their main streets with streamers for Easter Day parades. It's inevitable that in neighborhoods filled with highly mobile residents—clusters like Bohemian Mix—conflicts arise in the melange of religious practices. In a townhouse condominium development in the Bohemian Mix area of Philadelphia's Queen Village, some residents nearly came to blows over a proposal to share the cost of stringing Christmas bulbs throughout the development. One woman, who'd recently moved in from a Grain Belt town in Iowa, expressed shock at the resistance—though she shouldn't have. Bohemian Mix has six times as many Jews as Grain Belt, where they are a paltry .75 percent of all households.

Liz Michel, a 31-year-old attorney and one of the resistors, maintains that religious tolerance is one of the values that Bohemian Mixers hold dear. "I know our neighbor would have been happier living in a small, Christian community where the houses look alike and the neighbors come out of the same cookie-cutter mold," says Michel, a statuesque blond and former Protestant who converted to Judaism at the time of her marriage in 1980. "She couldn't understand why the Jewish residents didn't appreciate the Christmas decorations. And she didn't like the confusion. She'd grown up one way, had lived her life one way and didn't want to change. But in this neighborhood, with poor blacks living next to wealthy whites, where there's a 200-year-old church on one block and a synagogue being converted into condos on the next, you have to be flexible."

By contrast, in the family-filled small towns of Coalburg & Corntown, homogeneous values still bind the community and color their holiday celebrations. With their small centers of commerce, Coalburg & Corntowners rely on fraternal and civic clubs to host community bashes; the cluster ranks among the top for club membership. When July Fourth comes around, the residents of Columbia City, Indiana, throw a noisy extravaganza resembling a scene from *The Music Man*. In this heartland community, patriotism flourishes amid shady streets and businesses punctuated with American flags. According to town fathers, Columbia City has long prided itself on the number of volunteers it musters when the U.S. military calls. "You get the impression that people blindly love God, country and Columbia City," says David Heritier, a rotund, 41-year-old attorney and first vice commander of the American Legion.

"They send their sons off to war and welcome them back graciously."
With such patriotic fervor, Columbia City's social center understandably
is the American Legion: of 5,100 city residents, nearly 1,100 are members. While the service club is frequently the setting for weekend dances
and bingo games, it inevitably outdoes itself with an old-fashioned Independence Day celebration.

For Columbia City's July 4, 1986, the American Legion hosted a pig
roast and day-long carnival at DeVol Field, where local civic groups sold
pizza, fried dough and ice cream to raise money for their various causes:
the high-school swim team, the pee-wee football squad or the town
archaeological society. While children painted themselves with stars-
and-stripes makeup, their parents listened to a makeshift bluegrass band
playing from the back of a flatbed truck. Whole families—and extended
families—flopped down on the park's surrounding hillside, their Cole-
man coolers brimming with picnic staples. Larry Paulus, a 38-year-old
resident, showed up for the festivities with parents, wife and sons in
tow. He noted that many families can trace their roots in the community
back a hundred years. When he applied for a job at Dana's Weatherhead
division, he ran out of room on the application listing all the relatives
who worked at the company. "It was three weeks before I realized that
my supervisor was a second cousin," he says. "Everyone knows me and
my parents. If my kids do something wrong, it often gets back to me
before the kids get home. The local joke is that everyone knows what
everyone's doing already, but they get the newspaper just to find out
who got caught."

By nightfall that Fourth of July, every available inch around DeVol
Field was covered with people reclined on blankets or seated in the
backs of pickups. Crickets chirped and toddlers squirmed impatiently in
their fathers' arms. Finally, the first curling comets shot into the sky,
bursting into huge flowers of red and blue. Children and adults alike
cheered, screeched and applauded—as they had for a hundred years and
as they would no doubt for another hundred years to come. In Columbia
City as in many American communities, holiday celebrations don't
change much from generation to generation. But as our society embraces more divergent lifestyles and nurtures them in communities like
New Beginnings and Bohemian Mix, we will find more causes for celebration and more ways to celebrate them.

7

POLITICS: FROM PRECINCT TO THE PRESIDENCY

*"Knowledge of human nature is the begin-
ning and end of political education."*
—historian Henry Brooks Adams, 1907

Political targeting began with the first candidate who decided to work the wards to drum up support, when shoe-leathering, hand-shaking and one-on-one contact were essential to successful politicking. But in this decade, computers have joined the campaign arsenal, allowing politicians to use population classification systems like the PRIZM clusters instead of factory-gate appearances to learn voter concerns. While often criticized by political purists, these computerized efforts cannot be ignored. In 1983, opponents of that legendary political rapscallion, Louisiana Democrat Edwin Edwards, learned the hard way that the cluster system can provide more insight than traditional voter pulse-taking.

On July 27 of that year, Edwards formally announced his third bid to become governor of Louisiana. Edwards, then 56, was a Cajun-blooded free spirit who lived up to his nickname as Fast Eddie by his fondness for dice and beautiful women—and his history of narrowly escaping guilty verdicts on bribery, fraud and racketeering charges. During two earlier terms as governor, between 1972 and 1980, he'd earned a mixed report card—credited with boosting the state's economy while criticized for letting Louisiana slip in the standings for literacy, prenatal care and prison-reform programs.

But by early 1983, voters were tired of the stories of his exploits in Las Vegas and his appearances before New Orleans grand juries. And he faced an uphill battle to unseat Republican Governor David Treen, whose stolid, deliberate style was in sharp contrast to Edwards's shoot-from-the-lip flamboyance. "Treen," Edwards liked to say, "is the only man in the world who takes an hour and a half to watch '60 Minutes.' "

At the start of the campaign, polls showed Edwards with a base of support among black and Cajun voters, a slim coalition still tolerant of their back-country populist. But he lacked broad appeal among the middle class of northern Louisiana, where voters respected Treen's reputation for honesty, hard work and moral conduct. Edwards's integrity issue, as it became known, contributed to Treen's endorsement by the state's leading newspaper, the New Orleans *Times-Picayune.*

To restore that middle-class confidence, the Edwards campaign turned to the cluster system in what was then its political infancy. In May 1983, Edwards strategists contacted Targeting Systems, Inc., the firm based in Rosslyn, Virginia, that was licensed by Claritas to develop political applications for the clusters. TSI promptly polled 1,800 Louisiana voters, recording their campaign concerns and candidate preferences by neighborhood type.

The survey results generally confirmed what was already suspected: Edwards's weakness among voters in a dozen middle-class clusters. But they also pinpointed three midscale blue-collar clusters where voters were still up for grabs: Blue-Chip Blues—suburban neighborhoods of highly paid skilled workers and their families; Norma Rae-Ville—less affluent mill towns populated by minimally educated factory workers and their families; and Coalburg & Corntown—picket-fence communities built on light industry and farming.

Conventional political wisdom called for a media campaign to appeal to all of Louisiana's middle-class voters. But TSI proposed an untraditional, highly targeted direct-mail effort to reach the three clusters of undecideds. Lynn Pounian, TSI's 33-year-old chief, believed that an Edwards political pitch, written in three distinct voices, could speak directly to the concerns of different middle-class neighborhoods. A dynamic Chicago native and advocate of witty direct-mail advertising, she had honed her skills in numerous national and state political campaigns and as vice president of operations for The Naisbitt Group (which produced the book *Megatrends*). Before joining TSI in 1982, she had witnessed the effectiveness of the clusters during Democrat Bill Gunner's 1980 Florida race for the Senate, bringing a longshot in a crowded field to within a photo finish of an upset.

For the Louisiana campaign, Pounian decided on a series of brochure mailers to present Edwards's message to the trio of neighborhood types. "We'd seen enough surveys to understand the values of each cluster—the cluster gestalt, if you will," says Pounian. "And it was obvious that people in the different clusters had specific responsive chords. So it became a matter of presenting a message to hit that chord and pull people into our camp who wouldn't normally be there."

Among Louisiana's Blue-Chip Blues residents, purse-strings sounded the correct chord. Despite having risen to the top of their pay scales, these voters were still insecure about their jobs, acutely money-conscious and worried about the state's growing budget deficit. TSI's response: a four-page, red-lettered mailer opening with the question: "$1.7 BILLION. AND WHAT HAVE WE GOT TO SHOW FOR IT?" The brochure's inside copy went on to explain that the Treen administration, with a budget $1.7 billion larger than Edwards had ever enjoyed, had still caused skyrocketing unemployment, a worsening business climate and a growing state debt. An "open letter" from Edwards concluded that these problems were not insurmountable—naturally, with an experienced leader like Edwards back in office.

The message to Norma Rae-Ville was more direct, given that the residents in these poorer mill towns don't believe they have much power in the political process. "They perceive themselves as bystanders, affected by whatever happens," explains Pounian. To motivate these apathetic voters, TSI attacked the issue head-on in another mailer: "EDWIN EDWARDS. DAVID TREEN. DOES IT REALLY MAKE A DIFFERENCE?" the front page asked. Opening the brochure, the reader found the answer: "YOU BET IT DOES," and the text detailed Edwards's favorable record in the areas of employment, education and state finances. The amount of copy was about half that of the Blue-Chip Blues mailer because, as Pounian notes, "we know they're not going to read too much in Norma Rae-Ville. They're lucky if they graduated from high school."

In Coalburg & Corntown, small-town communities where the residents long for a simpler past, TSI appropriately turned nostalgic. Survey results indicated the voters were concerned about crime and unemployment, so the brochure began wistfully: "IT SEEMS LIKE SO LONG AGO . . . WHEN WE COULD WALK DOWN OUR OWN STREETS, AND FEEL SAFE. WHEN WE COULD PASS THE UNEMPLOYMENT OFFICE AND NOT SEE A LINE.

WHEN WE WERE PROSPERING." Inside, the text harkened back to four years ago, when Edwards was governor and the living was easy—or at least easier. The mailer concluded with a pitch to recreate those happier days by voting Edwards back into the governor's mansion. "THE BEST OF YESTERDAY AND A BETTER TOMORROW," the copy promised.

The results, recalls Pounian, were startling. "Slowly, the numbers began changing in the polls," she says.

Although surveys showed Treen and Edwards evenly matched in the spring, when voters went to the polls on October 23rd, they gave Edwards a landslide victory, with 63 percent of the ballots. State analysts reported that Edwards had, in fact, cut into Treen's power base in the middle-class parishes of northern Louisiana. "The clusters let us

---

TARGETING A POLITICAL DIRECT-MAIL CAMPAIGN

In 1983, Louisiana gubernatorial candidate Edwin Edwards targeted three clusters of undecided voters—clockwise from upper left: Norma Rae-Ville, Coalburg & Corntown and Blue-Chip Blues—customizing a direct-mail campaign to each. They helped him turn a potential defeat into a victory.

SOURCE: Targeting Systems, Inc., 1983.

know what the hell was going on out there, what these people cared about," says Pounian. "It wasn't magic to target a message to fit their perspective. Actually, it came down to common sense."

■ A NEW POLITICAL WEAPON

At the turn of the century, when city neighborhoods were viewed as virtual sovereign states, residents typically voted for the party that provided the best prospects for improving the neighborhood. Traditional partisan politics were linked to neighborhood precincts because victorious candidates could award jobs to loyal campaign workers who turned neighbors into supporters. Big-city political machines, with their army of ward workers, allowed a Mayor Richard Daly to "deliver Chicago" to the candidate of his choice election after election.

But the decline of the spoils system, apathy and the increasing nonpartisanship of the American voter steadily eroded the ranks of party loyalists. Big-city machines gave way to single-issue organizations, and candidates turned to special-interest groups for endorsements. These voting blocs—women, blacks, senior citizens, business, labor—became powerful forces in the '70s as post-Watergate ethics laws reduced the amount of money individuals and corporations could donate to candidates.

Sympathetic special-interest groups could provide endorsements from their members and money from their associated political action committees. The liberal AFL-CIO, with its political arm (Committee on Political Education) and its computerized mailing list of 13.8 million names, was free to spend unlimited amounts of money "educating" its members—and getting out the vote. Meanwhile, its power was more than matched by the membership lists of conservative groups which, aided by Richard Viguerie, created the art of constituency-by-direct-mail. Viguerie's Falls Church, Virginia, direct-mail operation, with its computer tapes of 20 million conservative supporters, helped finance such New Right institutions as the National Conservative Political Action Committee (NCPAC), the Conservative Caucus and the Fund for the Survival of a Free Congress. They exerted their political muscle not only by endorsing conservative candidates but also by developing controversial negative campaigns against targeted liberals.

Still, organizations don't cast ballots, their members do. And in the early '80s, polls began demonstrating that monolithic voting blocs were no longer reliable in determining voter preferences. A 1983 Gallup poll in Michigan found that a union endorsement turned off as many rank-and-file members as it turned on. Ken Moch, a biotech executive from the God's Country community of Plainsboro, New Jersey, epitomizes this unaligned phenomenon when he proclaims, "I think of myself as a conservative liberal, voting for the best person, no matter the party. Call me a Republicrat or Demičan."

In a stratified nation where the majority still rules, this sentiment sends shock waves among political strategists. How can candidates build coalitions of voters who ricochet from issue to issue like errant pinballs?

Neighborhood lifestyles, it turns out, prove to be a natural system for predicting political behavior. Because they are based on multiple socioeconomic indicators, clusters mirror voters' values more closely than do partisan labels, single issues or single factors like ethnic background, sex or geographic location. "True coalitions form according to lifestyle," says Charles Welsh, a TSI vice president and political analyst. "How people live—whether they're married, have kids or are footloose —all influence how they'll vote."

In this age of shrinking party identification, clusters can explain why some issues cross party lines yet remain true to neighborhood lifestyles. Trade protectionism, for instance, is popular among Young Suburbia voters who have lost jobs to foreign competition, such as textile workers in South Carolina, semiconductor workers of the Silicon Valley and autoworkers in Michigan and Missouri. This bipartisan issue allowed the normally Republican voters of Young Suburbia outside of St. Louis to split the ticket and elect Republican Senator John Danforth and Democratic Representative Richard Gephardt, who both supported trade barriers that would benefit the local auto industry. In contrast, the issue attracted few votes from Young Influential residents of the south side of St. Louis for whom global competition means cheaper Porsches, Guccis and Sonys. "To Young Influential voters," says Welsh, "protectionism is an economically primitive concept. They believe in free trade."

Indeed, geodemography may best explain why traditional voting blocs are no longer practical. When the women's movement rallied to pass the Equal Rights Amendment in the late '70s and early '80s, leaders counted on a nationwide grass-roots rebellion of all women to support the effort. But a cluster analysis of its core backers—the membership of the National Organization for Women, Common Cause and the American Civil Liberties Union—revealed that these people were concentrated in only a few clusters: the affluent, cosmopolitan neighborhoods of Urban Gold Coast, Bohemian Mix and Money & Brains. Only a small percentage of ERA supporters lived in the hinterland clusters of Grain Belt, Back-Country Folks and Tobacco Roads. Unable to woo these rural and small-town Americans to the cause, the ERA was doomed, as one southern state legislature after another rejected it. Had they crafted a message to reach these folks, we might today have an Equal Rights Amendment in the Constitution.

The breakup of the long-time partnership between organized labor and the Democratic Party is another story best told through neighborhood types—actually, two clusters, Heavy Industry and New Homesteaders. For a generation, Heavy Industry, a predominantly white, lower-working-class cluster of urban neighborhoods, represented the

---

NOW MEMBERS

The core members of the National Organization for Women live in upscale urban neighborhoods. The lack of representation in rural America was one reason NOW efforts to pass the Equal Rights Amendment ultimately failed.

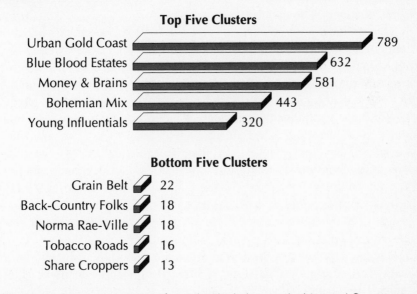

Top Five Clusters

Urban Gold Coast	789
Blue Blood Estates	632
Money & Brains	581
Bohemian Mix	443
Young Influentials	320

Bottom Five Clusters

Grain Belt	22
Back-Country Folks	18
Norma Rae-Ville	18
Tobacco Roads	16
Share Croppers	13

Numbers indicate percentages of people who belong to the National Organization for Women, indexed against the national average. Data based on a survey of 150,000 NOW members. An index of 100 equals the U.S. average: .5%. An index of 789 means a cluster has 7.89 times the national average, or about 4%. Source: Claritas Corp., 1986.

great American proletariat. Since the New Deal, its blue-collar workers had believed the Democrats represented the party of prosperity.

But in the '70s, factory jobs that provided union workers with decent wages dwindled in the face of global competition. Between 1972 and 1982, foreign goods gained a higher share of the U.S. market in thirty of forty-two industries. Unemployment began to pervade Heavy Industry's neighborhoods, typically built amidst a city's old factory district. As the skilled laborers moved to better opportunities in the right-to-work states of the Sunbelt, they adapted to the prevailing Republican climate that warmed the frontier boomtowns of New Homesteaders. Meanwhile, Democratic—and union—support among those remaining in Heavy Industry crumbled under the weight of double-digit inflation and mounting unemployment. Between 1970 and 1980, the industrial neighborhoods aged rapidly and deteriorated to the point where they are no longer a major force in party fundraising. During that decade, Heavy Industry dropped seven notches on the ZQ scale to rank thirty-fourth.

"Now when you talk about prosperity in Heavy Industry, people say 'Republican,' " says Welsh, a gravel-voiced 35-year-old with a laid-back manner and quick wit. "When residents lost their jobs, they no longer had the pro-Democratic influence of the union, one of their main sources of information. Now they're casting about."

This political saga is being played out in Hamtramck, Michigan, a Heavy Industry enclave of 22,000 surrounded by Detroit. At one time, more than 55,000 people jammed into the neighborhood's narrow streets of modest duplexes, Polish butcher shops and Russian bakeries. Jobs were plentiful in the flourishing auto industry and, like other ethnic communities that fueled the smokestack industries, Hamtramck became known as a Democratic stronghold. Democratic presidential candidates —Truman, Kennedy, Humphrey and Mondale—all made campaign stops in the community that locals called Poletown. "Truman said that this was the most Democratic town in the country," remembers Leo Kirpluk, a 67-year-old retired baker and former Democratic precinct delegate. "Growing up, we didn't even know what a Republican was. The voters here were 98 percent Democratic."

But the shutdown of the Dodge Main plant in 1980 changed everything. By the mid-'80s, the lack of adequate housing—many of Hamtramck's two-bedroom duplexes are valued at under $20,000—and the exodus of young people to the suburbs had taken their toll on the Democratic workers. In 1984, 41 percent of Hamtramck's voters backed President Reagan, the highest percentage any Republican had received

BLUE-COLLAR POLITICS

The decline in American manufacturing has sent unionized factory workers from Heavy Industry neighborhoods to expanding right-to-work New Homesteaders communities in the Sunbelt. In the process, a traditional Democratic constituency has drifted into hard-core Republican territory. Despite their more conservative bent, family-oriented New Homesteaders support anti-nuclear policies; the heavily Catholic Heavy Industry residents, however, are stronger on issues of moral traditionalism.

Heavy Industry		New Homesteaders
	Party Identification	
98	Democrat	76
90	Republican	120
36	Independent	30
102	Political apathy	94
	Political Ideology	
94	Liberal	82
156	Moderate	72
64	Conservative	142
100	1984 Mondale vote	80
	Concerns	
102	Anti–nuclear arms	116
64	Reducing budget	82
104	Unemployment	120
128	Moral traditions	112

Numbers indicate attitudes of voters, indexed against the national average. An index of 100 equals the U.S. average. An index of 150 means a cluster has 1.5 times the national average. Source: Targeting Systems, Inc., 1985.

in Hamtramck history. Cluster-wide, Heavy Industry residents gave President Reagan 59 percent of their votes.

In Hamtramck, voters like Leo Kirpluk explained the Democratic defections on moral grounds. Like 30 percent of Heavy Industry's residents, Kirpluk is Catholic, and he opposed abortion, birth control education in the schools and other issues championed by the liberal wing of the Democratic Party. "I believe in love, marriage and babies, but all in the proper order," says Kirpluk, a chunky man with thick glasses and white hair who keeps a reproduction of Michelangelo's *Pietà* in his living room. "I don't believe in previews."

Father Stanley Ulman, pastor of Hamtramck's St. Ladislaus Roman

Catholic Church, confirms the shift in political allegiances among many of his aging parishoners. "In a sense the Democrats brought it upon themselves," says Ulman, a husky second-generation Hamtramck resident who conducts Sunday mass in English and Polish. "They've espoused so many liberal causes that these people have revolted and said, 'Hey, that's not why I joined the Democratic Party. Just because my parents and grandparents were Democratic doesn't mean I can't vote for a Republican.' "

Today Hamtramck's out-of-work and retired autoworkers spend their days in the dingy bars on Caniff and Joseph Campau streets, sometimes talking of a community renaissance. In 1985, General Motors opened a new plant on the old Dodge site, an automated facility employing 4,500 workers and 260 robots that turns out Cadillac, Buick and Oldsmobile luxury cars. The opening of this Poletown plant, the first new assembly factory to be built in Detroit in fifty years, brought with it the demolition of 1,500 homes, businesses and churches as well as bitter protests over the dislocations. But city planners declared the plant's injection of new jobs to be in the public interest. And the old Democratic wards were bulldozed under, the image of a rejected party swept aside like an outdated machine.

Albeit grudgingly, Hamtramck's residents have come to regard the GOP as the party of the future. Indeed, for the first time in Father Ulman's memory, a member of his family is running for Congress on the GOP ticket. "My Dad must be turning over in his grave," sighs Ulman, whose relatives include many former Democratic Party officials. "But his chances are good because people know that he's Polish and he's going to watch out for us. They're saying to themselves, 'Hey, it ain't all that bad to be a Republican.' "

That view would hardly be disputed in New Homesteaders, a cluster composed of rustic towns like Redding, California, Yuma, Arizona, and Loveland, Colorado. While Heavy Industry has been fighting off decline, New Homesteaders communities throughout the Sunbelt comprise one of the nation's largest and fastest-growing neighborhood types. Many new residents are young urban exiles who've sought a countrified setting in which to raise their children—far from the maddening crowds. They typically report some college schooling, middle-class incomes and low-tech jobs.

And they're Republican, a classic case of upward mobility and suburbanization eroding urban Democratic ties. GOP officials have looked forward to this trend since the first Eisenhower victory, when a Democratic poll was supposed to have said, "The suburbs beat us." In 1984,

THE PESSIMISM INDEX

The most pessimistic Americans—the voters who think the country is "moving in the wrong direction"—tend to live in predominantly black urban neighborhoods. The exception is Bohemian Mix, home to America's counterculture.

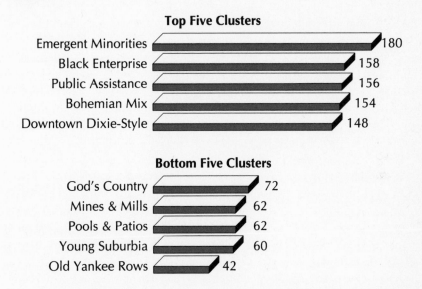

Top Five Clusters

Emergent Minorities	180
Black Enterprise	158
Public Assistance	156
Bohemian Mix	154
Downtown Dixie-Style	148

Bottom Five Clusters

God's Country	72
Mines & Mills	62
Pools & Patios	62
Young Suburbia	60
Old Yankee Rows	42

The numbers indicate nonvoting behavior by cluster—residents who failed to register or vote in 1984 compared to the national average. An index of 100 equals the U.S. average. An index of 180 means a cluster has 1.80 times the national average. Source: Targeting Systems, Inc., 1985.

New Homesteaders handed Reagan 69 percent of their vote and a year later gave him his highest approval rating among all the clusters. Having fled the city problems of crime and poverty, New Homesteaders represent a new breed of American voter: young, anti–big government and Republican.

Loveland, Colorado, is typical of Republican-leaning New Homesteader communities on the rise. During the '70s, its population doubled to 31,000, making it one of the fastest-growing cities in the nation. Located about an hour's drive north of Denver, the town has attracted a steady flow of technical workers to such firms as Hewlett-Packard, Kodak and Colorado Crystal. In fact, businesses in Loveland have had trouble keeping pace with the rush of newcomers and maintain that underemployment is a big problem. "We have waiters and waitresses with master's degrees," says Dennis Anderson, Loveland's Chamber of Commerce president. "They come here for the beauty, then wait around for jobs to open up." He remembers the time in 1986 when Wal-Mart opened a new store and 1,500 people lined up to apply for 130 positions.

The exodus to New Homesteaders communities like Loveland represents an '80s version of the back-to-the-land movement. The young singles who dropped out for backwoods communes during the '60s today are married parents looking for decent schools, scenic vistas and an unhassled pace. In Loveland, they show up for the regular art-gallery openings wearing workboots and jeans, their toddlers tucked inside backpacks. On summer afternoons, they stroll among the contemporary outdoor sculptures at Benson Park, their fishing poles in hand, ready to try their luck in a bordering stream. At the nearby Palmer Gardens shopping center, they can stop off for frozen yogurt, floppy discs, fish bait and shotgun shells.

"It's freer out here than in the city, but we're still unsure of our identity," observes Becky Orr, a 31-year-old reporter for the Loveland *Daily Reporter Herald* and a lifelong resident. "People are happy that the landscape isn't ruined with a bunch of factories and that they can see the mountains when they go off to work. A popular bumper sticker around here is 'Don't Californicate Colorado.' Once newcomers get out here, they want to shut the door so it won't grow any bigger."

Victor Wowk is one who made it to Loveland while the door was still open. The son of an immigrant autoworker from Hamtramck, he enrolled in the University of Michigan's mechanical engineering program to avoid following in his father's footsteps on an auto assembly line. After a stint in the Air Force brought him to Colorado, he decided to stay out West to work, tossing out his machinists' union card when he joined Hewlett-Packard. "It seemed to me that the union workers were less interested in doing a good job than getting revenge on management," says Wowk, a lean 38-year-old with sandy hair and angular features. "Around here, people say that companies that are unionized probably deserve to be."

A self-described conservative Republican in a town where registered GOP voters outnumber Democrats by nearly two to one, Wowk speaks admiringly of the Reagan administration's military buildup and reductions in social welfare programs. "People in Loveland don't take kindly to welfare recipients," he says. "There's little tolerance for social parasites, for people who don't earn a living or grow their own food." With his wife and three children, ages 1 to 5, Wowk lives in a modest plywood rambler in a transitional neighborhood with other "escapees from the

East," as he puts it. Despite his Hamtramck upbringing—or perhaps because of it—he harbors little sympathy for striking by autoworkers, declaring, "They get paid too much already. Most consumers feel they're paying for the high union wages with the increased cost of automobiles."

In New Homesteaders towns like Loveland, residents try to distance themselves from the ills of urban America. When Hewlett-Packard announced a voluntary severance program in 1986 due to stiff foreign competition, Wowk considered moving his family back to his roots. But a house-hunting expedition to Detroit and one too many freeway rush hours changed his mind. "There are too many problems I wanted my children to avoid—drugs, violence, the pressures of a high-density population," he says. "The pace is fast but the people are more pushy, too." Wowk decided to stay in Loveland, knowing he'll probably have to take a cut in his $42,000-a-year salary. "We're willing to do that in order to stay out here in the wide open spaces," says Wowk. In a community where people just want to be left alone, there's a lot of appeal in the GOP's government-off-our-backs philosophy.

"THE NEW MAGIC"

Clusters first entered the political arena in 1978 when Missouri voters faced a right-to-work referendum that would bar union contracts across the state. The United Labor Committee of Missouri, a coalition of union groups, was mobilized after an early poll indicated 63 percent of the public favored the measure, 30 percent opposed it and 7 percent were undecided. More disturbing to the labor organizers, even 57 percent of the state's union members had expressed support for it, siding against their own unions. Matt Reese, a political consultant hired by the labor group to turn the vote around, blamed union members' position on confusion. "The union workers didn't understand their self-interest," says Reese, a burly campaign operative who came to Washington with the Kennedy administration. "If you asked someone if he was for the right to work, he'd answer 'Of course.' If you asked him why, he'd say, 'Because it sounds good. It sounds American. How could anyone be against one's right to work?' "

In August 1978, the labor coalition hired pollster William Hamilton to survey 1,367 respondents who represented, proportionately, the clusters that existed within the state's borders. The poll asked subjects how they lived and what they thought about in the political arena.

Claritas then linked the addresses of the respondents to each of the state's 6,000 clustered block groups (typically a four-square-block area) and analyzed the poll data to identify the initiative's firm supporters, staunch opponents and persuadable voters. Eighteen clusters appeared to hold significant concentrations of persuadables, and they became the labor campaign's prime targets. By identifying voters from other phone and direct-mail lists who lived in the persuadable clusters, the coalition eventually targeted 595,000 Missourians to hear labor's message.

With the swing voters identified, the labor coalition debated strategies to secure their support. Concerned that a highly publicized effort would arouse the right-to-work backers, organizers earmarked only 15 percent of their $2.2 million budget for television, the mass medium of influence. Instead, they opted for a relatively quiet campaign of mail, telephone and personal contacts to reach persuadables without disturbing the referendum's sleeping supporters. "The campaign was so carefully targeted," Hamilton says, "that one resident of Springfield, Missouri, might think that defeating the initiative was the most important thing since the invention of sliced bread. Meanwhile, a few blocks away, someone might not even know that the initiative was on the ballot."

In early October, organizers launched their get-out-the-labor-vote drive, having developed several strategies to speak to the concerns of the eighteen targeted clusters. Voters in rural Grain Belt and Agri-Business clusters, for instance, heard what was described as the "pocketbook argument," which held that passage of the initiative would financially hurt not just union workers but those farmers who sold produce to union members. The skilled craftsworkers in Blue-Collar Nursery received the "fairness" message, which praised the current system's requirement of a majority of workers to decide on the formation of a union shop. In Coalburg & Corntown, where polled voters expressed concern that the economy was changing for the worse, organizers offered a "status quo" appeal, noting that other right-to-work states near Missouri had become home to the nation's poverty-stricken underclass.

All told, organizers prepared eighteen custom-tailored letters, varying the paragraphs according to Hamilton's cluster findings. As Election Day neared, the "favorables" and "undecideds" began receiving multiple mailings with the tailored message. Then, postcards and phone calls right before the election reminded them to vote.

Joseph Mockus, one of the political operatives backing the referendum in the campaign, remembers the campaign's intensity: "It is difficult to describe the voter-contact program initiated by the Reese team in Missouri without the word 'harassment' coming to mind," he wrote in

Campaigns & Elections magazine. "Besides the official mailings, there were calls from centralized telephone banks and from volunteers in their homes." Indeed, the labor campaign volunteers seemed consumed by their cluster attack. Wrote Mockus: "Late at night, after 14-hour days, the Reese group would occasionally gather in hotel bars and joke about Mr. and Mrs. Cluster Fourteen, the leading couple in a fantastic soap opera in which the right-to-work issue replaced adultery as the principal area of concern."

In two short months, the United Labor Committee had gone from early underdog to election-day favorite. When 1.5 million Missouri voters went to the polls in November 1978, the final tally represented a complete reversal of the early poll data: 60 percent of the voters rejected the right-to-work proposition. The victory didn't come cheap: the clustering effort alone cost $300,000—about 20 percent of the Labor Committee's campaign budget. But labor leaders were convinced the extra cost more than made up for the fact that less money was wasted on appeals to unpromising groups of voters. Political columnist James J. Kilpatrick observed after the vote, "Union supporters knew exactly where to throw the curve, where to throw the fast ball and where not to waste their time."

Clustering's impressive debut in Missouri prompted politicos like Reese to dub it "the new magic" and predict that it would revolutionize the face of political campaigning. In 1980, Reese began offering the PRIZM cluster system to presidential candidates, extolling targeting's virtues for helping a candidate single out those areas where he should do well, areas where he had no chance and areas where he might be able to persuade people. He courted several presidential contenders, but no contracts materialized.

In fact, in the years since the Missouri labor victory, clusters have figured in only a handful of successful congressional campaigns, among them the Senate bids of Missouri Democrat Thomas Eagleton in 1980 and West Virginia Democrat Jay Rockefeller in 1984 (though it's difficult to assess the cluster system's contribution when it was just one of many weapons in Rockefeller's colossal $20 million arsenal). The Reagan for President Committee in 1984 and the Democratic National Committee in 1985 both cluster-coded nationwide political polls to better understand voter concerns, but no individual candidate used cluster technology in the 1986 election. And in 1988, only special-interest groups employed the clusters to raise funds for candidates who back their political causes.

Why are politicians passing up the cluster bandwagon? Some point to the price: the bill for surveying a moderate-sized state by cluster groups and then supplying the messages to reach targeted voters can reach $100,000. "It costs too much to generate a decent-sized survey," says political consultant Eddie Mahe, who's provided cluster technology to the Republicans. "You're talking $30 to analyze each interview." And many pols simply rely on their intuition and years of experience in communicating with their constituency.

Admittedly, cluster analysts have found it easier to "sell" a referendum issue, with its static concerns, than a mercurial candidate whose image changes daily during a campaign. In this age when most voters receive their political information from television, their feeling about a candidate can shift with the nightly news. Even if a candidate develops a carefully targeted direct-mail campaign to get his or her message across, an opponent can still negate it with a well-timed blitz of TV commercials.

"TV can communicate a message much more clearly than the careful work you've done setting up the targeted messages through telephone and direct mail," TSI's Welsh concedes. "And it can undo your work in some groups." Although clusters can help strategists select the best TV programs to reach voters in specific clusters—whether "Miami Vice" or "Murder, She Wrote"—a wealthy opponent who blankets the airwaves can overwhelm any low-budget, spot-buying approach, no matter how well the ads are targeted. "In the face of an all-out, big-budget media campaign," says Welsh, "clusters have their limits. They have more power in referenda campaigns when you're not dealing with candidate personalities."

The clusters' creators have also been dogged by another source of criticism—the question of ethics. Some political observers fear that the clustering "magic" might involve more than a little Orwellian voodoo. "I wonder if it wouldn't be pretty easy to lose the human touch in all the tapes and codes and banks," Kilpatrick has written, concerned that political candidates could be sold "like so many tubes of toothpaste."

Political economist Robert Reich worries that we've already entered the era of packaged candidates who run for office because they're perceived as electable commodities rather than as effective leaders. Speaking at a League of Women Voters broadcast on the eve of the 1986 election, he charged that most contemporary political campaigns had already turned into Madison Avenue sell-jobs that relied on armies of TV advisors, pollsters and consultants. "The problem is that a democracy depends upon leadership, not marketable commodities," said Reich, a Harvard University professor and author of *Tales of a New*

America. "You need people who are going to create new visions and inspire the citizens, not simply pander the way we do with commercial products."

In his book, *The Rise of the Computer State,* journalist David Burnham raises similar questions about the impact of cluster politicking on the democratic process. With computerized direct-mail machines able to craft a multitude of messages directed to millions of prescreened voters, writes Burnham, "the truth about a candidate and his promises may be obscured for both the individual voters and even the most aggressive reporters." Receiving only pieces of a candidate's platform filtered through a cluster perspective makes it impossible for a voter to make an educated decision about the complete platform, claims Burnham. In the marketplace of ideas, the selective disclosure of truth is the moral equivalent of lying.

Yet many political strategists disagree with this criticism, noting that computerized data banks are only replacing old-fashioned ward heelers. Looking good to voters is the name of the game, they say, and the way politicking has been played throughout American history. If cluster technology allows a candidate to send letters discussing Israel to Two More Rungs voters and others, written in Spanish, stressing family values to Hispanic Mix residents, so be it. TSI's Welsh notes that targeting is only the latest tool in the marketing of American candidates. "The image of John Kennedy walking along the beach with his coat slung over his shoulder with nice music in the background is what turned politics into marketing," he says. "And those soft-sell spots were aired in 1960."

Given the infrequent use of clusters in recent political campaigns, ethical concerns may be premature. Cluster targeting has found a more receptive audience among corporate clients attempting to influence public policy and arouse the citizenry. For instance, during the centennial fundraising campaign to renovate the Statue of Liberty, TSI developed a series of glossy mailers to tap the patriotic pockets of residents in each cluster. For the neighborhoods of Two More Rungs, where affluent first-generation Americans view the United States as a land of golden opportunity, the TSI pitch emphasized the statue's role in welcoming the waves of European immigrants. "A Nation of Immigrants," reads the brochure headline below a turn-of-the-century photograph of an immigrant family on a steamer. "Her Story Is Our Story," declares the copy inside.

In Shotguns & Pickups, however, where nationalism is strong and residents blame foreigners for taking away jobs, any praise of immigrant contributions just wouldn't do. Accordingly, their brochure opens with a photo of the Statue of Liberty framed by a billowing American flag. The caption, "Stand Tall for the Lady, So She Can," could have been a quote from Rambo.

While these messages may simply amount to conventional tugs on the heartstrings of two groups predisposed to patriotism, imagine the challenge of trying to reach the residents of Young Influentials, America's materialistic yuppies. These people yawn at immigrant nostalgia and smirk at any blatant flag-waving. The solution? Beside a Peter Max–like illustration of the Statue of Liberty holding a bouquet, a free-hand scrawl admonishes readers, "Don't Send Flowers. The Lady Needs a New Dress." Bingo: patriotism equated with going shopping, one of Young Influentials' favorite pastimes. In Young Influentials, residents respond to a trendy, funky approach to patriotism.

CLUSTERS AND THE REAGAN REVOLUTION

Since the first nationwide political survey was analyzed by neighborhood type in 1980, the clusters have charted voter trends throughout the nation. Six months before Ronald Reagan won the 1980 presidential election, cluster analysts were predicting a Democratic defeat based on a nationwide sampling of 6,600 voters. With respondents grouped by cluster, the Hamilton poll revealed the traditional New Deal coalition unraveling at both ends of the party's political spectrum. In Hard Scrabble, the poor, rural cluster of mountain folk who traditionally voted Democratic by better than two to one, Reagan attracted 52 percent of the vote compared to Jimmy Carter's 32 percent and independent John Anderson's 6 percent. Meanwhile, among liberals in the high-rise neighborhoods of Urban Gold Coast, Anderson led with 37 percent of the vote, compared to 33 percent for Carter and 23 percent for Reagan.

According to the poll, conservative southern Democrats were becoming even more conservative, and blue-collar workers who had fled depressed northern cities for nonunion Sunbelt states were now adopting the values of their Republican neighbors. "We knew the Democratic Party had been breaking up for some time," recalls William Hamilton from his Chevy Chase, Maryland, office, strewn with photos of political clients from past campaigns. "But the cluster poll confirmed what was taking place."

Reagan's eventual victory in the 1980 presidential election surprised

POLITICAL IDEOLOGIES: LIBERALS

The greatest concentration of Americans who describe themselves as liberals lives in the nation's big cities—a neighborhood coalition of urban blacks, upper-middle-class Jews and young singles. The liberal label is liked least by the poor voters of farming and mining communities.

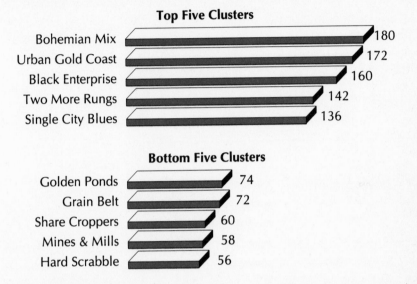

Top Five Clusters

Bohemian Mix	180
Urban Gold Coast	172
Black Enterprise	160
Two More Rungs	142
Single City Blues	136

Bottom Five Clusters

Golden Ponds	74
Grain Belt	72
Share Croppers	60
Mines & Mills	58
Hard Scrabble	56

Numbers indicate attitudes of voters, indexed against the national average. An index of 100 equals the U.S. average. An index of 150 means a cluster has 1.5 times the national average. Source: Targeting Systems, Inc., 1985.

few political observers. But the large-scale support he received from young blue-collar voters whom the Democrats had long counted as their own came as a shock. To cluster analysts, the defection of Blue-Collar Nursery residents exemplified this shift to the GOP. These starter-home suburbs, leading the nation in skilled craftsworkers—the elite of the blue-collar world—are still economically insecure. Residents remain vulnerable to inflation, employment downturns, stiff interest rates and the strains of oversized mortgages. In West Jordan, Utah, a cluster community outside of Salt Lake City, the 1985 shutdown of the Kennecott mines forced men who once earned $15 an hour digging copper to take $5-an-hour jobs stocking supermarket shelves.

Says TSI's Welsh of Blue-Collar Nursery residents nationwide, "Theirs is a precarious lifestyle. Families may be making $30,000 a year, but that's not good enough to give them security with two or three kids

POLITICAL IDEOLOGIES: MODERATES

Those in the middle of America's political road live in predominantly lower-middle-class communities. Typically, they are economic populists who vote liberally on economic issues and conservatively on matters of social policy.

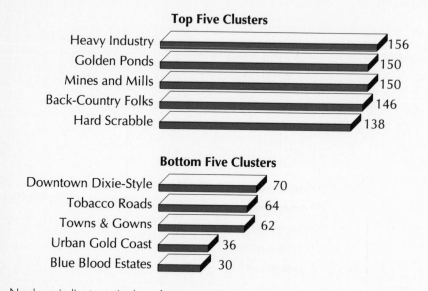

Top Five Clusters

Heavy Industry	156
Golden Ponds	150
Mines and Mills	150
Back-Country Folks	146
Hard Scrabble	138

Bottom Five Clusters

Downtown Dixie-Style	70
Tobacco Roads	64
Towns & Gowns	62
Urban Gold Coast	36
Blue Blood Estates	30

Numbers indicate attitudes of voters, indexed against the national average. An index of 100 equals the U.S. average. An index of 150 means a cluster has 1.5 times the national average. Source: Targeting Systems, Inc., 1985.

and a house they're trying to buy. These people are scrambling to keep their middle-class lifestyle."

The failures of the Carter administration at home and abroad drove Blue-Collar Nursery voters out of the Democratic camp. Some lost well-paying skilled jobs in the shift from a factory-based producing nation to a service-oriented economy in the late '70s. Still others became frustrated by foreign policies that allowed economic encroachment by the Japanese and diplomatic humiliation at the hands of the Iranians. "What did these people get from the Carter administration?" asks Welsh. "A lot of inflation, no jobs and Americans getting humiliated abroad. Then Reagan comes on and says, 'I'm going to cut your taxes. And we're not going to take anything from anyone abroad.' That has a lot of appeal to voters in Blue-Collar Nursery."

The 1984 presidential campaign did little to recapture the Blue-Collar

POLITICAL IDEOLOGIES: CONSERVATIVES

American conservatives fall into three categories: affluent economic conservatives (Blue Blood Estates), downscale social conservatives (Tobacco Roads, Share Croppers) and the beleaguered middle class (Blue-Collar Nursery, New Homesteaders), which embraces both ideologies to protect its values and pocketbooks.

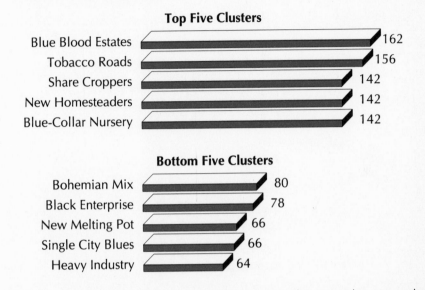

Top Five Clusters

Blue Blood Estates	162
Tobacco Roads	156
Share Croppers	142
New Homesteaders	142
Blue-Collar Nursery	142

Bottom Five Clusters

Bohemian Mix	80
Black Enterprise	78
New Melting Pot	66
Single City Blues	66
Heavy Industry	64

Numbers indicate attitudes of voters, indexed against the national average. An index of 100 equals the U.S. average. An index of 150 means a cluster has 1.5 times the national average. Source: Targeting Systems, Inc., 1985.

Nursery's disaffected voters for the Democrats. Only 26 percent of Blue-Collar Nurseryites voted for Walter Mondale. A 1985 poll found that many credited Reagan administration policies with the economic recovery and eyed with suspicion Mondale's call for a tax increase. A majority of Blue-Collar Nurseryites believed Republican charges that Democrats had become the pawns of special-interest groups. And Mondale's vice-presidential selection process—meeting successively with a black, a Hispanic and a female candidate—did little to alter that impression. The Democrats had high hopes that Geraldine Ferraro would attract the Blue-Collar Nursery moderates disillusioned with Reagan's opposition to women's rights. But these young suburbanites found little appealing in the tough-minded liberal from Queens, and few had deep Democratic roots.

MONDALE 1984

In the 1984 presidential election, Democrat Walter Mondale's core supporters were typically black urban voters—a profile that closely parallels that of pessimistic Americans (see earlier chart). In contrast, Ronald Reagan's chief supporters came from a diverse mix of affluent elderly and young suburban communities.

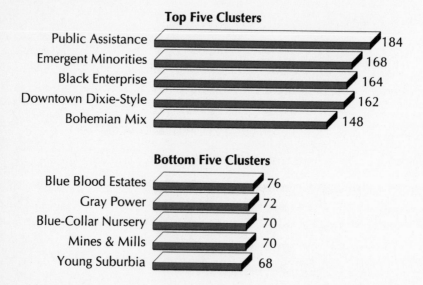

Top Five Clusters

Public Assistance	184
Emergent Minorities	168
Black Enterprise	164
Downtown Dixie-Style	162
Bohemian Mix	148

Bottom Five Clusters

Blue Blood Estates	76
Gray Power	72
Blue-Collar Nursery	70
Mines & Mills	70
Young Suburbia	68

Numbers indicate percentages of Mondale voters, indexed against the national average. An index of 100 equals the U.S. average. An index of 150 means a cluster had 1.5 times the national average of Mondale supporters. Source: Targeting Systems, Inc., 1985.

"Their memories don't extend to John F. Kennedy," says Welsh. "If you're 30 years old in this country, you only have a glimmering of Watergate and Nixon. Your memory goes back to trying to get a job and make a living, about 1976 onward."

When all the votes were counted in 1984, it appeared that the Democrats had become a party of have-nots, with Mondale's strongest support coming from the hourly wage earner, the poor and the jobless. Mondale did best among the three clusters with the highest percentage of black voters: Public Assistance (where Mondale won 83 percent), Black Enterprise (78 percent) and Emergent Minorities (75 percent).

Despite the socioeconomic gulf between the upscale Black Enter-

POLITICAL PARTY ANIMALS

The nation's political party workers tend to be affluent, educated and opinionated. They don't, however, share the same ideology: they represent liberals (Bohemian Mix, Urban Gold Coast) and conservatives (Blue Blood Estates, God's Country, Pools & Patios). Not surprisingly, these are the same people who are most likely to vote and write letters to the editor.

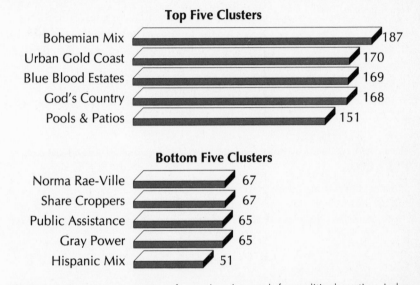

Top Five Clusters

Cluster	Index
Bohemian Mix	187
Urban Gold Coast	170
Blue Blood Estates	169
God's Country	168
Pools & Patios	151

Bottom Five Clusters

Cluster	Index
Norma Rae-Ville	67
Share Croppers	67
Public Assistance	65
Gray Power	65
Hispanic Mix	51

Numbers indicate percentages of people who work for political parties, indexed against the national average. An index of 100 equals the U.S. average: 8.25%. An index of 121 means a cluster has 1.21 times the national average, or about 10%. Source: SMRB 1984/85, Claritas Corp., 1987.

prise areas and the ghettos of Public Assistance, voters in both clusters tend to view the Democrats as the compassionate party and the GOP as advocates for the privileged. According to a 1985 survey, both clusters support U.S. foreign-policy measures based on social justice and humanitarian concerns rather than national interest. While achieving middle-class status made the GOP more attractive to residents of Blue-Collar Nursery, an improved social standing didn't undermine Democratic support in Black Enterprise neighborhoods. Part of this loyalty no doubt stems from barriers Black Enterprises still encounter to further upward mobility. And voters remember the Democratic Party as their ally in the civil rights struggle. "Republicans are shadows, not even spoken of around here," says Rev. Hosea Williams, an Atlanta city councilman from the Black Enterprise neighborhood of East Lake. "When you win the Democratic primary, you're in."

In contrast, the three clusters that proved Republican to the core in 1984 were Grain Belt—which constitutes the party's farming wing (70 percent for Reagan), Pools & Patios—the party regulars comfortable with their backyard-mellow lifestyle in older, postwar suburbs (72 percent) and Blue Blood Estates—representing the corporate boardroom of the GOP (also 72 percent). Such landslide percentages were not delivered solely on the charisma of a successful incumbent president. In Grain Belt, for instance, where administration policies have provided little relief for the farm crisis, Reagan's strong showing was a result of that cluster's traditional partisan voting behavior. Unlike the sophisti-

WHO VOTES

There is a direct correlation between education and voting participation in America. More than one out of three residents from the top five neighborhood types are college graduates, compared to one out of seventeen from the clusters whose residents vote the least.

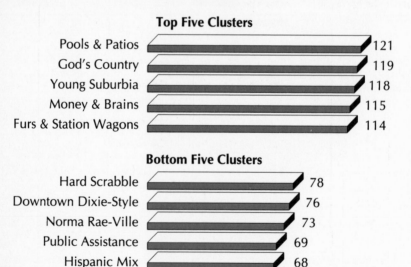

Top Five Clusters

Pools & Patios	121
God's Country	119
Young Suburbia	118
Money & Brains	115
Furs & Station Wagons	114

Bottom Five Clusters

Hard Scrabble	78
Downtown Dixie-Style	76
Norma Rae-Ville	73
Public Assistance	69
Hispanic Mix	68

Numbers indicate percentages of registered voters, indexed against the national average. An index of 100 equals the U.S. average: 42.9%. An index of 121 means a cluster has 1.21 times the national average, or about 52%. Source: SMRB 1983/84, Claritas Corp., 1987.

cates of Blue Blood Estates who dislike the pulpit politics of figures like Pat Robertson, Grain Belt voters appreciate the mix of religion and Republican conservatism. "Religion is important because you depend on Mother Nature," says Neil Mason, a Republican farmer from Early, Iowa, who voted twice for Reagan. "We consider it a compliment to be called 'conservative.' "

If the 1984 election signaled an ideological shift to the right, the 1986 congressional contest demonstrated that no permanent party realignment had taken place. About a year before, the Democratic National Committee conducted a nationwide public opinion survey of 5,500 voters, classifying the results by cluster. The findings helped local Democratic fundraisers target their appeals: heavy in deep-pocket party strongholds like Urban Gold Coast and Black Enterprise, light in GOP bastions like Blue Blood Estates and Furs & Station Wagons. And the

APATHETIC AMERICANS

Political apathy is most prevalent among America's poor and powerless. The inclusion of clusters like Mines & Mills and Middle America reflects the economic hard times that have befallen the nation's industrial core. Simply put, those who don't have, don't care.

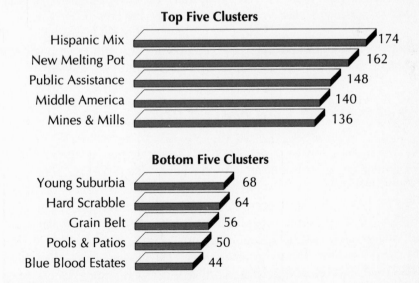

Top Five Clusters

Cluster	Index
Hispanic Mix	174
New Melting Pot	162
Public Assistance	148
Middle America	140
Mines & Mills	136

Bottom Five Clusters

Cluster	Index
Young Suburbia	68
Hard Scrabble	64
Grain Belt	56
Pools & Patios	50
Blue Blood Estates	44

Numbers indicate percentages of nonvoters, indexed against the national average. An index of 100 equals the U.S. average. An index of 150 means a cluster has 1.5 times the national average. Source: Targeting Systems, Inc., 1985.

survey, widely distributed to state party leaders and congressional candidates, aided campaign strategists in understanding the mood of the
electorate, neighborhood by neighborhood, on a variety of issues. Anti-
nuclear advocates, for instance, lived in Young Suburbia communities,
while foreign-policy hawks could be found in Shotguns & Pickups towns.
At the height of Reagan's second term, voters across the clusters
revealed clear images of the two parties. "Overall, the people saw
the Republicans as the party that knew how to manage," says Frank
O'Brien, then director of direct-mail for the DNC. "They saw the Democrats as having their hearts in the right place but being unable to deliver
on what they believed."

Ultimately, says O'Brien, the DNC survey provided the 1986 Democratic candidates with the guidelines "for uniting the 'passion wing' of
the party and the 'managerial wing' of the party." No congressional
hopefuls built their campaigns solely around the neighborhood types—
"clusters don't work as well in themeless campaigns," O'Brien says. But
he claims that the Democratic victories in the Senate and House bode
well for future cluster politicking. "As time passes, the electorate will
be made up of fewer people who have firm, culturally held views of the
parties," says O'Brien, now a managing partner of the direct-mail firm
of Coyle, Malchow & O'Brien. "More and more voters can be better
characterized as political consumers than party regulars, people who
look at campaigns year by year, candidate by candidate. And the more
you have that kind of fluid electorate, the more useful targeting is. The
most successful campaigns of the future will put together ad hoc coalitions of different lifestyle groups." Strange bedfellows indeed.

NEW-COLLAR VOTERS

Of all the coalitions to emerge over the last decade, none has proved
more challenging to politicians than the new-collar voters. Conceived by
Ralph Whitehead, a public-service professor at the University of Massachusetts, the label sprang from his observation in the '70s of a generation gap between younger, disaffected, blue-collar workers and those
who were older and more complacent.

As the counterculture trickled down to the working class, Whitehead
observed the rise of a new breed of worker who embraced '60s-style
values. Aged 21 to 40, with incomes between $20,000 and $40,000, new
collars are to the middle class what yuppies are to the upper-middle

class. They tend to hold down jobs in that gray area between blue-collar laborers and white-collar professionals, jobs such as teachers, computer programmers, nurses, secretaries and fast-food restaurant managers. But what new collars lack in individual wealth compared to yuppies, they gain in numbers. As one-third of the baby boom, they comprise nearly 15 percent of the electorate—some 25 million Americans. With their mercurial allegiance to politicians and parties, they represent a crucial swing vote that can decide elections.

"Politically, new-collar voters are a different breed," says Whitehead. "There's a great deal of volatility among them and they split their ticket to a high degree." In 1984, new collars helped return Reagan to the White House by a margin of 58 percent to 42 percent, precisely the national norm. But in congressional races, they voted for Democrats over Republicans by a 52-percent to 42-percent spread (with 8 percent for other candidates). "Nearly two out of three new-collar voters split their tickets," says Whitehead. "New-collar voters are the most deeply individualistic generation in American history."

Whitehead first developed a national portrait of the new-collar class in 1985, when political strategists realized that yuppies comprised less than 3 percent of the electorate and were numerically insignificant at the polls. Working with Claritas analysts, Whitehead determined that new-collar voters lived in six clusters: New Homesteaders, Young Suburbia, Black Enterprise, Blue-Chip Blues, New Beginnings and Blue-Collar Nursery. What they have in common is that many accept the traditional values held by their blue-collar parents, such as a commitment to home, family and country. But they are more liberal than their parents on issues such as abortion, premarital sex and marijuana use. And they're more tolerant of unconventional attitudes toward marriage and the changing roles of the sexes.

"Remember, they've been through sex, drugs and rock'n'roll," says Whitehead, who identifies one of their current pop culture heroes as Bruce Springsteen. It's no coincidence that both Reagan and Mondale tried unsuccessfully to court Springsteen's endorsement during the 1984 election.

In many ways, Colorado Democrat Gary Hart was the new-collar presidential candidate of 1984. He portrayed himself as a kind of isolationist, anti-union, pro-working-class American. Much of his core support during the 1984 Democratic primary came from New Homesteaders, white-collar residents who live beyond suburbia in rustic towns but who frequently commute to city jobs. Though for a time it looked as if

Hart might represent a synthesis of their views, a CBS-TV postelection poll found that fully 34 percent of the Democrats who supported Hart in the primaries voted for Reagan in the general election.

In 1984, Massachusetts Democratic Senator John Kerry determined that tailoring his advertising to the new-collar constituency was a key to his campaign's success. During focus group research with baby-boom voters, Kerry strategists learned that new-collar voters disliked Kerry's silver spoon image compared to the up-by-the-bootstraps past of his conservative opponent, Ray Shamie. To counter that perception, the Kerry campaign developed a TV commercial showing their candidate in jeans and sweater, standing in a hardware store condemning the prices the Pentagon was paying for items like screws and diodes. The spot closed with Kerry declaring, "If anyone thinks we can't do better, they must have a screw loose."

Among baby boomers, the ad was unexpectedly divisive. "The yuppies hated it because they thought it was too cute and clever," recalls Tom Kiley, a Democratic pollster from Boston. "But the new collars loved it. They weren't good at articulating their philosophy, but they took it personally. And they had a sensitivity to wasted tax dollars." Throughout the campaign Kerry media advisers bought time for the spot on the new collars' favorite TV shows: "Cagney & Lacey," ice hockey games and the World Series.

Kerry's Senate victory owes much to new-collar support. Yet, as a political force, new collars continue to receive little attention because, as Kiley puts it, "these people don't see themselves as new-collar voters until you tell them they are. They know they're not yuppies, but they're still struggling for a political self-identity." Kiley believes their rootlessness reflects an overriding distrust of big government, corporations and many public institutions—including traditional party politics. During their lives, these baby-boomers grew up with traumatic political experiences: assassinations, civil rights riots, the Vietnam War and Watergate. While their parents learned from the Depression and the New Deal that government could be beneficial, their own experiences taught them to be skeptical. "New collars are largely de-aligned," Ralph Whitehead says, "or have never gotten aligned in the first place."

By Whitehead's definition, Alan Lucenta fits the classic new-collar portrait: a 39-year-old registered Independent who "votes the man." From his ranch house bordering a Young Suburbia neighborhood in North Framingham, Massachusetts, he recounts his 1984 record at the polls, voting for Ronald Reagan and John Kerry—a seeming contradiction in partisan politics that makes sense in new-collar terms. "They're both my kind of people, aggressive and kind of heroic," says Lucenta, a coffee shop manager who's married with two children. "When I vote for a guy, he may be hurting my parents or relatives, but I'm more concerned about my immediate family. I'm just trying to live for today."

With a household income in the low $30s, Lucenta admits that he's saving little for the future. He holds a degree in business management but describes himself as a poor reader who rarely watches the national news. "There's too much to know," he complains. He supports nuclear power, conceding, "It's probably unsafe right now but we need nuclear power to survive. Besides, so many things are unsafe these days—milk, cranberry sauce, what have you. If I sat home and worried about all this stuff, I'd go crazy." Indeed, Lucenta lets the future take care of itself. "We have enough to worry about for today," he smiles. "In five years, I'll probably be just where I am right now, not rich but pretty happy."

Economic concerns remain the top priority of new-collar voters around the country. Though they were raised in the heady economic times of the '50s and '60s, they tend today to be fiscally conservative. Given the recession and high inflation through the '70s, their sense of security has evaporated. Many have been disappointed to find that a college degree and white-collar job don't guarantee financial security. Unlike their yuppie peers, they don't have the money to dine at upscale restaurants or hang out at chi-chi fern bars. While they work hard, new-collar men and women are not obsessed with their careers, and they enjoy their leisure time. At the top of their reading lists are *People* and *TV Guide*.

"What I'm seeing is a new kind of trapped American in this age group," Republican political consultant Lee Atwater has observed. "This generation was basically brought up at a time when there was unprecedented optimism. But many voters are finding out for the first time that the American dream will not work out the way they thought it would." Atwater foresees this populist working class eventually producing a tax revolt and an anti-establishment rebellion.

For now, the new-collar voters are simply seeking a voice to champion their concerns. As the 1988 presidential campaign heats up, candidates like New York Republican Jack Kemp, Tennessee Democrat Abert Gore and Missouri Democrat Richard Gephardt will increasingly court new-collar support with baby-boomer themes—lost dreams and fresh ideals, old protests and new activism. While they've received scant notice—a *New-Collar Handbook* is yet to be published—they'll doubtless be heard from more often as politicians vie for this megagroup's vote. Says Whitehead, "No matter whether they're Democrat or Republican, a candidate will have to speak to their concerns to command their attention, if not their vote." To Whithead, political campaigns of the future may yet revert to "working the wards"—appealing not to voters' party affiliation but to their shared lifestyle concerns.

8

CHANGING CLUSTERS

"To me, Loveland, Colorado, is going through its teenage years. We're growing but we're still a little gangly."
—Dennis Anderson, Loveland, Colorado (New Homesteaders)

The swimming pool was nearly empty when Holly Gordon plopped her Adolpho tote bag down and eased her golden-brown body into a chaise lounge under the white-hot sun baking Northeast Dallas. Around her, a handful of tanned young men in skimpy Speedo trunks were flinging Frisbees as Rolling Stones and Eurythmics music blared from two boom boxes. Occasionally, they'd whoop, curse and slap "high fives" after a deft catch, hoping to attract the attention of Gordon and other poolside heartbreakers. Whenever a Frisbee fell too close to one of the young ladies—all too often, it seemed—the errant thrower would offer the standard gentlemanly apology: "Hey, sorry babe."

As a resident of The Village, which bills itself as the largest singles' apartment complex in the nation, Holly Gordon is used to such antics. She lives with 11,000 mostly unattached men and women in a self-contained world of exercise, entertainment and boundless energy. Nestled amid 400 acres of garden apartments are thirty-seven swimming pools, twelve tennis courts and a lighted jogging trail. The development's country-club restaurant is notorious for hosting day-long rock concert pool parties—Woodstocks for the Madonna Generation. And every month, glossy posters publicize a heavy lineup of cheap-drink mixers, big-screen movie shows and beer bashes, all with one blatent intent: luring singles into a romantic connection.

"Living at The Village is like a perpetual Club Med vacation," says Gordon, 27, as she smoothes her shiny black maillot swim suit. "The big concerns are 'what are we going to wear tonight,' 'where are we going to go' and 'who are we going to go with.' Everyone talks about going for the gusto."

In many ways, this gusto-grabbing group at The Village is at the vanguard of social change. Throughout the Sunbelt, singles-filled communities of the New Beginnings cluster have sprouted to accommodate the shifting values of America's baby boomers. A generation ago, these young people would have married and started their own families in the suburbs. But today, they marry later (median age: 25.7 for men, 23.1 for women), have fewer children (0.98 children under 18 years old per family) and divorce at higher rates than their parents (one out of every two marriages).

Such trends weren't reflected in the nation's neighborhood structure in 1970, when these communities belonged to an aging blue-collar cluster nicknamed Bunker's Neighbors after the working-class TV character. Back then, these residents were fond of big American sedans, cruise ships, best-selling books and diet soft drinks. But during the '70s, the communities underwent a radical turnover as aging couples moved out to retirement homes and young, educated boomers took over their trim bungalows and garden apartments and packed into newly built singles complexes. Gradually, the lifestyle surveys picked up the newcomers' taste for Japanese subcompacts, backpacking abroad, jazz and Mexican food. Many of these neighborhoods emerged in the South and West— places like Northeast Phoenix and Parkmoor outside San Francisco— reflecting the decade's demographic shift from the Frostbelt to the Sunbelt. New Beginnings was the answer for the legions of young people who didn't pair off after college, like Noah's animals, to settle in a split-level on Long Island.

The Village's evolution mirrors many compelling social trends of the last twenty years. Launched in 1967 as a year-round adult summer camp of sorts, The Village was built partially to allow its country-club restaurant to sell liquor by the drink in what was then a dry, rural county. But the developers, Lincoln Properties, also hoped to lure the wave of baby boomers pouring into the Sunbelt in search of new jobs and deep tans. And they succeeded; at one time, 65 percent of The Village's tenants hailed from outside of Texas. The drawing card featured youth-oriented activities that pushed many overt and subliminal "hot buttons." One early ad showed a young lady's bottom in tight hip-hugger jeans patched with the names of The Village's different sections. "Looks have always been important here," observes Gordon, who grew up in Connecticut and came to Dallas for the warm weather and a nursing job at the Baylor School of Medicine. "There used to be a lot of quick meetings and then hopping into bed."

But by the early '80s, with AIDS and herpes scaring some residents sexless, the preoccupation of singles communities had shifted from sex to fitness, and today most Village residents would cringe at the term "swinging single." A more recent ad displays a bathing-suit-clad woman, sipping a drink after an apparently energizing swim. The athletic activities of The Village are extolled under the headline, "After Your 9–5, Experience Our 5–9." The lifestyle, however, is still geared for the young and good-looking—the age range is 24 to 27—and residents admit that cruising remains as popular as calisthetics. Nightclubs fringe the complex on Greenville Avenue, and the aisles of the local grocery store, the Tom Thumb, have become a favorite meeting spot—especially near the TV-dinner case. "It's not uncommon to go to Tom Thumb on a Friday night and have a date for Saturday night," says marketing director Carol Winfrey, who arrived at The Village in 1973 as a wide-eyed college grad. "But people are more sophisticated about how they party. They're more interested in moving here to make friends rather than looking for casual sex."

Sophisticated partyers? In the summer of 1986, Village residents could be found dancing in the laundry room, singing in the mail room and holding hibachi cookouts inside their car trunks in the parking lot. But most realize that theirs is a passing fantasy, not a perpetual rerun of *The Harrad Experiment.* The average length of stay at The Village is just three years, one major reason being the toll marriages take on roommates. Another reason is that a normal, healthy single can stand only so many years of institutionalized whoopee. Village resident Rick Corse, a 30-year-old preppy real estate broker who moved to the complex when Houston's oil boom went bust, recalls nights when he's been awakened by beer-filled revelers splashing in the hot tub below his balcony or by the shouts from an impromptu broom hockey game being played in the parking lot. "It's been a little hard for me to adjust since moving here," he concedes. "Sometimes I just want to open my window and not look out into someone else's party and not hear a band from the country club."

Admittedly, Corse is not certain how long he can maintain his New Beginnings lifestyle, with the Lean Cuisine dinners in the freezer, barbells by his bedroom computer and favorite jogging trail only a stairwell away. "There are good and bad features to living among people who are all young, on the make and going for the brass ring professionally," he says, pausing as his attention is diverted by a brunette passing below his balcony. "I like the fact that there are a lot of people seeking to meet other people around here." As a pioneer in a singles lifestyle that was unimagined by Bunker's Neighbors of the past, Corse understands the drawbacks of this uncharted territory. He's learned that the laundry room is for dancing.

■■■■■■■■■■ AS THE CLUSTER TURNS

Throughout America, communities flourish and decline like civilizations in microcosm. Just as singles complexes of New Beginnings were built to absorb the influx of middle-class baby boomers in the rental market, neighborhood landscapes constantly shift to accommodate the needs of a changing populace. Between 1970 and 1980, several clusters grew in population, others decreased in size and some underwent so much transition that they warranted new profiles, ZQ scores and nicknames. These new neighborhood types reflect the strongest social and economic trends at work. In the popular debate that accompanies every census—"Are the changes evolutionary or revolutionary?"—these clusters offer some answers.

Take Black Enterprise, the middle- and upper-middle-class black neighborhood type that emerged on the outskirts of the nation's big cities. In the 1970 cluster system, these communities were designated Sun-Belt Singles and contained predominantly white singles and families in comfortable homes and garden apartments. Residents tended to favor jogging, driving Plymouth hatchbacks, eating yogurt, drinking Scotch and reading *Glamour* magazine. But over the next decade, the migration of urban blacks to the better housing of inner-ring suburbs gradually shifted the racial makeup of Sun-Belt Singles: as white homeowners moved farther out in the suburbs, upwardly mobile black professionals ("buppies") moved in. By 1980, Black Enterprise represented more than 400 zip codes, which were racially mixed (about 60 percent black) and economically well off (nearly one-quarter earned over $50,000 annually). And surveys began picking up new interests—in playing tennis, owning Mercedes sedans, listening to contemporary jazz, drinking malt liquor and reading *Essence* magazine.

One place that underwent great change was Cascade Heights, now an affluent black enclave of large Tudor, ranch-style and colonial homes on the western boundary of Atlanta. After many of the area's white residents moved out in the late '60s, the 2.5-square-mile section became home to Atlanta Mayor Andrew Young, former baseball great Hank Aaron and a host of black college administrators, doctors, lawyers and entrepreneurs. In 1986, Cascade Heights witnessed the fruition of the civil rights movement when a congressional contest pitted two one-time aides to Martin Luther King—Julian Bond and John Lewis—against each other. As Andrew Young observed in the heat of the campaign (ultimately won by Lewis): "This is what the movement was all about, to be able to choose from the best among us." Today, real estate agents say the presence of such movers and shakers is luring back some of the whites who fled twenty years ago.

Another urban neighborhood type, Single City Blues, also emerged after the 1980 census as a result of the coming of age of lower-middle-class baby boomers during the inflation-racked '70s. Unable to afford the homes of their parents, these young people sought cheap housing in downscale industrial areas nicknamed Ethnic Row Houses in the 1970 cluster system. Then filled with a mix of Eastern European, black and Hispanic families, these households ranked high in purchases of roomy Chryslers, imported beer, cold cuts and burglar alarms—after all, these were rough, high-crime areas. But the press of boomer singles slowly pushed out the aging ethnics to other dense urban areas like Emergent Minorities and Heavy Industry. And in their place came the Single City Blues households with a taste for bottom-of-the-line Volkswagens, racquetball, natural cheeses and even more burglar alarms (apparently the criminal element never moved out). Unlike the former residents, who tended to contribute to political parties but not schools, the well-educated members of Single City Blues (one-third went to college) support their alma maters while remaining politically apathetic.

The Southeast section of Portland, one of the oldest residential and industrial areas in the city, reflects this transformation. As the community shifted from stable German Lutheran families to younger, lower-income singles—and more than a few gays—corner taverns were joined by used-record stores and organic food take-outs. Creaky Victorian brownstones were carved up into triplexes and sixplexes that sold for under $50,000. One high school was shut down and reopened as a theatrical performance center. And the newcomers, described by one as "aging hippies," introduced unheard-of referenda on election ballots, including a proposal to make their community a nuclear-free zone. (It failed.)

The influx of younger people didn't completely remake Southeast Portland, however: it's still a seedy area that attracts bikers to its X-rated video parlors and panhandlers to its liquor stores, which sell cheap fortified wine, banned in more affluent parts of Portland. But the newcomers have begun to reclaim vacant lots for parks, and some have formed cooperatives to renovate the homes—not for gentrification, mind you, but to ward off a decline. "We're what you call a transitional area," explains Steve Rudman, director of the Southeast Uplift community organization. "But we're trying not to slide further as we change."

AMERICA'S CLUSTERS, 1970 VS. 1980

The social and economic trends of the decade from 1970 to 1980 transformed the nation's neighborhoods. Eight new clusters (designated by †) emerged from the 1970 PRIZM system (the disappearing clusters designated by a single asterisk) and five others received new nicknames (designated by a double asterisk). Three other clusters, Heavy Industry, Pools & Patios and Levittown, U.S.A., underwent significant internal evolution, becoming older and less affluent and having fewer children.

	1970 Clusters		1980 Clusters
ZQ	Nickname	ZQ	Nickname
1	Blue Blood Estates	1	Blue Blood Estates
2	Money & Brains	2	Money & Brains
3	Furs & Station Wagons	3	Furs & Station Wagons
4	Two More Rungs	4	Urban Gold Coast
5	Urban Gold Coast	5	Pools & Patios
6	Pools & Patios	6	Two More Rungs
7	Young Influentials	7	Young Influentials
8	Young Suburbia	8	Young Suburbia
9	Blue-Chip Blues	9	God's Country
10	God's Country	10	Blue-Chip Blues
11	Levittown, U.S.A.	11	Bohemian Mix
12	Bunker's Neighbors*	12	Levittown, U.S.A.
13	Sun-Belt Singles*	13	Gray Power†
14	Bohemian Mix	14	Black Enterprise†
15	Old Melting Pot*	15	New Beginnings†
16	Blue-Collar Catholics**	16	Blue-Collar Nursery

Established neighborhoods don't always undergo transition as a result of young people pushing out the elderly. The '70s also marked the graying of America and its neighborhoods. Because of improved fitness and such medical advances as open-heart surgery, pacemakers and miracle drugs, the number of over-65s increased by 28 percent to 25 million —representing 11 percent of the population. And a greater proportion than ever before began reaching old age in good physical and financial health. Housing the nation's first generation of elderly living away from their families, two new clusters emerged in the 1980 cluster system: Gray Power and Golden Ponds.

Gray Power, the nation's planned retirement communities, popped up in the rural landscape of the Sunbelt, far from metropolitan areas. Sun City Center, Florida, a Gray Power town of 8,500 south of Tampa, used

	1970 Clusters		1980 Clusters
ZQ	Nickname	ZQ	Nickname
17	Middle America	17	New Homesteaders
18	Eastern Europeans*	18	New Melting Pot†
19	Young Homesteaders**	19	Towns & Gowns†
20	Blue-Collar Nursery	20	Rank & File†
21	Old Brick Factories**	21	Middle America
22	Down-Home Gentry*	22	Old Yankee Rows
23	Coalburg & Corntown	23	Coalburg & Corntown
24	Hispanic Mix	24	Shotguns & Pickups
25	Ethnic Row Houses*	25	Golden Ponds†
26	Emergent Minorities	26	Agri-Business
27	Heavy Industry	27	Emergent Minorities
28	Mines & Mills	28	Single City Blues†
29	Shotguns & Pickups	29	Mines & Mills
30	Big Fish/Small Pond*	30	Back-Country Folks
31	Agri-Business	31	Norma Rae-Ville
32	Marlboro Country*	32	Smalltown Downtown
33	Norma Rae-Ville	33	Grain Belt
34	Dixie-Style Tenements**	34	Heavy Industry
35	Back-Country Folks	35	Share Croppers
36	Urban Renewal**	36	Downtown Dixie-Style
37	Grain Belt	37	Hispanic Mix
38	Share Croppers	38	Tobacco Roads
39	Tobacco Roads	39	Hard Scrabble
40	Hard Scrabble	40	Public Assistance

SOURCE: Claritas Corp., 1983.

THE NEW CLUSTERS OF 1980

Eight new clusters emerged following the 1980 census, reflecting a host of '70s demographic changes played out in the nation's neighborhoods. Some of the new neighborhood types, like New Melting Pot, clearly evolved from earlier clusters. Others, like Black Enterprise and Gray Power, represent radically new communities on the American landscape.

Current Name	Trend
Black Enterprise	The rise in black affluence created upper-middle-class minority neighborhoods.
New Beginnings	Singles communities emerged in once-blue-collar family areas.
Towns & Gowns	The increase in college-educated baby boomers transformed campus communities from rural backwaters to sophisticated towns.
Gray Power	Senior retirement communities grew in number.
Rank & File	The number of young people living in industrial urban neighborhoods declined.
New Melting Pot	The decade's influx of immigrants, many of them middle-class Asians and Latin Americans, was the largest ever.
Single City Blues	Lower-middle-class baby boomers moved to downscale urban areas.
Golden Ponds	The number of middle-class retirees settling in rustic towns increased.

SOURCE: Claritas Corp., 1987.

to be a cattle ranch. The developers of Sun City, Arizona, laid out that city's circular streets on what were once 8,900 acres of cotton fields; early residents complained of boll-weevil infestations. In the 1970 cluster system, such communities were designated Marlboro Country and were characterized by family households who spent double the national average on baby foods, power boats, bowling, fishing gear and white bread. Consistent with their downscale economics (ZQ32), they rarely traveled abroad, played golf or bought champagne.

From the green pastures and croplands grew Gray Power communities with their golf courses, artificial lakes and stucco ranch houses landscaped with rows of colored pebbles. By the mid-'70s, one survey counted sixty-nine such retirement villages across the nation, some with populations above 10,000. Far different from the farm settlements of prior decades, these new developments are filled with well-off elderly Americans who tend to travel extensively, play golf and drink enough champagne and hard liquor to make alcoholism a serious problem. And Gray Power has attracted enough affluent residents—often through careful screening procedures—to secure a ZQ rank of 13. One street in Sun City, Arizona, has fourteen banks on it, and longtime resident Charles McKinnis boasts, "There are investment clubs here as astute as any on Wall Street."

Like Gray Power, the Golden Ponds cluster of retirement resorts also emerged from rural, family communities in the Sunbelt. Called Down-Home Gentry in 1970, the cluster was frequently found near military bases and contained blue-collar workers who were twice as likely as average Americans to live in mobile homes, drive vans, own power boats and buy cloth diapers and disposable baby bottles—no sign of the grandparents yet. But over the next decade, these rustic towns

CHANGING TASTES: 1970 TO 1980

As the demographic characteristics of neighborhoods change over time, so do the tastes of their residents. This sampling of products shows how consumption rates changed in clusters that underwent significant shifts during the 1970s. Credit cards were scarce among the residents of farmland Marlboro Country, for example, but when those rural areas turned into settlements for the upscale elderly, credit-card use nearly tripled.

1970 Cluster	Index	Product	1980 Cluster	Index
Bunker's Neighbors	145	Diet colas	New Beginnings	98
Marlboro Country	56	Credit cards	Gray Power	142
Ethnic Row Houses	105	White bread	Single City Blues	64
Sun-Belt Singles	40	Laundry detergent	Black Enterprise	99
Down-Home Gentry	117	Liquid makeup	Golden Ponds	98

Numbers indicate percentages of people who buy each product, indexed against the national average. An index of 100 equals the U.S. average for that category. An index of 200 means a cluster buys twice the national average for that category. Source: SMRB 1976/77, 1985/86, Claritas Corp., 1987.

saw the economic advantages of becoming scenic resorts and were soon luring vacationing tourists as well as year-round retirees. Buses brought 30,000 senior citizens from Philadelphia and New York City every year to visit the oceanside resort of Cape May, New Jersey. Some of those people later returned to plant roots.

Typically, these elderly citydwellers changed the country character of Golden Ponds communities, bringing with them a demand for arts-and-crafts shops, year-round supermarkets and well-stocked pharmacies. Cluster residents now boast high rates of book purchases, country club membership, domestic travel and cable TV hookups, and could care less about powerboats, bowling and baby oil. "We've gone cosmopolitan," explains Bruce Minnox, the former mayor of Cape May, not entirely happy about the transformation. "Suddenly we're seeing people dressed to the teeth as if they're going to the Waldorf. Everyone used to be happy going to dinner in jeans and sport shirts."

▬▬▬ CATCH THE WAVE

Communities like Cape May, Southeast Portland and Cascade Heights are more than just demographic blips on the cluster map. They represent the new directions American society is turning toward. Of the eight new clusters that emerged after the 1980 census—New Beginnings, Black Enterprise, Single City Blues, Gray Power, Golden Ponds, New Melting Pot, Towns & Gowns and Rank & File—the last three in particular reflect the greatest demographic movements that transformed the nation during the '70s. These communities will continue to serve as barometers of the powerful social and economic megatrends affecting the country through the end of the century.

▬ NEW MELTING POT

To demographers, the '70s were the Decade of the Immigrant. The increase of 4.5 million in America's foreign-born population represented the largest immigrant influx of any decade in U.S. history. Latin America and Asia accounted for 78 percent of the new immigrants, signifying a shift away from the Middle European stock that had dominated the American immigration scene since the turn of the century. The 1970 census still reported communities of aging immigrants living in an ethnic cluster of Chinatowns, Little Italys and Poletowns dubbed Old Melting Pot. But during the next decade, many of these original settlers died off, their children moved out to the suburbs and a new generation of immigrants took over the inner-city housing.

With the 1980 census, a New Melting Pot cluster emerged, absorbing the latest immigrant waves from Vietnam and Cambodia, El Salvador and Honduras, Lebanon and Iran. The settlers created new ethnic neighborhoods in the Jackson Heights section of New York, Los Feliz in Los Angeles and the Clarendon district of Arlington, Virginia, an enclave locals now call Little Saigon. But unlike the illegal aliens from Latin countries who've settled in the Hispanic Mix barrios of Texas and New York, the residents of New Melting Pot aren't poor. Their ZQ ranking is 18, their median home value ($113,616) is far above the national midpoint, and one-third of all residents earn over $35,000. In fact, immigrants from Japan boast a higher median income than average Americans. New Melting Pot residents are four times as likely to own Chevrolet Impalas, three times as likely to acquire mutual funds and twice as likely to belong to health clubs—signs of assimilation into mainstream American society.

In Los Feliz, the community's immigrant roots appear on the signs above Thai restaurants, Syrian delis, Armenian groceries and carry-outs advertising egg rolls, tacos and hot dogs—all on the same banner. Once a Hollywood playground and home to Walt Disney, Los Feliz has long sheltered diverse nationalities, most recently as an entry point for Mideastern and Oriental newcomers who settled in the town's pastel cottages and low-rise apartments. In contrast to city neighborhoods, where die-hard prejudices separate ethnic and racial groups, Los Feliz boasts a melding of cultures. Many parents oppose bilingual education in the schools—and voted in favor of the 1986 measure making English the state's official language—in order to accelerate their children's adoption of their new country's customs.

"Our yuppies don't only come in white faces," says local librarian Tony Shay, whose Aloha Street neighbors include Philippinos, Syrians, Chinese and Japanese. Many residents treat the Los Feliz Public Library as a social center, checking out magazines in a dozen languages and circulating books on music, dance and travel. Shay himself celebrates the area's cultural plurality through Avaz, a fifty-member international dance troupe he founded that performs the traditional dances and songs of many of the residents' homelands. And his programs, like Los Feliz's ethnic flavors, are constantly expanding. "Once a community absorbs one immigrant group," says Shay, "it becomes easy to accept the next one."

MIDDLE-CLASS IMMIGRANTS: NEW MELTING POT

Unlike the immigrants who live in the nation's poor Hispanic Mix barrios, the settlers in New Melting Pot have a middle-class lifestyle. They can afford to travel abroad, belong to health clubs and attend theatrical events.

	National Average	New Melting Pot	Cluster Index
Mutual funds	.8%	2.8%	356
Frozen yogurt	4.6	12.8	279
Convertibles	.9	2.2	248
Watch/listen to/attend horse races	2.0	4.3	215
Imported brandy/cognac	5.4	11.3	210
Valid passports	8.1	15.3	189
Travel by charter plane	2.4	4.2	176
Health clubs	2.8	4.9	174
Calculators	2.4	4.1	170
Attend live theater	17.6	25.5	145

Numbers indicate percentages of people in each category, indexed against the national average. An index of 100 equals the U.S. average for that category. An index of 200 means a cluster has twice the national average for that category. Source: MRI and SMRB data bases, Claritas Corp., 1987.

For Young Shin Chung, acceptance has been an important goal since her arrival from Korea in 1972. A 40-year-old wife and mother of three, she recently purchased the Silver Lake Cleaners bordering Los Feliz to supplement her husband's salary as a chemist. Though trained as a teacher in Korea, the language barrier here forced Chung out of the classroom and eventually into this storefront cleaners where she works 60-hour weeks. "My husband complains that I spend too much time here, but I want to become higher class," says the dark, petite woman who always seems to be in motion. "I don't have much time for bowling," she chuckles. At her four-bedroom home, spacious by Korean standards, Chung has tried to adapt to local customs like backyard barbecues. She subscribes to *Sunset* magazine for its "American" recipes and tunes into the daytime TV soaps to improve her language skills. Despite becoming a U.S. citizen in 1978, Chung fears there are certain fine points of American culture she'll never pick up. She has trouble figuring out the plot twists on "Dallas," and she can't understand why Americans put their parents in old age homes. "I spend a lot of my heart on my kids and, when they grow up, I want them to give me the same love," she says. "I guess I still think in Korean."

▄ TOWNS & GOWNS

When the wave of baby boomers went off to college in the '60s, few realized they'd alter campus communities long after their sit-ins and peace marches ended. But after becoming the most educated generation in the nation's history—from 1960 to 1980, the number of students earning bachelor's degrees more than doubled, to 1 million annually— many new graduates couldn't bear to leave their alma maters. The 1980 census revealed an explosion in the size of campus communities throughout rural America—places like Carbondale, Illinois, Gainesville, Florida, and State College, Pennsylvania. Known as Big Fish/Small Ponds in 1970, these country towns were characterized by residents who tended to camp, hunt, can their own produce and vacation with relatives. At the time, their local colleges were incidental to community life.

But by 1980, enough campus graduates and professors had settled in the communities to alter the demographic and create the new Towns & Gowns cluster. Many of the newcomers were former citydwellers who, once lured to the intellectual atmosphere and picket-fence pace of their college towns, had no desire to return to the noise and nuisance of urban life. And their presence gradually turned the rural "small ponds" into sophisticated towns, the seats of summer arts festivals and the homes for high-tech enterprises. Lifestyle surveys demonstrate the popularity of country clubs, gourmet cooking, listening to folk music and writing articles for publication.

Of all the new clusters, Towns & Gowns has the most unorthodox profile, a split personality that's typically one-quarter students and three-quarters townfolk. Cluster communities contain high concentrations of 18- to 24-year-old singles with high educational and professional levels living in group quarters, as well as longtime residents with modest incomes and home values. It's a mix that creates the kind of tension portrayed in the film *Breaking Away,* set on Indiana University's Bloomington campus. The plot centered on a bike race that pitted fraternity students against townies, who were known as "cutters" because of the local quarry workers who provided the stone for campus buildings. In real life, even the media tastes of the two groups are distinct: the college types read *GQ* while the townies favor *Family Weekly.*

Often shopkeepers in Towns & Gowns communities try to develop

THE GREAT DIVIDE: TOWNS & GOWNS

America's college communities, which comprise the Towns & Gowns cluster, typically have a split personality. While the students are jogging, joining fraternities and listening to folk music, the townies would rather go hunting, belong to civic clubs and tune in to "beautiful music."

	National Average	Towns & Gowns	Cluster Index
Civic clubs	1.2%	2.9%	246
Water-skiing	4.9	11.0	224
Jogging shoes	8.7	16.7	192
Downhill skiing	4.2	7.5	175
Veterans life insurance	4.3	7.3	170
Folk records	1.6	2.7	168
Hunting	7.6	12.2	160
Fraternal orders	3.3	5.1	155
"Beautiful music" records	3.6	5.2	144
Horseback riding	4.6	6.2	134

Numbers indicate percentages of people in each category, indexed against the national average. An index of 100 equals the U.S. average for that category. An index of 200 means a cluster has twice the national average for that category. Source: MRI and SMRB data bases, Claritas Corp., 1987.

a particular patronage, but allegiances can shift. Ithaca, New York, a classic Towns & Gowns community, harbors about 20,000 local residents and 20,000 students attending Cornell University and Ithaca College. For years, Fall Creek House bar was a hangout for the rough, middle-class employees of the nearby Ithaca Gun Works. But in the late '60s, Cornell's hockey players began showing up, accepted by the locals because they were tough enough to be the physical equals of the factory workers. When the team began winning national championships, however, celebrating students followed the hockey players to the bar and slowly elbowed out the townie tipplers. Eventually, the bar turned into a college hangout—Heinekens having replaced Pabst Blue Ribbons.

Located in the cloud-covered Allegheny Mountains far from any major city, State College, Pennsylvania, is another world unto itself, with 12,000 year-round residents and 24,000 students. The home of Penn State University, it epitomizes the Towns & Gowns transformation. In the thirty years mayor Arnold Addison has lived there, he's watched State College change from a rural village to a research center, a place where the white-collar workers outnumber the blue-collars six to one.

Condos have replaced the ramshackle boarding houses leading to the campus, and the fast-food franchises have been joined by restaurants featuring Indian, Chinese and American vegetarian cuisine. "It used to be that the town work force was almost completely associated with the university," says Addison, a staid, retired industrial-relations professor. "But as time went on, we started seeing spinoffs in the consulting field, defense contractors and chemical companies."

Today, State College tries to live up to its nickname, Happy Valley, thanks to an educated citizenry that frequently elects Penn State's urban-planning professors to town posts. There's constant traffic across College Avenue between campus and community: the townies use the university's library, gym facilities and creamery, and the students head for the local bookstores, clothing shops and watering holes like the Rathskeller and the Tavern. To be sure, tensions do exist between State College's students and townies. There are still blue-collar bars around town where, locals insist, university types would be beaten up if they entered. But the presence of students lends an atmosphere of youthful vigor rarely found in small towns and residential suburbs. "As you jog, you talk about Page Smith or *The Hunt for Red October* or whatever's going around the campus," says Dave Schuckers, a Penn State University administrator. "Sometimes," he adds, touching his gray-streaked hair, "you have to look in the mirror to tell you're getting older."

▤ RANK & FILE

In 1970, Rank & File's ancestor cluster was called Eastern Europeans for its high percentage of Polish and Czech families living in working-class neighborhoods. But a decade of factory shutdowns took its toll on cluster communities like Baltimore's Sparrow's Point, Pittsburgh's Carnegie and Detroit's Downriver suburbs. As young people left in search of better job opportunities, their aging blue-collar parents tried to make the best of their declining rowhouse neighborhoods. While cluster residents escaped the worst of the industrial downturn—residents can still afford to buy Renault Alliances, camping equipment, cameras and electronic video games at above-average rates—their future is gray. For now, Rank & File leads the nation in durable-manufacturing workers (one-quarter of the labor force), indicating that enough factories are still actively turning out goods to provide middle-class incomes for cluster households—but no one will predict for how long.

Lincoln Park and Wyandotte, two Rank & File suburbs of Detroit, are typical of cluster communities that have already seen their share of layoffs. According to one area study, over 70,000 people lost their jobs between 1950 and 1970. In 1975, a local columnist described Lincoln Park as a "ghost town" with 137 vacant stores and 300 blighted homes that failed to meet housing codes. But Downriver's gritty residents dug in, ignoring their community's reputation for being as foul as the odor from the nearby Detroit Filtration Plant. At least they still had jobs, at Ford's massive River Rouge plant, the Chrysler factory in Trenton and Great Lakes Steel nearby. And they still took pride in their squat brick ramblers with the sidewalks cleaned daily with hoses and pushbrooms. Today, only an occasional visitor senses something vaguely amiss on Downriver streets, something you can't quite put your finger on. Then suddenly the realization: the streets are empty of men and women in their 20s. At the Cee-Em bar in Lincoln Park, the average age of patrons is about 50. The bartender serving Blatz beer and shots of whisky is a grandmother wearing fuzzy pink house slippers.

Many Downriver Detroiters have discovered the best way to lure their kids home is through summertime ethnic festivals. Every week at the Benjamin Yack Arena, an enclosed coliseum the size of a football

---

STICKIN' TO THE UNION: RANK & FILE

The Eastern European immigrants who settled in the working-class city neighborhoods of Rank & File have escaped the worst of the downturn in American industry. Many still have union jobs and middle-class salaries—enough of a cushion to take camping trips and enjoy ice skating. But their rowhouses are aging, and Rank & Filers do their own home maintenance.

	National Average	Rank & File	Cluster Index
Ice skating	2.9%	5.7%	195
Yard trimmers	.9	1.5	166
Watch/listen to boxing	5.3	8.8	166
Domestic subcompacts	7.7	12.6	164
Instant developing cameras	7.5	12.1	162
Blended whisky or rye	7.3	11.2	154
Overnight camping trips	8.3	12.4	149
Exterior painting by household member	11.5	17.1	149
1960s rock records	5.8	8.5	146
Book clubs	9.7	13.4	138

Numbers indicate percentages of people in each category, and indexed against the national average. An index of 100 equals the U.S. average for that category. An index of 200 means a cluster has twice the national average for that category. Source: MRI and SMRB data bases, Claritas Corp., 1987.

field, new flags and booths go up as one of the local ethnic groups throws itself a party, complete with spicy food and spirited dances from the homeland, be it Poland, Italy, Germany, Czechoslavakia or Greece. The marquee outside sometimes reads like a Berlitz promotional poster: "German Festival–May 30, Hungarian Festival–June 6, Pan Slavic Festival–June 20."

What unites the Rank & File residents is a belief in close-knit families and in preserving their hyphenated cultures. "Everybody around here comes from a different background, but we tend to want the same thing out of life—a decent home and good neighborhood for our kids," says Leo DeJohn, president of the Downriver Italian-American Club and a union electrician at Ford. The business community continues to cater to the diverse residents with establishments like Ehrlich's Jewelers, Barney's Bar and Erika's German Cuisine Restaurant. But DeJohn, a courtly, heavy-set man with horn-rims and slicked-back gray hair, notes that most workers spend their off-time relaxing in the many ethnic clubs or working around the house. "There aren't many nightclubs here so the majority of people enjoy their VCRs at home," he says. "After spending eight hours in the plant, they're happy to go home and take care of their lawns."

■ COMMUNITIES IN TRANSITION

Communities evolve slowly, rarely enough over a ten-year period to create a new cluster. Yet changes do occur in all neighborhoods, invisibly, like the eroding of stone by water. They age, empty-nest, undergo gentrification and experience migratory trickles that don't always give way to demographic floods. To cluster analysts these minor neighborhood tremors are hints of what lies ahead in the next decade.

Because America enjoys so few ties to ancient cultures, modern architects, developers and builders play significant roles in the evolution of community lifestyles. The high-rise neighborhoods of Urban Gold Coast could not have existed before the mid-nineteenth century when new metal construction techniques and mechanical elevators permitted buildings to climb to the heavens. A half-century later, developer William Levitt built his space-efficient subdivisions to make room for the armies of house-hungry G.I.s fleeing congested city neighborhoods. In the '60s, self-sufficient "new towns" like Columbia, Maryland, sprang up as alternatives to those car-reliant Levittown, U.S.A. subdivisions, then out of vogue for their dearth of libraries, shopping centers and businesses.

James Rouse, Columbia's creator and the driving force behind such developments as Boston's Faneuil Hall and Baltimore's Inner Harbor, recalls of those days, "We weren't out to design a contemporary utopia." But building a city from scratch amounts to carte blanche for developers to create a new American lifestyle.

Columbia, for instance, was conceived in 1962 when the Rouse Company learned of an impending population explosion in Baltimore and Washington. Rouse and his colleagues decided to develop a planned community of homes and offices halfway between both cities and "responsive to the needs of 100,000 people," says Rouse. According to early promotional literature, Columbia would allow residents to live, work and play in the same setting, a community that had it all. After raising the money to acquire 14,000 acres of farmland, Rouse assembled a team to plan this model community from the mud up. "We called together a group of fourteen people who knew about health, education, religion, transportation and employment," he remembers wistfully. "We met two days a week, every other week for four months, basically exploring one main question: 'What would a rational city be?'" To attract a racially and economically diverse populace, the Rouse Company hired both black and white sales reps and pushed for integrated community planning boards.

Today developers praise Columbia as a triumph of urban planning and social pluralism. Rouse is quick to point out that among the 70,000 residents in 1986 were more than 300 Chinese families. But its billing as a place for people to live and work was never completely realized and, like other executive bedroom suburbs, it's still dependent on the car. Indeed, Columbia is classified as a Furs & Station Wagons community. Nationwide, the "new towns" concept never took off to create a new cluster, and now even Rouse downplays the planner's role in creating a community lifestyle. As he puts it, "Developers can build projects, but only people make a community."

And yet developers can unmake a community, too. Consider what's happening to Smalltown Downtown. While the suburbanization of the country is the largest settlement trend since World War II, it's had disastrous results in this cluster of downtown districts contained in hundreds of small industrial cities. These once-thriving commercial centers—cities like Jacksonville, Florida, Joplin, Missouri, and Parkersburg, West Virginia, designated Old Brick Factories in 1970—typically were settled by blue-collar workers living in homes surrounding urban factories. But as the industries shut down and the suburbs opened up, town residents moved to greener lifestyles. In 1980, the cluster was renamed

Smalltown Downtown to reflect the disappearing smokestacks, the economic downturn (a ZQ slide from 21 to 32) and the lost populations that have caused the cities to revert to small towns—with small-town affections for fishing, gospel music, Roller Derbies and Tupperware parties. "The automobile killed our downtown," claims Jim Snyder, city editor of the *Parkersburg News,* summing up the situation in so many of these communities. "The malls brought people out of downtown and they stayed."

A trip through Parkersburg (pop. 40,000), illustrates the shift in fortunes for many Smalltown Downtown communities. An early-twentieth-century boomtown tied to coal, chemicals and ceramics, Parkersburg has been steadily losing people and jobs since the 1970 census, and dozens of stores have closed in the heart of the city. Housing developers and merchants have followed the suburban exodus toward the Grand Central Mall, and not enough new industries and moderate-income families have moved into Parkersburg to keep the downtown young and vibrant. "This is a wonderful place to live but not a wonderful place to work," says Edwin Dil, owner of the largest retail outlet in the city, Dil Brothers' Department Store. Opened in 1900 in the center of town, Dil's now finds its customers have become increasingly older, more conservative and less affluent, and it's cut back its hours of business accordingly. These days it's open only one night a week; the average sale, $12.50. "People are buying closer to their need," says Dil. "You won't see a lot of flashy, frivolous purchases around here."

For longtime residents of Parkersburg, the changes overtaking their Smalltown Downtown are unsettling. Shirley Smith, who was born 44 years ago in a nearby house where her mother still lives, praises the unhurried atmosphere, where people sit on porches at night, throw backyard cookouts on the weekend and share hedge trimmers with neighbors. But she also worries about her neighborhood's proximity to downtown blocks that have become magnets for seedy nightclubs and boarded-up shops. "The bad has come in like termites eating out this area," says Smith, a no-nonsense blonde who works part time for American Crosstitch, a mail-order house. "At Christmas, you used to be able to shop in a downtown store and go outside into the cold to find the streets jammed with people. But that's an era our kids will never see. Sure, the mall's convenient, but I miss our downtown." Lately, even Smith has discussed with her husband the idea of moving out, fearful of the encroaching blight. "I worry about this area," she says quietly. "In ten years, the property values may go down and we'll be stuck."

In Downtown Dixie-Style, a cluster of lower-class communities con-

STOOP SITTERS: SMALLTOWN DOWNTOWN

In the decaying neighborhoods of America's small industrial cities, residents have a far different standard of living than their former neighbors who have moved to suburbia. The lower-middle-class Smalltown Downtowners belong to fraternal clubs, are active in their churches and political parties—mostly Republican—and enjoy gospel music.

	National Average	Smalltown Downtown	Cluster Index
Cafeterias	16.7%	32.7%	196
Canned meat spreads	7.5	14.5	194
Gospel records/tapes	4.0	7.7	193
Room air conditioners	4.5	7.9	175
Salt-water fishing	5.3	8.0	151
AM/FM radio cassette recorders	4.2	6.0	144
Fraternal orders	3.3	4.5	138
Tupperware parties	14.5	19.3	133
Electronic video games	5.6	6.8	126
Work for political party/candidate	3.2	4.0	124

Numbers indicate percentages of people in each category, and indexed against the national average. An index of 100 equals the U.S. average for that category. An index of 200 means a cluster has twice the national average for that category. Source: MRI and SMRB data bases, Claritas Corp., 1987.

centrated in several dozen mostly southern cities, residents are experiencing transition of a different sort. In communities like Queen Village in Philadelphia, whites have gentrified formerly black districts, and in others such as West Jackson, Mississippi, young black families have moved into aging white neighborhoods. In both cases, a largely neglected neighborhood is struggling to better itself, but the racial flux makes any concerted effort difficult. Downtown Dixie-Style is the nation's only neighborhood type whose favorite magazines include *Jet, Rudder, Soap Opera Digest* and *GQ*.

"We're a hybrid community, not an integrated community," explains Sylvester Vickers, a 43-year-old black contractor and longtime resident of West Jackson. "The white community is clustered and the black community is clustered. They're pretty separate from each other."

West Jackson, a classic Downtown Dixie-Style area dotted with discount markets and clothing thrift shops, is not a pretty place. A lot of the bungalow-style homes sag and the roads are notched with potholes. Drugs, unemployment and youth gangs are intransigent problems. And the wave of young black families moving into aging, working-class white neighborhoods has created further racial tensions and white flight. FOR SALE signs mark many homes and yard sales are commonplace, held by fleeing residents, whom white highway worker Tommy Brewer calls "die-hard segregationists. In this part of Jackson, you still find people of the old generation who don't accept you unless your skin is as white as theirs." In a neighborhood with such sentiments, gaining acceptance is no picnic for black newcomers like Rosena Parker, a 66-year-old retired federal administrator and one of the first to integrate her block in 1984. Within weeks of moving in, her home was burglarized. Since then, she's established cordial relations with her white neighbors, though their conversations "usually stick to crime in the neighborhood or what's going into someone's garden," she says. "I don't think I was wanted when I arrived, but I think that I'm now accepted."

Whether true racial harmony will ever come to Downtown Dixie-Style communities like West Jackson is still in doubt. Marcia Weaver, the area's city councilwoman, knows her constituents' fears. "The biggest issue of the last campaign was the changing neighborhood," says Weaver, a white former schoolteacher. "A lot of the elderly whites were frightened of change. But I'd say there's not a lot of difference between them and the younger blacks. They're all working-class people with a lot of pride and self-sufficiency." And all are frequent church-goers—mostly Baptist—though few belong to integrated congregations. Rare still in this urban vestige of the Old South is interracial socializing. When Tommy Brewer and his wife decided to host an integrated New Year's Eve party in 1985, they first called their white friends to prepare them. "We told them that if it's going to be a problem, then they'd better stay away," says the lanky 50-year-old, who chain-smokes Winstons. A dozen of his white friends didn't show up, Brewer acknowledges with a shrug. "I've always said that you can have good and bad white people as well as black people. There's nothing worse on God's green earth than white trash."

The neighborhood issues are rarely that divisive in two suburban clusters, middle-class Levittown, U.S.A. and upper-middle-class Pools & Patios. But in the last decade, residents of both have undergone another kind of cluster trauma—empty-nesting—as high housing costs have shut young couples out of these comfortable subdivisions. Many developments contained what were considered starter homes when they were built for the postwar boom thirty years ago. But these split-levels and Cape Cods aged gracefully, received frequent improvements and appreciated in value as their slim saplings grew into shady elms and oaks. After parents packed their teenagers off to college, they found that

POOR BUT PROUD: DOWNTOWN DIXIE-STYLE

In these poor, racially mixed areas, typically in southern cities, the living ain't easy. Residents travel by bus, treat themselves for medical problems and seek ways to save money any way possible; note the high purchase rates for home permanents and meat/fish extenders.

	National Average	Downtown Dixie-Style	Index
Soul records	2.5%	6.5%	262
Malt liquor	8.3	20.6	248
Travel by commercial bus	1.4	3.2	229
Asthma relief remedies	2.1	4.2	199
Denture adhesives	6.4	12.2	190
Men's leisure suits	1.4	2.6	187
Canned stew	2.8	4.6	163
Meat/fish extender	16.4	24.1	147
Follow horse races	4.3	6.1	141
Home permanents	8.9	12.2	137
Toothache/gum remedies	15.3	20.3	133

Numbers indicate percentages of people in each category and, indexed against the national average. An index of 100 equals the U.S. average for that category. An index of 200 means a cluster has twice the national average for that category. Source: MRI and SMRB data bases, Claritas Corp., 1987.

few young couples could afford their $150,000 starter homes. In Levittown, U.S.A. and Pools & Patios households across the country, cribs now stand in bedrooms once decorated with psychedelic black-light posters—awaiting periodic visits from faraway grandchildren. And both clusters mirror lifestyle patterns generally associated with retirement communities: high rates for golf, cruises, home remodeling, security systems and mutual funds.

But the empty-nesting process in these clusters isn't as gentle as the falling of autumn leaves. Residents in both Pools & Patios and Levittown, U.S.A. were torn apart over the issue of closing neighborhood schools, long the source of many communities' vitality as well as their insurance against plummeting property values. The realignment of fiscal priorities helped breed perhaps the strongest single attack on government seen in the last decade—the tax revolt. Since 1978, when Californians passed Proposition 13 slashing property taxes, nearly half the states have clamped ceilings on taxes and spending. The Pools & Patios community of La Crescenta, a hilly suburb of 30,000 overlooking Los Angeles, has closed one junior high and consolidated two elementaries.

Without kids in the streets, Neighborhood Watch programs have been launched to fend off daytime burglaries.

Much of La Crescenta consists of postwar tract developments built for the young workers at the nearby Jet Propulsion Laboratory. Now senior managers and retirees, these residents have watched the price tags on their ranch houses and split-levels climb to $200,000, though the community's close-in location figures into the cost. Residents have planted tall shade trees and built high walls, not to preserve their privacy —some homes are less than a car's length apart—but to create the illusion of being far from L.A.'s smoggy downtown. "Everyone tries to create Yosemite in their backyards," says Ollie Blanning, district representative for city councilman Michael Antonovitch. On weekends, backyard barbecues are a year-round activity, but longtime resident Dorothy Rumsby has noticed a difference in the last few years. "Now that the kids are raised, a lot of pools sit there unused," she says. "People just sit around and visit."

A recent demographic twist may change that somewhat. Just when they thought they had finished the job, many parents of suburban baby boomers find their children returning to the nest, their dirty laundry, financial straits and emotional difficulties in tow. According to the 1970 census, approximately 13 million young adults between the ages of 18 and 34 either had returned to or had yet to leave their parents' homes. By 1984, that number had grown to almost 20 million. Analysts attribute the increase to several factors: postponement of marriage, the rise in divorce, a tight job market and high housing costs. At a time when Pools & Patios and Levittown, U.S.A. communities are empty-nesting, census surveys show many young adults returning to their old homes—as well as their old habits, according to some parents.

In Norwood, Massachusetts, a Levittown, U.S.A. suburb southwest of Boston, family nests are chirping again. A one-time industrial town, Norwood underwent a postwar baby boom that swelled the population from 10,000 to 50,000. Development along Boston's Route 128 created a stable economic base for upper-middle-class families. White-shuttered, wood-framed houses went up, schools were built, and churches offered family memberships to accommodate congregants with eight to ten children. Frances Harwood, a homemaker and mother of four, was like many young mothers who became involved in their children's activities, serving as Girl Scout leader, swim meet chaperone, school band booster. "I called myself a compulsive volunteer," says Harwood, an energetic 56-year-old with wavy gray hair pulled back in a bun. "Whenever my children became involved, I became involved."

Then, during the '70s, Norwood residents had to readjust their image of a community forever young. At the town's largest church, St. Catherine's, the number of baptisms dropped from 600 a year to 150. By 1985, the town had more nursing homes than nursery schools, and more senior citizens marched in the Fourth of July parade than children. Every week during the summer, a town square concert attracted members of the lawn-chair set who marveled at the real-estate boom that made houses they bought for $30,000 now worth $200,000. And the children who once played in Norwood's sandboxes found themselves priced out of the market, so they headed for distant suburbs near the New Hampshire border. "This town used to be the boonies to people," says Loretta O'Brien, a Norwood attorney. "But now kids think of this town as Boston and the other towns as suburbia. Ten miles outside of Norwood can mean a $30,000 difference in the price of a home."

Like many baby-boom parents in Levittown, U.S.A. communities, Harwood figured her nurturing days were over when youngest daughter Carol went off to business school in Rhode Island. She planned to turn

---

EMPTY-NESTING SUBURBS: POOLS & PATIOS VS. LEVITTOWN, U.S.A.

America's postwar suburbs have begun to empty-nest, the grown-up baby boomers on their own, the aging couples left behind adopting lifestyle patterns of other retirees—heavy on golf and cruises, light on roller-skating and video games. The upper-middle-class residents of Pools & Patios also have more money for leisure activities than the middle-class residents of Levittown, U.S.A.

Pools & Patios		Levittown, U.S.A.
253	U.S. Treasury notes	162
160	Domestic tour packages	143
129	Knitting	133
209	Travel by cruise ship	132
192	Golf balls	124
55	Infant cereal	121
92	Toddler's toys	114
83	Motorcycles	88
95	Roller-skating	76
97	Pregnancy tests	51

Numbers indicate percentages of people in each category, indexed against the national average. An index of 100 equals the U.S. average for that category. An index of 200 means a cluster has twice the national average for that category. Source: MRI and SMRB data bases, Claritas Corp., 1987.

a part of the house into a rental apartment so she and her husband could increase their retirement savings and not just rely on income from his dental practice. But in 1984, 21-year-old Carol moved back to the family nest when she couldn't find an apartment that suited her modest salary as a manager of a Filene's Department Store. Carol found the money she saved on rent meant she could afford designer clothes and vacations in California and Europe. Frances found unexpected companionship— her daughter livened up such everyday routines as cooking and shopping. But slowly Carol began reverting to some of her adolescent ways. "There was the expectation that I would be doing her cooking and cleaning for her," says Frances, "which was fine up to a point. But I've already raised my kids and I don't think I should be tied down any longer. My husband and I like to go to dinner and the theater, and we'll travel anyplace and everyplace: Bermuda, Greece, Canada . . ." her voice trails off.

Across the nation, Levittown, U.S.A. communities are at a crossroads, many households empty-nesting while others witness grown children returning to the nest. Demographers and residents offer various predictions about what lies ahead—whether the cluster will turn into retirement communities, havens for extended families or something close to their original starter neighborhoods as the baby boomers finally attain the earning power necessary to afford their parents' pricey real estate. The only fact on which they can agree: their communities will never become static.

■ CLUSTERS OF THE FUTURE

How will the cluster system change in the future? In keeping with past findings that 20 percent of the nation's neighborhoods change every decade, America can expect eight new clusters to emerge in 1990. And if the past truly is prologue, some qualified forecasts can be made about how the 1990 census will reveal itself on a neighborhood level. Working from what demographers already know about America, cluster analysts offer an irresistible if clouded crystal ball. Among the new neighborhood types they envision:

■ Young Rustics. The 1990 census may reveal a new exurban cluster, reflecting the continued dispersal of the population from cities that began after World War II. At least 3.5 million people moved into non-metropolitan counties in the '70s, a sharp increase from the 2.8 million who left such areas in the previous decade. Technological advances in computers and telecommunications will facilitate the migration of workers away from central corporate offices. Bell Labs is already experimenting with a national office where people can interact through modems and television cameras, holding conferences with workers thousands of miles apart. Computers will allow these new migrants to get their educations, shop for clothes and have medical checkups without ever leaving home. By 1990, these middle-class singles and couples may form a new Young Rustics cluster, a place where residents prefer *Omni* to *Saturday Evening Post,* "Max Headroom" to "Murder, She Wrote" and microwave pasta dishes to canned ravioli.

■ Boomlet Families. The baby boomlet that social observers reported in the mid-'80s may produce another cluster in the Young Suburbia mold. Between 1980 and 1984, the suburbs gained more than 5.8 million people, whom social commentators have called "lapsed yuppies." After rushing to achieve jobs, wealth and personal fulfillment beyond their elders, career-oriented women have responded to the ticking of their expiring biological clocks. As the baby-boom generation moves into middle age, its members will look to raise their kids in stable suburbs—ironically, the very places they spent so much of their lives trying to escape. One economic forecast predicts that 35- to 44-year-olds will account for 44 percent of all new-home purchases between 1985 and 1995, up from 25 percent during the previous decade. With Boomlet Families most likely will come another explosion of suburban health clubs, ethnic restaurants and employer-sponsored day-care centers.

■ Gentrification Chic. The gentrification movement may create a new cluster, situated economically between Bohemian Mix and Money & Brains. Between the 1970 and 1980 census, the population of metropolitan centers grew by 10 percent, especially in gentrifying rowhouse areas. With many marginal areas already upgraded by urban pioneers, once down-in-the-heels neighborhoods have achieved a trendy status all their own. Residents of Washington's Capitol Hill have restored ramshackle brownstones into beauties worthy of a spread in *Metropolitan Home.* In San Francisco's legendary Haight-Ashbury neighborhood, former head shops have become chi-chi boutiques with too-cute names: For Heaven's Cake (bakery), Play With It (toys) and Revival of the Fittest (antiques). Look for a cluster that might be called Gentrification Chic, where tea dances and antique-hunting will be favorite sports.

■ Suburban Retirees. According to census projections, the average age of the American population will continue to climb. By 1990, the number of seniors is expected to surpass 31 million, compared to a teenage population of 23 million. This trend could add a third predomi-

THE CLUSTERS OF 1990

A new cluster system will appear after the 1990 census, reflecting the major demographic shifts of the '80s. Forecasters predict eight new neighborhood types that portray a populace with more retirees, wealthier minorities and an increase in nontraditional communities beyond the urban sprawl. Stay tuned.

Possible Nickname	Trend
Young Rustics	Americans continue to migrate from the cities to exurban areas.
Boomlet Families	Suburban family neighborhoods grow following the baby boomlet of the mid-'80s.
Gentrification Chic	Gentrifying inner cities become affluent.
Suburban Retirees	Aging, empty-nesting suburbs become retirement communities.
New-Collar Condos	Singles townhouse and condo developments fill with new-collar service workers.
Minority Achievers	The nation's minority and immigrant groups rise in affluence.
Sunbelt Industries	Manufacturing plants from northeastern cities continue to migrate to small southern factory towns.
Urban Independents	A wave of nontraditional households—stepfamilies, single-parent families and unmarried couples—moves to quiet city neighborhoods.

nantly elderly cluster, joining Gray Power and Golden Ponds. If salaries don't keep pace with housing inflation, one of the empty-nesting suburban clusters—Pools & Patios or Levittown, U.S.A.—may turn into Suburban Retirees. Expect to see elementary schools renovated as nursing homes and community centers for the elderly. *Modern Maturity* will outsell all other magazines, and movie houses will do a big matinee business.

■ New-Collar Condos. Stanford University reports that twenty occupations will account for 35 percent of the new jobs in the '80s, but only two of them, elementary-school teaching and accounting, require college degrees. The AFL-CIO predicts that by 1990 the nation will be home to 500,000 "surplus college graduates" with outmoded skills. The end of the decade may bring about a cluster for the postindustrial age: New-Collar Condos. In city condo and townhouse developments, singles and couples will work in service-industry professions, as paralegals, computer programmers and medical assistants. Their lifestyles will be middle-class, their clothes from the Gap, their favorite show, "Hill Street Blues" reruns.

■ Minority Achievers. Americans of Hispanic origin, who increased by 61 percent in the '70s and now number 16 million, are expected to overtake blacks and become the largest minority by 1990. And Asian immigrants who arrived during the last decade have gained more than a toehold in their new country. Diligence, all-American hard work and sacrifice will earn these newcomers middle-class status and lifestyles. This new cluster could reflect the millions of successful, first-generation immigrant families who have joined the establishment. For the first time in U.S. history, communities of well-off Hispanics will be reported on the American landscape, their neighborhoods dotted with BMWs, Weber kettles and backyard pools.

■ Sunbelt Industries. The Sunbelt has lured high-tech, nonunion factories out to pasture. In cities like Smyrna and Spring Hill, Tennessee, communities are growing up around newly built factories and manufacturing plants. The 1990 census may reveal a cluster filled with new factory workers—black and white, married and divorced—who live in just-built ranch house and townhouse subdivisions. Many will be migrants from the Sunbelt supercities that fell on economic hard times in the '80s. According to a 1985 study by the National Association of Towns & Townships, about half of all U.S. adults say they would move to small towns if they could get jobs there—a sentiment that will help spawn the Sunbelt Industries cluster. With careful planning, these southern factory towns will escape the decay that overwhelmed the northern industrial cities, and residents will live comfortably with their discount food warehouses, health clubs and softball leagues.

■ Urban Independents. The divorce rate has leveled off, but Census Bureau demographer Art Norton still forecasts an increase in the number of nontraditional U.S. households: single-parent families, stepfamilies, unmarried couples, middle-aged singles. While the number of family households grew by 19 percent in the last decade, nonfamily households made up of unrelated couples or single people jumped by 89 percent and now account for more than one-quarter of all U.S. households. The figures add up to what may become a cluster of metropolitan communities where the majority of apartments and homes are filled with nontraditional households—the stuff of "Kate & Allie" and "One Day at a Time." The big concerns: programs for latch-key kids, over-30 mixers and visitation rights for stepgrandparents.

Of course, the 1990 census will not only result in new clusters on the American landscape. Heavy Industry and Mines & Mills clusters may disappear if the American manufacturing economy remains on a downswing. The continued decrease in farmworkers could bid farewell to the Grain Belt and Agri-Business neighborhood types. And tiny Urban Gold Coast, containing only half a percent of the nation's households, may be swallowed by the new Gentrified Chic cluster. The 1990 cluster system no doubt will also lose a corresponding eight clusters, ultimately reflecting a nation that is more college educated, better salaried, whiter-collared and more heterogeneous.

Like any forecast, these projections must be viewed with a healthy dose of skepticism. Who, for example, could have predicted the postwar baby boom's wrenching effect on American life? And who can predict the next medical breakthrough—a cure for cancer, a reliable mechanical heart—that may further increase our longevity? Only time, the census and the cluster system will tell.

■ FUTURE ZIP

America, a dozen years into the future. The nation's citizens have come to recognize that society is no longer divided along racial or ethnic lines but by neighborhood types. The business community has given up entirely on the mass market and now targets all its messages to mini-market niches. With zillions of new products and services available to them, consumers clamor for better cluster tailors to help them make their purchase. Politicians have accepted the demise of the two-party system and now draw their support from coalitions of single-issue constituencies. And the American people no longer worry about the homogenization of culture but about how to propel the nation's lifestyle diversity into a united renaissance.

Those who chart the future already foresee an economy based in part on the cluster technology. Forecaster Marvin Cetron maintains that as much as one-fourth of all retail sales will take place via telemarketing —where customers use their computers to order items through electronic catalogues. As the metropolitan sprawl slowly engulfs suburban towns along both coasts—creating megalopoli from Boston to Norfolk and Seattle to San Diego—marketers will rely on a knowledge of lifestyle segments to reach their customers. Sears catalogues will flash on the PCs of Young Suburbia, while The Sharper Image appears on Blue Blood Estates terminals. With more than half of all Money & Brains residents working at home (Cetron estimates that one-quarter of the nation's labor force may work at home in the year 2000) that upscale cluster will have access to the most extensive home shopping offerings. At the touch of their keyboard, they'll be able to order everything from file cabinets to home-delivered sushi.

Much of the nation's media—print and TV—will be programmed according to the cluster segments of the day. Already, the subscribers of the *Los Angeles Times* and the *Chicago Tribune* receive different ads and supplements depending on their neighborhoods. An insert for a wine sale now goes to the in-town Urban Gold Coast neighborhoods, while discount coupons for Pizza Hut arrive on the doorsteps in Hispanic Mix. Not limited to the advertising departments, these applications are harbingers for the editorial side of the media as well. Specialty lifestyle publications will become even more specialized, geared for specific neighborhood types. *Field & Stream* may offer different editions for Shotguns & Pickups and Blue-Chip Blues subscribers. Among in-flight magazines, a *Towns & Gowns Traveler* will appeal to college students in search of adventurous backpacking.

The few "general interest" magazines still on the newsstands—publications like *Reader's Digest* and *TV Guide*—will present different articles according to their readers' zip codes. The covers will change to suit the cluster location of their display racks. In Emergent Minorities, a headline may promote a story on the problems of single working mothers; in Blue-Collar Nursery, the hazards of violent TV shows for children.

Television will no longer be regarded as a mass medium but as a video boutique where each cluster will receive programs and commercials tailored to neighborhood interests. Already, WFAA-TV, the ABC affiliate in Dallas, has used cluster profiles to convince Madison Avenue that its nightly newscasts attract a much more suburban and affluent audience than any of the competition. That information allowed it to hike its commercial rates, snare classier advertisers and increase its share of upscale viewers. In the future, most commercial TV stations will feature programming geared toward one cluster or another—much as cable TV stations now present specialty programming. (In fact, 95 percent of all American households will be wired for cable in the year 2000.)

Living in a Black Enterprise cluster, for instance, will determine whether your TV stations offer reruns of "The Cosby Show" or "Punky Brewster."

America's marketplace of the future will still be dominated by The Mall. But builders like Western Development of Washington, D.C., are pondering ways of creating entire "life-cycle" shopping centers ideally suited to the consumption tastes of the surrounding neighborhood types. Researchers right now tromp through parking lots, jotting down license plates to determine how far people will travel to shop in a mall. In the near future, those records will be matched with purchase receipts to determine what kind of man will drive a mile for a camel-hair jacket. "It will help crystallize our image of mall customers," says Western's research director Mark Kissel, who dreams of devising "the perfect formula" of mall shops that would not only guarantee success for the merchants but provide one-stop shopping for area residents. And that perfect formula could be repeated in other communities around the country with similar cluster makeups.

Peripheral to this retailer's Oz are super-powerful microcomputers that would allow marketers instant access to the cluster customers for tens of thousands of products. Programmers today are developing software that one day will allow a business to key in an intersection in Cincinnati and instantly retrieve a cluster breakdown of the area neighborhoods and the products that would have the best chances for success. Other advances may one day allow the manager to track projected growth in those neighborhoods over a five- and ten-year span and predict which medium will successfully reach the changing populace over the long term. "Future managers will have at their fingertips as much data as they need to analyze any marketing decision without having to go through a lot of complicated research data," says Bruce Carroll, president of Claritas. And advances in artificial intelligence promise to make complex business problems solvable with user-friendly programs.

Indeed, this technological tomorrowland could mean computers of cluster-based technology in every doctor's office, florist's stand and suburban split-level. An Atlanta-based computer company called Express Search currently allows home- and apartment-shoppers to key the specs of their dream home into a computer, which then spits out the available listings by neighborhood. No great programming leap is needed to cluster-code the neighborhoods for desired home or office. Business relocation firms may also tap the cluster technology to help genetics firms find white-collar God's Country workers or industrial plants settle amidst nonunion Mines & Mills blue-collar types. In 1986, medical schools began cutting back their enrollments because of a "physician's glut" in upscale metropolitan areas. Cluster maps of the future will aid the medical profession not only in attracting students from neglected areas but also in placing doctors outside the big cities in communities with cushy lifestyles. Not every intern need be sent to a health-care backwater in Tobacco Roads.

Politically over the next few decades, powerful coalitions will form based not on party affiliation but on lifestyle needs. Rev. Jesse Jackson had the right idea in 1984 when he formed the Rainbow Coalition to represent disenfranchised Americans from disparate parts of the country: the inner-city underclass of Public Assistance with the struggling farmers of America's Grain Belt. But the lack of affluence of these voters relegated that coalition to a minor role in national politics. Still, political analysts foresee both major parties losing power in the future as ad hoc cluster coalitions form to support single-issue concerns. It won't be uncommon for an organization opposing a nuclear arms build-up (certainly the debate will rage into the future) to find most of its members from disparate clusters with high concentrations of teenagers: Furs & Station Wagons, Tobacco Roads, Blue Blood Estates and Hard Scrabble. Pundits might dub this cluster mix the "Save the Teens Coalition."

In another dozen years, most households will cast their votes for president as well as for local officials using a home computer. And two-way cable systems will encourage instant reactions from voters, cross-referenced according to clusters. As has already been portrayed in "Max Headroom," a politician may be able to chart the reaction to his or her speech while speaking, one line at a time. And some leaders will become known by their cluster constituency, "The powerful voice of Bohemian Mixers" or "The esteemed representative of Blue Blood Estates."

To be sure, this brave new clustered world won't be welcomed openly by everyone. Many will worry about the power of specialists to predetermine the products and media offered depending on neighborhood lifestyles. And there's plenty of evidence that Americans will prize diversity beyond their own cluster's circle of experience. At present, 40 percent of all Catholics and 33 percent of all Jews intermarry—trends increasing at the rate of about 1 percent a year. In the future, "Zippy's Clustered Dating Service" will facilitate such matches, no matter what the preferred pairings will be. While a clustered society, let alone a clustered dating service, may not appeal to everyone, the boredom of a homogenized nation could be overwhelming.

It is the clusters' ability to connect people with their values and desires that will make most of the headlines in the future. But if these trends sound vaguely familiar, it's because we must dream the future before we can create it. And in many ways, we've already begun to live that dream. American lifestyles are always evolving, slowly from one generation to the next, our progress imperceptible yet ever-present. Stability in the face of change—the clustering of America demonstrates that that unique quality is shared by all neighborhood types across the nation.

9

FREEZE FRAME: THE FORTY CLUSTERS

If the clusters tell us anything, it's that most people tend to live in a bubble of consciousness penetrated only by a close circle of acquaintances. They're familiar with the lifestyles of a few other neighborhood types near their own socioeconomic level. And they're vaguely aware of several more through movies or the media—the life in Grain Belt portrayed in *Country* or the Blue Blood Estates world of *Down and Out in Beverly Hills.* But many of the TV sitcom views of American life are stereotypical impressions of Hollywood writers whose sensibilities were also probably shaped by only a few clusters—Bohemian Mix, Urban Gold Coast, Money & Brains and Furs & Station Wagons.

In an effort to replace vague stereotypes with detailed images, what follows are snapshots of life in the forty clusters, based on a variety of sources: PRIZM-coded data compiled by Claritas from the U.S. Census Bureau, Simmons Market Research Bureau, Mediamark Research, Inc. and R.L. Polk; political polls conducted by Targeting Systems, Inc.; and scores of interviews with residents of representative cluster communities. Because the clusters are constantly evolving, the observations reflect the progress and trends of our culture only at this point in time. But by taking a lifestyle look at America's neighborhoods, we can learn more about who we are, where we came from and where we're going. How we make use of what we know will help us understand what's happening along the way.

▄▄▄▄▄▄▄▄▄▄▄▄▄ ZQ 1: BLUE BLOOD ESTATES

From the sprawling manses of McLean, Virginia, to the cliff-clutching villas of Malibu, California, Blue Blood Estates encompasses America's wealthiest neighborhoods. Often situated in the greenbelt suburbs of major cities, they're home to the nation's corporate kingpins, the upper-crustiest white-collar professionals like heart surgeons and entertainment lawyers, as well as the heirs of old-money fortunes. One in five earns over $100,000 annually. Half have homes costing over $200,000. You can usually identify their residences by their surroundings: tall iron gates, private security guards and well-tended shrubbery. Blue Blood Estates represents the pinnacle of success to which Americans traditionally aspire: Easy Street.

With one in ten millionaires living in Blue Blood Estates, cluster consuming patterns reflect their regal tastes. Residents play chess, buy imported champagne, acquire U.S. Treasury Notes and attend the theater at many times the national average. Compared to the general population, they donate five times as much money to colleges. On their coffee tables, they're four times as likely as average Americans to have magazines such as *Gourmet, The New Yorker* and *Architectural Digest.* Because Blue Blood Estates residents can afford almost anything, what they don't like is also revealing (though not entirely unexpected): canned stews and TV dinners at the supermarket, *Hunting* and *Grit* at the newsstand, Ford Fairmonts and Chevrolet Impalas from auto dealerships. For the citizens of Blue Blood Estates, vacations usually revolve around exotic locales: ski slopes, island beaches and exclusive golf courses. These are the people who sport that envied glow—the winter tan—from skiing holidays in Switzerland.

Although so much of their taste defines high status in America, the residents of Blue Blood Estates typically downplay their lifestyle to the uninitiated. Understatement is the vogue. Elayne Nathanson, a resident of Malibu, the entertainer-rich colony north of Los Angeles, notes that neighbor Neil Diamond "can run up to the drugstore in sweats and no one cares." Many residents save their glitz and glamor for public forays—the political fundraisers, philanthropic dinners and charity balls that fill their social calendar.

In Blue Blood Estates, if they have it, they give it, partly out of humanitarian concern, partly for tax reasons and partly "out of guilt for a lifetime of debutante seasons," writes Lisa Birnbach in *The Preppy Handbook.* "Around here, we don't pass up a charity," says West

ZQ 1: BLUE BLOOD ESTATES

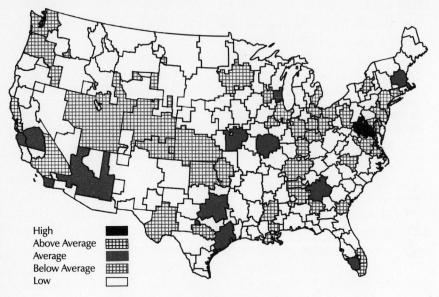

High
Above Average
Average
Below Average
Low

1.1% of U.S. households
Primary age range: 35–44
Median household income: $70,307
Median home value: $200,000+

Thumbnail Demographics
super-rich suburbs
single-unit housing
predominantly white families
college educations
white-collar jobs

Politics
Predominant ideology: conservative
1984 presidential vote: Reagan (72%)
Key issues: fiscal conservatism, nuclear arms

Sample Neighborhoods
Beverly Hills, California (90212)
Potomac, Maryland (20854)
Scarsdale, New York (10583)
Bloomfield Hills, Michigan (48013)
McLean, Virginia (22101)
Lake Forest, Illinois (60045)

Lifestyle

High Usage	Index	Low Usage	Index
U.S. Treasury notes	521	Tupperware	47
Irish whiskey	410	Pregnancy tests	46
Car rentals	398	Menthol cigarettes	44
Downhill skiing	322	Chewing tobacco	37
Travel by cruise ship	290	Groin irritation remedies	34
Bottled water	253	Denture adhesives	29
Tennis balls	251	Watch wrestling	21
Vermouth	250	Cigarillos	5

Magazines/Newspapers

High Usage	Index	Low Usage	Index
The New York Times	599	*Hot Rod*	27
Architectural Digest	499	*Sports Afield*	22
Gourmet	468	*1001 Home Ideas*	21
The Wall Street Journal	452	*Ebony*	4

Cars

High Usage	Index	Low Usage	Index
Rolls Royces	2554	Chevrolet Monte Carlos	51
Jaguars	1758	Chevrolet Chevettes	49
Ferraris	1648	Chevrolet Impalas	47
Mercedes 380/500/560	1387	Plymouth Gran Furys	35
BMW 5 Series	1108	Dodge Diplomats	28

Food

High Usage	Index	Low Usage	Index
Natural cold cereal	179	Meat tenderizers	75
Low-fat/skim milk	133	Canned meat spreads	67
Frozen dessert pies	119	TV dinners	61
Freeze-dried coffee	117	Powdered fruit drinks	55

Television

High Usage	Index	Low Usage	Index
"Late Night with David Letterman"	127	"The People's Court"	47
"The Tonight Show"	123	"Simon & Simon"	40
"60 Minutes"	113	"The Young and the Restless"	27
"20/20"	112	"American Bandstand"	4

Bloomfield, Michigan, resident Jon Greenberg, whose charitable offerings total $20,000 annually. "We call ourselves moneyed liberals, which
means we have sensitivity for the underdog but we don't work for the
issues. We give money instead."

Despite scattered Democratic pockets, Blue Blood Estates' political
leanings are mostly conservative Republican. In the 1984 election, 72
percent of the residents voted for Ronald Reagan, and they remain the
president's biggest boosters in the area of tax reform and free trade. No
cluster is more conservative on economic issues or more opposed to
government activism in welfare and affirmative-action programs. And
though Blue Blood Estates residents represent the GOP's biggest fundraisers, this cluster is also the biggest source of Democratic dollars
every election. Contributing is simply a habit.

▬▬▬▬▬▬ ZQ 2: MONEY & BRAINS

In the Georgetown section of Washington, D.C., it's easier to find a
tin of caviar in local shops than a box of nails. Houses in Georgetown
come with pedigrees to go with their price tags. And no dining room is
complete without Georgian silver on the table, ancestral portraits on the
walls and computer printouts of favorite recipes inside the Chippendale
hutch. On summer evenings, local teenagers leave their Federal-style
mansions to become street performers, ignoring the dirty-blues guitar
tradition to play from their experience: classical pieces for violin, flute
and cello.

Such is life in Money & Brains, the nation's cluster of exclusive,
in-town neighborhoods characterized by swank townhouses, renovated
condos and elegant apartments. Frequently located near prestigious city
colleges, Money & Brains ranks second among clusters in both educational achievement and affluence (nearly half the residents have college
degrees and earn over $50,000 annually). These are the neighborhoods
that attract the nation's well-off intelligentsia, the leaders of science,
academia and management. While residents enjoy the exclusivity of
their homes, they take more pride in their advanced degrees and ambitious jobs. These are the Americans who value conspicuous consumption not of goods but of taste.

And surveys confirm Money & Brains' ultrasophistication. Residents
buy investment property, sailboats, classical records and designer telephones at rates many times the national average. They're big purchasers
of salted nuts, snack cheeses and specialty wines—all the ingredients for

ZQ 2: MONEY & BRAINS

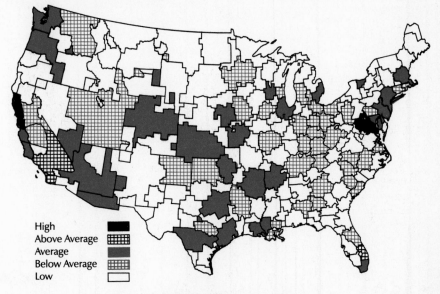

High
Above Average
Average
Below Average
Low

0.9% of U.S. households
Primary age range: 45–64
Median household income: $45,798
Median home value: $150,755

Thumbnail Demographics
posh in-town neighborhoods
single-unit housing
predominantly white families and singles
college graduates
white-collar workers

Politics
Predominant ideology: moderate/conservative
1984 presidential vote: Reagan (62%)
Key issues: foreign policy doves, nuclear arms

Sample Neighborhoods
Georgetown, Washington, D.C. (20007)
Grosse Point, Michigan (48236)
Palo Alto, California (94301)
Princeton, New Jersey (08540)
Park Cities, Dallas, Texas (75205)
Coral Gables, Florida (33146)

Lifestyle

High Usage	Index	Low Usage	Index
Travel/entertainment cards	358	Canning jars and lids	52
Aperitif/specialty wines	295	Fresh-water fishing	42
Classical records	289	Motorcycling	41
Valid passports	274	Country records/tapes	36
Imported champagne	261	Hunting	26
Sailing	252	Pickup trucks	26
Wine by the case	249	CB radios	24
Jazz records/tapes	237	Watch roller derby	17

Magazines/Newspapers

High Usage	Index	Low Usage	Index
Forbes	442	*Field & Stream*	33
Barron's	375	*Outdoor Life*	27
The New Yorker	364	*Mother Earth News*	23
Gourmet	358	*True Story*	14

Cars

High Usage	Index	Low Usage	Index
Rolls Royces	1683	Chevrolet Impalas	49
Jaguars	1119	Chevrolet Chevettes	48
Ferraris	1076	Chevrolet Monte Carlos	47
Mercedes 380/500/560	841	Plymouth Gran Furys	41
BMW 5 Series	800	Dodge Diplomats	40

Food

High Usage	Index	Low Usage	Index
Natural cold cereal	150	Canned meat spreads	74
Whole-wheat bread	131	White bread	68
Liquid nutritional supplements	131	Presweetened cold cereal	66
Frozen waffles	122	Canned stews	22

Television

High Usage	Index	Low Usage	Index
"At the Movies"	138	"The Facts of Life"	48
"Murder, She Wrote"	135	"Knots Landing"	46
"Cheers"	126	"Super Password"	40
"The Today Show"	121	"As the World Turns"	27

a cocktail party except stimulating conversation. And the cluster's most often purchased magazines provide fodder for that: residents are three times as likely as average Americans to read *Forbes, The New Yorker* and *Barron's.* Compared to the general population, they're more than twice as as likely to have written an article published in the last year.

Because their professional training tends to steep them in objective analysis, Money & Brains residents maintain a fair degree of political independence. While voters identify more with the GOP than the Democratic Party by a two-to-one ratio, they divide evenly when describing themselves as "liberal," "moderate" or "conservative." Money & Brains voters oppose the influence of Moral Majority–type groups in politics and side with moderate Democrats on foreign-policy issues. And pollsters decline to characterize the cluster as Reagan Country. In 1984, Reagan received no more votes here than the national average, and since then residents have expressed dissatisfaction with the direction the country is heading. No matter. When it comes to campaign contributions, this cluster is a prime source of dollars for both parties. Money & Brains residents write big checks.

ZQ 3: FURS & STATION WAGONS

"Plano, Texas, has been described as the nesting ground of the American executive," says city manager Bob Woodruff. And that's an appropriate characterization of its cluster type, Furs & Station Wagons, the kind of place where the lady of the house throws on a fur coat to schlep the kids to piano lessons in a station wagon.

Hugging the beltways of the nation's major cities, Furs & Station Wagons is typified by new money, parents in their 40s and 50s and sprawling houses filled with teenage children. Their newly built subdivisions may include shuttered colonials, all-glass contemporary structures or luxury townhouses, but all share hefty price tags: one in three is valued at more than $150,000. And they usually feature amenities such as tennis courts, swimming pools, bike paths and the rich soil to nurture elaborate gardens. In Furs & Station Wagons, a country-club membership is a fact of life—residents belong to them at more than four times the national average, out of geographical necessity as much as concern for status. "If you don't live out here, there's absolutely no reason to drive out here," says Kathy Bost, a resident of Paradise Valley, Arizona, "You have to drive a half an hour to get anywhere."

The residents of Furs & Station Wagons have "mastered all the

ZQ 3: FURS & STATION WAGONS

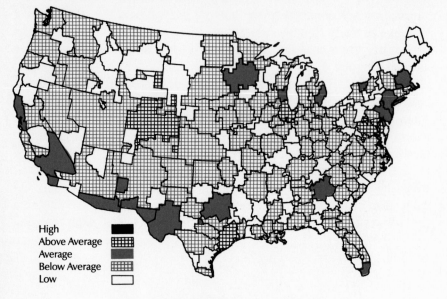

High
Above Average
Average
Below Average
Low

3.2% of U.S. households
Primary age range: 35–54
Median household income: $50,086
Median home value: $132,725

Thumbnail Demographics
executive bedroom communities
single-unit housing
predominantly white families
college educations
white-collar jobs

Politics
Predominant ideology: conservative
1984 presidential vote: Reagan (70%)
Key issues: nuclear arms, fiscal conservatism

Sample Neighborhoods
Plano, Texas (75075)
Reston, Virginia (22091)
Glastonbury, Connecticut (06033)
Needham, Massachusetts (02192)
Pomona, California (91765)
Dunwoody, Atlanta, Georgia (30338)

Lifestyle

High Usage	Index	Low Usage	Index
Country clubs	445	Motorcycles	76
Second mortgages	330	Laxatives	66
Wine by the case	275	Asthma relief remedies	64
Car rentals	255	Travel by commercial bus	64
Lawn furniture	244	Nonfilter cigarettes	54
U.S. Treasury notes	224	Hunting	38
Imported champagne	216	Denture adhesives	38
Business travel	211	Chewing tobacco	35

Magazines/Newspapers

High Usage	Index	Low Usage	Index
Gourmet	282	*Outdoor Life*	36
Architectural Digest	260	*Jet*	32
Bon Appetit	241	*Hunting*	27
Forbes	216	*Grit*	0

Cars

High Usage	Index	Low Usage	Index
BMW 5 Series	480	Chevrolet Chevettes	86
Jaguars	472	Chevrolet Impalas	84
Mercedes 300Ds	468	Dodge Diplomats	77
Audis	460	Pontiac Phoenixes	69
Mitsubishi Galants	450	Plymouth Gran Furys	64

Food

High Usage	Index	Low Usage	Index
Rye/pumpernickel bread	222	Nondairy creamers	80
Natural cold cereal	183	Meat tenderizers	80
Liquid nutritional supplements	127	Powdered fruit drinks	62
Low-fat/skim milk	125	Canned stews	43

Television

High Usage	Index	Low Usage	Index
"The Tonight Show"	131	"Highway to Heaven"	59
"60 Minutes"	122	"Wheel of Fortune"	57
"Nightline"	120	"Friday Night Videos"	51
"Newhart"	120	"Santa Barbara"	38

possibilities": They own numerous credit cards for airplane tickets, rental cars and entertainment, and they travel for business and pleasure six times as often as the general population. They're four times as likely as average Americans to drive such prestige cars as Cadillac, Mercedes, Porsche and Jaguar. They play golf, buy wine by the case, donate heavily to schools and hospitals and attend adult-education courses at above-average rates. And they think nothing of dropping $100 a week at the supermarket, duly picking up the ingredients listed in their copies of *Gourmet, Bon Appetit* and *Food & Wine* to create gourmet meals. Adults in this cluster hope that such trappings—the country clubs, exotic cars and gardening hobbies—won't be lost on their children. Furs & Station Wagons is the attempt by people who have been relatively successful to pass on their social status to the next generation.

Part of their heritage is support for the Republican Party. Furs & Station Wagons residents voted for Ronald Reagan by more than two to one in 1984 and believe the GOP is the superior party when it comes to managing the government. Though surveys find them unsettled by the right-wing extremists within the party, they support the GOP's ties to corporate America and appreciate the party's elitist airs. Voters here express extreme concern over the dangers of nuclear weaponry—probably reflecting the number of soon-to-be-draft-age sons. In many elections, these communities become GOP battlegrounds between voters who support their party's links to big business and their neighbors dismayed by the party's bellicose foreign policy. At backyard barbecues, guests stick to discussing mulch rather than military reform.

ZQ 4: URBAN GOLD COAST

As communities go, Urban Gold Coast literally stands above the rest. Composed of upscale high-rise neighborhoods in only a handful of big cities, Urban Gold Coast tops many demographic lists: most densely populated, most employed, most white-collar, most renters, most childless and most New York–based. Almost two-thirds live in residences worth more than $200,000, decorating their living rooms according to *Metropolitan Home,* buying their clothes at Brooks Brothers, frequenting the same hand-starch Chinese laundries. In Urban Gold Coast, residents have the lowest incidence of auto ownership in the nation; these cliff-dwellers get around by taxi and rental car.

Immersed in their metropolitan lifestyles, Urban Gold Coasters have little time to develop conventional consumption patterns. Residents

ZQ 4: URBAN GOLD COAST

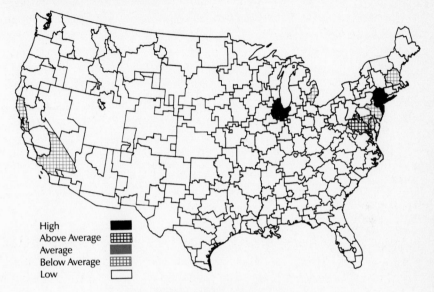

High
Above Average
Average
Below Average
Low

0.5% of U.S. households
Primary age groups: 18–24 and 65+
Median household income: $36,838
Median home value: $200,000+

Thumbnail Demographics
upscale urban enclaves
high-rise housing
predominantly white singles
college educations
white-collar jobs

Politics
Predominant ideology: liberal/moderate
1984 presidential vote: Mondale (60%)
Key issues: trade protection, jobs

Sample Neighborhoods
Upper East Side, Manhattan, New York (10021)
Upper West Side, Manhattan, New York (10024)
West End, Washington, D.C. (20037)
Fort Dearborn, Chicago, Illinois (60611)
Rincon East, San Francisco, California (94111)

Lifestyle

High Usage	Index	Low Usage	Index
Travel by railroad	1504	Powerboats	0
Aperitif/specialty wines	1243	Groin irritation remedies	0
Imported champagne	657	Feminine hygiene sprays	13
Car rentals	529	Nonfilter cigarettes	17
Valid passports	471	Fishing rods	19
U.S. Treasury notes	389	Tupperware	23
Tennis	388	Bicycles	27
Pregnancy tests	378	Motorcycles	28

Magazines/Newspapers

High Usage	Index	Low Usage	Index
New York	5015	*Motorcyclist*	0
The New York Times	3063	*Popular Hot Rodding*	0
Metropolitan Home	2227	*Hunting*	0
Atlantic Monthly	1756	*Car Craft*	0

Cars

High Usage	Index	Low Usage	Index
Rolls Royces	352	Chevrolet Novas	1
Jaguars	193	Chevrolet Sprints	1
BMW 5 Series	181	Bertone X19s	0
Ferraris	172	Mercury Sables	0
Mercedes 380/500/560s	170	Oldsmobile Omegas	0

Food

High Usage	Index	Low Usage	Index
Rye/pumpernickel bread	374	Pork sausages	35
Tomato/vegetable juice	150	TV dinners	26
Butter	129	Canned corned-beef hash	24
Fresh chicken	124	Canned meat spreads	0

Television

High Usage	Index	Low Usage	Index
"Nightline"	154	"Lifestyles of the Rich and Famous"	35
"Late Night with David Letterman"	152	"Simon & Simon"	30
"At the Movies"	117	"General Hospital"	28
"Entertainment Tonight"	117	"Dance Fever"	0

usually eat out for lunch and dinner, and their forays to grocery stores mostly yield breakfast items: yogurt, butter, orange juice and English muffins—all bought at slightly above-average rates. Compared to the general population, residents buy barely one-fifth the amount of such pedestrian treats as TV dinners, canned stews and powdered fruit drinks. Where these consumers do excel is at the liquor store: they buy imported champagnes, brandy, beer and table wine at twice the national norm, possibly to take the edge off stress-filled urban living. These are the Americans who arrange their dinner parties around the schedules of cooks and butlers. In this neighborhood type, residents live in the condo lap of luxury.

Politically, Urban Gold Coast is home to the nation's limousine liberals, the premier cluster of left-wing causes and Democratic fundraising. Sixty percent of its voters went for Walter Mondale in 1984, and 43 percent gave President Reagan an unfavorable rating in 1985. They support the Democratic Party's stand on civil liberties, liberal foreign policies and religious pluralism. With nearly a third of its households Jewish, Urban Gold Coast opposes the influence of the religious right on the GOP more than any other cluster. In these neighborhoods, the Reagan Revolution never materialized.

Still, some of the liberal fire seems to have left the Urban Gold Coast lately. In an apparent about-face from New Deal values, residents are more concerned about fiscal conservatism than the plight of the poor and the unemployed. In the words of one "formerly liberal" resident of the Upper East Side: "Crime has changed the way we think. We're tired of getting mugged simply because we come from better circumstances. The classic liberals here have stopped apologizing for being successful." The embers are still smoldering, however, as Urban Gold Coasters continue to contribute heavily to organizations like the American Civil Liberties Union and the National Organization for Women.

ZQ 5: POOLS & PATIOS

Once the nation's child-rearing suburbs, Pools & Patios has come of age—old age. Built during the postwar suburban boom, Pools & Patios communities have since been swallowed by metropolitan sprawl, making their spacious split-levels and ranch houses often too costly for younger families. Older couples now reside in these stable, prosperous and empty-nested subdivisions. With their double incomes and white-collar jobs, these residents enjoy laid-backyard comfort—a place for Saturday

ZQ 5: POOLS & PATIOS

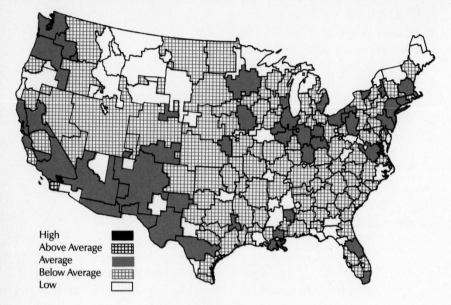

High
Above Average
Average
Below Average
Low

3.4% of U.S. households

Primary age range:	45–64
Median household income:	$35,895
Median home value:	$99,702

Thumbnail Demographics
aging, upper-middle-class suburbs
single-unit housing
predominantly white couples with grown children
college graduates
white-collar jobs

Politics
Predominant ideology: moderate/conservative
1984 presidential vote: Reagan (72%)
Key issues: fiscal conservatism, nuclear arms

Sample Neighborhoods
Fairfield, Connecticut (06430)
Morton Grove, Chicago, Illinois (60053)
Catonsville, Maryland (21228)
Mission, Kansas City, Kansas (66205)
La Crescenta, Los Angeles, California (91214)
Kettering, Ohio (45429)

Lifestyle

High Usage	Index	Low Usage	Index
Telephone purchases	301	Watch roller derby	76
Travel by cruise ship	209	Laxatives	73
Health clubs	200	Bowling	71
Common stock	196	Compact pickup trucks	71
Domestic champagne	182	Denture cleansers	69
Car rentals	178	Hunting	67
Money-market funds	176	Canning jars and lids	64
Civic clubs	172	Gospel records/tapes	62

Magazines/Newspapers

High Usage	Index	Low Usage	Index
Sunset	246	*Hot Rod*	51
The Wall Street Journal	234	*True Story*	44
Natural History	222	*Essence*	26
The New Yorker	222	*Grit*	14

Cars

High Usage	Index	Low Usage	Index
Alfa Romeos	250	Pontiac Phoenixes	85
BMW 5 Series	237	AMC Eagles	83
Mercedes 240/190s	234	Chevrolet Chevettes	82
Mercedes 380/500/560s	234	Pontiac T-1000s	79
Mitsubishi Galants	233	Dodge Diplomats	79

Food

High Usage	Index	Low Usage	Index
Natural cold cereal	148	White bread	84
Low-fat/skim milk	141	Powdered soft drinks	83
Liquid nutritional supplements	135	Whole milk	79
Instant iced tea	121	Canned stews	70

Television

High Usage	Index	Low Usage	Index
"60 Minutes"	119	"Knots Landing"	67
"At the Movies"	118	"American Bandstand"	62
"Newhart"	115	"Another World"	56
"Cheers"	115	"Friday Night Videos"	28

night cocktail parties, Sunday afternoon barbecues and drinks after a brisk round of golf. Not coincidentally, residents consume above-average amounts of pretzels, cheeses, canned cocktail mixes, Scotch, bourbon and brandy. "It's not a pretentious lifestyle," says John Rumsby, longtime resident of La Crescenta, California. "But we don't live too shabbily, either."

And marketing surveys confirm this portrait of pleasant living. Foreign sports cars like Alfa Romeos, Mercedes Benzes and BMWs line their driveways, and the latest electronic gadgetry fills their homes. For Pools & Patios residents, their idea of getting away from it all is a cruise or foreign airplane charter. At the supermarket, they typically spend more than $100 a week, mixing a concern for health—indicated by above-average purchases of low-cholesterol egg substitutes, yogurt and wheat bread—with a certain fondness for high-calorie foods like frozen pies, flavored rice mixes and brownie mixes. Pools & Patios people believe in enjoying the upper-middle-class fruits of their labors.

Still, there's a note of economic uncertainty in Pools & Patios. With many residents burdened by stiff mortgages and extended credit, they tend to be fiscal conservatives and staunch supporters of the GOP. They're among the beneficiaries of the 1987 tax cut and back the free-trade provisions that translate to cheaper prices in the marketplace. But a streak of political indifference runs among Pools & Patios residents that analysts have termed "a sort of mellow uninvolvement." Unlike other upscale Republican clusters, Pools & Patios is tolerant of Moral Majority–type conservative forces within the GOP. Cynics might argue that its residents are more concerned with their country clubs and health clubs—which they join at twice the national average. In their version of the good life, they just don't want to be bothered with politics. It's easier to get someone in Tibet to write a letter than to get someone in Pools & Patios write their member of Congress.

■ ZQ 6: TWO MORE RUNGS

At the turn of the century, the Statue of Liberty greeted millions of European immigrants seeking the land of golden opportunity. Today many of their grown sons and daughters have found their reward in Two More Rungs, a group of upper-middle-class ethnic neighborhoods located in a handful of big-city suburbs. These children of immigrants have reached upper-middle-class comfort through a mix of intelligence (48 percent have gone to college) and professional success (typically as

ZQ 6: TWO MORE RUNGS

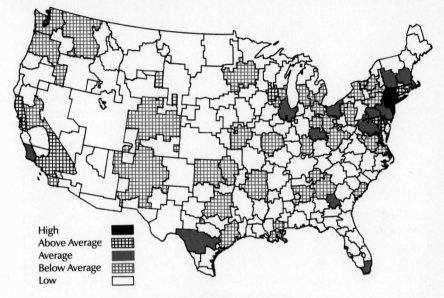

High

Above Average

Average

Below Average

Low

0.7% of U.S. households

Primary age range: 55+

Median household income: $31,263

Median home value: $117,012

Thumbnail Demographics

upper-middle-class, fringe-city neighborhoods

multi-unit housing

ethnic families and singles

college educations

white-collar jobs

Politics

Predominant ideology: liberal/moderate

1984 presidential vote: Reagan (56%)

Key issues: nuclear arms, poverty

Sample Neighborhoods

Skokie, Illinois (60076)

Flushing, New York (11365)

Fort Lee, New Jersey (07024)

Rancho Park, California (90064)

Bexley, Columbus, Ohio (43209)

McDonough, Baltimore, Maryland (21208)

Lifestyle

High Usage	Index	Low Usage	Index
Travel by chartered plane	284	Toy-sized dogs	50
Travel by cruise ship	283	Swimming pools	46
Distilled liquor	274	Canning jars and lids	46
Bottled water	216	Chewing tobacco	23
Golf balls	215	Hand tools	21
Convertibles	210	Hunting	18
Money-market funds	198	Gospel records/tapes	13
Environmentalist organizations	194	Watch roller derby	11

Magazines/Newspapers

High Usage	Index	Low Usage	Index
The New York Times	528	*Soap Opera Digest*	35
Scientific American	204	*Field & Stream*	34
Atlantic Monthly	197	*True Story*	8
Money	197	*Grit*	0

Cars

High Usage	Index	Low Usage	Index
Ferraris	342	Chevrolet Astros	62
Audi GTs	315	Dodge Diplomats	61
Rolls Royces	295	Pontiac T-1000s	59
Mitsubishis	293	Pontiac Phoenixes	49
Jaguar XJ-6s	287	AMC Eagles	48

Food

High Usage	Index	Low Usage	Index
Liquid nutritional supplements	215	Flavored gelatin desserts	84
Canned corned-beef hash	144	Pork sausages	83
Instant iced tea	143	Packaged piecrusts	74
Frozen entrees	125	Mexican foods	60

Television

High Usage	Index	Low Usage	Index
"Nightline"	189	"Falcon Crest"	61
"Late Night with David Letterman"	188	"Hunter"	58
		"Highway to Heaven"	55
"At the Movies"	170	"Days of Our Lives"	51
"The Tonight Show"	158		

teachers, social workers and small businesspeople). When they retire, they have no desire to leave their neighborhoods of aging but well-kept garden apartments, corner markets and Mom & Pop clothing shops—few fashion boutiques here. In a cluster community like Fresh Meadows, New York, some 300 retirees meet almost daily in front of the Hillcrest Jewish Center, sitting on park benches and schmoozing. As local rabbi Stephen Steingel observes, "There's a big bench society around here."

Compared to the nation, Two More Rungs residents are older (nearly a third are over 55), more ethnic (16 percent are foreign born) and more conservative in their spending habits. They drive sturdy, roomy, luxury cars like Cadillacs, Mercedes Benzes and Jaguars—more than three times as often as the general population. But they shy away from home gadgets—microwaves, video cassette recorders and electric toothbrushes are poor sellers—preferring an Old World practicality around the house. Socially and culturally aware, Two More Rungs residents are about twice as likely as average Americans to belong to environmental organizations, attend theatrical events and read *Scientific American* and *Barron's*. Their idea of fun is going on a cruise, which they take almost three times as often as average Americans, typically accompanied by their friends from the neighborhood.

This unusual cohesiveness may stem from Two More Rungs' status as the cluster with one of the highest concentrations of union members. Politically, that's helped make cluster voters among the Democratic Party's most fervent liberals and biggest contributors. But in 1984, Two More Rungs reversed tradition and handed Ronald Reagan a 56-percent majority vote, partly due to their financial fears of the higher taxes promised by Walter Mondale. They've bought the GOP line of government fiscal conservatism, however troubling to their liberal conscience. Phyllis Talmadge, a lifelong Democrat from the Kew Gardens section of Queens, New York, expresses this ideological dilemma when she says, "I support welfare programs because I can't see another way out. But it makes me sick that some ethnic groups can't become acclimated to the mainstream and others become scholarship winners five years off the boat." In Two More Rungs, your bootstraps should be well worn from frequent pulling.

■ ZQ 7: YOUNG INFLUENTIALS

Young Influentials is more than a neighborhood type; it's an adjective that qualifies the trendiest habits and purchases. A wine-tasting, for

ZQ 7: YOUNG INFLUENTIALS

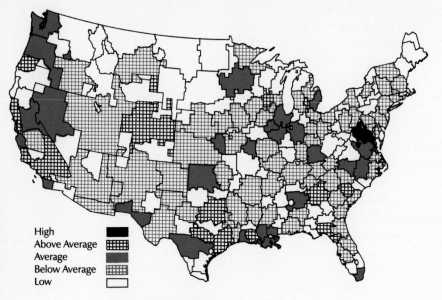

High
Above Average
Average
Below Average
Low

2.9% of U.S. households
Primary age range: 18–34
Median household income: $30,398
Median home value: $106,332

Thumbnail Demographics
yuppie inner-ring suburbs
apartment and condo dwellings
predominantly white singles and childless couples
college educations
white-collar jobs

Politics
Predominant ideology: moderate
1984 presidential vote: Reagan (61%)
Key issues: fiscal conservatism, nuclear arms

Sample Neighborhoods
Glendale, Denver, Colorado (80224)
North Side, Atlanta, Georgia (30339)
Greenbelt, Maryland (20770)
Redondo Beach, Los Angeles, California (90277)
Westheimer, Houston, Texas (77603)
Parkfairfax, Virginia (22302)

Lifestyle

High Usage	Index	Low Usage	Index
Environmentalist organizations	295	Bowling balls	66
Travel by cruise ship	282	Nonfilter cigarettes	58
Convertibles	280	Compact pickup trucks	53
Irish whiskey	278	Home permanents	52
Jazz records/tapes	271	Toy-sized dogs	48
Investment property	268	Outboard powerboats	42
Racquetball	228	Chewing tobacco	36
Valid passports	204	Watch roller derby	16

Magazines/Newspapers

High Usage	Index	Low Usage	Index
Rudder	370	*The Star*	43
Sea & Pacific Skipper	333	*Health*	40
Sunset	303	*Grit*	34
Barron's	277	*True Story*	5

Cars

High Usage	Index	Low Usage	Index
VW Cabriolets	322	Pontiac Bonnevilles	55
Alfa Romeos	309	Chevrolet Monte Carlos	55
Acuras	286	Plymouth Gran Furys	52
Porsche 911s	252	Chevrolet Impalas	47
BMW 5 Series	245	Dodge Diplomats	44

Food

High Usage	Index	Low Usage	Index
Yogurt	155	Whole milk	73
Whole-wheat bread	154	White bread	71
Mexican foods	139	Powdered soft drinks	70
Low-fat/skim milk	136	Canned meat spreads	62

Television

High Usage	Index	Low Usage	Index
"At the Movies"	130	"Knots Landing"	67
Sunday morning interview programs	121	"Hunter"	60
"60 Minutes"	116	"Wheel of Fortune"	42
"Cheers"	113	"Another World"	41

instance, is Young Influentials. So is trading up your Honda for a BMW. Or taking a ski vacation in the middle of the week.

Sometimes referred to as "Yuppieville," Young Influentials is home to the nation's young, upwardly mobile singles and dual-career couples —tomorrow's Money & Brains residents. Their neighborhoods, found in the inner-ring suburbs of major cities, are filled with expensive condos, recently built townhouses and midrise apartments decorated with the three Bs of interior design: Breuer, butcher-block and Barcelona. Many residents have the kind of high-tech, white-collar jobs that provide substantial incomes (38 percent earn over $35,000) and that allow leisure-intensive lifestyles. On a sunny weekend, Young Influentials residents can often be found jogging, biking or speed-walking—sometimes to a bar for drinks and dancing. Young Influentials don't care about good schools, because they don't have children. They want a mall with a sushi bar, gourmet cookie shop, travel agency and psychotherapy center.

With their double incomes and acquisitive ways, Young Influentials are a fast-track marketer's dream. They're more likely than average Americans to own a convertible, travel abroad, drink domestic champagne and attend musical performances. Serious about fitness, they spend twice as much time as the general population sailing and skiing, playing racquetball and tennis. And they eat to win, as seen by their tendency to fill their shopping carts with healthy snack foods such as yogurt, nuts, cheese and wheat bread. Their lack of interest in television viewing can be explained by their go-go pace. When they sit down, they want to read magazines that can help them climb the ladder—be it corporate, status or yacht-club competition. *Barron's, Rudder* and *Travel & Leisure* are all purchased at more than twice average U.S. rates. In Young Influentials, life is still a game—albeit a competitive one.

This preoccupation with winning is reflected in their politics, too. Typically, these children of Democrats switched allegiance and joined the Republican Party during the '80s. In polls, they express admiration for the GOP's management ability and President Reagan's talent for reducing taxes. Some of these otherwise conservative careerists have a liberal bent, left over from their collegiate days in the antiwar movement; they still oppose nuclear weapons and hawkish foreign policies. But their political views seem just an extension of their pursuit of material goods. Listen to Tim Collins, a 30-year-old Republican from Glendale, Colorado, who supports Lee Iacocca for president: "We have to balance the budget before we can look to luxuries like sending helicopters to Central America or paying for Star Wars."

████████████ ZQ 8: YOUNG SUBURBIA

When the baby-boom generation discovered that housing prices in suburbia had gone through the roof, they simply pushed farther out into the country. Today, Young Suburbia is the nesting ground for the nation's nuclear families of Mom, Dad and the kids.

Scattered around the country's metropolitan fringes, this cluster ranks near the top in total population and the concentration of married couples with children. Young Suburbia has the kind of lifestyle amenities trumpeted in real-estate ads: new homes, modern schools, gleaming shopping centers and a reasonable commute downtown. So what if the freshly built subdivisions are often a maze of uniformity, with brick veneer split-levels pressed together like sausages? In some suburbs, you can drive for miles without seeing another human being. In Young Suburbia, people are everywhere—jogging through the streets, swinging golf clubs in their yards, discussing the intricacies of self-propelled lawn mowers.

With their expanding households, Young Suburbanites are strong consumers of most family products. Supermarket shoppers are 20 percent more likely than average Americans to buy fruit juices, cheese spread, baked beans, pretzels, dry soups and frozen pizzas. At hardware stores, they are 40 percent more likely to buy lawn mowers and hedge clippers, automatic garage-door openers and sheet vinyl flooring, lumber and varnishes. An athletic group, Young Suburbanites spend their leisure time ice-skating and playing racquetball and tennis, and to stay on top of their sports they read magazines like *World Tennis, Skiing* and *Golf.* Having achieved a toe-hold on the upper middle class, Young Suburbanites splurge a little when it comes to owning a car. They put down payments on flashy Nissan 300ZXs, Chevrolet Corvettes and Porsche 924s at more than twice the national average. In this neighborhood type, success is measured by the width of your garage.

Like those "little white houses of suburbia" that gave President Eisenhower his comfortable victories, Young Suburbia neighborhoods are solidly Republican. Over three-quarters of the residents voted for President Reagan in 1984, and a majority support the GOP's agenda on conservative fiscal matters and laissez-faire government activism. Un-

ZQ 8: YOUNG SUBURBIA

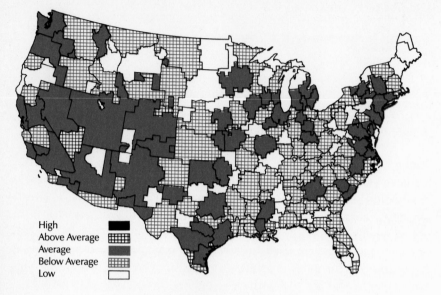

High
Above Average
Average
Below Average
Low

5.3% of U.S. households

Primary age range: 25–44
Median household income: $38,582
Median home value: $93,281

Thumbnail Demographics

upper-middle-class outlying suburbs
single-unit housing
predominantly white families
college educations
white-collar jobs

Politics

Predominant ideology: conservative
1984 presidential vote: Reagan (76%)
Key issues: fiscal conservatism, trade protection

Sample Neighborhoods

Eagan, Minnesota (55124)
Dale City, Virginia (22193)
Pleasanton, California (94566)
Smithtown, New York (11787)
Ypsilanti, Michigan (48197)
Lilburn, Georgia (30247)

Lifestyle

High Usage	Index	Low Usage	Index
Rental cars	239	Laxatives	81
Swimming pools	228	Convertibles	80
Mutual funds	227	Malt liquor	78
Health clubs	217	Hair tonic	74
Ice-skating	213	Civic clubs	65
Racquetball	179	Soul records/tapes	63
Home computers	178	Watch pro wrestling	38
Foreign tour packages	158	Snuff	29

Magazines/Newspapers

High Usage	Index	Low Usage	Index
World Tennis	255	*National Enquirer*	76
Sea & Pacific Skipper	208	*True Story*	47
Skiing	187	*Grit*	41
Golf	177	*Rudder*	13

Cars

High Usage	Index	Low Usage	Index
Mitsubishi Galants	263	Plymouth Gran Furys	98
Ford EXPs	215	Chevrolet Impalas	97
Toyota vans	209	Dodge Diplomats	97
Nissan 300ZXs	208	Rolls Royces	39

Food

High Usage	Index	Low Usage	Index
Cheese spreads	138	Canned meat spreads	91
Pretzels	134	Whole milk	91
Frozen waffles	133	Canned stews	87
Rye/pumpernickel bread	131	Powdered fruit drinks	76

Television

High Usage	Index	Low Usage	Index
"Cheers"	130	"Knots Landing"	78
"Night Court"	123	"Highway to Heaven"	78
"Newhart"	116	"The Young and the Restless"	62
"Family Ties"	115	"Friday Night Videos"	61

like other upscale Republican clusters, Young Suburbia supports trade protectionism, a sign that cluster residents still find their jobs vulnerable to competition from abroad. Many are only a generation removed from the blue-collar world, and those involved in industrial firms are often threatened by economic recessions. In this current version of the American Dream, many of the baby boomers' progeny attend day-care so Mom can work to help meet the mortgage and pay for Big Wheel tricycles.

▬▬▬▬ ZQ 9: GOD'S COUNTRY

They're America's latest pioneers, those urban exiles who've gone back to the land following the migration of high-tech companies. In God's Country, they've created rural boomtowns with the highest socioeconomic levels outside the nation's major metropolitan areas. God's Country residents are among the nation's best educated (47 percent have gone to college), most solidly employed (63 percent hold professional, managerial and other white-collar jobs) and most mobile. Newcomers arrive for the work, enjoy the often breathtaking scenery and then move on when handed a promotion. In Plainsboro, New Jersey, a God's Country town bordering the Princeton-Forrestal Center, local voter rolls undergo astonishing turnover rates every four years. "By the time residents get interested in local politics," says town clerk Patricia Hullfish, "they're about ready to move away."

Given their education and affluence, God's Country residents have a kind of frontier sophisticate lifestyle. Outdoors, they hunt, ski, camp and canoe nearly twice as often as average Americans. Indoors, they tend to cultivate such hobbies as cooking, coin-collecting and painting. They drive sporty foreign cars like Subarus, Saabs and Peugeots at twice the national average. But they're not above performing routine maintenance—or at least finding a good mechanic—to keep the cars running for weekend jaunts to the city. Residents of God's Country communities haven't completely lost their urban tastes. They prefer brandy to malt liquor, racquetball to fishing, video cassette recorders to AM-FM radios. These are the folks who watch "The Today Show" and "60 Minutes" at above-average rates to keep up with the latest scandals scaring the city dwellers they left behind.

With urban tastes transplanted to the country, residents' political attitudes in God's Country tend to be Republican—with a twist. Nearly 70 percent of the cluster's voters supported President Reagan during

ZQ 9: GOD'S COUNTRY

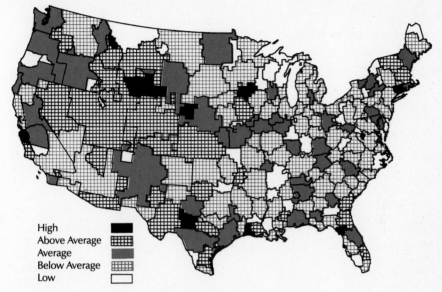

High
Above Average
Average
Below Average
Low

2.7% of U.S. households
Primary age range: 25–44
Median household income: $36,728
Median home value: $99,418

Thumbnail Demographics
upscale exurban boom towns
single-unit housing
predominantly white families
college educations
white-collar jobs

Politics
Predominant ideology: conservative
1984 presidential vote: Reagan (70%)
Key issues: fiscal conservatism, nuclear arms

Sample Neighborhoods
Woodstock, New York (12498)
Plainsboro, New Jersey (08536)
Corrales, Albuquerque, New Mexico (87048)
Lake Arrowhead, California (92352)
Aspen, Colorado (81611)
Clancy, Montana (59634)

Lifestyle

High Usage	Index	Low Usage	Index
Investment property	675	Convertibles	58
Microwave ovens	410	Laxatives	56
Movie cameras	286	Comedy records/tapes	52
Truck-mounted campers	284	Cigarillos/small cigars	47
Target-shooting	228	Civic clubs	46
Above-ground swimming		Watch professional wrestling	43
pools	215	Nonfilter cigarettes	38
Dest-top calculators	168	Car-leasing	10
Painting and drawing	163		

Magazines/Newspapers

High Usage	Index	Low Usage	Index
Flying	212	*Field & Stream*	74
Ski	200	*Glamour*	73
Inc.	183	*National Enquirer*	54
Food & Wine	161	*Ebony*	35

Cars

High Usage	Index	Low Usage	Index
Saabs	227	Chevrolet Monte Carlos	90
Subarus	222	Dodge Diplomats	87
VW Vanagons	219	Rolls Royces	80
Porsche 944s	198	Plymouth Gran Furys	72
Audi 4000s	195	Chevrolet Impalas	69

Food

High Usage	Index	Low Usage	Index
Canned meat spreads	136	White bread	92
Natural cold cereal	134	Canned ham	87
Whole-wheat bread	125	Frozen corn-on-the-cob	70
Instant soup mix	125	Rye/pumpernickel bread	51

Television

High Usage	Index	Low Usage	Index
"Kate & Allie"	120	"The People's Court"	66
"CBS Evening News"	119	"Dynasty"	64
"Newhart"	118	"At the Movies"	63
"Entertainment Tonight"	113	"Dance Fever"	56

his 1984 re-election campaign, and a year later, residents backed GOP domestic policies at three times the national average. But on environmental issues, these voters turn positively anti-Republican. Residents support heavy government regulation of toxic wastes to protect their beautiful vistas. And they also express Democratic sympathies on related issues like historical preservation and conservation of folkways. They made a conscious decision to settle in rustic surroundings, and they want to enjoy nature at its purest.

▬▬▬▬ ZQ 10: BLUE-CHIP BLUES

The nation's most affluent blue-collar households are concentrated in Blue-Chip Blues, composed of postwar suburban subdivisions in major metropolitan areas. Here lives a blue-collar version of the American dream: the majority of adults have high-school educations, earn between $25,000 and $50,000 annually and own comfortable, middle-class homes. Boasting one of the highest concentrations of married couples with children, Blue-Chip Blues is the kind of neighborhood type with fast-food restaurants attached to every shopping center, baseball diamonds in the parks and motorboats in the driveways. "Status," says cluster resident Rick Packer of Coon Rapids, Minnesota, "is related to the kinds of adult toys you keep at the house: the snowmobiles, boats and pools."

Indeed, consumer surveys reveal that Blue-Chip Blues residents have the money to indulge their salt-of-the-earth tastes. Compared to the national average, Blue-Chippers go camping twice as often, fish 34 percent more often, visit theme parks 33 percent more often and bowl 28 percent more often. Residents are group oriented, typically belonging to unions, traveling with foreign tour charters and staying active in fraternal organizations. They're also do-it-yourselfers who are 25 percent more likely than the general population to build additions to their homes and maintain their own cars. In this neighborhood type, owning a mint-condition Ford Mustang or Pontiac Grand Am is considered the height of cool.

Blue-Chip Blues residents tend to vote Republican, but their support is far from unequivocal. President Reagan captured their 1984 votes by a 26-percent margin, but many express strong pessimism concerning current administration policies. These hard-working family types worry about the long-range implications of the nuclear arms buildup, the budget deficit and government waste. Residents support tax relief for the

ZQ 10: BLUE-CHIP BLUES

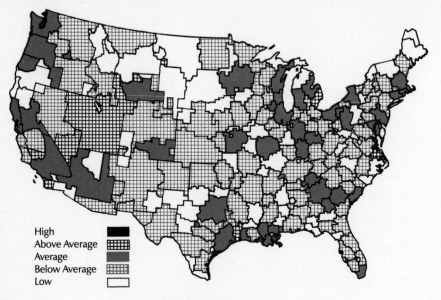

High
Above Average
Average
Below Average
Low

6% of U.S. households

Primary age group: 25–44
Median household income: $32,218
Median home value: $72,563

Thumbnail Demographics
midscale working-class suburbs
single-unit dwellings
predominantly white families
high-school educations
blue-collar jobs

Politics
Predominant ideology: moderate
1984 presidential vote: Reagan (63%)
Key issues: fiscal conservatism, nuclear arms

Sample Neighborhoods
Coon Rapids, Minnesota (55433)
South Whittier, California (90605)
Mesquite, Texas (75149)
Ronkonkoma, New York (11779)
St. Charles, St Louis, Missouri (63301)
Taylor, Detroit, Michigan (48180)

Lifestyle

High Usage	Index	Low Usage	Index
Above-ground swimming pools	197	Civic clubs	81
Watch ice hockey	173	Watch roller derby	77
CB radios	155	Imported champagne	76
Bicycles	154	Latin records/tapes	70
Travel by chartered plane	149	Malt liquor	69
Racquetball	145	Chewing tobacco	63
Unions	139	Jazz records/tapes	54
Contact lenses	134	Movie cameras	51

Magazines/Newspapers

High Usage	Index	Low Usage	Index
Skin Diver	192	*The Wall Street Journal*	77
Bride's Magazine	162	*The New Yorker*	74
4 Wheel & Off Road	159	*Harper's*	69
Golf	154	*Town & Country*	54

Cars

High Usage	Index	Low Usage	Index
Chevrolet Sprints	194	Mercedes 380/500/560s	51
Buick Rivieras	175	BMW 5 Series	49
Plymouth Turismos	174	Ferraris	46
Pontiac Grand Ams	171	Jaguars	41
Ford EXPs	171	Rolls Royces	23

Food

High Usage	Index	Low Usage	Index
Natural cold cereal	130	Canned corned-beef hash	94
Children's vitamins	126	Whole milk	92
Frozen pizzas	125	Cold cereal	89
Mexican foods	122	Canned stews	84

Television

High Usage	Index	Low Usage	Index
"Entertainment Tonight"	121	Sunday morning interview programs	77
"Night Court"	114	"American Bandstand"	75
"Family Ties"	112	"As the World Turns"	74
"Who's the Boss?"	111	"Super Password"	70

middle class and trade protectionist legislation to stem the loss of jobs from American soil. But their mix of traditional GOP and Democratic concerns means the votes of Blue-Chip Blues are usually up for grabs. At the ballot box, they traditionally vote for the candidate, not the party.

▬▬▬▬▬ ZQ 11: BOHEMIAN MIX

Sociologists would have a field day charting the evolution of Bohemian Mix. Since the 1950s, these urban hodge-podge neighborhoods have nurtured, in succession, beatniks, flower children, public-interest crusaders and gays.

Concentrated in the nation's major harbor cities, Bohemian Mix is an eclectic melange of never-married and divorced singles, young turks and older professionals, blacks and whites. Its community of students, artists, writers and actors has created a unique income profile: a U-shaped graph with many high- and low-income residents but only a small middle class. An air of adventure pervades the funky brownstones and gentrifying apartment houses, sidewalk cafes and benefit dances for the Sandinistas. Avant-garde both in political and social attitudes, Bohemian Mix is America's answer to the Left Bank of Paris.

As consumers, Bohemian Mixers tend to cultivate both mind and body. Squash, racquetball and jogging are popular pasttimes, and sales rates of *Atlantic Monthly, Harper's* and *GQ* are more than five times the national average. Area residents read paperback books twice as often as the general population and go to the movies three times as often. Like other inner-city clusters whose single residents frequent bars and coffee shops for food and gossip, Bohemian Mixers consume only a handful of supermarket products at rates above the U.S. average: whole-wheat bread, fruit and vegetable juices, cheese spread, dry soup, tea and frozen TV dinners. When they do sit down in front of a TV, they tend to pass up most prime-time fare for hip, midnight-hour programs like "Late Night with David Letterman" and "Saturday Night Live." You won't find a lot of locals tuning in to televangelists.

In Bohemian Mix, liberalism has long translated into strong Democratic support. During the 1984 election, residents gave Walter Mondale 65 percent of their vote, one of only two nonminority, white-collar clusters that provided Democratic majorities. Indeed, the cluster ranks second in the amount of money contributed to the Democratic Party. While Bohemian Mixers identify themselves as liberal by a margin of two to one, the national swing to the right has taken its toll even in this

ZQ 11: BOHEMIAN MIX

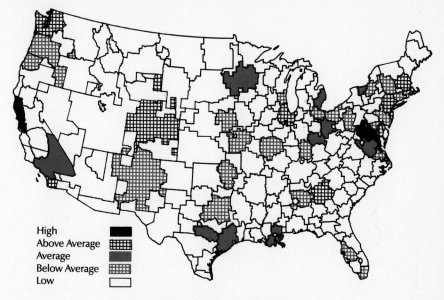

High
Above Average
Average
Below Average
Low

1.1% of U.S. households

Primary age range:	18–34
Median household income:	$21,916
Median home value:	$110,668

Thumbnail Demographics

bohemian inner-city neighborhoods
multi-unit housing
racially mixed singles
college graduates
white-collar jobs

Politics

Predominant ideology:	liberal
1984 presidential vote:	Mondale (65%)
Key issues:	nuclear arms, federal budget

Sample Neighborhoods

Greenwich Village, New York, New York (10014)
Dupont Circle, Washington, D.C. (20036)
Cambridge, Boston, Massachusetts (02139)
Lincoln Park, Chicago, Illinois (60614)
Shadyside, Pittsburgh, Pennsylvania (15232)
Haight-Ashbury, San Francisco, California (94117)

Lifestyle

High Usage	Index	Low Usage	Index
Environmentalist organizations	573	Cigars	35
Travel by railroad	475	Hunting	26
Downhill skiing	306	Wall paneling	19
Drink Irish whiskey	303	Standard-size cars	13
Country clubs	287	Christmas/Chanukah clubs	10
Classical records/tapes	273	CB radios	7
Wine by the case	254	Chewing tobacco	7
Common stock	248	Watch roller derby	0

Magazines/Newspapers

High Usage	Index	Low Usage	Index
Atlantic Monthly	727	*Seventeen*	19
Harper's	645	*Saturday Evening Post*	19
Gentlemen's Quarterly	593	*Working Woman*	15
The New Yorker	489	*1001 Home Ideas*	13

Cars

High Usage	Index	Low Usage	Index
Alfa Romeos	516	Buick LeSabres	16
Saabs	261	Ford Crown Victorias	16
Peugeots	222	Mercury Grand Marquises	15
BMW 3 Series	219	Dodge Diplomats	13
Mitsubishi Mirages	218	Pontiac Bonnevilles	10

Food

High Usage	Index	Low Usage	Index
Whole-wheat bread	144	White bread	65
Frozen waffles	120	Pretzels	56
Fruit juices and drinks	116	Frozen pizzas	54
TV dinners	115	Meat tenderizers	49

Television

High Usage	Index	Low Usage	Index
"Late Night with David Letterman"	245	"Who's the Boss?"	59
"At the Movies"	227	"Highway to Heaven"	44
"Nightline"	165	"CBS Sports Saturday"	38
"Good Morning America"	141	"Santa Barbara"	15

left-wing province. Residents are not as politically active as they were in decades past, and they're more concerned about fiscal issues than about the plight of disadvantaged groups. Chalk it up to political midlife crisis. Bohemian Mixers have begun joining the system they once marched against.

ZQ 12: LEVITTOWN, U.S.A.

When builder William Levitt began constructing his first Long Island subdivision in 1948, he probably never foresaw the way his cookie-cutter developments would take over the nation. Today Levittown, U.S.A. represents the legions of tract house communities built to accommodate the postwar baby boom. Initially starter homes for white-collar and well-paid blue-collar families, Levittown, U.S.A.'s suburban neighborhoods have since grown up and largely empty-nested. Older couples now inhabit the mass-produced homes, having altered the standard styles by adding garages, second stories and backyard swimming pools. On summer nights, old-time jazz concerts have replaced Little League baseball games. Along checkerboard streets, you can almost hear the houses whisper, "The Old American Dream."

In Levittown, U.S.A., the living is easy, according to marketing surveys. Levittowners have the cash to buy electric gadgets such as slide projectors, electric toothbrushes and electric grills at above-average rates. They're modest in their automotive tastes (Yugos, AMC Alliances, Dodge Aries) and they don't mind putting in time caring for their cars. To Levittowners, maintaining stability is more important than flashiness. Their shopping lists show a preference for sit-down, home-cooked meals: stuffing mixes, chicken coatings, powdered puddings, frozen seafood, flavored rices and baking mixes are all bought at above-average rates. Inside Levittowners' family rooms, the walls are decorated with signs of success: high-school diplomas, bowling trophies and a Norman Rockwell reproduction of a moving van unloading a family's possession into a new suburban home.

The concentration of aging suburban families has contributed to Levittown, U.S.A.'s Republican-leaning political views. In 1984, residents voted to re-elect President Reagan by a three to two margin, and they continue to give him a high performance rating. They prefer the policy-making skills of the GOP to those of the Democrats and accept the growing power of the evangelical right. Still, these middle-class voters disapprove of the influence of big business and the rich on the

ZQ 12: LEVITTOWN, U.S.A.

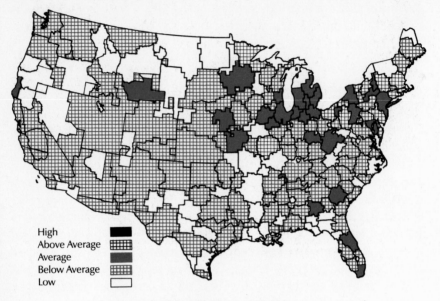

High

Above Average

Average

Below Average

Low

3.1% of U.S. households

Primary age group:	55+
Median household income:	$28,742
Median home value:	$70,728

Thumbnail Demographics

middle-class suburban neighborhoods
single-unit housing
predominantly white couples
high-school educations
white-collar jobs

Politics

Predominant ideology: moderate
1984 presidential vote: Reagan (59%)
Key issues: fiscal conservatism, foreign policy doves

Sample Neighborhoods

Norwood, Massachusetts (02062)
Cuyahoga Falls, Ohio (44221)
Donelson, Nashville, Tennessee (37214)
Stratford, Connecticut (06497)
Cheswick, Pittsburgh, Pennsylvania (15024)
Mercerville, New Jersey (08619)

Lifestyle

High Usage	Index	Low Usage	Index
Watch ice hockey	181	Feminine hygiene sprays	75
Ale	170	Hair tonic	75
Bowling	156	Archery	66
New roofs	147	Convertibles	64
Depilatories	144	Travel by bus	63
Golf	140	Malt liquor	59
Knitting	133	Pregnancy tests	51
Travel by cruise ship	132	Small cigars	43

Magazines/Newspapers

High Usage	Index	Low Usage	Index
Industry Week	193	*Playgirl*	62
Stereo Review	178	*Food & Wine*	57
Barron's	158	*Metropolitan Home*	54
Golf Digest	153	*Jet*	17

Cars

High Usage	Index	Low Usage	Index
Yugos	234	Mercedes 380/500/560s	77
Mercury Marquises	173	BMW 5 Series	77
Dodge Aries	163	Ferraris	65
AMC Alliances	163	Jaguars	63
AMC Encores	162	Rolls Royces	54

Food

High Usage	Index	Low Usage	Index
Instant iced tea	147	Packaged cold cuts	84
English muffins	133	Canned chicken	81
Stuffing mixes	128	Mexican foods	80
Pretzels	124	Pizza mixes	65

Television

High Usage	Index	Low Usage	Index
"St. Elsewhere"	138	"Miami Vice"	90
"Lifestyles of the Rich and Famous"	128	"Hunter"	87
"Newhart"	127	"Friday Night Videos"	59
"Sale of the Century"	124	"American Bandstand"	56

Republican Party. Resembling white-collarites in their fiscal conservatism and blue-collarites in their support of government welfare programs, Levittown, U.S.A. voters are eagerly courted by both parties at election time. Their credo is to vote for whoever promises to leave them alone.

ZQ 13: GRAY POWER

To newcomers, the sight is striking: homeowners driving golf carts along public streets, stopping to pick up litter and rotting oranges that have dropped from the decorative trees. But volunteer street sweepers are typical in Gray Power, that cluster of active retirement communities that has sprung up in the last generation.

Primarily concentrated in the Sunbelt states along both coasts, Gray Power communities have the nation's highest concentration of childless married couples, typically living in condos, low-rise apartments and modest retirement homes. Most Gray Power communities are self-contained environments where retirees live free of urban concerns like crime and rush-hour traffic. In their place are recreation centers, golf courses and hobby clubs dedicated to the nonstop pursuit of leisure. Those with an individualist's streak ignore the activities and putter around the backyard or leaf through magazines like *Natural History* or *Golf Digest.*

Many of Gray Power's residents originally came from sophisticated middle-class suburban communities in the Northeast, and they're well-off enough to afford some of life's luxuries. With the time and money to travel, they use rental car charge cards and buy movie projectors to show films of their trips at rates twice the national average. They're social butterflies who host dinner parties and cocktail parties more often than the general population. In cars, they look to luxury sedans designed to last for years: Lincoln Continental, Cadillac Seville and Mercedes Benz are all purchased at rates three times the national norm. In contrast to clusters with younger residents, Gray Power TV viewers shy away from the sitcoms and soap operas like "Kate & Allie" and "Ryan's Hope" in favor of news and sports programs like "Nightline" and "NBC Sportsworld." Among "Miami Vice" viewers, the nation's lowest concentration live in Gray Power.

At the ballot box, it comes as no surprise that the cluster with the wealthiest senior citizens is one of the most solidly Republican. "Affluence is Republican, poverty is Democratic," observes Sylvia Cartso-

ZQ 13: GRAY POWER

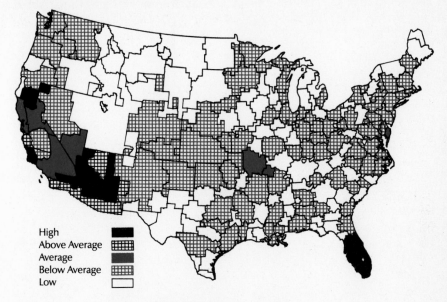

High
Above Average
Average
Below Average
Low

2.9% of U.S. households

Primary age group:	55+
Median household income:	$25,259
Median home value:	$83,630

Thumbnail Demographics

upper-middle-class retirement communities
multi-unit housing
predominantly white couples
some college educations
white-collar jobs

Politics

Predominant ideology:	conservative
1984 presidential vote:	Reagan (73%)
Key issues:	fiscal conservatism, nuclear arms

Sample Neighborhoods

Sun City, Arizona (85373)
Laguna Hills, California (92653)
Hallandale, Florida (33009)
South Yarmouth, Massachusetts (02664)
Danville, Virginia (24541)
Sarasota, Florida (33577)

Lifestyle

High Usage	Index	Low Usage	Index
Movie projectors	249	Pianos	57
Civic clubs	202	Bowling	52
Sailing	199	Wall paneling	45
Foreign tour packages	187	Unions	45
Salt-water fishing rods	177	Christmas/Chanukah clubs	38
Country clubs	162	Hunting	31
Host dinner parties	161	Watch rodeo	28
Wine by the case	159	Swimming pools	26

Magazines/Newspapers

High Usage	Index	Low Usage	Index
Rudder	520	*Sporting News*	63
Architectural Digest	339	*Self*	62
Golf Digest	226	*Working Woman*	44
Natural History	216	*True Story*	32

Cars

High Usage	Index	Low Usage	Index
Rolls Royces	471	Bertones	50
Cadillac DeVilles	281	Ford EXPs	40
Lincoln Continentals	279	AMC Eagles	35
Cadillac Fleetwoods	270	Chevrolet Novas	22
Mercedes 380/500/560s	267	Mercury Sables	10

Food

High Usage	Index	Low Usage	Index
Canned corned-beef hash	143	Cheese spreads	81
Rye/pumpernickel bread	135	Canned meat spreads	79
Natural cold cereal	130	Powdered soft drinks	78
Frozen dessert pies	119	Liquid nutritional supplements	39

Television

High Usage	Index	Low Usage	Index
"Good Morning America"	194	"Family Ties"	73
"NBC Sports World"	145	"Kate & Allie"	67
"Nightline"	142	"Ryan's Hope"	39
Sunday morning interview programs	138	"Loving"	34

nis, a Sun City, Arizona, social worker. Most residents have nothing but applause for their fellow senior, President Reagan; 74 percent gave him a favorable rating in a 1985 national poll. And though they are comparatively well-off, with hefty pensions supplementing Social Security checks, they still vote as fiscal conservatives and oppose government-aided welfare programs—except when the issues relate to Social Security or assistance for senior citizens. Despite their small numbers, Gray Power voters have electoral punch at the ballot box. They'll bolt the party whenever they believe their interests are threatened.

ZQ 14: BLACK ENTERPRISE

The emergence of Black Enterprise reflects the rise of America's black middle class. Since passage of the 1964 Civil Rights Act, the increasing rates of professional employment and higher educational achievement among blacks have created predominantly black, upper-middle-class neighborhoods. Today, Black Enterprise is the preferred address for many of the nation's black achievers and intelligentsia who want to settle down outside the urban core. In these integrated communities, residents boast high educational achievement (34 percent have gone to college), enviable salaries (47 percent earn over $35,000) and brick-solid homes (27 percent cost between $80,000 and $150,000). The local value system holds that hard work and discipline lead to color-blind success. In Washington, D.C.'s Gold Coast, black families send their children to exclusive private schools, belong to well-connected social clubs like Jack and Jill and spend their vacations on Martha's Vineyard—alongside their white neighbors. In Black Enterprise, money is the great racial equalizer.

When it comes to politics, the Reagan Revolution never reached Black Enterprise. In this cluster, more residents identify with the Democratic Party than anywhere else in the nation. Voters gave Walter Mondale one of his best showings in the 1984 election with 78 percent of their ballots, and they continued to vote Democratic in 1986. Black Enterprise is one of the few neighborhood types to claim that the Democrats are the best party when it comes to national leadership and image, and they're twice as likely as the average American to mention the party's concern for "the average American" when explaining their political preferences. In polls, Black Enterprisers express less concern with fiscal matters than with unemployment and poverty. They're unable to forget the party's contribution to the civil rights movement.

ZQ 14: BLACK ENTERPRISE

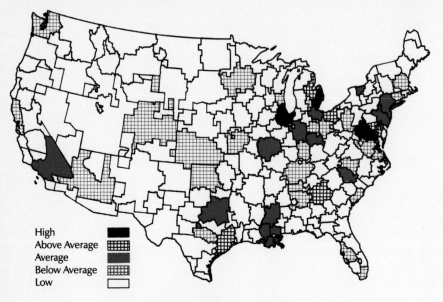

High
Above Average
Average
Below Average
Low

0.8% of U.S. households
Primary age range: 35–54
Median household income: $33,149
Median home value: $68,713

Thumbnail Demographics
middle-class inner suburbs
predominantly black families
single-unit and duplex housing
some college educations
white-collar jobs

Politics
Predominant ideology: liberal
1984 presidential vote: Mondale (78%)
Key issues: jobs, trade

Sample Neighborhoods
Capitol Heights, Maryland (20743)
Auburn Park, Chicago, Illinois (60620)
Seven Oaks, Detroit, Michigan (48235)
Mount Airy, Philadelphia, Pennsylvania (19119)
South De Kalb, Atlanta, Georgia (30034)
Cranwood, Cleveland, Ohio (44128)

Lifestyle

High Usage	Index	Low Usage	Index
Travel by railroad	428	Imported red wine	75
Sangria/pop wine	346	Hotels/motels	74
Malt liquor	334	Travelers checks	73
Small cigars	318	Electric hair dryers	68
Disco records/tapes	294	Draft beer	65
Unions	145	Microwave ovens	64
Hardcover books	140	Personal loans	61
Travel by bus	140	Car-camping	54

Magazines/Newspapers

High Usage	Index	Low Usage	Index
Essence	716	*Barron's*	45
Ebony	610	*Mother Earth News*	45
Jet	554	*New York*	42
Ms.	302	*Ski*	9

Cars

High Usage	Index	Low Usage	Index
Yugos	436	Porsches	59
Mitsubishi Tredias	255	Subaru DL4s	49
Peugeots	245	AMC Eagles	40
Mitsubishi Cordias	235	Mercury Sables	39
Cadillac Sevilles	228	Ferraris	22

Food

High Usage	Index	Low Usage	Index
Nondairy creamers	144	Cheese spreads	84
Meat tenderizers	122	Tomato juice	78
Frozen dessert pies	119	Canned stews	76
Freeze-dried coffee	116	Low-fat/skim milk	68

Television

High Usage	Index	Low Usage	Index
"American Bandstand"	203	"St. Elsewhere"	74
"Nightline"	200	"Highway to Heaven"	72
"Hotel"	158	"Newhart"	67
"Miami Vice"	153	"CBS Evening News"	65

As the first minority cluster to have achieved genuine middle-class status, Black Enterprise has consuming patterns that reflect educated, midscale tastes. More than eighty magazines are purchased at above-average rates; *Essence, Jet* and *Ebony* lead them all at more than five times the national norm. While status is a Mercedes in many Black Enterprise neighborhoods, cluster driveways are 50 percent more likely than the average to hold diesels, convertibles and sports cars. In their family rooms, residents are three times as likely as the average person to listen to disco records, 50 percent more likely to read a hardcover book and 15 percent more likely to own three TV sets—the better to watch favorite shows like "Hotel," "Miami Vice" and "Nightline." Though the rate of viewership for "The Cosby Show" may be higher in other neighborhoods, in Black Enterprise, residents are living the script.

ZQ 15: NEW BEGINNINGS

In Bloomington, Minnesota, New Beginnings is home to a 49-year-old financial analyst and divorced mother of three who lives in an aging rambler and is active in Parents Without Partners. In Dallas, Texas, New Beginnings is where a 27-year-old nurse lives in a new singles complex and hangs out at the country-club pool. What they both have in common is a neighborhood type that's predominantly young, middle-class, unmarried and involved in recreation and entertainment.

New Beginnings is the result of an adult population that is one-third single. Divorced, widowed or delaying marriage perhaps indefinitely, singles have proliferated and so have these communities characterized by rental housing and residents with high rates of mobility, some college educations and lower-echelon white-collar jobs (46 percent of the households earn between $15,000 and $35,000 annually). Many of the neighborhoods are located in Sunbelt cities and have become havens for the steady flow of northern migrants in search of new job opportunities and sociable lifestyles. In New Beginnings, standard amenities include bars, fitness clubs and self-help organizations ranging from open universities to video dating services. All the better to meet Mr. or Ms. Right.

This ready-to-mingle attitude is evident in the above-average consumption of many youth-oriented products and services. Residents enjoy going to concerts, theater and health clubs—all at rates 25 percent above the norm. They're big on travel and are 46 percent more likely than average Americans to fly abroad and 98 percent more likely to rent

ZQ 15: NEW BEGINNINGS

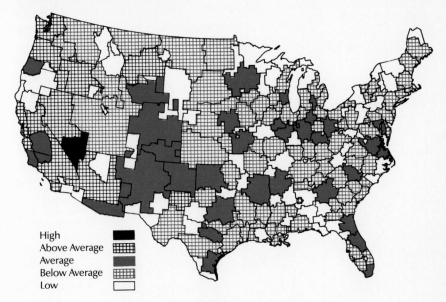

High
Above Average
Average
Below Average
Low

4.3% of U.S. households
Primary age group: 18–34
Median household income: $24,847
Median home value: $75,364

Thumbnail Demographics
middle-class city neighborhoods
single and divorced apartment dwellers
some college educations
white-collar jobs

Politics
Predominant ideology: moderate
1984 presidential vote: Reagan (64%)
Key issues: fiscal conservatism, nuclear arms

Sample Neighborhoods
Bloomington, Minnesota (55420)
Northeast Phoenix, Arizona (85016)
Reseda, Los Angeles, California (91335)
Englewood, Denver, Colorado (80110)
Parkmoor, San Francisco, California (95126)
Park Place, Houston, Texas (77061)

Lifestyle

High Usage	Index	Low Usage	Index
Slide projectors	229	Pianos	74
Car-leasing	200	Outboard powerboats	69
Civic clubs	174	Snuff	65
Tequila	171	Hunting	63
Salt-water fishing	171	Gospel records/tapes	58
Jazz records/tapes	163	Watch roller derby	51
Backpacking/camping		Canning jars and lids	43
equipment	160	Investment property	39
Valid passports	152		

Magazines/Newspapers

High Usage	Index	Low Usage	Index
Scientific American	185	*Redbook*	80
Shape	180	*Popular Mechanics*	79
Rolling Stone	169	*True Story*	68
Travel & Leisure	160	*Family Handyman*	59

Cars

High Usage	Index	Low Usage	Index
Mitsubishi Mirages	171	Chevrolet Caprices	67
Hyundais	169	Pontiac Bonnevilles	67
Isuzus	163	Dodge Diplomats	64
VW Cabriolets	161	Pontiac 6000s	63
Acuras	153	Chevrolet Impalas	60

Food

High Usage	Index	Low Usage	Index
Bottled water	154	Whipped topping	87
Whole-wheat bread	137	Powdered soft drinks	81
Low-fat/skim milk	122	White bread	79
Natural cheeses	109	Canned stews	75

Television

High Usage	Index	Low Usage	Index
"Late Night with David		"Entertainment Tonight"	81
Letterman"	130	"Falcon Crest"	73
"Who's the Boss?"	114	"The $25,000 Pyramid"	64
"Night Court"	112	"As the World Turns"	55
"Cheers"	112		

cars to travel domestically. They're heavy purchasers of travel-related items like slide projectors, passports and 35-mm cameras. And they're party animals: they buy rock and pop records at rates 40 percent above the norm and consume alcoholic beverages at rates more than 30 percent above average (their three favorite drinks are tequila, Irish whiskey and imported brandy).

Even without the alcohol, living in New Beginnings can be intoxicating. Residents are recreation buffs who ski, backpack, fish and play racquetball at above-average rates. TV execs state that shows like "Cheers," "Who's the Boss?" and "Night Court" have "good demographics" because of their popularity with this cluster's budding consumers. At the supermarket they tend to mix health-conscious and convenience foods: whole-wheat bread, skim milk, frozen dinners and natural cheese are all purchased at above-average rates. And shoppers don't mind mixing business and pleasure. In New Beginnings, even the grocery stores double as "meet markets."

Like their blue-collar parents, the typical residents of New Beginnings are conservative in their economic values. Many are pro-GOP because of Ronald Reagan's appeal, but their loyalty falls short of hero worship. These veterans of the '60s era of sex and drugs and rock'n'roll support a liberal social agenda. And they're more attuned to the special-interest groups linked to the Democratic Party than to the big-business associations of the GOP. Still their political loyalties are sometimes suspect. The prevailing cluster transiency results in apathy among voters, and registration and ballot counts are well below average. In this starter group, many residents are more absorbed in their careers and social lives than in politics.

ZQ 16: BLUE-COLLAR NURSERY

They are America's starter-family neighborhoods, places where the baby bust never occurred. In Blue-Collar Nursery, young, middle-class families first settle down in a landscape of recently built subdivisions and overcrowded schools. Often located on the fringe of midwestern cities, these communities of modest ramblers and split-levels are home to union men employed as skilled laborers and machine operators, homemakers and working women who serve as nurses and secretaries and their elementary-school–age children, who look exactly like their postwar predecessors on skateboards and two-wheelers. More traditional families—married couples with children—live in Blue-Collar Nursery

ZQ 16: BLUE-COLLAR NURSERY

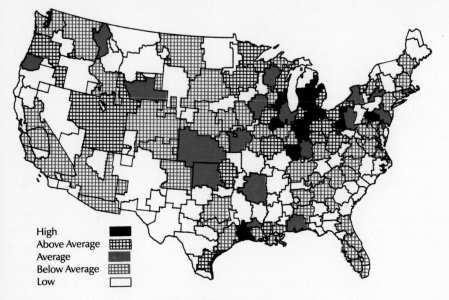

High
Above Average
Average
Below Average
Low

2.2% of U.S. households
Primary age range: 25–44
Median household income: $30,007
Median home value: $67,281

Thumbnail Demographics
middle-class child-rearing towns
single-unit housing
predominantly white families
high-school educations
blue-collar jobs

Politics
Predominant ideology: conservative
1984 presidential vote: Reagan (74%)
Key issues: fiscal conservatism, nuclear arms

Sample Neighborhoods
West Jordan, Utah (84084)
Maryville, South Carolina (29440)
Princeton, Texas (75044)
Richmond, Michigan (48062)
Haysville, Kansas (67060)
Magnolia, Houston, Texas (77355)

Lifestyle

High Usage	Index	Low Usage	Index
Campers	222	Electric fry pans	47
Unions	192	Watch tennis	45
Christmas/Chanukah clubs	186	Foreign tour packages	45
Watch pro wrestling	186	Malt liquor	43
Toy-sized dogs	175	Money-market funds	41
Hunting	171	Environmentalist organizations	38
1960s rock records/tapes	164	Travel by railroad	21
Tupperware	141	Slide projectors	16

Magazines/Newspapers

High Usage	Index	Low Usage	Index
Lakeland Boating	287	*Forum*	37
Mother Earth News	202	*Fortune*	35
Industry Week	198	*Rolling Stone*	34
Skin Diver	176	*Atlantic Monthly*	12

Cars

High Usage	Index	Low Usage	Index
Ford EXPs	232	Jaguars	29
Chevrolet Chevettes	208	BMWs	28
Plymouth Turismos	196	Bertone X19	27
Ford Escorts	188	BMW 5 Series	20
Chevrolet Cavaliers	184	Mitsubishi Galants	18

Food

High Usage	Index	Low Usage	Index
Canned stews	141	Whole-wheat bread	85
Pretzels	119	Canned corned-beef hash	78
Children's vitamins	116	Canned orange juice	65
Baked beans	115	Frozen corn-on-the-cob	56

Television

High Usage	Index	Low Usage	Index
"St. Elsewhere"	143	"Miami Vice"	92
"Newhart"	132	"NBC Sports World"	80
"Night Court"	127	Sunday morning interview programs	64
"Highway to Heaven"	117	"American Bandstand"	53

than in any other neighborhood type. And in this cluster, the bigger the family, the prouder the parents.

With most Blue-Collar Nursery households solidly middle class (58 percent of Blue-Collar Nurseryites earn between $20,000 and $50,000), residents have a fair amount of disposable income burning holes in their jeans. Compared to American averages, they own twice as many campers, motorcycles and powerboats. Their mainstream values come out in their choice of cars (Ford Escorts, Chevrolet Chevettes), TV shows ("Highway to Heaven," "Night Court") and supermarket items, which naturally include many children's products (diapers, baby shampoo, powdered soft drinks). In the cluster community of West Jordan, Utah, the big holidays are Christmas and Halloween, as children don costumes to recreate the nativity scene or the flight of Luke Skywalker. Adults spend these occasions hiding anything breakable and hosting elaborate parties with throwaway paper products.

A one-time Democratic stronghold, Blue-Collar Nursery is typical of middle-American groups that have left the party out of disaffection with special-interest politics. Upward mobility and suburbanization have brought area residents physically and socially into traditional Republican camps. Conservative in their political and religious beliefs, Blue-Collar Nurseryites are against abortion and birth control and would rather see government funds go for defense than for social welfare programs. "Around here," says West Jordan Chamber of Commerce president Craig Dearing, "you don't mention Ted Kennedy's name if you want to get elected." Unlike upscale Republicans, however, cluster voters support buy-American trade policies. In their economically insecure position, Blue-Collar Nurseryites are vulnerable to inflation, economic downturns and the strains of oversized mortgage payments. In this patch of Reagan country, residents think the GOP is smarter at managing the economy.

ZQ 17: NEW HOMESTEADERS

Dave Kimberlin left his home in Harrisburg, Pennsylvania, and accepted a lower-paying job for the chance to live in rustic Loveland, Colorado. "When I first came here, I thought there was too much blue in the sky for it to be normal," he recalls. Detroit-born Victor Wowk settled his family there because he liked the easy pace. "People drive slower than the speed limit around here," says Wowk. "And you just don't worry about the crime and violence you have in a big city."

ZQ 17: NEW HOMESTEADERS

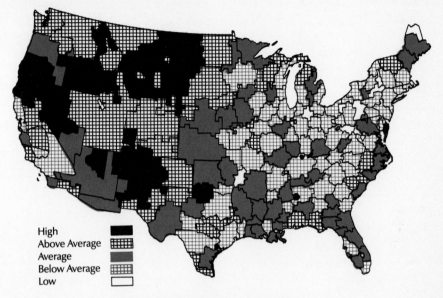

High
Above Average
Average
Below Average
Low

4.2% of U.S. households

Primary age range:	18–34
Median household income:	$25,909
Median home value:	$67,221

Thumbnail Demographics

middle-class exurban boomtowns
single-unit housing
predominantly white families
some college educations
blue- and white-collar jobs

Politics

Predominant ideology:	conservative
1984 presidential vote:	Reagan (69%)
Key issues:	jobs, fiscal conservatism

Sample Neighborhoods

Loveland, Colorado (80537)
Alamogordo, New Mexico (88310)
Redding, California (96001)
Yuma, Arizona (85364)
Pocatello, Idaho (83201)
Billings, Montana (59101)

Lifestyle

High Usage	Index	Low Usage	Index
Microwave ovens	247	Video cassette recorders	74
Convertibles	233	Tennis	72
Travel by cruise ship	212	Bowling	71
Environmental organizations	205	Mutual funds	68
Tequila	198	Christmas/Chanukah clubs	52
Overnight camping	174	Men's leisure suits	50
Country records/tapes	165	Jazz records/tapes	45
Cable TV	164	Watch soccer	40

Magazines/Newspapers

High Usage	Index	Low Usage	Index
Sunset	199	*Esquire*	61
Car Craft	186	*World Tennis*	52
Audio	183	*Ebony*	50
Harper's Bazaar	180	*New York*	31

Cars

High Usage	Index	Low Usage	Index
Chevrolet Sprints	225	Alfa Romeos	53
VW Station Wagons	154	Mitsubishi Galants	48
Subaru DL4s	147	Rolls Royces	47
Oldsmobile Omegas	143	Jaguars	41
Toyota Vans	138	Yugos	30

Food

High Usage	Index	Low Usage	Index
Mexican foods	157	Spaghetti sauce	90
Canned meat spreads	140	Packaged piecrusts	80
Whole-wheat bread	138	Canned corned-beef hash	78
Fruit juices	121	Rye/pumpernickel bread	55

Television

High Usage	Index	Low Usage	Index
"Super Password"	128	"Cagney & Lacey"	86
"At the Movies"	115	"Miami Vice"	81
"60 Minutes"	114	"Another World"	71
"ABC Wide World of Sports"	113	"Ryan's Hope"	68

New Homesteaders communities like Loveland have that effect on city dwellers. One of the largest and fastest-growing clusters, New Homesteaders is the principal recipient of the great western migration witnessed in the last decade. Its remote towns, predominantly in the West, are set amid natural wonders like mountains, lakes and canyons. A socioeconomic step down from its cluster twin, God's Country, New Homesteaders is characterized by residents with some college education (only 16 percent actually have their diplomas), middle-class incomes (half the households earn between $20,000 and $50,000) and military jobs (service families live in this cluster six times more often than the national average). Many of its residents are urban exiles who've sought out a countrified setting with room for kids to grow. Except in some offices of eastern-based corporations, blue jeans are the standard dress for men, women and children.

Given the wide-open spaces surrounding many New Homesteaders communities, it's no wonder that surveys show residents to be outdoor types. Campers, powerboats, minibikes and motor homes are all popular among New Homesteaders. Supermarket surveys show these western families buying above-average quantities of Mexican food and corn chips, cloth diapers and baby oil, as well as convenience foods like canned ham and fruit juices. Compared to the general population, residents belong to environmental organizations, take adult-education courses and spend their leisure time painting or drawing at twice the national average. A lot of New Homesteaders take their hobbies more seriously than their jobs.

Politically, New Homesteaders are Republican-leaning and gave President Reagan 69 percent of their votes in 1984. Residents support GOP policies in the areas of reduced federal spending and limited government. But their environmentalist bent translates into opposition to both nuclear arms and a hawkish foreign policy. Having moved to exurbia to get away from city problems, New Homesteaders don't want anyone threatening their affordable house or their pristine view.

ZQ 18: NEW MELTING POT

America's new-immigrant neighborhoods are found most often in the port cities along the East and West coasts. Once home to older immigrant groups, in the nation's Chinatowns and Little Italys, they've now absorbed the latest wave of foreign born: Hispanic, Asian and Middle Eastern. Unlike the illegal aliens from Central America who've settled

ZQ 18: NEW MELTING POT

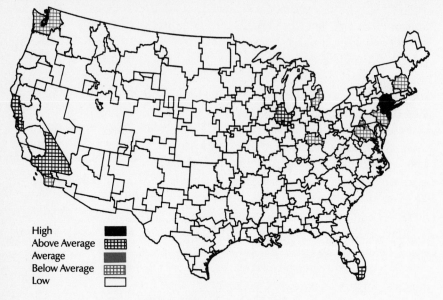

High

Above Average

Average

Below Average

Low

0.9% of U.S. households

Primary age range:	55+
Median household income:	$22,142
Median home value:	$113,616

Thumbnail Demographics

new-immigrant urban neighborhoods
multi-unit dwellings
ethnic singles and families
college educations
white-collar jobs

Politics

Predominant ideology:	moderate
1984 presidential vote:	Reagan (64%)
Key issues:	poverty, social programs

Sample Neighborhoods

Los Feliz, Los Angeles, California (90027)
Jackson Heights, New York, New York (11372)
Rogers Park, Chicago, Illinois (60660)
Geary, San Francisco, California (94121)
Little River, Miami, Florida (33138)

Lifestyle

High Usage	Index	Low Usage	Index
Mutual funds	356	CB radios	50
Convertibles	248	Packaged dry dog food	49
Latin records/tapes	240	Travel by cruise ship	47
Men's leisure suits	225	Sailing	46
Imported brandy/cognac	210	Canning jars and lids	33
Health clubs	174	Pipe tobacco	32
Watch horse racing	169	Hunting	30
Wine by the case	164	Pickup trucks	16

Magazines/Newspapers

High Usage	Index	Low Usage	Index
The New York Times	769	*Mother Earth News*	8
Barron's	264	*Southern Living*	1
The New Yorker	207	*Grit*	0
Metropolitan Home	166	*Modern Bride*	0

Cars

High Usage	Index	Low Usage	Index
Chevrolet Impalas	434	Mercury Capris	19
Mitsubishis	220	AMC Eagles	19
Hyundais	165	Ford Aerostars	18
Alfa Romeos	149	Ford EXPs	11
Audi GTs	131	Mercury Sables	0

Food

High Usage	Index	Low Usage	Index
Pumpernickel/rye bread	225	Deviled ham	49
Yogurt	165	Breakfast/snack bars	46
English muffins	164	Pizza mixes	44
Instant iced tea	147	Mexican foods	44

Television

High Usage	Index	Low Usage	Index
"Late Night with David Letterman"	252	"At the Movies"	72
"Dance Fever"	216	"General Hospital"	69
"St. Elsewhere"	154	"Days of Our Lives"	59
"Cagney & Lacey"	121	"Good Morning America"	51

in border barrios, New Melting Pot residents aren't poor. With a third having attended college and almost half reporting home values of more than $100,000, these residents have consumer and political tastes comparable to other sophisticated urban clusters like Bohemian Mix and Urban Gold Coast. On the streets, chop suey joints vie for space with wine and cheese shops.

In worldly New Melting Pot, the most popular magazines include *The New Yorker, Barron's* and *Metropolitan Home.* The top three automotive brands are snappy imports: Mitsubishi, Alfa Romeo and Hyundai. With a high concentration of aging singles deposited during previous immigrant waves, the cluster's supermarket behavior leans towards quick-and-easy food items: instant hot lunches, yogurt, pumpernickel bread, frozen corn-on-the-cob and instant iced tea. The foreign roots of so many cluster residents also explain their purchase of Latin records, imported brandy and passports at rates above the national average. In New Melting Pot, residents prefer horse-racing and chess to bowling and hunting. Says Tony Shay, a librarian from the cluster community of Los Feliz, California, "We think of ourselves as the Manhattan of Los Angeles."

With its polycultural lifestyles, New Melting Pot identifies itself with liberal causes. Voters favor the Democratic Party's support of government programs for the disadvantaged. A 1985 survey showed that New Melting Pot topped all clusters in disapproving the link between the GOP and the nation's business elite. Yet the cluster's influence is lessened by its political apathy. New Melting Pot was the only liberal white-collar cluster that failed to give Walter Mondale a majority of its votes in 1984 (only 36 percent). No doubt, the cluster's makeup of recent immigrants partially explains this uninvolvement. But with better jobs and schooling than Hispanic Mix immigrants, they also suffer less poverty and discrimination. These residents think more like preppies than proletarians.

■■■■■■ ZQ 19: TOWNS & GOWNS

In this cluster of remote college towns, students dominate the way of life. Retail stores are filled with school-colored sweatshirts and university-crested beer mugs, football weekends bring traffic to a standstill, and neighborhoods close to campuses may be noisy student ghettos. Among neighborhood types, Towns & Gowns displays a unique profile typically composed of three parts locals to one part students. Census data show high percentages of well-educated 18- to 24-year-olds with high-paying professional jobs living alongside older, blue-collar workers with modest means. The colleges not only provide work for residents as faculty members and support personnel, they also sponsor concerts, plays and sporting events for the communities' entertainment. "The town is us, we are the town," says Dave Schuckers, a Penn State University administrator of State College, Pennsylvania, though his observation applies to all Towns & Gowns communities.

Thanks to the mixed white- and blue-collar labor force, this cluster exhibits an enormous breadth of tastes. Residents subscribe to *Natural History, Scientific American* and *Omni,* not to mention *Cycle, Lakeland Boating* and *Family Weekly*—all at more than twice the national average. Many of the top choices in cars are all foreign compacts, with Mazda GLC, Subaru DL4 and Toyota Tercel among the leaders. Outdoor activities dominate, reflecting the rural settings of most Towns & Gowns campuses as well as the athletic proclivities of its residents. Jogging, tennis and downhill skiing are twice as popular here as in the general population. Residents also hunt, fish and camp at rates nearly twice the U.S. average. Because most students, assistant professors and service workers don't earn much money, life isn't all beer and backpacking, according to supermarket surveys. Cluster residents rarely spend more than $50 a week on groceries, and what they do buy is of the "grazer" variety: canned stews, meat spreads and frozen pizzas are among the most popular items. In Towns & Gowns, many residents have never held a steady job and carry little more than loose change.

For political analysts, Towns & Gowns is difficult to read, what with its heterogeneous mix of students, faculty members and blue-collar natives. Residents lean toward the GOP (Mondale received only 40 percent of the cluster's votes in 1984) but their high educational levels can result in nonconformist behavior. Like those in many white-collar clusters, voters dislike trade protectionism and favor nuclear disarmament. Despite the activism that fermented in many Towns & Gowns communities in the '60s, the '80s have been marked by complacency. Where they once might have marched against the war, students today gather for job-search seminars and join established campus organizations like Young Republicans and Campus Libertarians. "Now that the war is over," says Penn State's Schuckers, "students

ZQ 19: TOWNS & GOWNS

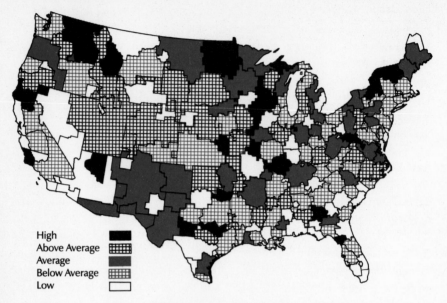

High
Above Average
Average
Below Average
Low

1.2% of U.S. households
Primary age group: 18–34
Median household income: $17,862
Median home value: $60,891

Thumbnail Demographics
middle-class college towns
single-unit dwellings
predominantly white singles
college graduates
white-collar jobs

Politics
Predominant ideology: conservative
1984 presidential vote: Reagan (60%)
Key issues: nuclear arms, fiscal conservatism

Sample Neighborhoods
State College, Pennsylvania (16801)
Bloomington, Indiana (47401)
Ithaca, New York (14850)
Gainesville, Florida (32608)
Corvallis, Oregon (97330)
College Station, Texas (77840)

Lifestyle

High Usage	Index	Low Usage	Index
Civic clubs	246	Unions	64
Tennis rackets	226	Toy-sized dogs	61
Water skiing	224	Vans	51
Country clubs	189	Foreign tour packages	44
Folk records/tapes	168	Men's leisure suits	44
Factory-loaded ammunition	168	Microwave ovens	38
Charcoal grills	157	Burglar alarm systems	25
Watch college basketball	150	Mutual funds	14

Magazines/Newspapers

High Usage	Index	Low Usage	Index
Natural History	364	*Industry Week*	30
Modern Bride	300	*Baby Talk*	26
GQ	216	*The New York Times*	25
Family Weekly	182	*Motorcyclist*	14

Cars

High Usage	Index	Low Usage	Index
Mercury Sables	226	Mercedes 420s	36
Subaru DL4s	165	Hyundais	31
Pinin Farinas	163	Rolls Royces	31
Toyota Tercels	153	Jaguar XJ-6s	24
Mazda GLCs	151	Mitsubishis	18

Food

High Usage	Index	Low Usage	Index
Mexican foods	128	Canned ham	85
Canned meat spreads	127	Cheese spreads	84
Canned stews	125	Natural cold cereal	75
Whole-wheat bread	119	Liquid nutritional supplement	51

Television

High Usage	Index	Low Usage	Index
"Late Night with David Letterman"	180	"Dynasty"	73
		"The Facts of Life"	72
"Good Morning America"	142	Sunday morning interview programs	72
"The Tonight Show"	125		
"Magnum, P.I."	115	"The People's Court"	57

are hitting their books and thinking conservative thoughts—like how to get a job."

ZQ 20: RANK & FILE

Centered in the aging factory suburbs of the Rust Belt, Rank & File is composed of old ethnic neighborhoods that grew up around the nation's smokestack industries. This cluster leads all others in durable-manufacturing jobs (81 percent above the national average) and ranks near the top in its concentration of union members (26 percent of the working population). Many residents are blue-collar workers who cling to their ethnic roots—be they Slavic, Italian or Irish—through social clubs and churches where English is not the first language. Their middle-class salaries (41 percent earn between $25,000 and $50,000) allow them to live comfortably in prewar duplexes, railroad flats and tightly packed cottages. But the economic crisis that's struck many industry-based clusters has left them worried about maintaining their way of life. Rank & Filers fear urban decay almost as much as gentrification.

Like other neighborhood types still tied to organized labor, Rank & File leans to the Democratic Party and is one of the few middle-class clusters that hasn't swung to the GOP. Although cluster voters nation-wide gave President Reagan a 56-to-44-percent edge in the 1984 election, a majority supported Democratic congressional candidates in 1986 and expressed dissatisfaction with the lack of "people programs" under the GOP administration. In surveys, residents express fears that the way of life they have labored for years to build is vanishing. Rank & Filers are concerned about jobs and competition from abroad, registering their support for import restrictions. "Other countries subsidize their factories," notes Leo DeJohn, a union electrician from Lincoln Park, Michigan. "So, in a sense, they're sending their unemployment over to us."

Given such sentiments, you're not likely to find Toyotas or Hondas here. Rank & Filers are buy-American consumers whose favorite cars tend to be Detroit models like the Buick Skyhawk, Chrysler Cordoba and Dodge Omni. And they're homebodies, for whom status is maintaining their homes and paying off the mortgage. They're 66 percent more likely than average Americans to buy yard trimmers and 49 percent more likely to lay their own sheet vinyl flooring. They also enjoy entertaining friends and family at home: they're 46 percent more likely to throw monthly parties and 21 percent more likely to host barbecue cookouts.

ZQ 20: RANK & FILE

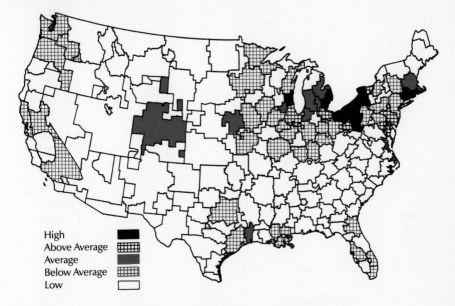

High
Above Average
Average
Below Average
Low

1.4% of U.S. households
Primary age range: 55+
Median household income: $26,283
Median home value: $59,363

Thumbnail Demographics
middle-class inner suburbs
rowhouse dwellings
racially mixed couples
high-school educations
blue-collar jobs

Politics
Predominant ideology: moderate
1984 presidential vote: Reagan (56%)
Key issues: trade protection, social programs

Sample Neighborhoods
Wyandotte, Detroit, Michigan (48192)
Sparrow's Point, Baltimore, Maryland (21222)
Fairview, Milwaukee, Wisconsin (53219)
Clearing, Chicago, Illinois (60638)
Carnegie, Pittsburgh, Pennsylvania (15106)
Meriden, Connecticut (06450)

Lifestyle

High Usage	Index	Low Usage	Index
Oral irrigators	275	Fraternal orders	50
Electric toothbrushes	228	Snuff	46
Ice-skating	195	Foreign tour packages	44
Yard trimmers	166	Host cocktail parties	43
U.S. Savings Bonds	166	Gospel records/tapes	28
Women's girdles	155	Convertibles	17
Camping trips	149	Mutual funds	0
Dog biscuits	146	Movie projectors	0

Magazines/Newspapers

High Usage	Index	Low Usage	Index
Chicago	303	*The New Yorker*	22
Audio	236	*Architectural Digest*	19
Essence	224	*Fortune*	11
Lakeland Boating	220	*Food & Wine*	10

Cars

High Usage	Index	Low Usage	Index
Pontiac Sunbirds	177	Isuzus	29
Buick Skyhawks	176	BMW 5 Series	18
AMC Encores	169	Jaguars	13
Plymouth Caravelles	164	Ferraris	13
Dodge Omnis	161	Rolls Royces	0

Food

High Usage	Index	Low Usage	Index
Rye/pumpernickel bread	171	Canned chili	77
Cheese spreads	161	Breakfast/snack bars	67
Toaster products	153	Whole-wheat bread	65
Canned tuna	149	Frozen yogurt	53

Television

High Usage	Index	Low Usage	Index
"Hotel"	147	"The Cosby Show"	80
"ABC Wide World of Sports"	144	"Friday Night Videos"	62
"General Hospital"	142	"Entertainment Tonight"	42
"CBS Sports Saturday"	115	"Santa Barbara"	42

Still the highlight of the social season to many Rank & Filers is the ethnic festival that features Old-Country foods, music, crafts and enough liquor to inspire community storytellers.

ZQ 21: MIDDLE AMERICA

Middle America is well named on several counts: its midsized, middle-class towns are close to the nation's midwestern center as well as to the U.S. average on most measures of age, ethnicity, household composition, even political attitudes. Nearly 40 percent of the cluster's residents have high-school degrees, blue-collar jobs and middle-class incomes (earning between $25,000 and $50,000 annually). Their placid communities are characterized by turn-of-the-century homes, family businesses and a devotion to local sports that makes high-school athletes town heroes. No one seeks out a Middle America town in order to dine in a trendy restaurant or pick up a baguette. Locals can grow up without ever seeing a mall.

As consumers, Middle Americans reflect the tastes of their plain, unpretentious towns. Indeed, what they're not attracted to is revealing: foreign travel, imported cars, tennis, jewelry and frozen yogurt—mainstays of an affluent, worldly society. Residents tend to drive modest Detroit models like the Plymouth Horizon, Dodge Shadow and Chevrolet Chevette, along with a lot of minicycles and mopeds. Ever cost-conscious, Middle Americans like to redeem supermarket coupons when buying their TV dinners, pizza mixes, canned stews, snack dips, skim milk, canned vegetables and whipped toppings. And there's no lack of young families in Middle America, as shown by their above-average purchase of diapers, children's clothing, preschool games and pet foods (for both dogs and cats). These are the people who claim their communities are "Burger King towns," though they patronize most other fast-food places as well. On a Saturday night, the biggest attraction in Middle America is still the drive-in that makes the best milk shakes.

In 1984, Middle America voters reflected the general population in their support of President Reagan and the GOP's policies of fiscal conservatism. They're not without economic anxieties, however, and remain fearful of government overspending and the lack of programs that help the middle class. Accordingly, Middle America remains a swing cluster, receptive to Democrats who play up their links to the middle class and to Republicans who play down their ties to the wealthy. "Middle Americans," according to one Targeting Systems, Inc., report,

ZQ 21: MIDDLE AMERICA

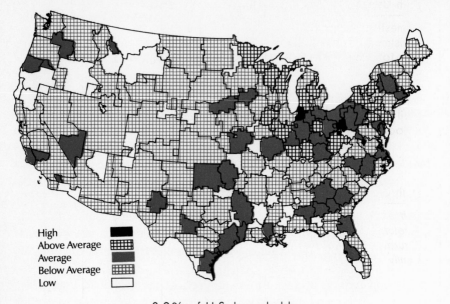

High
Above Average
Average
Below Average
Low

3.2% of U.S. households
Primary age range: 45–64
Median household income: $24,431
Median home value: $55,605

Thumbnail Demographics
middle-class suburban towns
single-unit housing
predominantly white families
high-school educations
blue-collar jobs

Politics
Predominant ideology: moderate
1984 presidential vote: Reagan (63%)
Key issues: trade protection, fiscal conservatism

Sample Neighborhoods
Marshall, Michigan (49068)
Sandusky, Ohio (44870)
Hagerstown, Maryland (21740)
Oshkosh, Wisconsin (54901)
Stroudsburg, Pennsylvania (18360)
Elkhart, Indiana (46514)

Lifestyle

High Usage	Index	Low Usage	Index
Domestic air charters	169	Country clubs	66
Christmas/Chanukah clubs	160	Classical records/tapes	68
Pipe tobacco	145	Swimming pools	64
Electric drills	145	Malt liquor	59
Truck-mounted campers	142	Foreign tour packages	56
Motorcycles	140	Burglar alarm systems	53
Mail-order catalogues	140	Depilatories	37
3-door hatchbacks	138	Travel by bus	36

Magazines/Newspapers

High Usage	Index	Low Usage	Index
Grit	171	*New York*	34
Lakeland Boating	168	*Rudder*	32
Saturday Evening Post	162	*American Photographer*	31
Family Handyman	145	*Skin Diver*	16

Cars

High Usage	Index	Low Usage	Index
Plymouth Sundances	147	Mercedes 380/500/560s	37
Chevrolet Chevettes	145	BMW 5 Series	36
Dodge Shadows	143	Mitsubishi Galants	34
Plymouth Horizons	135	Jaguars	28
Chevrolet Citations	134	Rolls Royces	17

Food

High Usage	Index	Low Usage	Index
Pizza mixes	128	Canned ham	85
Canned tea	126	Natural cold cereal	85
Low-fat/skim milk	119	Liquid nutritional supplements	79
TV dinners	117	Canned meat spreads	60

Television

High Usage	Index	Low Usage	Index
"The Facts of Life"	129	"Donahue"	86
"Simon & Simon"	115	"Nightline"	76
"Newhart"	115	"Friday Night Videos"	69
"Family Ties"	112	"Loving"	63

"identify with the middle class, but they're genuine working-class people. They made a down payment on the American dream, but they can't afford the mortgage."

ZQ 22: OLD YANKEE ROWS

Not all middle-class families have fled the city in search of the suburban American Dream. In Old Yankee Rows, a mix of blue- and white-collar ethnic neighborhoods in the Northeast, young people grow up and remain in the old neighborhood. This makes for close family ties as well as an insular lifestyle: men go to the same bar night after night, single women live at home until they're married, and several generations of families christen their babies at the same church. "On any given day, you can find four generations down at the town park," says William "Peco" Myers of Revere, Massachusetts. "The kids will be playing in the tot park, their parents will be shooting hoops at the basketball court, their grandparents might be playing over-40 softball and their great-grandparents will be playing bocce."

Cluster residents are typically high-school educated (only 23 percent have gone on to college), middle class (48 percent earn between $25,000 and $50,000) and of European descent (12 percent are foreign born). As the cluster nickname suggests, they're three times as likely as average Americans to live in rowhouses, duplexes or triple-deckers. Leases are passed on to relatives like china heirlooms.

As marketing surveys indicate, times are still good in Old Yankee Rows. These group-oriented residents—union membership is 27 percent above the national average—tend to bowl, travel by chartered plane, and belong to Christmas clubs at rates above the national average. Due to the cluster's concentration in the Northeast, ice hockey, ice-skating and salt-water fishing are the most popular sports. Old Yankee Row media tastes, however, are eclectic, ranging from *The New Yorker* to the *Star,* from the Sunday morning interview programs to "Who's the Boss?" Only politics unites local interest: in Revere, Massachusetts, cable telecasts of city council meetings rival soap operas in ratings.

In a sense, economic prosperity has made Old Yankee Row political attitudes uncertain. Forty-five percent identify themselves as "Independents" with no affinity for either party: Yankees object to the GOP's ties to the wealthy and to Democratic links to special-interest groups. Although 68 percent of the cluster voters backed President Reagan in 1984, a political poll a year later found an overriding dissatis-

ZQ 22: OLD YANKEE ROWS

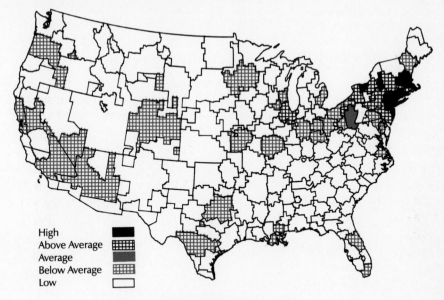

High

Above Average

Average

Below Average

Low

1.6% of U.S. households

Primary age range:	55+
Median household income:	$24,808
Median home value:	$76,406

Thumbnail Demographics

middle-class rowhouse districts

mixed families and singles

high-school educations

blue- and white-collar jobs

Politics

Predominant ideology:	moderate
1984 presidential vote:	Reagan (68%)
Key issues:	nuclear arms, poverty

Sample Neighborhoods

Revere, Massachusetts (02151)

Ozone Park, New York (11417)

Bayonne, New Jersey (07002)

Cranston, Rhode Island (02910)

West Haven, Connecticut (06516)

Melrose Park, Illinois (60160)

Lifestyle

High Usage	Index	Low Usage	Index
Latin records/tapes	262	Environmentalist organizations	43
Watch ice hockey	215	Business travel	42
Christmas/Chanukah clubs	205	Sailing	42
Salt-water fishing rods	194	Folk records/tapes	41
Host dinner parties	178	Powerboats	39
Ale	171	Toy-sized dogs	25
Disco records/tapes	166	Chewing tobacco	19
Stamp collecting	144	Convertibles	17

Magazines/Newspapers

High Usage	Index	Low Usage	Index
The New York Times	365	*Car & Driver*	15
New York	352	*Cycle World*	15
Self	206	*Town & Country*	7
Star	144	*Grit*	3

Cars

High Usage	Index	Low Usage	Index
Yugos	202	Isuzus	36
Mercury Marquises	169	VW Station Wagons	32
Subaru GLFs	154	Chevrolet Sprints	31
Plymouth Reliants	150	Ferraris	15
Buick Regals	149	Rolls Royces	0

Food

High Usage	Index	Low Usage	Index
Orange juice	200	Shortening	67
English muffins	173	Packaged cold cuts	57
Instant iced tea	164	Canned chili	49
Yogurt	135	Pizza mixes	39

Television

High Usage	Index	Low Usage	Index
"St. Elsewhere"	137	"Simon & Simon"	75
"Who's the Boss?"	132	"Magnum, P.I."	74
"Cagney & Lacey"	124	"Late Night with David Letterman"	64
Sunday morning interview programs	122	"American Bandstand"	61

faction with the GOP leadership and split their vote in 1986. In Old Yankee Rows, residents vote according to whether they have a job to go to and money to buy food. And in towns like Revere, where the unemployment rate is a slender 5 percent, the GOP is still on the upswing.

▬▬▬▬▬▬ ZQ 23 COALBURG & CORNTOWN

Composed of small midwestern towns, Coalburg & Corntown is a slice of Americana where one might imagine the Music Man would live. Most residents are high-school educated, earn under $35,000 a year and live in neighborhoods of white clapboard homes. The cluster's nickname reflects an economic base split between farming and light industry. But the phrase also alludes to an old-fashioned way of life, where residents still wave Old Glory in their front yards and the biggest teenage problem is kids cruising Main Street—à la *American Graffiti*. In Coalburg & Corntown, communities may be too tiny to have a major-league sports franchise, but they're also too intimate to worry about major-league crimes.

Politically, the small-town attitudes of Coalburg & Corntown are as hard-core Republican in real life as they are in fable. Residents vote two to one in favor of GOP candidates and gave President Reagan 65 percent of their ballots in 1984. Dispassionate in the debate between fiscal conservatism and government welfare programs, cluster voters do take a stand on the issue of trade protectionism: residents proudly display "Buy American" bumper stickers on their cars and belong to unions 75 percent more often than the national average. "A lot of people don't buy out of the community," says Columbia City, Indiana, mayor Joseph Zickgraf, "much less anything that's foreign made."

Indeed, nationwide surveys confirm that Coalburg & Corntown residents favor cars built by American Motors, Ford and General Motors at 50 percent above the national average. The rural setting of its towns can be seen in purchases of canning jars, chain saws and wood-burning stoves at twice the rate of the general population. It's hard to keep Coalburg & Corntowners indoors, given their tendency to buy canoes, powerboats and snowmobiles three times as often as average Americans. When it comes to reading, their top four magazine choices are *Motor Boating & Sailing, 4 Wheel & Off Road, Hunting* and *Motorcyclist* —all at rates twice as high as the general population. Residents fill their shopping carts with larger-than-average amounts of such standards as

ZQ 23: COALBURG & CORNTOWN

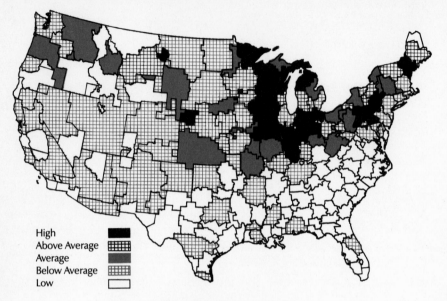

High
Above Average
Average
Below Average
Low

2.0% of U.S. households
Primary age groups: 35–44 and 65+
Median household income: $23,994
Median home value: $51,604

Thumbnail Demographics
middle-class small towns
predominantly white families
high-school educations
blue-collar workers

Politics
Predominant ideology: moderate
1984 presidential vote: Reagan (65%)
Key issues: trade protection, moral traditions

Sample Neighborhoods
Columbia City, Indiana (46725)
Oil City, Pennsylvania (16301)
Canton, Illinois (61520)
Seymour, Kentucky (47274)
Ticonderoga, New York (12883)
Red Wing, Minnesota (55066)

Lifestyle

High Usage	Index	Low Usage	Index
Canning jars and lids	337	Bottled water	39
Canoes/rowboats	336	Travel by cruise ship	31
Hunting	273	Imported champagne	29
Mutual funds	215	Burglar alarm systems	26
Wood-burning stoves	210	Classical records/tapes	18
Wall paneling	201	Soul records/tapes	12
Chewing tobacco	187	Electric toothbrushes	0
Toy-sized dogs	175	Latin records/tapes	0

Magazines/Newspapers

High Usage	Index	Low Usage	Index
Motor Boating & Sailing	355	*Scientific American*	40
4 Wheel & Off Road	275	*Harper's*	32
Hunting	250	*New York*	25
Motorcyclist	242	*Gentlemen's Quarterly*	10

Cars

High Usage	Index	Low Usage	Index
AMC Eagles	239	Hyundais	16
Mercury Sables	225	VW Cabriolets	13
Mercury Lynxes	191	Jaguars	12
Chevrolet Citations	174	Porsche 924s	9
Ford Aerostars	173	Mitsubishis	8

Food

High Usage	Index	Low Usage	Index
Canned orange juice	137	Frozen vegetables	90
Frozen pizzas	132	Meat tenderizers	83
Powdered soft drinks	132	Flavored rice	78
Canned spaghetti	130	Whole-wheat bread	66

Television

High Usage	Index	Low Usage	Index
"Scrabble"	151	"Entertainment Tonight"	67
"Super Password"	150	"Good Morning America"	65
"Simon & Simon"	149	"Lifestyles of the Rich and	
"Highway to Heaven"	132	and Famous"	63
		"At the Movies"	59

powdered soft drinks, cold cuts, TV dinners, white bread, canned spaghetti and draft beer. Not a great place to hawk yogurt, organic fruit drinks, frozen tofu and PBDBs (Palm Beach Dog Biscuits).

■■■■■■■■ ■ ZQ 24: SHOTGUNS & PICKUPS

Beyond the metropolitan sprawl, past the rolling farmland and into the foothills of the nation's mountains, you'll generally find a Shotguns & Pickups community: a rugged crossroads village dotted with a few dingy bars, grocery stores and gun & tackle shops. This cluster of rural outposts, centered in the northern tier of the country, serves the breadbasket and lumber needs of the nation. Shotguns & Pickups has high concentrations of large families, high-school-educated craftsworkers and midscale incomes (half the households earn between $20,000 and $50,000). Residents tend to live in modest ranch houses and wood-frame ramblers. With mobile homes holding 11 percent of all households, more people live on blocks here than anywhere else in the nation. No matter that the yards are tablecloth-sized and neighbors are only a whisper away. In Shotguns & Pickups, even the smallest home can come equipped with a giant-sized TV, wood stove, a ceramic bird collection and a dusty pickup in the driveway. "We think of this as a dream environment," says Shirley Lyons, Chamber of Commerce president of Molalla, Oregon. "Where else can you hunt from your backyard and ride a horse through town?"

With their large families and modest means, Shotguns & Pickups residents like to stretch their budgets with frozen pizzas, dry soups, TV dinners and powdered soft drinks. They also install their own mufflers and repair the brakes on their Mercury, AMC and Subaru cars. For leisure, women enjoy needlepoint, men enjoy woodworking and hunting, and the family likes gardening; residents buy canning jars 79 percent more often than average Americans. In Shotguns & Pickups, no one has to pretend a fondness for outdoor living: deer season ranks up there with Christmas for favorite holidays.

Politically, Shotguns & Pickups voters act like conservative populists who are suspicious of both major parties. They followed the national voting pattern in the last presidential election but gave the Reagan administration a low approval rating in a 1985 survey. Interestingly, for all the cluster's fondness for guns, hunting and target-shooting, residents are pacifists when it comes to the nuclear arms buildup. Hard hit economically by foreign imports, Shotguns & Pickups communities sup-

ZQ 24: SHOTGUNS & PICKUPS

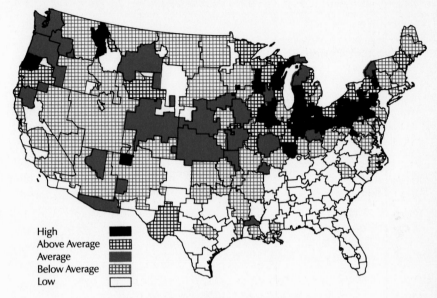

High
Above Average
Average
Below Average
Low

1.9% of U.S. households
Primary age range: 35–54
Median household income: $24,291
Median home value: $53,222

Thumbnail Demographics
lower-middle-class crossroads villages
single-unit housing
predominantly white families
high-school educations
mixed blue-collar and farm jobs

Politics
Predominant ideology: conservative
1984 presidential vote: Reagan (61%)
Key issues: trade protection, moral traditions

Sample Neighborhoods
Molalla, Oregon (97038)
Zanesville, Ohio (43701)
Ringgold, Pennsylvania (15770)
Monroe, Indiana (46772)
Jewett, West Virginia (43986)
Moravia, New York (13118)

Lifestyle

High Usage	Index	Low Usage	Index
Gas chain saws	379	Valid passports	47
Wood-burning stoves	276	Irish whiskey	42
Truck-mounted campers	227	Country clubs	40
Snuff	213	Travel by chartered plane	40
Canoes	209	Money-market funds	39
Canning jars and lids	179	Solid gold jewelry	37
Hunting	163	Car rentals	32
Outdoor gardening	141	Latin records/tapes	27

Magazines/Newspapers

High Usage	Index	Low Usage	Index
Grit	318	*Tennis*	32
Organic Gardening	265	*Southern Living*	30
4 Wheel & Off Road	244	*Gourmet*	21
Pickup Van & 4 Wheel Drive	237	*Audio*	7

Cars

High Usage	Index	Low Usage	Index
AMC Eagles	259	Mitsubishi Cordias	18
Chevrolet Citations	173	Ferraris	16
Mercury Lynxes	159	Mitsubishi Mirages	15
Subaru DL4s	158	Jaguars	13
Pontiac Phoenixes	154	Rolls Royces	8

Food

High Usage	Index	Low Usage	Index
Powdered soft drinks	137	Frozen dessert pies	79
Frozen potato products	127	Natural cold cereal	74
Dry soups	124	Canned meat spreads	68
Whipped topping	123	Frozen corn-on-the-cob	35

Television

High Usage	Index	Low Usage	Index
"Hunter"	152	"Hotel"	88
"Highway to Heaven"	138	"Dynasty"	69
"Days of Our Lives"	137	"At the Movies"	64
"Another World"	135	"Nightline"	56

port strong trade measures to protect American jobs and productivity. Already the tough times faced by the timber industry have turned residents into an angry, alienated group.

That view recently found expression in Molalla when lumberman Vern Reisch explained why he voted against a school bond issue. "I'm taxed to death and making less than I ever did," he says. "If our kids were coming out of schools knowing something, it might be different. But the drugs are smoking up the brains of kids before they've had time to develop. The only way to complain is by voting down the school bond issue."

▬▬▬▬▬▬ ZQ 25: GOLDEN PONDS

Gulls, geese and ducks have known about these waterfront locations for some time. Today, Golden Ponds is attracting a population mix of the "three Rs": retirees, resort lovers and rural townsfolk. Once confined to remote areas of Maine and Arkansas, the cluster has spread throughout the country in the last decade. Its communities are neither as affluent nor as age-restrictive as those of the other retirement cluster, Gray Power: two-thirds of the Golden Ponds households earn between $15,000 and $50,000 and about a quarter of the locals are over 55 years old. In Golden Ponds towns, gray-haired women in golf visors typically share beaches with teenage girls in punk shades. And everyone hangs out at the Sunday crafts shows. Golden Ponds is where retirees go when they don't want to live out their final years staring at other retirees.

As a cluster, Golden Ponds has consumer tastes heavily influenced by a rural, middle-class sensibility. Residents tend to buy made-in-Detroit cars—the Renault 18I is the only foreigner among their twenty favorite models. Many Golden Ponds communities rely on cable TV for decent reception, and though they watch few commercial programs at rates above the national average, they're big on spectator sports, enjoying football, track and wrestling on cable. A lot of cluster residents have the time to enjoy leisure activities, and they're more likely than average Americans to fish, knit, play checkers and bowl. At the supermarket, residents show their age in their frequent purchases of denture cleansers, hair-setting products and face powder. They also tend not to make meals a big deal, as evidenced by their purchase of no-fuss foods: TV dinners, frozen chicken, meat extenders and pizza mixes. At mealtimes, residents would rather be out beachcombing.

Golden Ponders are a politically moderate lot, self-described Demo-

ZQ 25: GOLDEN PONDS

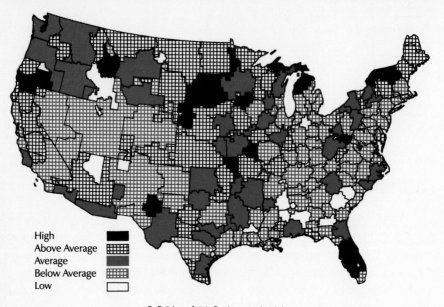

High
Above Average
Average
Below Average
Low

5.2% of U.S. households
Primary age range: 55+
Median household income: $20,140
Median home value: $51,537

Thumbnail Demographics
middle-class rustic towns
single-unit housing
predominantly white couples
high-school educations
blue- and white-collar occupations

Politics
Predominant ideology: moderate
1984 presidential vote: Reagan (71%)
Key issues: trade protection, nuclear arms

Sample Neighborhoods
Cape May, New Jersey (08204)
Ocala, Florida (32670)
Big Spring, Texas (79720)
Needles, California (92363)
St. Michaels Island, Maryland (21663)
Hudson, New York (12534)

Lifestyle

High Usage	Index	Low Usage	Index
Civic clubs	203	Imported champagne	54
Hand tools	201	Domestic tour packages	48
Truck-mounted campers	188	Environmentalist organizations	46
Cable TV	175	Travel by railroad	42
Snuff	158	Microwave ovens	39
Auto loans	142	Burglar alarm systems	34
Horse racing	140	Convertibles	27
Toy-sized dogs	139	Health clubs	26

Magazines/Newspapers

High Usage	Index	Low Usage	Index
World Tennis	230	*New Woman*	50
Family Food Garden	209	*Modern Bride*	44
Audio	178	*New York*	39
True Story	175	*Self*	32

Cars

High Usage	Index	Low Usage	Index
Dodge Diplomats	153	Audi GTs	38
Plymouth Gran Furys	142	Acuras	38
AMC Eagles	140	Alfa Romeos	37
Mercury Grand Marquises	137	Porsche 924s	28
Renault 18ls	135	Mitsubishis	27

Food

High Usage	Index	Low Usage	Index
Canned meat spreads	124	Presweetened cold cereal	86
Frozen waffles	117	Packaged piecrusts	85
TV dinners	114	Canned corned-beef hash	75
Canned ham	113	Natural cold cereal	70

Television

High Usage	Index	Low Usage	Index
"Another World"	179	"CBS Sports Saturday"	91
"Super Password"	158	"NBC Sports World"	90
"The Days of Our Lives"	148	"Magnum, P.I."	87
"The $25,000 Pyramid"	148	"Late Night with David Letterman"	55

crats who feel free to cross party lines and support President Reagan at the ballot box. They take no strong stand on the nuclear arms debate, budget-cutting or foreign-aid programs. In fact, the only issues that seem to turn Golden Ponders into vocal activists are the environment and threats to their rustic communities. "The love of the region over-comes conservatism," says Tony Bevivino, an innkeeper from Cape May, New Jersey. "The whole community rallies around restoring the beachfront and fighting off toxic wastes." At these demonstrations, no one acts their age.

ZQ 26 AGRI-BUSINESS

The farm slump has brought wrenching change to the American Midwest, but the Agri-Business cluster has escaped the worst of it. Centered in America's plains and mountain states, Agri-Business is composed of stable ranching, farming and mining communities. Despite bustling shops and middle-class incomes (46 percent earn between $25,000 and $75,000), Agri-Business faces the same troubles that have so devastated the Grain Belt cluster: low prices and high surpluses that are choking the cluster's towering grain elevators. At coffee shop coun-ters, burly men in coveralls and peak caps commiserate over the bleak economy that's sent most young people packing. In Agri-Business, three-quarters of the residents never made it to college and one-quarter of them are over 55. A Sunday night ritual is the long-distance phone call to children at far-flung colleges and big city jobs.

Befitting a country cluster, Agri-Business consumer surveys indicate an outdoors-oriented lifestyle. Residents are 50 percent more likely than average Americans to go camping, horseback riding and fresh-water fishing. They're second only to Blue Blood Estates in their fondness for gardening, and their harvests often end up in canning jars and freezers, which they purchase at above-average rates. Agri-Business motorists shy away from imports and subcompacts—"you can't plough much snow with one of those little four-cylinder jobs," as one cluster resident explained—and instead purchase mid- and full-sized domestic sedans more often than the general population. Far removed from the nation's commercial centers—as well as national chains and shopping malls—most residents buy through catalogues or the local Sears mail-order outlet. Yet the rural atmosphere breeds a feeling of community that makes Agri-Business one of the leading clusters for civic club member-ship—residents join up at more than twice the national average. "We

ZQ 26: AGRI-BUSINESS

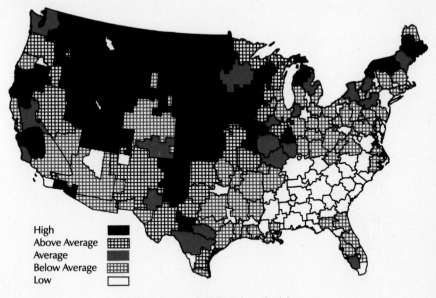

High
Above Average
Average
Below Average
Low

2.1% of U.S. households
Primary age range: 55+
Median household income: $21,363
Median home value: $49,012

Thumbnail Demographics
midscale farming and ranching communities
single-unit housing
predominantly white families
high-school educations
blue-collar and farm occupations

Politics
Predominant ideology: conservative
1984 presidential vote: Reagan (71%)
Key issues: trade protection, fiscal conservatism

Sample Neighborhoods
Clarion, Iowa (50525)
Burlington, Colorado (80807)
Humboldt, Kansas (66748)
Blackfoot, Idaho (83221)
Thief River, North Dakota (56701)
Orland, California (95963)

Lifestyle

High Usage	Index	Low Usage	Index
Hunting	208	Racquetball	45
Standard pickup trucks	188	Sailing	39
Chewing tobacco	170	Bottled water	37
Motorcycles	145	Health clubs	35
Fresh-water fishing	140	Imported champagne	28
Horseback riding	140	U.S. Treasury notes	11
Travel by bus	139	Convertibles	7
Outdoor gardening	130	Depilatories	0

Magazines/Newspapers

High Usage	Index	Low Usage	Index
Grit	259	*New York*	45
Mother Earth News	228	*World Tennis*	42
Hunting	202	*Baby Talk*	36
Sports Afield	195	*The Wall Street Journal*	35

Cars

High Usage	Index	Low Usage	Index
AMC Eagles	211	Jaguars	15
Dodge Diplomats	123	Acuras	14
Chevrolet Impalas	119	Porsche 924s	11
Plymouth Caravelles	117	Mitsubishis	11
Ford LTD Crown Victorias	115	Alfa Romeo Milanos	7

Food

High Usage	Index	Low Usage	Index
Pizza mixes	135	Frozen yogurt	73
Cottage cheese	126	Canned hash	71
Instant tea	125	Frozen waffles	52
Shortening	118	Egg substitutes	44

Television

High Usage	Index	Low Usage	Index
"The Today Show"	131	"Miami Vice"	85
"Falcon Crest"	119	"Murder, She Wrote"	82
Sunday morning interview programs	114	"Friday Night Videos"	63
"Dallas"	111	"Dance Fever"	48

don't like strangers around here," says Bruce Bierma, town manager of Clarion, Iowa. "So we make them our friends."

Politically, Agri-Business residents are friends to the Republicans, too. They gave Ronald Reagan 71 percent of their votes in 1984 and continued to give GOP candidates strong margins of support in 1986. Despite the farm crisis that arrived with the Republican administration, Agri-Business voters continue to exhibit tolerance and applaud the GOP's management capabilities. Their conservatism extends to both cultural and economic issues. According to political surveys, they select the conservative label over the liberal one by a margin of two to one, explaining in part their disapproval of government welfare programs. In Agri-Business, farmers see themselves as small-town capitalists who, even in economic straits, reject government aid as a handout from Uncle Sam.

ZQ 27: EMERGENT MINORITIES

In these mostly black, mostly lower-class and largely neglected neighborhoods, residents are struggling to emerge from poverty. And it is a struggle, played out against a cityscape of decaying projects and graffiti-scrawled stores. In Emergent Minorities, unemployment is high (nearly double the national average at 10 percent), incomes are low (38 percent of the households earn under $10,000 annually) and college graduates are rare (41 percent never completed high school). Almost half the cluster children grow up with a single parent—"We have too many babies having babies" is a frequent lament among residents. And, as in most dense, urban communities, crime is a major problem. Many residents know which alleys are used for drug transactions. But from the vantage of their stoops, they still take comfort in knowing it could be worse—in the hard-core ghettos of Public Assistance, from which many have escaped.

As consumers, residents of Emergent Minorities reflect black, working-class tastes. Compared to the general population, they're twice as likely to buy malt liquor, pop wines and 45-rpm records—comedy, black and jazz types. Because modern supermarkets typically are located outside of their urban neighborhoods, many of the most popular grocery items are those that can be picked up at corner Mom & Pop stores: canned orange juice, candy bars, soft drinks and canned stews. At home, cluster residents tend to watch programs like "Dance Fever" and "CBS Sports Saturday" and are six times as likely to read minority-focused

ZQ 27: EMERGENT MINORITIES

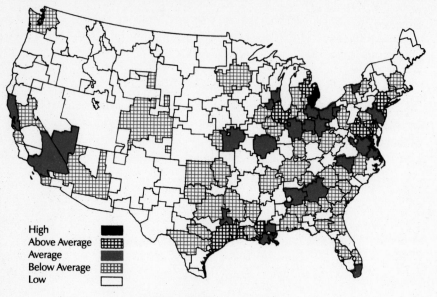

High
Above Average
Average
Below Average
Low

1.7% of U.S. households

Primary age range:	18–34
Median household income:	$22,029
Median home value:	$45,187

Thumbnail Demographics
working-class urban neighborhoods
multi-unit housing
predominantly black, single-parent families
some high-school educations
blue-collar and service occupations

Politics

Predominant ideology:	moderate
1984 presidential vote:	Mondale (75%)
Key issues:	jobs, social programs

Sample Neighborhoods
Anacostia, Washington, D.C. (20020)
Strathmoor, Detroit, Michigan (48227)
East Orange, New Jersey (07017)
South Park, Houston, Texas (77033)
Newburg, Cleveland, Ohio (44105)
Rimpau, Los Angeles, California (90019)

Lifestyle

High Usage	Index	Low Usage	Index
Contemporary black records/tapes	287	Cat food	59
Comedy records/tapes	277	Powerboating	56
Convertibles	241	Mutual funds	54
Menthol filter cigarettes	188	Outdoor gardening	54
Canned tea	162	Ice-skating	51
Watch track & field	161	Health clubs	47
Malt liquor	158	Country clubs	40
Burglar alarms	157	Stamp-collecting	34

Magazines/Newspapers

High Usage	Index	Low Usage	Index
Jet	656	*Grit*	17
Ebony	565	*Skin Diver*	16
Essence	525	*Mother Earth News*	12
Rudder	405	*Skiing*	8

Cars

High Usage	Index	Low Usage	Index
Chevrolet Novas	137	AMC Eagles	29
AMC Alliances	129	Chevrolet Astros	24
Chevrolet Spectrums	126	Ford Aerostars	23
Yugos	126	Subaru DL4s	16
Chevrolet Chevettes	123	Rolls Royces	10

Food

High Usage	Index	Low Usage	Index
Canned orange juice	189	Yogurt	68
Frozen yogurt	172	Pretzels	64
Egg substitutes	124	Canned mushrooms	59
Canned spaghetti	112	Mexican foods	57

Television

High Usage	Index	Low Usage	Index
"Friday Night Videos"	221	"Kate & Allie"	76
"Dance Fever"	200	"Who's the Boss?"	73
"CBS Sports Saturday"	160	"Newhart"	64
"Donahue"	152	"Cheers"	56

magazines like *Jet* and *Ebony*. Emergent Minorities communities are among the nation's worst markets for campers, ski clothing, station wagons and slide projectors. These consumers are just trying to make ends meet.

Like other predominantly black clusters, Emergent Minorities is firmly in the Democratic camp. Next to Black Enterprise voters, residents here identify with the Democratic Party more than in any other cluster, and in 1984 they gave Walter Mondale 75 percent of their vote. Partially out of self-interest, Emergent Minorities leads all clusters in its support of government activism to provide more jobs, better housing and improved welfare programs. Unlike some working-class clusters, which are slipping into the Republican camp, Emergent Minorities sees the Democrats as the party of hope.

ZQ 28: SINGLE CITY BLUES

It has been called "a poor man's bohemia," the home of downscale singles who never gave a thought to becoming yuppies. Single City Blues is made up of America's inner-city neighborhoods ignored by gentrification. Typically located near colleges, this cluster has a split educational profile: while a third have gone to college, another third haven't made it through high school. What unites them is their universally low salaries—57 percent of all the households report incomes under $20,000—defying the usual link between education and affluence. Within ramshackle houses and funky apartments live immigrants, minorities and working-class whites, aging hippies, blue-collar laborers and struggling artists. Despite their rundown neighborhoods, Single City Blues residents still report high subscription rates for magazines like *Harper's, Ms.* and *Atlantic Monthly.*

Consumer surveys of Single City Blues communities reflect this odd profile. As recruits in the natural foods revolution, locals are 50 percent more likely than the average American to shop at health-food stores and are big consumers of frozen yogurt, bottled spring water and natural cheeses. But because they're on tight budgets, they travel by bus and train more than twice as often as the general population. Single City Blues residents would rather jog and ski than bowl or play golf. Activist-minded, they write letters to TV and radio stations, belong to environmental organizations and work for political candidates at above-average rates. When they want to wind down, they turn up the music, buying '60s rock and new-wave records more than twice as often as the general

ZQ 28: SINGLE CITY BLUES

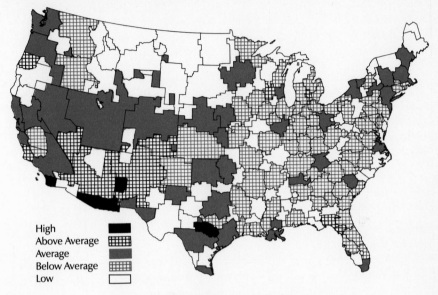

High
Above Average
Average
Below Average
Low

3.3% of U.S. households
Primary age range: 18–34
Median household income: $17,926
Median home value: $62,351

Thumbnail Demographics
downscale city districts
multi-unit housing
racially mixed singles
some college educations
blue- and white-collar occupations

Politics
Predominant ideology: moderate
1984 presidential vote: Mondale (50%)
Key issues: nuclear arms, federal budget

Sample Neighborhoods
Southeast Portland, Oregon (97214)
Mount Rainier, Maryland (20712)
Fort Sutter, California (95816)
Westport, Kansas City, Missouri (64111)
North Austin, Texas (78751)
West Dodge, Nebraska (68131)

Lifestyle

High Usage	Index	Low Usage	Index
Travel by railroad	579	Video games	47
Watch roller derby	309	Hunting	42
Travel by bus	248	Organs	40
Environmentalist		Wood-burning stoves	30
organizations	246	Country clubs	28
New-wave rock records/		Canoes/rowboats	22
tapes	180	Push power mowers	20
Downhill skiing	176	Microwave ovens	0
Personal loans	142		
Backgammon	135		

Magazines/Newspapers

High Usage	Index	Low Usage	Index
Harper's	252	*Flying*	55
Modern Bride	243	*Hunting*	48
Architectural Digest	238	*Organic Gardening*	42
Atlantic Monthly	236	*Nation's Business*	41

Cars

High Usage	Index	Low Usage	Index
Mitsubishi Mirages	115	Buick Electras	34
VW Sciroccos	105	Pontiac 6000s	34
Toyota Tercels	103	Mercury Grand Marquises	29
Mitsubishi Cordias	102	AMC Eagles	25
Honda Civic 1200/1300s	101	Mercury Sables	11

Food

High Usage	Index	Low Usage	Index
Canned corned-beef hash	135	Presweetened cold cereal	81
Whole-wheat bread	134	Cheese spreads	74
Low-fat/skim milk	121	Meat tenderizers	68
Packaged pasta	104	Children's vitamins	67

Television

High Usage	Index	Low Usage	Index
"Dance Fever"	157	"Hunter"	85
"Friday Night Videos"	155	"Another World"	82
"Nightline"	153	"Simon & Simon"	74
"Miami Vice"	143	"Days of Our Lives"	70

population. A favorite pastime is hanging out at the local bar with a jukebox full of the Grateful Dead.

With its populace of unattached, working-class residents, Single City Blues is a Democratic-leaning cluster. Voters are strong believers in the Democrats as the party of compassion and of leftist special-interest groups whose members tend to live in Single City Blues. Yet surveys also find cluster residents opting for the GOP's superiority in public policy issues, and Walter Mondale only broke even here in the 1984 balloting. As in most clusters with a lot of rootless young people, there's usually a low voter turnout in Single City Blues. Though they dislike the conservative social agenda, they sometimes don't vote in high enough numbers to make their views count.

ZQ 29: MINES & MILLS

The sight of smokeless smokestacks has come to represent Mines & Mills, the nation's cluster of mining villages and steeltowns. Concentrated in the Northeast between New England and Lake Michigan, these company towns prospered during the heyday of America's industrial age, from the turn of the century to as recently as 1960. But foreign competition has forced many Mines & Mills towns into retrenchment. Today, 46 percent of the cluster's households earn under $20,000 annually. In many of these grimy neighborhoods dwarfed by rusting factories, the local population is aging, the tax base is declining and local shops and restaurants are boarding up their doors. Many are on the way to becoming ghost towns.

In terms of consumption patterns, Mines and Mills resembles other lower-middle-class clusters. Residents buy above-average quantities of processed foods: canned stews and pastas, jarred vegetables and spaghetti sauce. They take home lots of cleaning products to scrub off the soot that coats many homes and streets. Bathroom cleaners, rug deodorizers, floor wax and in-bowl toilet cleaners are all bought at above-average rates. Having produced the steel for Detroit's factories, area motorists tend to buy AMC Eagles, Dodge Diplomats and Mercury Lynxes. As for recreation, the sports-minded Mines & Mills dwellers are fond of activities that can be accompanied by a six-pack of beer: fishing, bowling and camping. These are the Americans whose family rooms are graced with stuffed deer heads on the wall, *Sports Afield* and *Popular Mechanics* on the easy chair and hiking boots in the corner.

In Mines & Mills, the economic situation has produced the politics

ZQ 29: MINES & MILLS

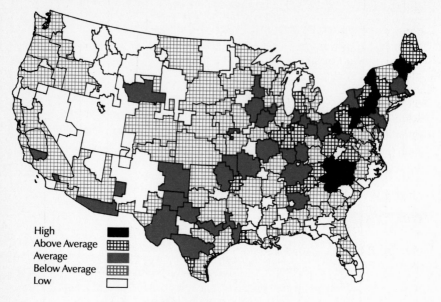

High
Above Average
Average
Below Average
Low

2.8% of U.S. households
Primary age range: 45–64
Median household income: $21,537
Median home value: $46,325

Thumbnail Demographics
lower-middle-class milltowns
single-unit housing
predominantly white families
high-school educations
blue-collar jobs

Politics
Predominant ideology: moderate
1984 presidential vote: Reagan (75%)
Key issues: social programs, moral tradition

Sample Neighborhoods
Monessen, Pennsylvania (15062)
Thomasville, North Carolina (27360)
Millville, New Jersey (08332)
Sebring, Ohio (44672)
New Philadelphia, Pennsylvania (17959)
Franklin, Massachusetts (03235)

Lifestyle

High Usage	Index	Low Usage	Index
Cigars	232	Valid passports	34
Wood-burning stoves	204	Environmentalist organizations	24
Outboard powerboats	198	Sailing	18
Watch pro wrestling	197	Common stock	12
Chewing tobacco	187	Comedy records/tapes	7
Watch rodeo	170	Microwave ovens	0
Bowling	167	Mutual funds	0
Dog food	151	Country clubs	0

Magazines/Newspapers

High Usage	Index	Low Usage	Index
Industry Week	328	*Gentleman's Quarterly*	13
Grit	233	*World Tennis*	0
Popular Mechanics	195	*New York*	0
Sports Afield	191	*Forbes*	0

Cars

High Usage	Index	Low Usage	Index
Chevrolet Spectrums	199	Acura Integras	26
AMC Eagles	196	VW Cabriolets	22
Pontiac Bonnevilles	155	Alfa Romeos	15
Dodge Diplomats	145	Jaguar XJ-6s	12
Mercury Lynxes	144	Mitsubishis	11

Food

High Usage	Index	Low Usage	Index
Canned meat spreads	140	Fresh chicken	80
Canned corned-beef hash	133	Whole-wheat bread	66
Toaster products	127	Natural cold cereal	63
Packaged piecrusts	120	Mexican foods	57

Television

High Usage	Index	Low Usage	Index
"Loving"	191	"CBS Sports Saturday"	79
"Ryan's Hope"	167	"NBC Sports World"	78
"Guiding Light"	158	"Nightline"	70
"Another World"	157	"The Today Show"	69

of turmoil. People here are uncertain about their communities' future, and political allegiances have faded. Once solidly Democratic, Mines and Mills voters could muster only 25 percent of their 1984 vote for Walter Mondale, and today the cluster is evenly divided between Democrats and Republicans on the one hand and undecided voters on the other. According to political surveys, Mines & Mills voters express a fine blend of economic liberalism and right-wing populism: they support government welfare programs for the disadvantaged, oppose free-trade policies and express isolationist tendencies when it comes to foreign policy. But like other rural, working-class clusters, Mines & Mills residents suffer from apathy, with one of the highest proportions of unregistered voters in the nation. The remoteness of their communities and their dependence on paternalistic manufacturers—now departed—have weakened their solidarity with the liberal national trade-union movement. When they're out of work, Mines & Mills residents have a short political attention span.

▬▬▬▬▬▬ ZQ 30: BACK-COUNTRY FOLKS

They live in the nation's backwater regions: Appalachia, the Ozarks and the southern uplands. They work as lumberjacks, shrimp seiners, oil-rig workers and dairy farmers. And there's a kind of shabby gentility to these Back-Country Folks. Residents have modest educations (47 percent never completed high school), large households (49 percent have children) and low incomes (37 percent earn under $15,000 annually). Still they have a multigenerational pride in their lives and livelihoods. A lot of kids grow up to stay down on the farm. At coffee shops, Back-Country Folks discuss stockyards as animatedly as city dwellers debate stock markets.

"This community seems lost in time," says author Peter Jenkins of Spring Hill, Tennessee, in a comment apropos to the entire cluster. "The moral values have been constant for the past one hundred years. People dress like they have for many decades. They get attached to their old pickups and never want to get rid of them."

Democratic conservatives in their political thinking, Back-Country Folks nonetheless voted for President Reagan by a two-to-one margin in the 1984 election and continue to give him high marks. Like other rural populists, Back-Country Folks are less concerned with budget-balancing than with government programs for the unemployed. They support the party that's more generous with government aid—usually

ZQ 30: BACK-COUNTRY FOLKS

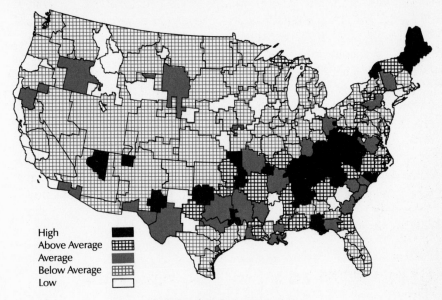

High
Above Average
Average
Below Average
Low

3.4% of U.S. households
Primary age groups: 35–44 and 65+
Median household income: $19,843
Median home value: $41,030

Thumbnail Demographics
downscale rural and remote towns
single-unit housing
predominantly white families
some high-school educations
blue-collar jobs

Politics
Predominant ideology: moderate
1984 presidential vote: Reagan (68%)
Key issues: poverty, moral tradition

Sample Neighborhoods
Dothan, Alabama (36301)
Spring Hill, Tennessee (37174)
Caribou, Maine (04736)
Ball Ground, Georgia (30107)
Mount Airy, North Carolina (27030)
Larose, Louisiana (70373)

Lifestyle

High Usage	Index	Low Usage	Index
Compact pickups	190	Comedy records/tapes	35
Canning jars and lids	172	Travel agents	35
Chewing tobacco	168	Live theater	34
Wood-burning stoves	162	Imported champagne	34
Snuff	157	Money-market funds	30
Civic clubs	145	Health clubs	29
Hunting	145	Downhill skiing	25
Cable TV	141	Environmental organizations	18

Magazines/Newspapers

High Usage	Index	Low Usage	Index
True Story	208	*Omni*	45
Southern Living	162	*Fortune*	37
Outdoor Life	152	*Inc.*	31
Soap Opera Digest	135	*Gourmet*	22

Cars

High Usage	Index	Low Usage	Index
Dodge Diplomats	160	Ferraris	13
Pontiac Bonnevilles	140	Mitsubishi Tredias	10
Chevrolet Monte Carlos	137	Mitsubishi Cordias	9
AMC Eagles	136	Pinin Farinas	9
Ford Crown Victorias	136	Rolls Royces	5

Food

High Usage	Index	Low Usage	Index
Canned meat spreads	207	Instant soups	73
Canned orange juice	158	Low-fat/skim milk	54
TV dinners	125	Canned corned beef hash	41
White bread	120	Rye/pumpernickel bread	17

Television

High Usage	Index	Low Usage	Index
"Knots Landing"	152	"Late Night with David Letterman"	73
"The Young and the Restless"	151	"Cheers"	71
"Dallas"	127	"Lifestyles of the Rich and Famous"	67
"Wheel of Fortune"	114	"St. Elsewhere"	65

the Democrats. Yet that backing rarely extends to campaign contributions: in these rural hamlets, constituents just can't afford it.

Nor can Back-Country Folks purchase products at rates too far above the national average. They fill their supermarket carts with low-cost, processed foods like white bread, frozen potato products, pork sausages and TV dinners—all slightly more often than the general population. And the number of large families in the cluster influences their frequent purchase of children's clothing, baby shampoo and children's pain relievers. Residents show a preference for products you'd expect in a rural cluster: they're more likely than average Americans to buy compact pickups, canning jars, chewing tobacco and cable television. Their idea of a good time is attending a Tupperware party or a country music concert. Their two favorite magazines are *True Story* and *Southern Living,* and they'd rather watch "Knots Landing" than "Cheers." Drunk driving is not a serious problem here, as Back-Country Folks has one of the lowest liquor consumption rates: less than one-third of the U.S. average. With much of the cluster located in the nation's Bible Belt, many residents can't even buy a drink in their communities.

ZQ 31: NORMA RAE-VILLE

Nicknamed for the Sally Field movie about a union organizer in a southern textile mill, Norma Rae-Ville consists of the nation's milltowns and industrial suburbs sprinkled throughout the Appalachian and Piedmont mountains. Residents work in nondurable manufacturing more than any other field and thus have been hit hard by foreign competition in the '80s. Most workers are nonunion, poorly educated (49 percent never completed high school) and accustomed to low-salaried manual labor (38 percent earn under $15,000 annually). In the milltown of Dalton, Georgia, even carpet factories paying meager $3.35-an-hour wages are closing down. For too many workers in Norma Rae-Ville, there's never been an American Dream.

As befits its downscale lifestyle, Norma Rae-Ville consumes more basic necessities than luxury items. Shoppers buy twice as much canned stew and meat spread as the general population and above-average amounts of canned ham, canned spaghetti, rice and white bread. These racially mixed residents also throw into their grocery bags *The National Enquirer, Southern Living, Jet* and *Ebony.* Norma Rae-Ville is the kind of southern outpost where the good ol' boys chew tobacco, watch wrestling and install shock absorbers on their cars—all at rates above

ZQ 31: NORMA RAE-VILLE

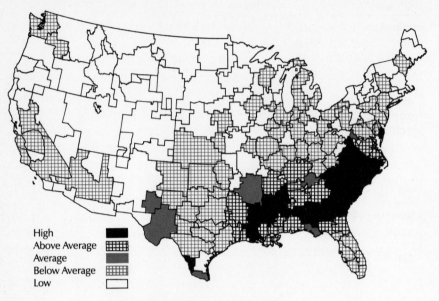

High
Above Average
Average
Below Average
Low

2.3% of U.S. households
Primary age groups: 18–24 and 45–54
Median household income: $18,559
Median home value: $36,556

Thumbnail Demographics
lower-middle-class milltowns
single-unit housing
racially mixed families
some high-school educations
blue-collar jobs

Politics
Predominant ideology: conservative
1984 presidential vote: Reagan (69%)
Key issues: trade protection, jobs

Sample Neighborhoods
Dalton, Georgia (30720)
Danville, Virginia (24541)
Rock Hill, North Carolina (29730)
Burlington, North Carolina (27215)
Alexander, Alabama (35010)
Anderson, South Carolina (29621)

Lifestyle

High Usage	Index	Low Usage	Index
Feminine hygiene sprays	196	Mutual funds	41
Asthma relief remedies	180	Chess	41
Chewing tobacco	175	Travel by domestic airline	40
Watch pro wrestling	175	Bottled water	35
Energy drinks	163	Downhill skiing	30
Sleeping tablets	154	Camping equipment	18
Compact pickup trucks	136	Valid passports	16
Menthol cigarettes	134	Convertibles	11

Magazines/Newspapers

High Usage	Index	Low Usage	Index
Southern Living	258	*Architectural Digest*	2
Ebony	228	*Metropolitan Home*	0
National Enquirer	174	*Dun's Business Month*	0
Weight Watchers	126	*Town & Country*	0

Cars

High Usage	Index	Low Usage	Index
Pontiac Bonnevilles	184	Subaru RXs	28
Chevrolet Spectrums	174	Jaguars	26
Pontiac T-1000s	169	Ferraris	25
Buick LeSabres	135	Saab 9000s	23
Buick Regals	127	Mitsubishis	11

Food

High Usage	Index	Low Usage	Index
Canned stews	248	Natural cheese	78
Canned spaghetti	131	Whole-wheat bread	72
Frozen pies/cakes/pastries	117	Yogurt	48
Bottled barbecue sauce	111	Low-fat/skim milk	41

Television

High Usage	Index	Low Usage	Index
"As the World Turns"	205	"Night Court"	75
"Loving"	168	"The Today Show"	72
"Knots Landing"	149	"St. Elsewhere"	70
"Falcon Crest"	129	"The Tonight Show"	69

the norm. And the women are heavy purchasers of hair-styling combs, home permanents and feminine hygiene deodorant sprays. Without the money for private physicians, residents treat themselves with laxatives, asthma remedies and cough syrup. They rarely travel, especially abroad —but when they do, they're more inclined to stay in a Days Inn than a Holiday Inn, to eat at a Hardee's than a Friendly's, to go fishing or hunting than play tennis or ski. If they need special clothes for a sport, these residents aren't interested in trying it.

Norma Rae-Ville's economic depression has prompted cluster voters to identify themselves as Democrats, but prevailing apathy makes them only lip-service partisans. As Dalton congressional aide Robin Sponberger puts it, "Most of your millworkers are just existing from day to day and aren't interested in getting politically involved." Nationwide, these residents feel squeezed. In opinion surveys questioning which party is best able to handle the nation's toughest problems, they respond with "both" or "neither." Like other southern populists, Norma Rae-Ville residents relate to the problems of the poor and the unemployed, supporting trade protectionist policies out of self-interest. Foreign imports are taking away their jobs.

▰▰▰▰▰▰▰ ZQ 32: SMALLTOWN DOWNTOWN

A century ago, the nation's railroads connected booming factory towns—from Binghamton to Baton Rouge, from Savannah to Spokane. Skilled immigrant labor moved into working-class neighborhoods and built prosperous middle-class lives. But the technological revolution bypassed these industrial communities, and today Smalltown Downtown represents inner-city areas left in the dust after the great suburban migration. In this blue-collar cluster, 52 percent of the residents make less than $20,000, 41 percent haven't finished high school and 42 percent rent apartments. While their more successful peers have fled for a home in the 'burbs, Smalltown Downtowners remain renters living near the plant. They'd rather hang out on a city stoop.

With lower-middle-class budgets, Smalltown Downtowners simply can't afford extravagant tastes. They tend to travel less by plane or train than average Americans, and they buy few cars at above-average rates. Their idea of a vacation is to go camping, fishing and hiking, and their home-based leisure pursuits would make a preppy blanch: they like to watch wrestling and Roller Derby, go out for a cafeteria dinner or a Tupperware party and listen to gospel and country music. Locals are

ZQ 32: SMALLTOWN DOWNTOWN

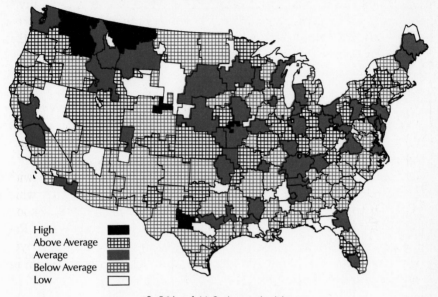

High
Above Average
Average
Below Average
Low

2.5% of U.S. households
Primary age groups: 18–24 and 65+
Median household income: $17,206
Median home value: $42,225

Thumbnail Demographics
industrial inner-city districts
multi-unit housing
predominantly white families and singles
high-school educations
mixed blue- and white-collar jobs

Politics
Predominant ideology: moderate
1984 presidential vote: Reagan (62%)
Key issues: trade protection, jobs

Sample Neighborhoods
Parkersburg, West Virginia (26101)
Joplin, Missouri (64801)
North Central Spokane, Washington (99205)
Murray Hill, Jacksonville, Florida (32205)
East San Diego, California (92105)
Dayton, Ohio (45410)

Lifestyle

High Usage	Index	Low Usage	Index
Salt-water fishing rods	205	Travel by chartered plane	40
Watch pro wrestling	202	Imported champagne	38
Cafeterias	196	Motorcycles	37
Gospel records/tapes	193	Host cocktail parties	35
Outboard motors	192	Chewing tobacco	30
Hair tonic/dressing	178	Travel/entertainment cards	29
Watch Roller Derby	153	Racquetball	25
Fraternal orders	138	Money-market funds	18

Magazines/Newspapers

High Usage	Index	Low Usage	Index
Colonial Homes	211	*Atlantic Monthly*	0
True Story	207	*Harper's*	0
Southern Living	186	*Barron's*	0
Sporting News	163	*Skin Diver*	0

Cars

High Usage	Index	Low Usage	Index
Isuzus	119	Fiats	26
Chevrolet Chevettes	111	Mercury Sables	12
Plymouth Gran Furys	109	Bertone X19s	12
Chevrolet Spectrums	108	Rolls Royces	11
Pontiac Bonnevilles	107	Ferraris	7

Food

High Usage	Index	Low Usage	Index
Canned meat spreads	194	Whole-wheat bread	80
Packaged instant potatoes	143	Instant iced tea	74
Nondairy creamers	126	Mexican foods	71
TV dinners	117	Natural cold cereal	68

Television

High Usage	Index	Low Usage	Index
"Scrabble"	165	"Donahue"	79
"The Today Show"	143	"Newhart"	79
"NBC Sports World"	127	"Late Night with David Letterman"	66
"ABC Wide World of Sports"	115	"The Tonight Show"	53

trusting enough to install burglar alarms at a rate 40 percent below the national average and to buy products from door-to-door salesreps at a rate 125 percent above the norm. Despite their bleak surroundings, Smalltown Downtowners are more civic-minded than the general population, belonging to fraternal orders, working for political candidates and contributing to their local hospitals. Their credo is to give what they can.

Politically, Smalltown Downtown is a moderate place where voters include both Democrats and Republicans. Although 62 percent backed President Reagan in 1984, close to that percentage supported Democratic candidates in 1986. With many Smalltown Downtown communities dotting the nation's Bible Belt, residents happily support the evangelical right and the recent presidential candidacy of Rev. Robertson. On issues involving foreign policy and nuclear arms, however, they rarely take strong stands. The downtowners of a town like Parkersburg, West Virginia, are more interested in local problems than international diplomacy. Explains local newspaper editor Jim Snyder: "The people here are just more concerned about a prison riot at Moundsville Prison up the road than an American journalist being held in Beirut."

ZQ 33: GRAIN BELT

The farm crisis has devastated the Grain Belt, the cluster of America's most sparsely populated rural communities. In tiny farm towns throughout the Midwest and Northern Plains, an increasing number of households are reporting "negative incomes." Unlike its cluster twin, Agri-Business, Grain Belt is characterized by smaller family farms, lower incomes (25 percent of the households earn under $10,000) and minimal educational levels (39 percent failed to complete high school.) With the increasing number of farm foreclosures, whole communities have quietly slid into poverty: the storefronts boarded up, the streets empty of traffic, families moving away. "We're in a period of hurting," says Methodist minister Gary Byrd of Early, Iowa, and it could be said of many Grain Belt communities. "People are just hunkering down and trying to work through it."

Living on the edge of solvency, many Grain Belt residents have reverted to their self-sufficient pioneer roots. To provide for their family farmsteads, they buy guns, gas chain saws and hand tool kits twice as often as the general population. They lead the nation in ownership of cats, no doubt to deal with the mice attracted to the cluster's grain stores. With fresh meat and vegetables available on the farm, big sellers

ZQ 33: GRAIN BELT

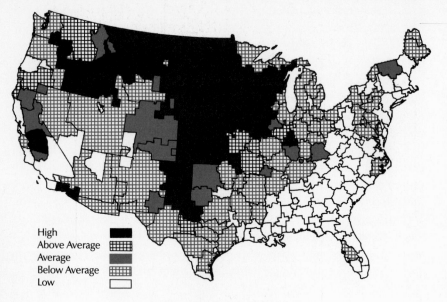

High
Above Average
Average
Below Average
Low

1.3% of U.S. households

Primary age range:	55+
Median household income:	$21,698
Median home value:	$45,852

Thumbnail Demographics

sparsely populated farm communities
single-unit housing
predominantly white families
high-school educations
blue-collar/farm occupations

Politics

Predominant ideology:	moderate
1984 presidential vote:	Reagan (70%)
Key issues:	moral tradition, fiscal conservatism

Sample Neighborhoods

Early, Iowa (50535)
Lehr, North Dakota (58460)
Jetmore, Kansas (67854)
Butte, Nebraska (68722)
Granville, Iowa (51022)
Chokio, Minnesota (56221)

Lifestyle

High Usage	Index	Low Usage	Index
Electric fry pans	263	Jazz records/tapes	24
Second mortgages	256	24-hour teller cards	22
Gas chain saws	210	Travel by cruise ship	20
Motorcycles	197	Irish whiskey	18
Cats	172	Sailing	12
Watch rodeo	171	Common stock	6
Vinyl flooring	171	Christmas/Chanukah clubs	2
Canning jars	166	Burglar alarm systems	0

Magazines/Newspapers

High Usage	Index	Low Usage	Index
Grit	398	*Harper's*	6
Lakeland Boating	222	*Scientific American*	2
Organic Gardening	219	*Food & Wine*	0
Hunting	168	*Audio*	0

Cars

High Usage	Index	Low Usage	Index
Chrysler E-Classes	191	Mitsubishi Galants	1
AMC Eagles	183	Mitsubishi Mirages	1
Chevrolet Impalas	168	Rolls Royces	0
Ford Crown Victorias	167	Yugos	0
Dodge Diplomats	167	Bertones	0

Food

High Usage	Index	Low Usage	Index
Canned stews	148	Frozen dessert pies	69
Powdered fruit drinks	130	Frozen waffles	54
Cookie-baking chips	128	TV dinners	54
Frozen pizzas	118	Frozen corn-on-the-cob	49

Television

High Usage	Index	Low Usage	Index
"Simon & Simon"	129	"Hotel"	61
"Magnum, P.I."	126	"At the Movies"	61
"The Today Show"	125	"Entertainment Tonight"	50
"CBS Evening News"	122	"Dynasty"	48

in cluster markets are starchy processed foods: cake mixes, white bread, frozen pizzas, canned stews and spaghetti. A list of Grain Belter's favorite magazines captures the cluster's rugged personality: *Grit, Organic Gardening* and *Hunting.* These Americans trust in providence to protect them: their purchase rate for burglar alarms is zero.

In Grain Belt, rural independence translates to Republican Party allegiance. There are more than two GOP supporters for every Democrat in these farm towns. In 1984, Walter Mondale could scrape together barely 30 percent of their ballots, and cluster voters ranked dead last in their commitment to the Democratic Party. But economic desperation has tempered the cluster's GOP affections. Ronald Reagan recently received only a middling approval rating among Grain Belt residents, and his administration has earned low marks for its economic policies. Still, cluster residents are more conservative than any others on issues involving moral values, and they continue to vote as rightest populists. In Grain Belt, as one resident put it, "People go to church, believe in God and are loyal to the Republican Party."

ZQ 34: HEAVY INDUSTRY

The decline of American manufacturing has resulted in the deterioration of Heavy Industry, the nation's inner-city factory neighborhoods. Concentrated in the older industrial cities of the Northeast, these working-class districts typically were settled by European immigrants at the turn of the century. Today, Heavy Industry communities report high numbers of Hispanics (14 percent) and the foreign born (13 percent)—both figures are more than double the national average. And its population is aging (25 percent are over 55 years old) and poor (27 percent earn under $10,000 annually). On streets lined with sagging duplexes and rowhouses, locals debate the value of bulldozing a block that resembles a war zone. But most houses remain standing for the same reason that Heavy Industry residents go to the same bars, bingo games and fraternal clubs year after year.

"The people here are comfortable with the niche they've carved out for themselves," says Father Stanley Ulman, a Catholic pastor in Hamtramck, Michigan. "They still have their cronies, their family and the places that are familiar to them."

Heavily Democratic from its days as an immigrant entry point, Heavy Industry has turned into a moderate swing group. No doubt the loss of union jobs has reduced labor's traditionally liberal influence on its blue-

ZQ 34: HEAVY INDUSTRY

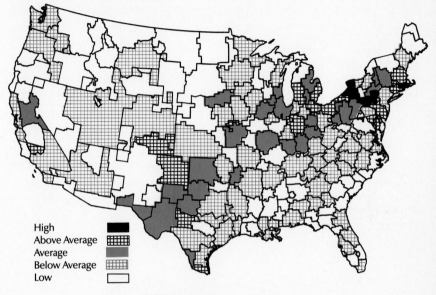

High
Above Average
Average
Below Average
Low

2.8% of U.S. households
Primary age group: 55+
Median household income: $18,325
Median home value: $39,537

Thumbnail Demographics
lower-working-class urban neighborhoods
ethnic families and singles
some high-school educations
blue-collar jobs

Politics
Predominant ideology: moderate
1984 presidential vote: Reagan (59%)
Key issues: moral tradition, social programs

Sample Neighborhoods
Hamtramck, Detroit, Michigan (48212)
Ironbound, Newark, New Jersey (07105)
New Bedford, Massachusetts (02740)
Pawtucket, Rhode Island (02860)
Kedzi Grange, Chicago, Illinois (60618)
Southside Scranton, Pennsylvania (18505)

Lifestyle

High Usage	Index	Low Usage	Index
Travel by railroad	230	Gas credit cards	62
Asthma relief remedies	205	Circular saws	61
Wall paneling	188	Video games	60
Nonfilter cigarettes	175	Digital watches	58
Cat litter	152	Billiards	57
Ale	142	Compact pickup trucks	51
Bowling balls	137	Water-skiing	42
Watch auto-racing	136	Mutual funds	27

Magazines/Newspapers

High Usage	Index	Low Usage	Index
Lakeland Boating	222	*Nation's Business*	26
The Star	184	*Harper's*	25
Barron's	168	*Sunset*	10
Modern Bride	161	*Grit*	3

Cars

High Usage	Index	Low Usage	Index
Yugos	140	Mercedes 300Ds	23
Renaults	133	Jaguars	23
AMCs	129	Audis	22
Plymouth Horizons	117	Porsches	21
Dodge Aries	115	BMW 5 Series	20

Food

High Usage	Index	Low Usage	Index
Instant iced tea	150	Mexican foods	69
Meat sticks	140	Pizza mixes	68
English muffins	129	Frozen yogurt	59
Canned spaghetti	121	Canned chili	55

Television

High Usage	Index	Low Usage	Index
"Nightline"	191	"Cheers"	93
"St. Elsewhere"	142	"Simon & Simon"	85
"Donahue"	133	"The Today Show"	77
"Cagney & Lacey"	120	"The Facts of Life"	70

collar workers. In addition, Heavy Industry's voters, 39 percent of whom are Catholic, are less accepting of the Democrats' support of gay rights and pro-abortion programs. On foreign-policy issues, Heavy Industry voters are moderate, their protectionist sentiments tempered by ties to the Old Country. "Middle-of-the-road" is their favorite ideological label. But they resoundingly support government programs for the poor, the jobless and the victims of urban decay. In Heavy Industry, such programs can mean the difference between living above or below the poverty line.

As consumers, Heavy Industry residents have tastes that reflect their age and modest means. They make above-average purchases of denture cleansers, Medicare insurance, women's girdles and pain-relieving rubs, and they rely on under-$10,000 cars for transportation. These family-oriented communities host parties 50 percent more frequently than the general population and purchase instant-developing cameras at twice the national average—frequently to capture the relatives on film. When it comes to athletic activities, they'd rather bowl than do anything else. In Heavy Industry, the favorite alcoholic drinks are Cold Duck, ale and port—all purchased at rates 30 percent above the norm. On their tight budgets, these residents try to save money by putting up their own wall paneling, installing their own shock absorbers and using kerosene room heaters rather than running up stiff electric bills. During Hamtramck's long, broiling summers, resident Leo Kirpluk will use his air conditioner only at night. "You do what you can with what you've got," he says in what might be the cluster motto.

▆▆▆▆▆▆▆ ZQ 35: SHARE CROPPERS

When Jimmy Carter put Plains, Georgia, on the map, he also brought to the national consciousness the lifestyle of southern hamlets designated Share Croppers. Found throughout the states comprising the Old Confederacy, Share Croppers is a cluster of crossroads villages typically devoted to dairy farming, pulpwood cutting and chicken breeding. In recent years, the Sunbelt migration and nonunion labor pool have attracted light industry, making Share Croppers the nation's largest rural cluster. But outdated racial attitudes keep this cluster from becoming part of the Progressive South. Predominantly poor blacks comprise 15 percent of the population: in Plains, they literally live on the other side of the railroad tracks in shanties and apartment projects a quantum leap away from the white clapboard homes of their white neighbors. And

ZQ 35: SHARE CROPPERS

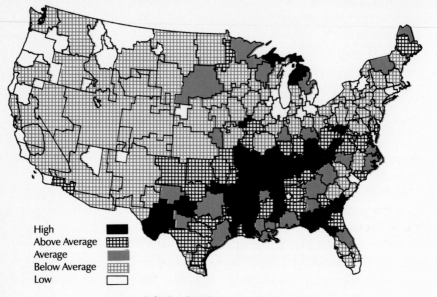

High
Above Average
Average
Below Average
Low

4.0% of U.S. households

Primary age range: 55+
Median household income: $16,854
Median home value: $33,917

Thumbnail Demographics
downscale rural villages
single-unit housing
racially mixed families
grade-school educations
blue-collar and farm jobs

Politics
Predominant ideology: conservative
1984 presidential vote: Reagan (64%)
Key issues: moral traditions, jobs

Sample Neighborhoods
Plains, Georgia (31780)
Shiloh, Virginia (27974)
Okeechobee, Florida (33472)
Cold Spring, Texas (77331)
Booneville, Arizona (72927)
Oak Hill, West Virginia (45656)

Lifestyle

High Usage	Index	Low Usage	Index
Chewing tobacco	259	Bottled water	25
Outboard powerboat	228	Imported brandy/cognac	20
Snuff	216	Sailing	19
Hunting	186	Environmentalist organizations	15
Gospel records/tapes	159	Downhill skiing	14
Wood-burning stoves	151	Jazz records/tapes	13
Wall paneling	149	Health clubs	10
Laxatives	141	Microwave ovens	8

Magazines/Newspapers

High Usage	Index	Low Usage	Index
Southern Living	222	*Stereo Review*	21
Colonial Homes	157	*Bon Appetit*	19
Hunting	155	*Atlantic Monthly*	15
Decorating and Craft Ideas	130	*The Wall Street Journal*	13

Cars

High Usage	Index	Low Usage	Index
Dodge Diplomats	164	Alfa Romeos	14
Pontiac Bonnevilles	155	VW Cabriolets	13
Chevrolet Impalas	152	Porsche 911s	12
Lincoln Town Cars	148	Saab 9000s	11
Ford LTD Crown Victorias	148	Mitsubishis	9

Food

High Usage	Index	Low Usage	Index
Deviled ham	155	Frozen entrees	56
Canned orange juice	146	Instant iced tea	55
Snack cakes	127	Yogurt	51
Pork sausage	110	English muffins	44

Television

High Usage	Index	Low Usage	Index
"As the World Turns"	194	"Entertainment Tonight"	68
"The Today Show"	154	"Late Night with David Letterman"	67
"Wheel of Fortune"	138	"The Tonight Show"	57
"Knots Landing"	136	"At the Movies"	53

community life revolves around churches and schools, most of which are racially segregated—by choice, according to Hugh Carter, Jimmy's cousin and a local antique-store owner. "This is still a transition period," he likes to say. "It'll take twenty-five years before the blacks can go along equally with the whites."

Other Share Croppers communities echo that view, and their political attitudes are characterized by conservative populism. President Reagan captured almost two-thirds of the cluster's ballots in 1984—Plains was an exception—but in 1986 voters declared their preference for Democratic candidates by a slim majority. Unlike other downscale clusters, Share Croppers is not impressed with the Democratic Party's links with "ordinary people." It's more concerned with the influence of liberal special-interest groups among Democrats than with the Moral Majority faction within Republican circles. In Share Croppers communities, religious fundamentalism is considered a virtue. "We don't like trash on TV or in magazines—those with a lot of violence or sex—that leave nothing to the imagination," explains Betty Lou Hagerson from the cluster hamlet of Concord, Georgia. "That's how the Scripture teaches us."

Such down-home farm values color the consuming habits of Share Croppers residents. They generally drive pickups and large, American-made sedans like the Ford LTD, Chevrolet Impala and Pontiac Bonneville. They tend to be homebodies—with a low rate of domestic and international travel—and prefer magazines that are home- and hobby-centered: *Southern Living, Hunting* and *Decorating and Craft Ideas.* At the grocery store, processed foods that can't be raised on the farm are popular: cold cuts, snack cakes, egg substitutes, powdered soft drinks and barbecue sauces. At diners, they're the sunburned men who eat without taking off their John Deere caps. To Share Croppers, relaxation means chewing, hunting, fishing and listening to country and gospel music. In these towns, change doesn't happen much—and people like it that way.

ZQ 36: DOWNTOWN DIXIE-STYLE

Centered in several dozen big southern cities, Downtown Dixie-Style is a cluster of downscale neighborhoods in transition. The population is half black, half grade-school-educated and mostly lower class (46 percent earn under $15,000 annually.) Yet in these poor but dignified neighborhoods, cluster residents have an average rate of sending children to college. Depending on the community, you may find young whites mov-

ZQ 36: DOWNTOWN DIXIE-STYLE

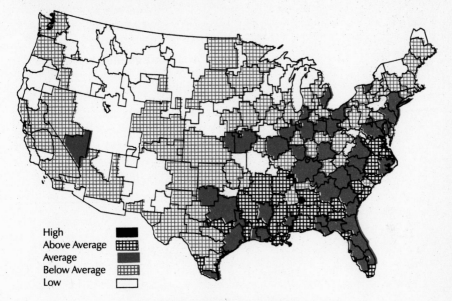

High ■
Above Average ▦
Average ▦
Below Average ▦
Low ▢

3.4% of U.S. households
Primary age ranges: 18–24 and 65+
Median household income: $15,204
Median home value: $35,301

Thumbnail Demographics

downscale inner-city neighborhoods
predominantly black singles and one-parent families
aging apartments
some high-school educations
blue-collar and service jobs

Politics

Predominant ideology: liberal
1984 presidential vote: Mondale (72%)
Key issues: poverty, social programs

Sample Neighborhoods

West Jackson, Mississippi (39209)
Lynchburg, Virginia (24504)
Selma, Alabama (36701)
Galveston, Texas (77550)
Lafayette, Louisiana (70501)
Fayetteville, North Carolina (28301)

Lifestyle

High Usage	Index	Low Usage	Index
Soul records/tapes	262	Desktop calculators	37
Jazz records/tapes	257	Men's tennis clothing	29
Malt liquor	248	Target shooting	28
Movie cameras	194	U.S. savings bonds	15
Men's leisure suits	187	Gas chain saws	15
Watch wrestling	182	Convertibles	10
Laxatives	146	Country clubs	10
Cafeterias	126	Microwaves	0

Magazines/Newspapers

High Usage	Index	Low Usage	Index
Ebony	414	*Ms.*	19
Jet	409	*Grit*	16
Soap Opera Digest	234	*Sunset*	2
GQ	153	*Natural History*	0

Cars

High Usage	Index	Low Usage	Index
Isuzus	124	Renault 18ls	29
Chevrolet Spectrums	114	Chevrolet Sprints	27
Yugos	105	Subaru DL4s	21
Bertone X19s	102	Ferraris	18
Peugeots	100	AMC Eagles	11

Food

High Usage	Index	Low Usage	Index
Canned stews	167	Frozen yogurt	67
Meat/fish extenders	147	Instant rice	63
Canned corned-beef hash	140	Low-fat/skim milk	55
Powdered soft drinks	114	Cottage cheese	54

Television

High Usage	Index	Low Usage	Index
"General Hospital"	161	"Scrabble"	75
"As the World Turns"	159	"Super Password"	67
"Dynasty"	150	"Cheers"	59
"Falcon Crest"	126	"Newhart"	56

ing into aging black neighborhoods or the racial reverse. What unites them is the predominantly ramshackle housing stock and a high crime rate that makes burglar alarms and Neighborhood Watch programs de rigueur. Leisure activities often revolve around church, but there's not a lot of socializing across racial lines—in or out of church. Locals know which schools, bars and diners are for whites or blacks and keep to their own. In Downtown Dixie-Style, integration is still discussed as a hypothetical concept.

Politically, Downtown Dixie-Style neighborhoods have all the ingredients of a strongly partisan Democratic cluster: a large black population, an inner-city location, lower-working-class jobs and southern location. Indeed, residents gave Walter Mondale his fourth-best showing among all the clusters, with 72 percent of their votes in the 1984 election. In surveys, they express interest in increasing government programs to help the poor and the unemployed, hardly for altruistic reasons. These Dixie-ites like to say that the Democrats are the party of the common people, and that label suits them fine. The major drawback for Democratic leaders in Downtown Dixie-Style, alas, is money. Residents rarely have enough to contribute to political fundraisers.

The cluster's down-at-the-heels financial status is reflected in marketing surveys: Downtown Dixie-Style residents rarely consume products or services far above the national average. In their pantries, they tend to stock low-cost, small-quantity, filler foods: canned stews, meat extenders, rice, pancake mix and hash—all purchased at above-average rates. They're about four times as likely as the average American to read *Ebony, Jet* and *Essence* and about twice as likely to read *True Story* and *Soap Opera Digest*. Although residents buy few new cars at rates greater than the norm, their favorite cars are inexpensive subcompacts: Isuzu, Yugo and Peugeot are favorite name plates. "You might live in a dump, but if you've got a late-model car, you're doing okay," says Mike Jefcoat, a 32-year-old shopkeeper from West Jackson, Mississippi. "There are no hot cars around here, just big old long ones."

ZQ 37: HISPANIC MIX

Hispanic Mix neighborhoods are spread throughout the nation: from the Puerto Rican communities of New York to the Cubano districts of Miami to the Mexican-American barrios of San Antonio and Los Angeles. These districts are filled with large families (nearly one in five households has more than five residents), low-wage earners (47 percent

ZQ 37: HISPANIC MIX

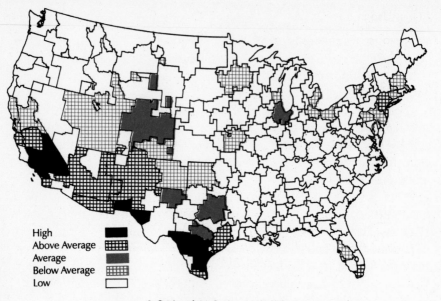

High
Above Average
Average
Below Average
Low

1.9% of U.S. households
Primary age range: 18–34
Median household income: $16,270
Median home value: $49,533

Thumbnail Demographics
poor inner-city enclaves
multi-unit housing
predominantly Hispanic singles and families
grade-school educations
blue-collar jobs

Politics
Predominant ideology: moderate
1984 presidential vote: Reagan (51%)
Key issues: social programs, foreign-policy doves

Sample Neighborhoods
West San Antonio, Texas (78207)
East Los Angeles, California (90022)
Bushwick, Brooklyn, New York (11232)
Pilsen, Chicago, Illinois (60608)
Riverside, Miami, Florida (33135)
Hoboken, New Jersey (07030)

Lifestyle

High Usage	Index	Low Usage	Index
Asthma relief remedies	262	Racquetball	60
Travel by bus	218	Dental rinse	57
Bottled water	187	Money-market accounts	54
Malt liquor	179	Golf	53
Domestic champagne	157	Water-skiing	49
Chess	136	Subcompact cars	48
Watch boxing	132	Travel by cruise ship	28
Portable radios and tape decks	124	Second mortgages	22

Magazines/Newspapers

High Usage	Index	Low Usage	Index
New York	448	*U.S. News & World Report*	7
The New York Times	279	*Travel & Leisure*	7
Travel/Holiday	134	*Rudder*	0
Jet	133	*Architectural Digest*	0

Cars

High Usage	Index	Low Usage	Index
Mitsubishis	83	Oldsmobile 98s	17
Yugos	79	Mercury Sables	16
Chevrolet Sprints	79	Pontiac 6000s	15
Alfa Romeo Milanos	76	AMC Eagles	14
Nissan Sentras	73	Merkurs	14

Food

High Usage	Index	Low Usage	Index
Egg substitutes	180	Pork sausage	80
Canned chicken	134	Low-fat/skim milk	76
Canned chili	128	Pizza mixes	73
Rice	109	Imported white wine	39

Television

High Usage	Index	Low Usage	Index
"Lifestyles of the Rich and Famous"	307	"The Today Show"	67
"Friday Night Videos"	222	"NBC Nightly News"	66
"American Bandstand"	193	"Newhart"	61
"Donahue"	158	"Kate & Allie"	41

earn under $15,000) and rows of aging apartments and bungalows interrupted by Spanish bodegas (markets), bars and restaurants. Hispanic Mix ranks first among all clusters for recent immigrants and second (behind New Melting Pot) in the concentration of foreign-born citizens —26 percent. But unlike other recent immigrants, Hispanic Mixers aren't sure they'll eventually move up and out of the barrio. "They say people will have three homes in their lifetime," says Maria Berriozabal, city councilwoman from San Antonio's West Side, "but we know we'll have just the one."

Consumption patterns in Hispanic Mix reflect residents' ethnicity and family makeup as well as their poverty. Residents are above-average purchasers of Mexican food, tortilla chips and canned chili as well as children's vitamins, cloth diapers and baby shampoo. Hispanic Mixers buy inexpensive filler foods—rice, pancakes, canned chicken and spaghetti—and treat themselves with asthma remedies, throat lozenges and first-aid products—all purchased at above-average rates. Compared to the national average, they watch 32 percent more televised boxing matches but only half as many tennis games. However, network surveys don't adequately gauge the audiences of foreign-language shows in Hispanic Mix. In Hispanic Mix households, the babysitter for many children is the novella—the Spanish soap opera.

Statistically, Democrats outnumber Republicans by a two-to-one margin in Hispanic Mix, but any impact at the ballot box is diluted by low voting rates. Indeed, when it comes to national politics, Hispanic Mix is the most apathetic of all clusters. One reason is the high number of illegal aliens who still live in Hipanic Mix. Another factor is the general disenfranchisement felt by many of the recent immigrants. Local political leaders maintain that greater participation occurs at the neighborhood level over issues like building parks, laying sewers and rehabbing houses. For Hispanic Mixers with a history of distrusting federal immigration and law enforcement officials, national politics holds little allure. "These people aren't asleep," says San Antonio's Helen Ayela, director of Communities Organized for Public Service. "They get involved in issues that affect them at home."

■■■■■■■ ZQ 38: TOBACCO ROADS

"We're just a small town," says Tom Turner, mayor of Belzoni, Mississippi, "a very small, rural southern town." That description of this

Missippi Delta community of 2,800 fits most of the nation's Tobacco Roads communities.

Located throughout the South, from the scrub pines of the Carolinas to the mud flats of Mississippi, Tobacco Roads is a cluster of racially mixed farm towns surviving in a benignly redneck atmosphere. Though blacks comprise 50 percent of the population, they're rarely the ones who own the farms, manage the shops, hold public office or belong to the arts groups. The cluster ranks last in the concentration of white-collar jobs, depending on farming, light industry and unskilled labor for its economic base. The results are hardly impressive: 67 percent of the workers earn less than $15,000 annually, 59 percent of the residents haven't finished high school, and too many of the homes are dilapidated shanties without indoor plumbing. In Tobacco Roads' one-block-wide towns, you see thrift shops, biscuit-and-gravy diners and laundromats; the only national chain store is a Sears catalogue outlet. Some of the communities resemble villages in a Third World country.

Like other poor, southern-based farm clusters, Tobacco Roads communities traditionally vote as Democratic conservatives. Residents are moral traditionalists on issues like abortion and prayer in public schools. But they support increases in farm-support programs, legal services for the poor and Medicaid. While President Reagan received a 56-percent majority in the 1984 election, that's not typical of GOP presidential showings. Tobacco Roads provides solid evidence that rural, blue-collar southerners still regard the Democrats as the party of the common people. Explains Herbert Allen, a black cotton farmer from Belzoni, "President Reagan doesn't know how poor people feel. He's a strong man, but he's of the wrong mind."

Although blacks and whites live in separate parts of Tobacco Roads, consumer surveys reflect their shared poor, rural tastes. Shoppers are more likely than average Americans to buy deviled ham, canned tea, egg substitutes and snack cakes. If they travel long distances, which is rare, they do so by bus. On the farm, everyone has a pickup and frequently a roomy, American-made second car: residents buy Pontiac Bonnevilles, Chevrolet Impalas and Ford Crown Victorias more often than the general population. Tobacco Roaders watch prime-time fare like "Hotel" and "Knots Landing" rather than "The Tonight Show" and "Nightline," possibly because many cluster residents are early-to-bed farmers who turn in before the late-night offerings come on. When you have to be

ZQ 38: TOBACCO ROADS

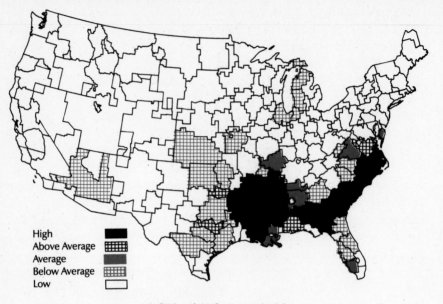

High
Above Average
Average
Below Average
Low

1.2% of U.S. households

Primary age range:	55+
Median household income:	$13,227
Median home value:	$27,143

Thumbnail Demographics

lower-class farm towns
single-unit farmsteads
predominantly black families
grade-school educations
blue-collar and farm jobs

Politics

Predominant ideology: conservative
1984 presidential vote: Reagan (56%)
Key issues: traditional values, jobs

Sample Neighborhoods

Belzoni, Mississippi (39038)
Sparta, Georgia (31087)
Hugers, South Carolina (29450)
Tunica, Mississippi (38676)
Warrenton, North Carolina (27589)
Gates, Virginia (27937)

Lifestyle

High Usage	Index	Low Usage	Index
Travel by bus	325	Knitting	41
Asthma relief remedies	296	Live theater	34
Room heaters	276	Bowling	34
Malt liquors	266	Travel by commercial plane	33
Feminine hygiene sprays	252	Smoke detectors	31
Pipe tobacco	225	Imported cars	30
Diesel cars	204	Billiards	28
Pregnancy tests	203	Electric shavers	27

Magazines/Newspapers

High Usage	Index	Low Usage	Index
Southern Living	343	*Ms.*	0
Grit	334	*Natural History*	0
Ebony	309	*House Beautiful*	0
Hot Rod	208	*Rolling Stone*	0

Cars

High Usage	Index	Low Usage	Index
Pontiac Bonnevilles	207	Mitsubishi Tredias	1
Chevrolet Impalas	203	Yugos	0
Ford Crown Victorias	164	Pinin Farinas	0
Buick LeSabres	152	Mitsubishi Cordias	0
Pontiac T-1000s	148	Ferraris	0

Food

High Usage	Index	Low Usage	Index
Canned tea	240	Natural cheese	59
Rice	169	Whole-wheat bread	39
Pizza mixes	150	English muffins	32
Shortening	131	Mexican foods	32

Television

High Usage	Index	Low Usage	Index
"American Bandstand"	454	"Nightline"	66
"Knots Landing"	299	"Scrabble"	41
"Hotel"	227	"Super Password"	15
"Dance Fever"	215	"The Tonight Show"	4

up at 5:30 in the morning, the thoughts of Johnny Carson suddenly have little meaning.

▬▬▬▬▬ ZQ 39: HARD SCRABBLE

The term "hard scrabble" is an old phrase meaning to scratch a meager living from hard soil. And that's just what residents of America's poorest rural areas are doing. From Appalachia to the Ozarks, from the Mexican border country to the Dakota Badlands, Hard Scrabble is a mix of depressed Indian reservations, mountain hollows and outback settlements of Chicano migrant workers. Residents in general are poor (58 percent earn less than $15,000 annually), undereducated (59 percent never finished high school) and live in substandard housing, with 12 percent residing in mobile homes. Hard Scrabble communities are too small to support even a business center for shops. In New Milton, West Virginia, which is little more than a post office and several hundred isolated homes in Appalachia, going out for fast food means a 25-mile drive over twisting roads to the closest Wendy's.

"It doesn't take a lot of money to be happy in this world," says Fern Cumpston, a New Milton retiree who estimates her household income at $6,000 a year. "We just live from day to day."

With residents barely eking out a living, Hard Scrabble naturally has below-average consumption rates of many products. Their near abstinence from beer and wine can partly be explained by the cluster's presence in many dry counties throughout the South. They depend on television as a major source of entertainment—satellite dishes are often planted alongside mobile homes—and residents are more likely than the general population to view programs such as "Falcon Crest," "Knots Landing" and "Highway to Heaven." Typical of rural clusters, motorists avoid lightweight imports for sturdy domestic cars like the Chevrolet Impala and Plymouth Gran Fury, the better to cope with local roads that are unpaved or full of mud. But no models are bought new at significantly above-average rates, and local hobbies include trying to keep the old car running. Hard Scrabble residents like gardening, hunting and fishing—not for relaxation but for survival.

Politically, Hard Scrabble voters are old-fashioned populists rather than either liberal or conservative ideologues. Although residents voted three to two in favor of Ronald Reagan in 1984, they still distrust the influence of the rich and big business on the GOP. And they're more

ZQ 39: HARD SCRABBLE

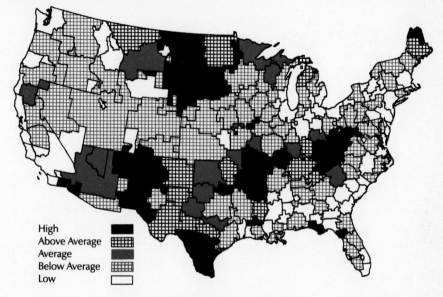

High
Above Average
Average
Below Average
Low

1.5% of U.S. households
Primary age range: 55+
Median household income: $12,874
Median home value: $27,651

Thumbnail Demographics
poor isolated settlements
single-unit dwellings
predominantly white families
grade-school educations
blue-collar and farm jobs

Politics
Predominant ideology: moderate
1984 presidential vote: Reagan (61%)
Key issues: moral tradition, trade protection

Sample Neighborhoods
New Milton, West Virginia (26411)
Chinle, New Mexico (86503)
Doniphan, Arizona (63935)
Montezuma, Utah (84534)
Booneville, Kentucky (41314)
Pineville, Tennessee (40977)

Lifestyle

High Usage	Index	Low Usage	Index
Latin records/tapes	452	Backpacking/hiking	13
Chewing tobacco	300	Adult-education courses	5
Campers/trailers	291	Downhill skiing	0
Compact stereos	243	Host cocktail parties	0
Canning jars and lids	214	Health clubs	0
Shock absorbers	170	Common stock	0
Power boats	158	Jazz records/tapes	0
Denture cleaners	148	Microwave ovens	0

Magazines/Newspapers

High Usage	Index	Low Usage	Index
Southern Living	259	*New York*	0
Hunting	186	*Ms.*	0
Prevention	174	*Modern Bride*	0
Field & Stream	155	*Self*	0

Cars

High Usage	Index	Low Usage	Index
AMC Eagles	131	Alfa Romeos	3
Dodge Diplomats	115	Mitsubishi Starions	2
Ford Crown Victorias	112	Mitsubishi Mirages	2
Chevrolet Impalas	111	Yugos	0
Plymouth Gran Furys	111	Pinin Farinas	0

Food

High Usage	Index	Low Usage	Index
Dry milk	146	English muffins	31
Frozen poultry	125	Instant soups	25
Canned chili	118	Rosé wine	22
Packaged cold cuts	118	Frozen yogurt	0

Television

High Usage	Index	Low Usage	Index
"Wheel of Fortune"	141	"The Bill Cosby Show"	65
"Highway to Heaven"	137	"Donahue"	53
"Falcon Crest"	132	"Friday Night Videos"	48
"Knots Landing"	121	"At the Movies"	19

likely to vote for candidates who push old-fashioned values than those who smack of big-city ways. Their favorite politicians are those who push economic development while preserving the local culture. City slickers beware.

ZQ 40: PUBLIC ASSISTANCE

Given a choice, few people would want to live in Public Assistance, the nation's poorest inner-city neighborhoods, where a major concern is simply survival. Located primarily in the aging ghettos east of the Mississippi River, Public Assistance is a world of crumbling housing projects and tenement rowhouses, boarded-up stores and trash-strewn lots. The people who live here comprise an underclass society of welfare mothers, teens with no job skills, the working poor and the destitute elderly—people with no choices. Demographically speaking, the cluster's population is 70 percent black, poorly educated (57 percent never graduated from high school) and financially indigent (49 percent earn less than $10,000 annually). "Poor people can't afford to move out of here," says Mabel Gray, a South Bronx resident for most of her sixty-two years. And three decades of urban renewal have thus far failed to improve conditions. In Public Assistance, the poverty rate is five times the national average. Just having a minimum-wage job is considered an achievement.

As consumers at the bottom of the socioeconomic scale, Public Assistance nonetheless purchases high levels of corner-store items like menthol cigarettes, canned orange juice, packaged cold cuts and soft drinks. Unable to afford private physicians, many are self-treaters who buy above-average quantities of laxatives, cough syrup and toothache remedies. In contrast to the rural poor who enjoy hunting, camping and fishing, Public Assistance residents would rather watch a wrestling match, go to the race track or play checkers. They're big consumers of alcohol—malt liquor, rum, pop wines and gin—as well as records—soul, jazz, disco and Latin. And they're more inclined to host home parties than the general population because it's frequently their only affordable entertainment. "We're poor, but there are ways of sharing a stereo or VCR among families," says South Bronx resident Blanca Ramirez. "In the South Bronx, status is being the first in your project to own a VCR to entertain your friends and relatives."

Despite the prevailing poverty, Public Assistance is rich in one area:

ZQ 40: PUBLIC ASSISTANCE

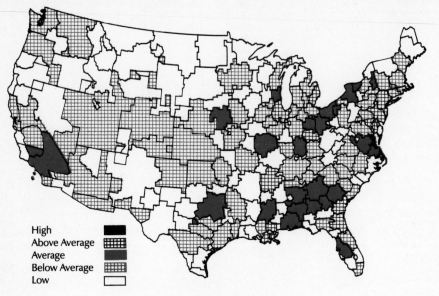

High
Above Average
Average
Below Average
Low

3.1% of U.S. households
Primary age groups: 18–24 and 65+
Median household income: $10,804
Median home value: $28,340

Thumbnail Demographics
inner-city ghettos
multi-unit housing
predominantly black singles and one-parent families
grade-school educations
mixed blue-collar and service jobs

Politics
Predominant ideology: moderate
1984 presidential vote: Mondale (83%)
Key issues: poverty, jobs

Sample Neighborhoods
West Philadelphia, Pennsylvania (19122)
Watts, Los Angeles, California (90002)
Fox Creek, Detroit, Michigan (48215)
Hyde Park, Chicago, Illinois (60653)
Downtown Louisville, Kentucky (40202)
Morrisania, South Bronx, New York (10456)

Lifestyle

High Usage	Index	Low Usage	Index
Soul records/tapes	415	Fraternal orders	30
Malt liquor	326	Hunting	25
Menthol cigarettes	199	Downhill skiing	22
Travel by bus	180	Wood-burning stoves	19
Hair tonic	155	Canning jars and lids	17
Sleeping tablets	154	Gas chain saws	10
Burglar alarms	154	Investment property	3
Salt-water fishing	153	Convertibles	3

Magazines/Newspapers

High Usage	Index	Low Usage	Index
Essence	718	*World Tennis*	0
Jet	622	*Boating*	0
Ebony	525	*Golf*	0
GQ	202	*Harper's*	0

Cars

High Usage	Index	Low Usage	Index
Yugos	90	Plymouth Voyagers	12
Chevrolet Novas	62	Chevrolet Astros	10
AMC Alliances	56	Subaru DL4s	9
Pontiac T-1000s	53	AMC Eagles	8
Chevrolet Spectrums	53	Pinin Farinas	0

Food

High Usage	Index	Low Usage	Index
Canned orange juice	191	Ground coffee	72
Frozen corn-on-the-cob	154	Cottage cheese	65
Canned chili	127	Mexican foods	64
Packaged cold cuts	112	Low-fat/skim milk	48

Television

High Usage	Index	Low Usage	Index
"Loving"	279	"60 Minutes"	85
"Ryan's Hope"	272	"Night Court"	80
"Friday Night Videos"	270	"NBC Nightly News"	79
"Dance Fever"	256	"Newhart"	74

Democratic support. In 1984, 83 percent of the cluster voted for Walter Mondale, his strongest showing among all clusters. In election after election, only one in ten Public Assistance voters goes Republican, the lowest percentage in the country. And this trend shows no signs of changing in the future: Democratic loyalty is too ingrained and compatible with the cluster's self-interest. Only apathy diminishes their clout. On election day, residents don't rush to line up at the voting booth.

APPENDIX

WHERE DO YOU FIT IN?

You know you live in one of the forty neighborhood types; you're just not sure where. Although you consider yourself a Bohemian Mix kind of gal or guy, all your neighbors drive Ford pickups and you buy jumbo Pampers at the K-mart. Your town might be a stronghold for the blue-collar elite of Blue-Chip Blues, but middle management seems to be encroaching in the form of Young Suburbia. And what if you take that first job out in God's Country: will you have climbed up or down the socioeconomic ladder?

While there's not enough room here to list all 250,000 neighborhoods or 36,000 zip codes in America, you can determine your cluster by answering a handful of questions that approximate the classification process Claritas first used when it created the forty-cluster PRIZM system. The following "Cluster Classifier" begins with a general question about your neighborhood's setting: city, country, suburb or small town. Each answer leads to another question along a path that narrows in on your community's characteristics.

Eventually, you should be able to figure out whether you're a resident of Single-City Blues or Emergent Minorities, Pools & Patios or Furs & Station Wagons. Then refer back to Chapter 9 for a more complete description of your neighborhood type. One day, of course, you may live in the millionaires' enclave of Blue Blood Estates and no longer wonder how you measure up. You'll know you've reached the top.

CLUSTER CLASSIFIER

1. Where is your neighborhood located?
   a) near the center of a big city (if yes, see #2)
   b) within a suburban community (if yes, see #19)
   c) close to or part of a remote city or small town (if yes, see #35)
   d) in rural surroundings (if yes, see #52)

URBAN AREAS

2. Which phrase best describes your area's racial and ethnic characteristics?
   a) predominantly white (if yes, see #3)
   b) predominantly older white immigrants (if yes, see #7)
   c) predominantly black (if yes, see #12)
   d) predominantly Hispanic (if yes, see #17)
   e) a significant proportion of young, recent immigrants (if yes, see #18)

3. How would you describe the housing style of your neighborhood?
   a) high-rise (over ten stories) condos, co-ops and apartments (if yes, see #4)
   b) a mix of gentrifying rowhouses, condos and low-rise (two- to nine-story) apartments (if yes, see #5)
   c) elegant single-family homes, townhouses or low-rise apartments in desirable areas (if yes, see #6)
   d) aging rowhouses, duplexes and triple deckers (if yes, see #7)
   e) rundown bungalows and decaying apartments (if yes, see #11)
   f) upper-middle-class single-family homes (if yes, see #19)

4. You probably live in Urban Gold Coast, the nation's upscale high-rise neighborhoods chiefly found in cities like New York, Chicago, Washington and San Francisco. If you think your area has more low-rise apartments and less affluent residents, consider #5.

5. Welcome to Bohemian Mix, a hodge-podge of funky apartments, gentrifying brownstones, students and artists, divorcees and gays. Don't let your neighbors catch you in Hush Puppies.

6. Relax, you've found the good life in Money & Brains, communities typically found near prestigious city colleges. Your dinner guests— corporate chieftains, college administrators and well-known philanthropists—are served from silver platters.

7. Which scene best reflects the way of life in your neighborhood?
   a) Irish and Italian families, ethnic delis and Catholic churches, after-work games of baseball or bocce (if yes, see #8)

    b) aging Eastern Europeans and young minorities, corner markets, rusting factories, laid-off factory workers drinking away their afternoons (if yes, see #9)

    c) union workers of Polish descent, Old-Country clubs and travel agencies, frequent cultural festivals (if yes, see #10)

8. You live in Old Yankee Rows, where several generations of families stick together in comfortable rowhouse neighborhoods, located particularly in cities of the Northeast. First-communion Sundays are big affairs in this heavily Catholic cluster.

9. Heavy Industry—a lower-working-class district concentrated in the industrial cities between New England and the Great Lakes—is your home. Here, your neighbors include Hispanics and the foreign born living in aging duplexes, periodically threatened by urban renewal.

10. You most likely live in Rank & File, that working-class cluster of suburban rowhouse neighborhoods chiefly found in the Northeast. Your motto: "Buy American."

11. You're probably singing the Single City Blues. This cluster contains those forgotten urban neighborhoods of working-class singles—white, black and Hispanic—untouched by gentrification. You and your neighbors congregate in corner bars and pick up whole-grain bread at local health food markets.

12. In your neighborhood, which of the following street scenes is most apropos?

    a) solid brick homes, new Mercedes Benzes in the driveways, well-tended yards (if yes, see #13)

    b) aging frame houses, duplexes and small apartment buildings, four-year-old Escorts on the street, graffiti on the Chinese carry-outs (if yes, see #14)

    c) ramshackle rowhouses and one-story bungalows, ten-year-old clunkers, clothing thrift shops (if yes, see #15)

    d) crumbling tenements and public housing projects, '65 Chevys on blocks, boarded-up liquor stores doing a big business in pint bottles of Muscatel (if yes, see #16)

13. Your Black Enterprise neighborhood is home to America's black upper middle class, typically living in city-fringe districts around the country. Lots of college grads and white-collar professionals lead "The Cosby Show" lives.

14. You probably live in the mostly black, mostly working-class cluster called Emergent Minorities. If so, these are turbulent times for

your neighborhood, with high rates of crime and unemployment, racial tension and a lack of city services.

15. Downtown Dixie-Style is where you feel at home. These southern-based neighborhoods typically are undergoing a racial transition from poor whites to poor blacks—or the reverse. Depending on the social tide, the most popular bar is called the Rebel Yell, where the Confederate flag is proudly displayed.

16. You've hit cluster bottom, living in one of the ghettos that comprise Public Assistance. You know the score: dangerous streets, families on welfare, unemployed men huddled around garbage-can fires. An optimist would say there's no place to go but up; neighbors believe otherwise.

17. There's a good chance you live in Hispanic Mix, the nation's primarily Hispanic, mostly poor communities, including the Puerto Rican districts of New York, the Cubano areas of Miami and the Mexican-American barrios of Los Angeles. Spanish spoken here.

18. As a resident of New Melting Pot, you're riding the new wave of immigrants: middle class and rapidly moving up the ladder. Area children dream of scholarships to college.

▤ SUBURBIA

19. What's the family status of most of your neighbors?
   a) married couples with many children at home (if yes, see #20)
   b) married couples with few children (if yes, see #24)
   c) a mix of singles and families (if yes, see #32)

20. Do your neighbors hold mainly blue- or white-collar jobs?
   a) blue (if yes, see #21)
   b) white (if yes, see #29)

21. How old are most of the neighborhood kids?
   a) toddlers and elementary-school age (if yes, see #22)
   b) teenagers (if yes, see #23)

22. Your schools are overcrowded, and the bulk-food supermarkets are always busy. That's life in Blue-Collar Nursery, where neighborhoods typically encompass recently built subdivisions. Peanut butter (economy-sized) is on your shopping list.

23. Blue-Chip Blues is Home Sweet Home for you. This cluster contains the nation's wealthiest blue-collar neighborhoods, where you're never too far from a Wendy's, McDonald's or Burger King.

24. Which phrase best describes your neighbors?
  a) older affluent families and young singles, homes worth several hundred thousand dollars, small lots in desirable neighborhoods (if yes, see #6)
  b) upper-crust couples with grown children, pricey suburban lots, million-dollar homes (if yes, see #25)
  c) well-fixed older couples, settled split-levels and ranch houses worth $150,000 or more, lots of patios and backyard pools (if yes, see #26)
  d) comfortably situated older couples, postwar tract houses valued at $100,000, well-maintained lots with added garages and second stories (if yes, see #27)
  e) aging couples and retirees living comfortably in high-rise and garden apartments, surrounded by Jewish and Italian delis (if yes, see #28)

25. There's no mistaking your neighborhood: Blue Blood Estates, consisting of the toniest towns from Scarsdale, New York, to Beverly Hills, California.

26. In your stable Pools & Patios suburb, you and your neighbors live in backyard comfort. With the children grown, your houses are big and empty, except for overflowing attics and basement storage areas.

27. Levittown, U.S.A. is your kind of place, with hundreds of cookie-cutter projects modeled after William Levitt's postwar habitat. Neighbors have added garages and second stories to differentiate —and help locate—their homes.

28. You probably live in Two More Rungs, composed of upper-middle-class ethnic neighborhoods surrounding a handful of big cities. Lots of sons and daughters of immigrants and a high percentage of Jews make their homes here, many reluctant to leave the old neighborhood when they hit retirement age.

29. Which description is more appropriate for your neighborhood?
  a) young executive families living in plush new homes surrounded by pools, tennis courts and bike paths (if yes, see #30)
  b) young middle-class families living in recently built starter homes decorated with swing sets and Weber grills (if yes, see #31)

30. Furs & Station Wagons is home for your new money, with good schools and country-club socializing. Last year you traded in the four-year-old Buick for a new Volvo.

31. If you've moved to the outer-lying suburbs in search of cheaper homes and newly built schools, you're most likely a resident of Young Suburbia. Part of the daily price, however, is an hour-long commute to your in-town job.

32. Which description is more appropriate for your neighborhood?
   a) young upwardly mobile singles and couples, apartment and townhouse developments, BMW dealerships and pasta parlors (if yes, see #33)
   b) young, middle-class, unmarried and divorced singles, modest bungalows and garden apartments, Toyota garages and singles Safeways (if yes, see #34)

33. As a resident of Young Influentials, on the fringe of major cities, you probably know all the area health clubs, singles bars and yuppie jokes. But if you're not sure of the difference between radicchio and arugula, you don't belong.

34. Your New Beginnings community caters to middle-class singles— unmarried, divorced and widowed. Your mail is filled with invitations to pool parties, church folksings and self-help groups.

■ SMALL TOWNS AND REMOTE CITIES

35. How would you describe the growth rate of your town?
   a) fast-growing boomtown (if yes, see #36)
   b) stable or barely-holding-its-own community (if yes, see #40)

36. Which phrase best characterizes your community's work force?
   a) high-tech professionals, white-collar executives and financial managers (if yes, see #37)
   b) industrial techies, blue-collar construction workers and military types (if yes, see #38)
   c) a mix of blue-collar workers and college students (if yes, see #39)
   d) few workers, mostly retirees (if yes, see #49)

37. God's Country is how you describe your new hometown to the friends you left behind in the city. This group of rapidly growing exurban towns is filled with white-collar grads staking claims on the Silicon Valleys of the '80s.

38. You live one rung down from God's Country in New Homesteaders, where young blue-collar families from city centers move to raise their families in rustic towns. You and your friends take your outdoor hobbies more seriously than your jobs.

39. You live in a Towns & Gowns neighborhood, where the rhythm of the local college dominates the rural lifestyles. Many state universities are located in these remote towns, which experience rush-hour traffic jams every Saturday during football season.

40. How would you describe your community's work force?
   a) factory workers (if yes, see #41)
   b) a mix of white-collars, farmworkers and mill workers (if yes, see #44)

41. What kind of factories are found in your area?
   a) durable manufacturing involving iron and steel (if yes, see #42)
   b) nondurable manufacturing such as textiles (if yes, see #43)

42. Your Mines & Mills community represents the nation's steeltowns and mining villages that prospered during America's industrial age. Today, factory shutdowns are turning many of these company towns into ghost towns.

43. As a resident of Norma Rae-Ville, your life is dominated by the local textile mill. Although named for the cinematic union organizer, such southern towns are typically filled with poor, black, nonunion workers.

44. Which phrase best describes the size of your community?
   a) a midsized town, several commercial streets, recreational parks and several white-tablecloth restaurants (if yes, see #45)
   b) a small town with courthouse square, one bowling alley and dinner-dances held at the American Legion (if yes, see #46)
   c) a crossroads village with a handful of shops in the center of town and one blinking stoplight (if yes, see #47)
   d) the aging industrial core of a small city, with pre–World War II housing and struggling businesses (if yes, see #48)

45. You're proud to live in the nation's heartland—Middle America—home of sleepy towns with average measures of income, ethnicity and age. This is no place for serious crime or trendy boutiques, and you like it that way.

46. Welcome to Coalburg & Corntown, a cluster of peaceful midwestern towns where your neighbors dance at the American Legion and wave the flag on holidays.

47. Shotguns & Pickups is where you live as well as what you own. Consisting of hundreds of rugged townships in the midst of grain farms and timberland, this neighborhood type is home to dedicated outdoorsmen and women. Antlers on the walls are common.

48. Many of your friends have moved to the suburbs, but you're still hanging on in an old city district known as Smalltown Downtown. In this cluster of once-thriving industrial neighborhoods, you still enjoy relaxing outside at night but fear the criminal element attracted to seedy bars nearby.

49. Which phrase best describes your community?
   a) planned retirement community (if yes, see #50)
   b) quiet retirement resort (if yes, see #51)

50. Gray Power represents those Sunbelt developments that have sprung up over the last quarter-century to accommodate active senior citizens like you. Among your cluster neighbors are residents of Sun Cities and Leisure Worlds across the nation.

51. In your Golden Ponds town, typically found on the banks of a lake or seashore, retirees share the rustic scenery with vacationers and local townsfolk. Henry Fonda won his only Oscar for being an "old poo" in a similar community.

▤ RURAL AREAS

52. In what region of the country is your community located?
   a) Midwest (if yes, see #53)
   b) South (if yes, see #56)

53. Which phrase best describes your community?
   a) a farmtown of several thousand with a several-blocks-square business district surrounded by vast farms, ranches and timber areas (if yes, see #54)
   b) a farm hamlet of several hundred with a single commercial street, several grain silos and isolated farmsteads about a quarter-mile from each other (if yes, see #55)

54. You live in Agri-Business, a middle-class group of bustling farmtowns and prosperous farmsteads. Hog futures and soybean prices are hot topics at the local diner, which serves nothing blackened or nouvelle style.

55. As a resident of Grain Belt, consisting of the nation's most sparsely populated lower-middle-class rural communities, you've been hard-hit by the farm crisis. If you had a college diploma, you'd be "outta here."

56. How would you describe the racial makeup of your community?
   a) predominantly white (if yes, see #57)
   b) predominantly black (if yes, see #60)

57. Which phrase best describes your community?
   a) a town of several thousand, with one high school, a small commercial district and a blue-collar work force (if yes, see #58)
   b) a poor, isolated settlement of several hundred with little more than a post office and a single general store (if yes, see #60)

58. You're probably of English ancestry, a trait you share with other neighbors in Back-Country Folks. This cluster contains remote rural towns typically located in the Ozark or Appalachian uplands. The Sears catalogue store is jammed on Saturday.

59. You are eking out a living in Hard Scrabble, the cluster of the nation's poorest rural settlements, from the mountain hollows of Appalachia to the outback areas along the Mexican border. Your neighbors still send money to televangelists.

60. Which phrase best describes the local landscape?
a) a Dixie hamlet of several hundred where the employment often involves dairy farming, chicken breeding or pulpwood processing (if yes, see #61)
b) a farmtown of several thousand where residents work on cotton and catfish farms or in textile or food processing plants (if yes, see #62)

61. Anti-apartheid sentiment never surfaced in your Share Croppers town, which consists of the nation's racially segregated farm villages. Whites live in modest cottages, while blacks subsist in shanties; both worship in their own churches and frequent their own clubs. Dirt roads outnumber the paved.

62. Your Tobacco Roads village has a high rate of black farmers, but many of your neighbors work for white landowners, following a way of life unchanged over the last century. Lots of sagging clapboard homes and a high rate of outdoor plumbing make living here decidedly downscale.

LIFESTYLE QUIZ

Test your understanding of American lifestyles by answering the following questions:

1. Robin Leach's interview subjects usually live in which neighborhood?

2. You've had a tough day in front of the computer terminal. When you get to your apartment-building elevator, you press the button to the 21st floor. Where do you live?

3. Which cluster is the odds-on favorite for finding a deli that sells chopped liver, gefilte fish and knishes?

4. Where did the pre- and postwar scenes from *The Deer Hunter* take place?

5. Where did Billy Carter go from gas-station owner to mobile-home entrepreneur?

6. A man comes up to a woman in a singles bar and asks, "Could you give me a lift to my townhouse? My BMW is boxed in at the brokerage." He's hoping for a ride to what cluster?

7. In what neighborhood does the local paper feature articles on "safe sex," marijuana decriminalization and the latest foreign film?

8. Having just received the distributorship for iron-rich Geritol, you'd head for which cluster?

9. Where's the last place you'd like to be if your Porsche broke down, leaving you stranded with only a Gold Card to barter with?

10. Which neighborhoods should you avoid if you're allergic to cats?

≡ ANSWERS

1. The host of TV's "Lifestyles of the Rich and Famous" rarely travels beyond Blue Blood Estates.
2. In Urban Gold Coast, pricy apartments loom high above the city core and residents work in service-sector businesses.
3. Two More Rungs has the highest concentration of first-generation Jewish Americans, and deli owners know what they like.
4. The rugged surroundings of the Robert DeNiro film present a portrait of Shotguns & Pickups.
5. In 1986, Jimmy's brother moved back to the family hometown of Plains, Georgia, a classic Share Croppers community.
6. This barfly is of the genus Young Influentials, subclass commodities broker.
7. Bohemian Mix is home to an eclectic mix of gays, leftists and film buffs.
8. The active retirees of Gray Power communities could hardly pass up pills to keep them going.
9. A toss-up: Public Assistance, with its crime-filled ghettos, is no place to dally. But in the destitute settlements of Hard Scrabble, your AmEx card won't get you too far either—no matter who you are.
10. With grain-filled silos looming over many of their farmhouses, the residents of Grain Belt report plenty of mice and the highest rate of cat ownership in the nation.

ACKNOWLEDGMENTS

Many people deserve thanks and recognition for their generous contributions to this book.

At the Claritas Corporation, a number of talented individuals gave their time and energy to compile the information that fills these chapters. Jonathan Robbin, whose vision brought the clusters to life, acted as my guide through the world of geodemography and provided endless insights into why people do the things they do. Witty marketing analyst Doug Anderson offered anecdotal gems while unlocking the data banks that gave shape and color to the clusters. Ace adman Robin Page developed the names and vernacular for describing the forty clusters and promoted the book at Claritas from day one. Sam Barton offered thoughtful recollections on the development of the PRIZM system. Bruce Carroll and Dick Raines lent executive support. Kevin Donnalley provided the maps. And many others helped in various invaluable ways: Mike Adams, Mark Capaldini, Nancy Deck, Fran Laura, Bruce MacNair, Tony Phillips, Rebecca Pietz, Denise Shaw, Jill Felts and April Wright.

Several people deserve special recognition for their assistance in the production of this book. My colleague and friend Joel Makower created the book's graphics and helped guide the project from its inception. My agent Raphael Sagalyn championed the book, offered astute advice and safeguarded my interests throughout the project. Clare Crawford-Mason, Lloyd Dobyns and Richard McWilliams all provided critical editing, suggestions and encouragement when they were most needed. Harper & Row's William Shinker and Carol Cohen ultimately made this book a reality.

Sincere thanks to all the new and old friends around the country who consented to probing interviews about their lives and communities. And a special note of appreciation to all the relatives and friends who furnished a bed, breakfast and tour during my research trips from Malibu to Lower Manhattan: David and Ginger Amoni, Karen and Bill Basham, Jill and Eddie Stanger, Sheila and Lee Mondshein, Golda Mandell, Joanne Ostrow, Natalie Salet and Wayne Michel.

Phyllis Stanger, my wife and love, deserves more praise than is tasteful for her patient support throughout my weeks on the road and months in writer's hibernation at home. The Weisses and Stangers, near and far, were always there with encouragement and sustenance. My parents, Vivian and Sidney Weiss, are simply the best.

Several others deserve heartfelt thanks for helping in diverse ways: Ken Ludwig, Charles Welsh, Emily Sheketoff, Lee Salet, Bruce Duffy, John Neubauer, Don Ryan and Marilena Amoni, Steve Fennell, Carol Ryder, Robert Sherbow, Matilda Helfenbein, the Morgensterns, the Ben-Amis, the Lusmans, Rosemary Connelly of Oakland Street Press, the staffs of the National Association of Neighborhoods and the National Association of Towns and Townships, the Poker Boys plus Jennifer the Muse.

Finally, my deepest gratitude goes to Christine Zylbert, my longtime editor and friend, who salvaged the manuscript on innumerable occasions and polished every page of every draft. Her clear-sighted editing has been vital to my writing for many years. And I am grateful for her artistry and painstaking care, on this and every project.

—M.J.W.

INDEX

416 ■ INDEX

Two More Rungs *(cont'd)*
158; magazines, 42, 108, 148; music tastes,
130; politics, 221, 223; television, 149, 150,
153, 155, 190; travel, 161, 164

Ulman, Stanley, 213–14, 370
Unemployment, 6, 8, 119–23
Unions, 217–19; and Democratic Party,
211–14; membership, 113, 328, 334, 337
United States Army recruitment, 15–16, 17
United States Census information, 10–11
University Park, Texas, 50
Upper East Side, Manhattan, 97–99, 193, 279
Upward mobility, 29–65
Urban Gold Coast, 4, 7, 12, 17, 21, 24–25,
69–71, 97–99, 120, 124–25, 251, 263,
278–81; buying habits, 134; children, 182;
drug abuse, 191; eating habits, 144,
193–96; employment, 94–96; finances, 165;
foods, 140, 145; health clubs, 192; home
maintenance, 132; investments, 163;
leisure, 156, 158, 159; magazines, 42, 147,
148; music tastes, 130; politics, 211,
222–24, 227, 229; single parents, 186;
smoking habits, 191, 192; television
viewing, 149, 153–55, 190; travel, 161–64;
working women, 105; young singles, 173
Urbanization, and buying habits, 129–31

Vickers, Sylvester, 254
Viguerie, Richard, 209
Volunteer work, 79, 106, 118
Voting practices, 21–25

Walton, Sam, 64
Warrenton, North Carolina, 384
Washington, D.C., 7, 72, 74, 97, 140, 141,
176; Anacostia, 35, 104, 106, 350; Capitol
Heights, 46; Dupont Circle, 1, 301;
Georgetown, 50, 202, 272, 273; Gold
Coast, 309; National Symphony Orchestra,
15; Parkfairfax, 179, 288; West End, 279
Watkins, Sylvia, 93
Wattenberg, Ben, 46
Watts, Los Angeles, California, 390
Weaver, Marcia, 255
Webb, Del, 55
Welsh, Charles, 3, 147–48, 210, 212, 220,
221, 223–24, 226
Westchester County, New York, 172
West Dodge, Nebraska, 353
West End, Washington, D.C., 279
West Haven, Connecticut, 335
Westheimer, Houston, Texas, 288

West Jackson, Mississippi, 254–55, 377, 379
West Jordan, Utah, 107, 181–85, 223, 316,
318
West Newark, New Jersey, 120–21
West Philadelphia, Pennsylvania, 390
Westport, Kansas City, Missouri, 353
West San Antonio, Texas, 197, 380
West Union, West Virginia, 33
White Anglo-Saxon Protestants, 89–93
White-collar jobs, 40, 78, 94, 97–103
Whitehead, Ralph, Jr., 24, 230–32, 234
White Plains, New York, 189–90
Williams, Hosea, 228
Wines, 47, 59, 61, 97, 144–45, 202,
281
Winfrey, Carol, 237
Wistow, Fred, 174
Wok ownership, 127
Women, in labor force, 93, 103–9
Women's magazines, 148
Woodruff, Bob, 190, 275
Woodstock, New York, 295
Working Woman, 47, 107–8
Working women, 45, 177–81
Work patterns, 89–123
Wowk, Victor, 216–17, 318
Wrestling, professional, 19–21
Wyandotte, Detroit, Michigan, 249, 329

Young, Andrew, 239
Young Influentials, 4, 12, 15, 17, 31, 32, 73,
75, 39–41, 120, 171, 178–81, 287–91; cars,
137, 139; buying habits, 127, 131–32;
foods, 142, 143, 168, 169, 195;
investments, 163; K-mart shoppers, 20;
leisure, 156, 158, 192; magazines, 42, 147,
148; music tastes, 130; politics, 23, 210,
211, 222; smoking habits, 191, 192;
television, 149, 154; travel, 161
Young Suburbia, 4, 7, 9, 12, 14, 31, 44–45,
47, 55, 69, 75, 127, 128, 291–94; cars, 139;
children, 182; finances, 164, 178; foods,
140, 144, 145, 168, 169; leisure, 160;
magazines, 108, 149; music tastes, 130;
politics, 210, 215, 226, 228, 229, 230, 231;
Sears shoppers, 20; television, 150, 153;
VCRs, 184; working women, 103–4
Ypsilanti, Michigan, 292
Yuma, Arizona, 214, 319

Zanesville, Ohio, 341
Zickgraf, Joseph, 18–19, 337
Zip codes, 2; ratings by, 11
Zip Quality (ZQ) scale, 12, 79